Machiavelli, Hobbes, and the Formation of a Liberal Republicanism in England

Certain English writers of the seventeenth and early eighteenth centuries, whom scholars often associate with classical republicanism, were not, in fact, hostile to liberalism. Indeed, these thinkers contributed to a synthesis of liberalism and modern republicanism. As this book argues, Marchamont Nedham, James Harrington, Henry Neville, Algernon Sidney, and John Trenchard and Thomas Gordon, the coauthors of a series of editorials entitled *Cato's Letters*, provide a synthesis that responds to the demands of both republicans and liberals by offering a politically engaged citizenry as well as the protection of individual rights. The book also reinterprets the writings of Machiavelli and Hobbes to show that each contributed in a fundamental way to the formation of this liberal republicanism.

Vickie B. Sullivan is Associate Professor of Political Science at Tufts University in Medford, Massachusetts. She is the author of *Machiavelli's Three Romes: Religion, Human Liberty, and Politics Reformed* and the editor of *The Comedy and Tragedy of Machiavelli: Essays on the Literary Works* and the coeditor of *Shakespeare's Political Pageant: Essays in Politics and Literature*. She has published articles in *American Political Science Review, History of Political Thought, Political Theory,* and *Polity*.

Machiavelli, Hobbes, and the Formation of a Liberal Republicanism in England

VICKIE B. SULLIVAN

Tufts University

CAMBRIDGE
UNIVERSITY PRESS

CAMBRIDGE UNIVERSITY PRESS
Cambridge, New York, Melbourne, Madrid, Cape Town, Singapore, São Paulo

Cambridge University Press
The Edinburgh Building, Cambridge CB2 2RU, UK

Published in the United States of America by Cambridge University Press, New York

www.cambridge.org
Information on this title: www.cambridge.org/9780521833615

First published 2004
This digitally printed first paperback version 2006

A catalogue record for this publication is available from the British Library

Library of Congress Cataloguing in Publication data
Sullivan, Vickie B.
    Machiavelli, Hobbes, and the formation of a liberal republicanism in England /
    Vickie B. Sullivan.
        p. cm.
    Includes bibliographical references and index.
    ISBN 0-521-83361-2
    1. Political science – Great Britain – History – 17th century. 2. Political science –
Great Britain – History – 18th century. 3. Republicanism – Great Britain – History –
17th century. 4. Republicanism – Great Britain – History – 18th century. 5. Liberalism –
Great Britain – History – 17th century. 6. Liberalism – Great Britain – History –
18th century. 7. Machiavelli, Niccolò, 1469–1527. 8. Hobbes, Thomas, 1588–1679.
9. Political science – Philosophy. I. Title.
JA84.G7S85   2004
320.51′0941′09032–dc22   2003061101

ISBN-13 978-0-521-83361-5 hardback
ISBN-10 0-521-83361-2 hardback

ISBN-13 978-0-521-03485-2 paperback
ISBN-10 0-521-03485-X paperback

To Daniel, Anne, and Joan
"O brave new world / That has such people in't!"
– Shakespeare

Contents

Acknowledgments

Michael Zuckert counseled me to turn my attention to the English Machiavellians and encouraged me in the production of the book – even before I had decided to write it – and generously read and commented on drafts at every stage. This book would not exist without his insight and help. I also wish to acknowledge the help and encouragement of my other teachers: Joseph Cropsey, Nathan Tarcov, and Catherine Zuckert.

My colleague in political theory at Tufts University, Robert Devigne, gave me thoughtful advice and commented with alacrity on any portions that I requested he read. His comments, as well as our conversations on modern political thought around the department, have aided me in numerous ways; some, I am sure, I do not even recognize. Another generous friend and colleague whose help and interest I value, Malik Mufti, read and commented on the entire manuscript. Paul Rahe, in his role as editor of *Machiavelli's Republican Legacy*, helped me to refine my arguments with respect to Algernon Sidney and Cato.

A Semester Leave Award from the Faculty Research Awards Committee at Tufts and a Fellowship Research Grant from the Earhart Foundation allowed me to produce an initial draft of the manuscript, and I gratefully acknowledge their help.

I had the benefit of talented Tufts undergraduates, Michelle Tolman Clarke, Katherine Levitt, and Justin Race, who served as research assistants. I also wish to acknowledge the chair of my department, James Glaser, who made the funds available for me to make use of their talents. I also wish to acknowledge the generous encouragement of another member of my department, Jeffrey Berry.

Tufts University provided me with access to Harvard University's Widener Library. I also wish to acknowledge the helpful staff of Harvard's Houghton Library, where the rare books that I cite are housed.

I wish to thank the readers for Cambridge University Press whose thoughtful comments improved the manuscript.

Finally, the dedication of this book expresses my appreciation to my family. Daniel has aided me with his insight over the years in ways too numerous to enumerate. Anne and Joan, too, offered inspiration in their own way, being present at every moment when I drafted a large portion of the manuscript, in the months before their birth.

Introduction

This work examines the writings of selected English thinkers of the seventeenth and early eighteenth centuries with republican sympathies. These writers, I argue, contribute to the reconciliation of elements of republicanism with liberalism that eventuates in a new synthesis – liberal republicanism. This particular formulation is intended to be disruptive of the current thinking on the relation between republicanism and liberalism, because republicanism was, and continues to be, a phenomenon associated, for the most part, with antiquity, whereas liberalism is decidedly a product of modernity. The republicanism of these English thinkers is fundamentally influenced, I will show, by the writings of Niccolò Machiavelli, and their liberalism derives primarily from transformed elements of Thomas Hobbes's thought. The reconciliation of two such apparently contradictory terms – liberalism and republicanism – is unlikely to be a simple story; in fact, the history of that reconciliation is a complicated one.

The philosopher Charles Louis de Secondat, baron de Montesquieu, for example, gives voice to the complicated character of the melding of republicanism and liberalism, of elements of antiquity and modernity. What this philosopher expresses as the entanglement of these elements has become in the thought of contemporary scholars and political thinkers a stark polarization: republicanism and liberalism are mutually contradictory. If thinkers evoke republican themes, then they are allied with antiquity and arrayed against the forces of liberal modernity. Because elements once understood as entangled are now simplified and portrayed as dichotomous, it is a crucially important task to clarify what each of the constituent elements is, how they interacted, and how each affected the other. The place to begin the unraveling is with Machiavelli and his English followers, who initiated this blending of antiquity and modernity and who have of late received a great deal of attention. That attention, though, cries out for even greater scrutiny of their writings because it has focused exclusively on the republican and ancient side and, hence, has oversimplified the character of their thought.

We can begin to see the complicated, intertwined nature of liberalism and republicanism when we turn to consider the constituent elements of the liberal republicanism of the English writers I treat. Liberalism posits that individuals are the bearers of natural rights and that all are by nature equal and free. Such natural equality and freedom dictate that there are no natural governors and no natural governed. In order for one individual to have political authority over another, that other must consent to be ruled. Political power, then, finds its origin in the consent of the governed. Contemplating the individual apart from the community on this understanding is not merely possible; in fact, it is absolutely necessary if we hope to understand the proper role and scope of government. Such a consideration reveals that individuals construct government as a mechanism that protects their natural rights. Governments are necessary in order to keep order, because rights can only be protected where law is known and settled and a power exists to enforce it against violators. Thus, liberalism emphasizes that government serves the individual by providing the security necessary to acquire property and to pursue private happiness and by refraining from infringing on the individual's liberty. On this view, government is a human construct intended specifically to serve the individual. The individual is prior to the state.

Because the individual receives such priority in liberalism, the status of the public realm, if not completely uncertain, is certainly diminished with respect to the private realm. The natural rights of individuals are exercised primarily in the private realm. This realm consists of the household, where people acquire possessions and educate their children, and of those voluntary associations, where they worship God and organize projects with like-minded neighbors, for example. The pursuit of these activities appears not to require political activity as such. Politics, of course, is in the background, for a life lived in private requires order, which necessitates that some others make the laws, enforce the laws, and judge and punish offenders. Because not all need tend to these functions, liberalism does not emphasize political participation and seems largely unconcerned with the type of regime, although John Locke, whose name provides an adjective by which to specify a type of liberalism, declares that property cannot be properly protected unless the legislative power "consists, wholly or in part, in Assemblies which are variable."[1] On the basis of this claim, Locke points to a moderate monarchy as a preferred form of government. His specification arises directly from a concern for individual rights, underlining that for the liberal what matters most about politics is the government's promotion of the individuals' interests and well-being.

Republics, particularly the city-states of antiquity, not monarchies, whether absolute or moderated by parliaments, evince the type of intense

---

[1] John Locke, *The Second Treatise of Government*, para. 138 in *Two Treatises of Government*, ed. Peter Laslett (Cambridge: Cambridge University Press, 1988), 361.

political involvement of the citizenry so contrary to a liberal society. Indeed, such republics, where the people conduct the business of the regime, seem not to accord with the primary interests of liberalism: acquisition, industry, and the private pursuit of happiness. It is difficult for individuals to pursue their own interests when they are constantly being pulled into the public arena to debate the proper measures for the common good and, then, asked to sacrifice in order to institute them.

This ready contrast between the political life of the ancient and modern polities did not escape those political philosophers who contemplated the implications of a liberalism on the ascendant. Montesquieu, for example, highlights the chasm between ancient and modern political life, by describing the awe-inspiring political dedication of the citizens of the ancient cities. In addition, though, he points to the possibility of a modern form of republicanism, quite different from the ancient form. Modern republicanism has, in his view, absorbed liberal purposes and improved upon ancient republican practices. In this way, he reveals a more complicated picture of the relation between modern liberalism and republicanism than the one contemporary commentators so often depict.

Montesquieu draws a stark contrast between the political life of the ancients and that of the moderns: "The political men of Greece who lived under popular government recognized no other force to sustain it than virtue. Those of today speak to us only of manufacturing, commerce, finance, wealth, and even luxury."[2] The engrossment in individual and private concerns, so characteristic of modernity, pushes aside the emphasis on the inculcation of political virtue, so characteristic of antiquity, Montesquieu suggests. He goes on to examine the consequences of that ancient republican emphasis on virtue when he comments that "[m]ost of the ancient peoples lived in governments that had virtue for their principle, and when that virtue was in full force, things were done in those governments that we no longer see and that astonish our small souls."[3] What the moderns find so striking about the deeds of the ancients is the degree to which the citizens put the interests of the state before their own: "[P]olitical virtue is a renunciation of oneself, which is always a very painful thing."[4] So self-denying does Montesquieu find the citizen virtue of the ancient republics that, in his chapter entitled "What Virtue Is in the Political State," he compares the ancient republican citizens with the extreme ascetics of the modern world: "Love of the homeland leads to goodness in mores, and goodness in mores leads to love of the homeland. The less we can satisfy our particular passions, the more we give

---

[2] Charles de Secondat, baron de Montesquieu, *The Spirit of the Laws* 1.3.3, trans. and ed. Anne M. Cohler, Basia Carolyn Miller, and Harold Samuel Stone (Cambridge: Cambridge University Press, 1989), 22–3.

[3] Ibid., 1.4.4, 35.

[4] Ibid., 1.4.5, 35.

ourselves up to passions for the general order. Why do monks so love their order? Their loves comes from the same thing that makes their order intolerable to them.... The more austere it is, that is, the more it curtails their inclinations, the more force it gives to those that remain."[5] In this manner, Montesquieu indicates the extent to which the demands of the ancient polities transformed the natural inclinations of those who inhabited them.

Although Montesquieu finds the principle of virtue as self-renunciation so necessary to the republics of antiquity, he does not associate that principle with republicanism simply. He finds that England is a "republic" that "hides under the form of monarchy,"[6] and England, as Montesquieu presents it, is certainly not a republic that promotes the self-renunciation of its citizens. That modern nation, where the citizens speak of commerce, finance, and even of luxury, takes not virtue for its principle, but rather "political liberty" for "its direct purpose." Political liberty he defines "in a citizen" as "that tranquillity of spirit which comes from the opinion each one has of his security."[7] Individual security, not selfless dedication to the polity, is the focus of the modern republic, he claims.

Moreover, the modern form of republic no longer demands that its citizens constantly debate and determine its policy. In modern practice, representation replaces participation; Montesquieu heartily approves of this innovation: "A great vice in most ancient republics was that the people had the right to make resolutions for action.... The people should not enter the government except to choose their representatives."[8] In this comment, he suggests the superiority of modern to ancient republicanism.

Montesquieu finds in England, therefore, not only a model for a new type of republicanism but, in some important ways, an improvement over the ancient type. His modern form of republicanism relies neither on the moral character of its citizens nor on their direct political participation. It is a republicanism that embraces the liberty of the individual, understood as the feeling of individual security, as its purpose. This modern republic relies on institutional means to achieve that purpose: the separation of powers as embodied in England's constitution.[9] Montesquieu's modern republicanism has thoroughly reconciled itself to liberal purposes.

Not only ancient practice but prominent elements of ancient philosophy, of course, furnish a stark contrast to liberalism's emphasis on individuals and their desires. Aristotle, after all, declares both that the city is prior to the individual and that it is natural.[10] Further, he explicitly denies that a

[5] Ibid., 1.5.2, 42–3.
[6] Ibid., 1.5.19, 70; see also 2.11.5, 156, and 3.19.27, 326–7.
[7] Ibid., 2.11.5, 156, and 2.11.6, 157.
[8] Ibid., 2.11.6, 160.
[9] Ibid., 2.11.6, 156–66.
[10] Aristotle, *The Politics* 1.2, trans. Carnes Lord (Chicago: University of Chicago Press, 1984), 1253a19–29.

city can be a product of a compact. Politics, according to his conception, is intended to improve citizens, not merely to prevent citizens from committing injustices against each other and to promote business transactions, bare requirements of political life, he concedes.[11] Although acknowledging that the latter purposes, which, in fact, closely approximate the liberal conception of politics, are necessary for a city, Aristotle declares that they do not approach the city's true function. On the basis of such declarations, of course, Aristotle's thought permits for a much wider swath of the intrusion of politics into the lives of citizens. Further, the ancient philosopher defines the political relationship as ruling and being ruled in turn.[12] Participation, again, calls liberalism to account. The aspirations both of ancient politics and political philosophy, then, in some salient respects oppose themselves to the very purposes of liberalism.

Contrary to Montesquieu's suggestion that some new variant of republicanism could, and had, in fact, accommodated itself to the individualism of the liberal regime – as evidenced by the political experience of the English – recent scholars of intellectual history and political theory argue that adherents of republicanism not only persevered in maintaining their allegiance to ancient thought but also successfully contained the encroachment of modern, liberal ideas, in England and in America as well. In this way, these scholars offer an excessively polarized view of the relation between republicanism and liberalism: republicanism is necessarily ancient and is thoroughly hostile to liberalism and its purposes.

This thoroughly dichotomous depiction of the relation of republicanism and liberalism has had a profound impact in a number of disciplines. Perhaps deepest is its impact on the study of the American founding. During the second half of the twentieth century, a group of scholars transformed the study of the thought surrounding the founding period in America, which conventional wisdom had ruled thoroughly Lockean, by maintaining that classical republicanism ruled the thoughts and motivated the actions of the Americans. Although the details of their assessments vary, they are united in claiming that liberalism derived from Locke was not foremost in the American mind at the creation of the United States. Instead, they claim, the Americans were shaped by the classical republican tradition that had found fecund soil in Renaissance Italy, and that had then traveled to England with the thought of Machiavelli, taking root in the thought of various Englishmen who opposed the crown during and after the English Civil Wars.[13] When it came time for the Americans themselves to oppose

---

[11] Ibid., 3.9, 1280a31–7.

[12] E.g., ibid., 7.14, 1332b24–6.

[13] The influential work of J. G. A. Pocock and Quentin Skinner is responsible for the view that Machiavelli is the source for classical republicanism in the modern world. Pocock's sweeping book, *The Machiavellian Moment: Florentine Political Thought and the Atlantic Republican*

the crown, they drew inspiration from their English predecessors.[14] These English thinkers, important scholars claim, had embraced the ancient and distinguished tradition of thought that spoke in terms of virtue rather than self-interest, looking to what the individual could sacrifice for the common life of the state.[15]

This historical scholarship, which interprets treatises from the Renaissance, tracts from the English Civil Wars, and pamphlets from the

Tradition (Princeton: Princeton University Press, 1975), presents Machiavelli as receiving the civic humanism of Aristotle, transmitting it to England where Harrington gave it further expression, an expression that served as inspiration for, in Pocock's formulation, the "neo-Harringtonians," members of the opposition both before and after the Glorious Revolution. These opposition writers, then, became the source for the civic humanist tradition in America that survived long after the period of the framing of the Constitution. Skinner, too, depicts Machiavelli as a classical republican, but one who owes much to "Roman stoic sources" (*The Renaissance*, vol. 1 of *The Foundations of Modern Political Thought* [Cambridge: Cambridge University Press, 1978], xiv).

[14] Caroline Robbins, *The Eighteenth-Century Commonwealthman: Studies in the Transmission, Development and Circumstance of English Liberal Thought from the Restoration of Charles II until the War with the Thirteen Colonies* (Cambridge: Harvard University Press, 1959), brings forward the notion that republican ideas were influential not only in England after the hope of their full implementation had long lapsed, but also in America. She shows, for instance, how the thought of innovators during the periods of the English Civil Wars and Restoration influenced the character of the Whig opposition after the Glorious Revolution through the reign of George III. Her commonwealthmen, however, are not opposed to liberalism. Indeed, she includes Locke's work in the "sacred canon" revered by the "Real Whigs of the next century" (4–5). Thus, she considers his thought (58–67) and considers the impact it had on the eighteenth-century thinkers (e.g., 253, 267, 297, 302, 306–8, 318, 325–6, 378, 383). Cf. Pocock's statement: "It is clear…that Locke played no predominant role in the formation of what Caroline Robbins has called 'the Whig canon' in the tradition of 'the eighteenth-century commonwealthmen'" (J. G. A. Pocock, "Authority and Property: The Question of Liberal Origins," in *Virtue, Commerce, and History: Essays on Political Thought and History, Chiefly in the Eighteenth Century* [Cambridge: Cambridge University Press, 1985], 66). Robbins's work clearly influenced Bernard Bailyn, *The Ideological Origins of the American Revolution* (1967; reprint and enlarged, Cambridge, Mass.: Belknap Press, 1992), 34–6. Like Robbins, Bailyn does not offer these seventeenth- and eighteenth-century writers as a stark alternative to liberal thought. He suggests instead not only that this tradition coexisted with Locke's thought but that Americans embraced both simultaneously, e.g., 36 and 45. Although Gordon Wood, *The Creation of the American Republic, 1776–1787* (Chapel Hill: University of North Carolina Press, 1969; reprint, New York: W. W. Norton, 1972), agrees with Robbins and Bailyn on the influence of the English opposition tradition in America, he considerably modifies its character from that which they describe. Citing an early article of Pocock ("Machiavelli, Harrington, and English Political Ideologies," *William and Mary Quarterly*, 3d ser., 22 [1965]: 549–83), he argues that when the Americans appealed to the English Whig opposition tradition they were, in fact, appealing to the classical antiquity that had traveled to England via Machiavelli (32–3). With this judgment, Wood offers the English radical Whigs as an alternative to Locke's modern and liberal influence.

[15] Joyce Appleby explains that "classical republicanism made civic virtue – the capacity to place the good of the commonwealth above one's own – the lynchpin of constitutional stability and liberty-preserving order" (*Liberalism and Republicanism in the Historical Imagination* [Cambridge: Harvard University Press, 1992], 21).

American Revolutionary War, has influenced contemporary political discussions. Many who reflect on contemporary politics and society ask with increasing frequency and urgency how, if governments are intended to serve individuals, do they elicit the service of citizens on their behalf, the very type of service that would nourish and promote the public realm. The community seems unequipped to make any claims on the individual. As a result, the community suffers as the claims of the individual are elevated. According to these thinkers, such a priority produces selfish individuals alienated from their communities and their fellow citizens; it teaches individuals to claim rights and to evade duties. Driven by their dissatisfaction with contemporary, liberal politics, they appeal to the republican tradition and its battle with liberalism (as depicted by the historians) in order to posit an alternative. Liberalism produces the unsatisfactory political life that marks the contemporary situation, and republicanism is its vanquished but intrepid opponent that harkens back to the vital politics of the Italian cities of the Renaissance and the city-states of Greece and of Rome. The worthier contender in this battle, these contemporary thinkers maintain, did not emerge victorious. The contemporary citizen would do well to learn from the experiences of a more fulfilling, because more selfless, political life.[16]

This book makes the case that the relation between republicanism and liberalism need not result in this hostile antinomy. Indeed, such a thing as a liberal republicanism is not only possible but was actually present very early in the history of liberalism. The process of reconciliation between the two, I argue, began even before Locke's *Second Treatise* was written, let alone promulgated. This reconciliation occurred in the thought of the

---

[16] Classical republicanism and civic humanism furnish an alternative standard by which scholars not only in political theory but in such fields as law and public policy can criticize what they view as liberalism's excessive influence on the individual. The so-called communitarian critics of liberalism became associated with this tradition. See, e.g., Michael Sandel, *Democracy's Discontent: America in Search of a Public Philosophy* (Cambridge, Mass.: Belknap Press, 1996). He states there, for instance, that "the republican tradition, with its emphasis on community and self-government, may offer a corrective to our impoverished civic life" (6). For his reliance on the depiction of the classical republican tradition put forth by Pocock and Skinner, see, e.g., 26 and n. 2. For a perspective on this tradition's impact on law, see, for example, the special issue "Symposium: The Republican Civic Tradition," *Yale Law Journal* 97 (1988): 1493–1723. Don Herzog offers a critical assessment of the implications of the application of civic humanism to contemporary American politics in "Some Questions for Republicans," *Political Theory* 14 (1986): 473–93. Jeffrey C. Isaac criticizes the republican and communitarian positions as oversimplifying liberalism and suggests that republicanism and liberalism need not be seen as irreconcilable in "Republicanism vs. Liberalism? A Reconsideration," *History of Political Thought* 9 (1988): 349–77. James Hankins provides a helpful and concise review of the impact of classical republicanism on the academy and politics in his introduction to *Renaissance Civic Humanism*, ed. James Hankins (Cambridge: Cambridge University Press, 2000), 1–7; see also Steven C. A. Pincus, "Neither Machiavellian Moment nor Possessive Individualism: Commercial Society and the Defenders of the English Commonwealth," *American Historical Review* 103 (1998): 705–11.

very English writers to whom recent scholars have pointed as the source of
the classical republican tradition for the later Americans, so radically opposed to liberalism.[17] These writers expressed varying degrees of republican
sympathies during and after the English Civil Wars.[18] These writings that I

[17] Blair Worden, a distinguished and prolific commentator on the writers in this English republican tradition, notes the presence of the salient doctrines that constitute a liberal understanding of politics: "Usually writing in opposition to the prevailing power, they drew
heavily on ideas of contract and resistance and of natural rights which were not peculiarly
republican" ("English Republicanism," in *The Cambridge History of Political Thought, 1450–
1700,* ed. J. H. Burns with the assistance of Mark Goldie [Cambridge: Cambridge University
Press, 1991], 443). Nevertheless, he does not examine the sources and significance of these
doctrines in any detail. Other scholars, too, have suggested that the republican tradition
need not be seen as hostile to liberalism. See, e.g., Steven M. Dworetz, *The Unvarnished
Doctrine: Locke, Liberalism, and the American Revolution* (Durham: Duke University Press,
1990), 101; Stephen Holmes, *Passions and Constraints: On the Theory of Liberal Democracy*
(Chicago: University of Chicago Press, 1995), 5 and 30; and Christopher Nadon, "Aristotle
and the Republican Paradigm: A Reconsideration of Pocock's *Machiavellian Moment,*" *Review
of Politics* 58 (1996): 677–98. Thomas L. Pangle states: "This new republicanism, this new
interpretation of the experience of the classical cities, was not at all as opposed to the spirit
of Locke's teaching, . . . as has been recently claimed" (*The Spirit of Modern Republicanism:
The Moral Vision of the American Founders and the Philosophy of Locke* [Chicago: University
of Chicago Press, 1988], 30). Paul A. Rahe challenges the classical republican interpretation
when he identifies a critical break between ancient and modern republicanism. He argues
that the modern republicans, beginning with Machiavelli, reject the Aristotelian premise that
locates the foundation for political life in the human capacity for *logos.* See Paul Rahe, *Republics Ancient and Modern: Classical Republicanism and the American Revolution* (Chapel Hill:
University of North Carolina Press, 1992). Rahe further undermines this interpretation by
showing how such modern republicans as Machiavelli and Harrington helped shape Locke's
thought, both when he embraced and rejected their ideas (469–79; on Machiavelli's influence
on Locke, see also Pangle, *Modern Republicanism,* 260). Pincus also questions the assumption
of an antimony between liberalism and republicanism by arguing that those who supported a
commerical economy in England during the seventeenth century invented "a new ideology"
"which valued human choice, the human capacity to create wealth, and epochal change
in human history" and which "can no longer be called classical republicanism but is better
understood as liberalism." He continues: "It is a liberalism, however, that should not be seen
as antagonistic to republicanism" ("Commercial Society and the Defenders of the English
Commonwealth," 708). Whereas Pincus accepts the designation of classical republican for
Machiavelli and Harrington, I do not. Although I agree that they do not support a commercial society, I argue that their ideas concerning politics cannot be said to be classical.
Michael P. Zuckert, *Natural Rights and the New Republicanism* (Princeton: Princeton University Press, 1994), argues that Locke's thought combined with Whig political science in the
early eighteenth century to form a new republicanism that would fundamentally influence
the American republic (see particularly 312–19). My study examines the formation of such
an amalgamation at an earlier stage. Richard Dagger, *Civic Virtues: Rights, Citizenship, and Republican Liberalism* (Oxford: Oxford University Press, 1997), finds it necessary to construct
a contemporary version of "republican liberalism," because one "has not truly *developed
historically*" (5).

[18] I use the term "republican" loosely. Those who wrote after the Restoration, for obvious
reasons, did not openly advocate republicanism. Nevertheless, the term does convey something important about their thought in that they are disposed to admire republics and seek

examine belong to Marchamont Nedham, James Harrington, Henry Neville, Algernon Sidney, and John Trenchard and Thomas Gordon (who together coauthored a series of editorials entitled *Cato's Letters*).[19] Their liberal republicanism eventuates in an understanding of politics that makes the private primary – that is, the rights of individuals – but relies heavily on a public means to effect that end. It brings the citizens into the public realm by relying on them not only to elect their representatives but also to be constantly vigilant so that they can act with dispatch and decisively – even vengefully – when those representatives forsake their interests and violate their rights. It blends liberalism with Machiavelli's republicanism.

The Foundations of Liberal Republicanism

The republicanism of the writers I examine derives primarily from Machiavelli's *Discourses on the First Ten Books of Livy* – a republicanism far removed from that which can be termed classical – and their liberalism primarily from certain themes Hobbes expounds in his various writings, which these writers transform to fulfill their liberal purposes.[20] Machiavelli

to emulate their practice to the extent that political circumstances in England permit. In addition, England's constitution did permit them to view their nation through the lens of the mixed regime, in a manner akin to Montesquieu's suggestion that England was at base a form of republic. In Worden's words the English republicans' "proposals were flexible, and the form of government often mattered less to them than its spirit. The term republican was not, on the whole, one which they sought, and was more commonly one of abuse. Nevertheless, a republican tradition can be identified which was to enter the mainstream of eighteenth-century political ideas in Britain, on the continent, and in America" ("English Republicanism," 443). Quentin Skinner, who had previously referred to thinkers in this tradition as republican, now expresses hesitation in so terming them (*Liberty before Liberalism* [Cambridge: Cambridge University Press, 1998], 11, n. 31; 54–5, n. 176). See also David Wootton's discussion of the word "republicanism" and its uses ("The Republican Tradition: From Commonwealth to Common Sense," introduction to *Republicanism, Liberty, and Commercial Society, 1649–1776*, ed. David Wootton [Stanford: Stanford University Press, 1994], 2–7).

[19] A case could be made for including additional writers. The thought of the particular writers I have selected for examination, I believe, tells a particularly coherent story. I have chosen not to treat John Milton, for example, who was a very prominent republican during the Civil Wars. Although at points his writings refer to a contract, ultimately his thought is too deeply embedded in biblical revelation to qualify as a precursor to liberal thought. See Zuckert's treatment of these issues, *Natural Rights and New Republicanism*, 79–93. Milton's commonplace book, where he transcribed passages from the works he was reading, shows him to be a student of Machiavelli. For more recent considerations of Machiavelli's influence on Milton, see Victoria Kahn, *Machiavellian Rhetoric: From the Counter-Reformation to Milton* (Princeton: Princeton University Press, 1994), and Blair Worden, "Milton's Republicanism and the Tyranny of Heaven," in *Machiavelli and Republicanism*, ed. Gisela Bock, Quentin Skinner, and Maurizio Viroli (Cambridge: Cambridge University Press, 1990), 225–45.

[20] Steven B. Smith, *Spinoza, Liberalism, and the Question of Jewish Identity* (New Haven: Yale University Press, 1997), maintains that a combination of elements from the writings of

and Hobbes, then, are the primary sources of this liberal republicanism, but the thought of each had to be radically transformed before either could contribute to this new combination. As my examination of the thought of each illustrates, neither Machiavelli nor Hobbes would endorse this synthesis had they known to what purposes their writings would be put. Liberal republicanism could hold no allure for either of them, although each offered essential components of it, nevertheless.

One of the most important elements that Machiavelli contributes to this particular form of republicanism is an intense dedication to a democratic republicanism. He, in fact, makes prominent claims in favor of the people and denounces, in their name, the tradition of "all the writers" on politics as being too aristocratic.[21] The supporters of an aristocratic republicanism, he observes, would reject out of hand Rome's political life, pronouncing that the people had too prominent a role there: not only were the people able to enforce their demands against the nobility, but one such demand resulted in the institution of the tribunate, which gave the people and their supporters a direct voice in the government. The people's prominent role in Rome's governance resulted in a chaotic political realm and contributed to the republic's ultimate collapse. In contrast, Machiavelli has no such scruples. He endorses Rome precisely because it embraced the people.

Liberal republicanism, as we shall see, concerns itself with the people and their pursuits. It seeks to serve their own ends. Machiavelli's republicanism, then, serves liberal republicanism's purposes by bringing this class forward as worthy to participate in government. Machiavelli, though, would not endorse liberal republicanism's ultimate position on the people. As my chapter on Machiavelli emphasizes, his endorsement of the people is not an end in itself but a means to his own end of war and empire. In his view, any state capable of acquiring and maintaining an empire must have as many people as possible armed as soldiers to fight in this cause. His overture to the people originates from this necessity. In Machiavelli's *Discourses*, his own concerns consistently trump the people's.

In order to produce an aggressive republic, Machiavelli sets himself the task of evaluating the appetites of the two classes, the people and the great. The people desire security and property, whereas the great desire dominance and honor. He constructs his republic squarely on the desires of each. He determines that his purpose is served – his purpose of creating a belligerent republic – if both classes can to a degree satisfy their desires. Neither, though,

Hobbes and of Machiavelli influenced what he terms Spinoza's democratic liberalism (see 23, 32–4, 131–4, and 146–7). Thus, not only England, but also the Continent saw Machiavelli's influence on later liberal thinkers.

[21] Niccolò Machiavelli, *Discourses on Livy*, trans. Harvey C. Mansfield and Nathan Tarcov (Chicago: University of Chicago Press, 1996), 1.58.1. I cite this edition by book, chapter, and paragraph number.

can satisfy its desires to too great a degree. If the satisfaction of either were to occur, either the people would have overturned the great or the great, the people. In either case, the resulting form of government would be incapable of maintaining an acquiring army. Again, his republicanism serves his overarching purpose of war and empire.

Because war is Machiavelli's purpose, his republic is deeply indebted not only to the people, who furnish the body of his army, but also to the great, whose desire for honor fuels the pursuit of war. He understands, however, the dangers of the intense desire for distinction that moves the great, dangers exacerbated by his militaristically acquisitive republic that both unleashes and fosters such a potentially dangerous desire. He recognizes that some citizens, in fact, will manifest the most intense form of that desire, the desire for tyranny. In order for the republic to counter this danger, he teaches ingratitude toward the most illustrious. For instance, when an individual, previously rewarded for great deeds, breaks the laws of the state, the state cannot balance the past benefits against the current wrong: it must punish most harshly without regard to past service. A republic, in his view, cannot afford to indulge in hero worship; rather, it must display a deep cynicism toward the great, being always alert to the dangers the most ambitious pose and constantly counteracting those dangers.

Even at this juncture, much can be gleaned from Machiavelli's thought. His republicanism embraces a civil life characterized by tumult. He rejects the teachings of classical philosophy that emphasize harmony in political life, because he relishes conflict and dissension. This struggle between the two classes originates from their desires and passions. He intends not to educate their passions, not to teach them to put the collective good before their own individual good. As he says in *The Prince*, "truly it is a very natural and ordinary thing to desire to acquire, and always, when men do it who can, they will be praised or not blamed."[22] His purposes are well served if the many and the few act on their own selfish passions – if the many act to acquire property and the few honor. All of this is to nurture war. Thus, he rejects Aristotle's claim that war is for the sake of peace.[23] He envisions no such peace.

The English republicans glean from the teachings of their Italian master that government should give the people a prominent place and should actually base itself on the passions of its citizens. Some even inure themselves to the prospect of civil strife. Indeed, some learn from Machiavelli to judge both that tumults in a state is a sign of its good health and that stern punishment is necessary to maintain a state's health. In addition, some even are drawn into Machiavelli's orbit precisely because of his unrepentantly bellicose

---

[22] Niccolò Machiavelli, *The Prince*, trans. Harvey C. Mansfield, 2d ed. (Chicago: University of Chicago Press, 1985), 3.14. I cite this edition by chapter, followed by page number.

[23] Aristotle, *Politics* 7.14, 1333a30–6, 1334a4–5, and 7.15, 1334a15.

republicanism. This attraction, though, would turn to repulsion in other thinkers before the liberal elements of the synthesis could fully gel.

Hobbes's thought, too, serves as a source for liberal republicanism. In order for the English republicans to draw on both thinkers, there must be some areas of compatibility between these two thinkers, and there are. Despite some salient and profound differences, certain elements of Hobbes's thought are fully compatible with Machiavelli's, and others, although certainly not compatible, are, in some sense, extensions of the Italian's positions – whether knowing extensions or not.[24] In many cases, those extensions of Machiavelli's positions serve what are incipient liberal positions. For example, Hobbes's thought serves those positions when he posits that human beings are equal, that citizens possess a natural right that can serve as a claim against the government, that the people should attain their desired peace, and, thus, that acquisition should result only from peaceful means.

The philosopher of Malmesbury, like Machiavelli, emphasizes the passionate nature of human beings and finds that government must be rooted in those passions.[25] When he delves deeply into the passions, he finds that at base all human beings fear for their lives. Machiavelli, as we shall see, would not necessarily disagree with this judgment, but Hobbes draws political ramifications from this principle far beyond what could win the Italian's approval. According to Hobbes, the fear of death induces people to consent to a government or to embrace a conquering power in order to preserve their lives. Because government serves the citizens who construct it, his government is specifically designed to serve them by protecting against the fear of violent death and promoting a positive attachment to a life that provides comfort. Peace is the thing most needful, in Hobbes's view, because only when it reigns can the fear of violent death be assuaged and a comfortable and pleasing life be promoted.

According to Hobbes, only an absolute, indeed, only a terrifyingly powerful sovereign can furnish stability and peace. No republican is he; republics, he judges, confound his purposes. They are too chaotic, too warlike, too filled with orators who seek their own personal advancement. More intensely than any liberal, he decries the tumultuous public realm and seeks sanctuary in the private realm with the wish that politics itself could evaporate. By

---

[24] It is certainly an important and interesting question whether Hobbes knew Machiavelli's work and intentionally transformed it. On the controversy regarding this question, see my subsequent discussion.

[25] Albert O. Hirschman finds that Machiavelli is the source both for a more realistic analysis of human behavior and for the notion that governments could produce favorable results by "pitting passions against passions" (*The Passions and the Interests: Political Arguments for Capitalism before Its Triumph* [Princeton: Princeton University Press, 1977], 41; see also 13 and 33). These notions, Hirschman finds, were to combine, and their united force was to play a transformative role in social, political, and economic thought through the seventeenth and eighteenth centuries.

accepting Machiavelli's notion that human beings are driven by their passions to acquire, but by rejecting Machiavelli's promotion of war, Hobbes endorses most zealously the central pursuit of liberalism, the acquisition of property through peaceful – rather than martial – pursuits.[26]

As opposed as their views are on the desirability of war, Hobbes's antipathy to war is again an outgrowth, albeit an extreme one, of Machiavelli's own position on the people. The Florentine advocates a prominent role of the people in a state because only when they have so prominent a role can a state put them under arms as the main force for empire. Machiavelli himself reveals the extreme danger of his argument in favor of the people. If the people had their way – if they were to become victorious in the internal war between the many and the great – they could act on their greatest desire, their desire for security. As a result, war would be eliminated. He, of course, wishes to avert such an eventuality, whereas Hobbes endeavors to promote it. If Machiavelli can be said to oppose the tradition of writers and philosophers when he jettisons their aristocratic sensibilities, it must be concluded that Hobbes goes completely over to the side of the people, endeavoring to make them and their passions prevail. He wishes for them to attain the rewards of their fondest hopes; peace, security, and a comfortable life.

Other aspects of Hobbes's thought bear the marks of his embrace of the people. He outlines a scenario in which all construct government. The establishment of government can occur when all individuals consent to turn over their right to all things to a mighty sovereign. Founders of political life, in his conception, are not half-mythological individuals possessing rare and awe-inspiring qualities, as they are in Machiavelli's. Instead, anyone at all can participate in a founding. Moreover, Hobbes does not describe his sovereign, this figure elected by all to protect them, as possessing special abilities. What makes Hobbes's sovereign so awe-inspiring, so fearful, is that he or she possesses the former rights of all. Hobbes does not endow his sovereign with unique attributes because he endows no one with them. He is a radical egalitarian, who challenges the notion that some individuals are more beloved by nature than others. No one, he argues, is privileged by being so strong or so smart that he or she has a marked advantage over others. Nature bestows its gifts equally to human beings, Hobbes argues, and, as a result, all feel the cold vulnerability of the state of nature, which is a state of war.

This overriding sense of vulnerability, Hobbes hopes, will drive all to embrace not only the comforts but also the inconveniences of civil society. People are driven to this state in order to protect their lives. Nature dictates,

---

[26] Paul A. Rahe maintains that a number of modern philosophers "turned against [Machiavelli's] exaltation of political glory" in this fashion ("Antiquity Surpassed: The Repudiation of Classical Republicanism," in Wootton, *Republicanism, Liberty, and Commercial Society*, 242).

he says, that individuals can never renounce this right to protect their lives. As a result, one can struggle justifiably, for instance, against the king's minister who takes one to the gallows. The right to life, then, is the only right of nature that individuals retain. Therefore, unlike Machiavelli, Hobbes posits the critical notion that the individual could, in certain circumstances, claim a right against the government.

Despite Hobbes's positing of this right to life, the only thing that prevents sovereigns, in Hobbes's understanding, from making their subjects their prey is the good sense that tells them that a sovereign whose people are rendered weak from the sovereign's own depredations is a weak sovereign. This is a thin veil, indeed, that separates the subjects' comfort, liberty, and security from a condition that could, in certain critical respects, be even worse than the state of nature. Locke says as much when he notes the illogic of simultaneously endowing a sovereign with so much power but failing to offer the individual protections against that power: "He being in a much worse condition who is exposed to the Arbitrary Power of one Man, who has the Command of 100000. than he that is expos'd to the Arbitrary Power of 100000. single Men."[27]

Hobbes is not a liberal thinker because he is not a partisan of a mild government that concerns itself with protecting the liberties and property of its citizens. Nevertheless, it is easy to see how another could use Hobbes's purposes against him in order to arrive at a liberal position: security is certainly not promoted when the monarch, still armed with all the rights of nature, is furnished with the force of all. All can become the prey of Hobbes's leviathan. This recognition forces the conclusion that if Hobbes's end is to be served, security must be protected by enlarging the scope of the natural rights that individuals retain under government to include the right to liberty and to property.

Some of the English Machiavellians did just that; they embraced some of Hobbes's doctrines and endeavored to find a better, more secure way to promote his ends. In the process, they became liberals. But also being the students of Machiavelli, they manifested decidedly republican sympathies as well. Indeed, they found that republicanism provided a means for the people themselves to protect their natural rights. Thus, the liberal republicanism of these English writers is a spirited liberalism, a liberalism in which there is decidedly a public space. That public space provides a place for citizens to contend for their own rights. That contention is so heated because citizens understand that self-interest motivates their leaders. As a result of the passions of the rulers, the ruled must be vigilant to protect their rights. A vigorous public realm is so necessary precisely because their republicanism is so hardheaded. Although the public realm they envision is vigorous, ultimately

---

[27] Locke, *Second Treatise*, para. 137, 359–60.

the activity that takes place there serves the private realm because it serves the individual's rights. Theirs is a modern, not an ancient, republicanism.

The English writers who fashioned this liberal republicanism had to be selective when they appealed to the thought of Machiavelli and Hobbes. They knew for what they were searching when they ransacked the works of these two thinkers to support the political life they envisioned. Both Machiavelli and Hobbes provided them with key elements of their understanding, but they embraced only some elements of each, transformed some of the rest, and eschewed those they could not appropriate or change.

The Formation of the Synthesis

This liberal republicanism did not emerge fully formed. Nedham, the first whose writings I examine, did much to transform Hobbes's teachings in a liberal direction, and thus much to effect this reconciliation, but each of the succeeding chapters in this study presents a stage in the process in the creation of this liberal republicanism. Each of the English republicans whom I treat draws on different elements of the thought of Machiavelli and Hobbes to offer a different combination of their teachings.

The final reconciliation occurs, I argue, in the thought of Trenchard and Gordon, writing as "Cato." In order to provide a fuller picture of what liberal republicanism is, I begin in this overview with what will be the end, with the conclusions that Cato, the expositor of a truly liberal republicanism, reaches. Cato is the only one of the thinkers I examine who had access to Locke's writings,[28] an access of which Cato obviously made generous use. For instance, not only does he appeal to Lockean doctrines, which, in fact, appear in some of the works of his predecessors as transformed Hobbesian doctrines – such as a state of nature in which all are equal and the notion that government itself is instituted through the consent of the governed in order to protect certain rights – but he also endorses the genuinely Lockean right of resistance to be wielded when governors fail to protect those rights. Cato is a true liberal.

Cato's Lockean liberalism, though, does not drive out some prominent and authentic Machiavellian sentiments. In particular, he evidences Machiavelli's own ambivalence toward the most ambitious in a state ("the great") on Machiavelli's own grounds. Cato displays at once a deep appreciation for the great because their passion for distinction can drive them to

---

[28] Blair Worden raises the intriguing question of what type of liberties did the editor of Algernon Sidney's *Discourses*, published in 1698, take with the manuscript. See Blair Worden, *Roundhead Reputations: The English Civil Wars and the Passions of Posterity* (London: Penguin Press, 2001). Although Locke's writings were not available to Sidney, they would have been available to the editor who prepared his manuscript for publication. See my discussion in Chapter 6.

magnificent accomplishments, as well as an acute awareness that their passions can pose a very grave threat to the state. To counter this danger, he closely follows Machiavelli's teaching on the necessity of ingratitude toward the most illustrious men when they commit crimes, an ingratitude that itself must issue in spectacular punishments. Because he allows the great such a large arena to pursue their desires and also allows the people the ability to challenge them, he not only accepts but relishes a tumultuous political life, as does Machiavelli.

As genuine as these Machiavellian sentiments are, Cato's teaching regarding the great is not strictly Machiavellian. Like Machiavelli, he offers glory seekers a great deal of latitude within the realm of politics, but he differs from the Italian in two important ways: he withholds from the ambitious access to the realm of war, where they traditionally sought honor, but proffers in its stead a new realm – that of commerce – where they can compete for honor. This move on Cato's part is most significant. Indeed, before republicanism could become truly liberal, it had to shed its romance with military adventures. Cato bids farewell to that lingering attraction that had prevented most of the earlier English Machiavellians from fully embracing liberalism. As a result, Cato commits his full allegiance to the party of the people, which seeks property and security. He agrees with Machiavelli that to desire to acquire is an ordinary and natural thing, but he will only follow the people's path to that increase – the path of peace rather than of war. As a result, Cato's Machiavellian spirit unflinchingly serves the protection of Lockean rights. This Machiavellian sensibility results in a spirited politics: the spirited great seeking distinction, and the spirited many vigilantly guarding their rights.

While Cato's reconciliation occurs in the early eighteenth century, well after the Bill of Rights and the Act of Settlement, Nedham, writing as a journalist during the Interregnum more than half a century earlier, without the writings of Locke on which to draw, offers a surprising anticipation of Cato's liberalism. At one point, he argues that political power should be distributed by the consent of the people, who establish government to protect their liberty and security, and that the people can withdraw their consent when the governors fail to provide for their security.

In addition, although famous as a turncoat, having written at different times in favor both of the king and Parliament, when in his republican mood Nedham seems to have learned his republicanism from Machiavelli's *Discourses*. He expresses admiration for republican Rome, retells many of Machiavelli's stories, and conveys the Machiavellian lessons deriving from those stories concerning such Machiavellian themes as the necessity of ingratitude, the desirability of tumults, and how the pursuit of individual passions can further the common good of a republic. Moreover, he learns from the Florentine to bring the people into the political realm, but he does not follow the logic that brings Machiavelli to the choice of a democratic republic. Nedham seems not overly concerned – as is Machiavelli – that the people, once in the political realm, be used for the prosecution of a republic's wars. Instead, this Englishman brings the people into the political realm in order for them to protect their own rights and liberties. In this, he is very much like Cato. Unlike Cato, however, he is extremely hesitant to cite Machiavelli's authority when he is clearly drawing on it. Thus, Nedham's fundamental differences with Cato derive from the facts that he could not draw on Locke's liberal political thought and that he is much more reticent to proclaim his debt to Machiavelli.

Harrington is a Machiavellian who focuses on some particular Machiavellian themes in order to dispute the Florentine's views. The depth of his disputes with Machiavelli is rather paradoxical, given the explicit praise he lavishes on him. The paradoxical character of the treatment he accords his sources is actually even deeper, because as much as he praises Machiavelli, he criticizes Hobbes. Despite all appearances, however, he agrees more with Hobbes than with Machiavelli on some of the most central issues of politics. Apparently, Hobbes receives his vociferous criticism and Machiavelli his praise, because the former supports monarchies and the latter republics. Nevertheless, he puts this disagreement regarding forms of government aside to follow Hobbes in being most wary of the ambitions of the great and in favoring a tranquil domestic realm. As a result of these Hobbesian concerns, he explicitly opposes Machiavelli's views with regard to tumults, and he dismisses Rome as too chaotic to provide an adequate republican model.

Rather than imitating ancient republican Rome, Harrington, in fact, devises his own model. In pursuing domestic tranquillity, he envisions a republic in which citizens do not strive to develop the moral character necessary to restrain their passions (as Aristotle recommends), but which can be perfect even if its citizens are imperfect. To effect this form of perfection, he relies on institutions and laws to contain what he regards as the politically deleterious passions of the citizens who populate his republic. His most famous device, in fact, is an agrarian law designed to limit the amount of property the republic's most wealthy citizens could hold. Such a provision, he believes, would go a long way to preventing the ravenous few from depleting the possessions of the many. In this way, it would help maintain the people in quiet. In this reliance on institutional remedies, Harrington is decidedly a modern, a fact attested to by a successor, Walter Moyle, a radical Whig and vocal admirer.[29] In *An Essay upon the Constitution of the Roman Government*,

[29] Moyle is another of the English republicans, and his thought contributes to the synthesis I outline here. I have chosen not to examine his thought in detail in this work because I do not believe it adds anything critical to the mix. Like Neville, Sidney, and Cato, he is an admirer of Harrington but finds himself diverging from his thought in important ways. In some of these ways, he anticipates the thought of Cato, but Cato's thought is much more developed. In fact, in 1697 Moyle collaborated with John Trenchard in writing *An Argument, Shewing that a Standing Army is Inconsistent with a Free Government, and Absolutely Destructive to the Constitution of the English Monarchy* (London, 1697), "the widest circulated and most

Moyle declares that an emphasis on property, which he knowingly borrows from Harrington, marks a significant divergence from ancient political thought. Indeed, Moyle notes that such an emphasis actually "confute[s]" Polybius's cycle of regimes. Polybius, declares Moyle, went wrong by declaring that the changes of regime derive from "moral reasons; such as vices and corruptions."[30]

Although Harrington is a modern because he diverges in this critical manner from the ancient emphasis on moral character, he evinces none of the liberal preferences, which later would become synonymous with modern political thought. Although an apt pupil of Hobbes, his political thought evidences no regard for a state of nature, consent as a basis of government, or a conception of individual rights.

Harrington's disinterest in liberal preferences is also evident in what amounts to a prominent agreement with Machiavelli and disagreement with Hobbes. Harrington designs his republic with the express purpose of pursuing offensive wars. When relishing the military accomplishments of his republic, which he does frequently, Harrington bares his Machiavellian teeth. Harrington is a Machiavellian, I suggest, largely because he endorses an aggressively belligerent republic. This endorsement also helps to undergird the political realm of Harrington's republic, which to a large extent is circumscribed by the constraining institutions that quell domestic conflict.

---

often reprinted tract of the coming century" (Caroline Robbins, introduction to *Two English Republican Tracts*, ed. Caroline Robbins [Cambridge: Cambridge University Press, 1969], 29). See also Z. S. Fink's *The Classical Republicans: An Essay in the Recovery of a Pattern of Thought in Seventeenth-Century England*, 2d ed. (Evanston, Ill.: Northwestern University Press, 1962), 29. The exact authorship of this pamphlet is still open to question. Blair Worden conjectures that Moyle, John Toland, and Trenchard "probably collaborated" on this pamphlet as well as on *A Short History of Standing Armies*, "although Moyle's is likely to have been the guiding pen" (Worden, "English Republicanism," 461). See also Worden, *Roundhead Reputations*, 105; Lois G. Schwoerer, "The Literature of the Standing Army Controversy, 1697–1699," *Huntington Library Quarterly* 28 (1965): 190–1.

[30] Walter Moyle, *An Essay upon the Constitution of the Roman Government*, in Robbins, *Two Republican Tracts*, 231. Classical republican scholarship makes the case that the ancient theory of mixed government fundamentally influenced Machiavelli and his followers in England. According to Fink, "the Greek historian Polybius" "was mainly responsible for giving the theory of mixed government its characteristic form" (*Classical Republicans*, 3). On Fink's understanding, because Machiavelli and the English embrace this type of mixed government, they are classical republicans. Fink ignores this distinction that Moyle draws between his own understanding of politics and that of Polybius. As a result, Fink declares that "Moyle's sentiments were those not only of a republican, but of a classical republican, the last really authentic specimen of the tribe" (*Classical Republicans*, 174). Pocock acknowledges the influence of Fink's work on his own depiction of these thinkers as indebted to an ancient conception of politics. See, for example, J. G. A. Pocock, "*The Machiavellian Moment* Revisited: A Study in History and Ideology," *Journal of Modern History* 53 (1981): 50, and "Machiavelli, Harrington and English Political Ideologies in the Eighteenth Century," in *Politics, Language, and Time: Essays on Political Thought and History* (New York: Atheneum, 1971), 106–7; all subsequent references to this article are to this version.

Harrington's fascination with war, then, forestalls liberal concerns for both the promotion of peace and the importance of the preservation of life. Moreover, always vulnerable to calls to arms in service of their country's military advancement, his republican citizens are prevented from pursuing their private and domestic happiness unimpeded. In this way, his republic's public life continually asserts itself into its citizens' private lives. Thus, unlike Hobbes's thought, there is a well-defined public space in Harrington's thought.

Like Nedham, therefore, Harrington uses the thought of both Hobbes and Machiavelli to construct his political thought. But he draws on elements different from those which attracted Nedham and would lead to a fully liberal republicanism. Harrington, in fact, radically diverges from the path that would appear to lead straight from Nedham's writings to those of Cato. Although he represents what might be seen as a detour in this story of liberal republicanism, his path must be followed because it leads through the very thinkers who represent the final destination. Neville and Cato admire Harrington for his prominent and distinctive notion that the distribution of property in a state determines what type of government it can sustain. Although they embrace this aspect of his teaching, they move away from another. The severe constraints that Harrington places on the passions in order to foster the domestic tranquillity he so values are fundamentally opposed to both Machiavelli's teaching and liberalism's intentions. Machiavelli and liberalism may value the free play of the passions for different purposes, but they are nevertheless united in valuing them. Neville, Sidney, and Cato all move away from Harrington's hesitations regarding the passions as they construct a liberal republicanism.

As much as he was a friend of Harrington and actively undertook to transmit his ideas, Neville introduces to the Harringtonian universe new ideas – liberal ones, in fact – that ultimately serve to undermine some of Harrington's own intentions. As a result, Neville represents that first step away from Harrington. Neville reveals Hobbes's influence – but an influence different from the one that Hobbes exerts on Harrington's thought – when he describes a state of nature in which its residents possess a right to all things. Following Hobbes, Neville pronounces that the universal right to all collapses into a state of war. Like Nedham, and in contrast to Harrington, Neville refers to the fact that people consent to government in order to live a secure life. The purpose of government, according to Neville, is to provide for security. Again, like Nedham, Neville takes a step beyond Hobbes to declare that citizens may judge their governments on the basis of how well they provide that security.

Neville is also clearly devoted to Machiavelli. In addition to displaying a propensity to term the Florentine "divine," he produced an English translation of the collected works of Machiavelli. Thus, he was acquainted with the details of his thought, and that authentic knowledge of Machiavelli is evident, because he draws on Machiavellian themes that had not been transmitted by Harrington. The political situation Neville faces is different from the one that confronts Harrington, and the use he makes of Machiavelli's thought accords with those changed circumstances. After the monarchy has been restored, Neville does not vociferously declare in favor of a republic for England, as Harrington does when the monarchy had been overturned. Still apparently harboring republican sentiments after the Restoration, though, Neville emphasizes Machiavelli's teaching that sometimes significant political change can occur so subtly that the depth of the change is not evident to all. That is precisely the type of change Neville proposes to remedy England's political ills – namely, to modify most subtly the king's power in the direction of a republic. Writing during the Exclusion Crisis that occurred during the reign of Charles II, when England's Protestants feared that their next king would be a Catholic, he draws on what he finds to be another appealing aspect of Machiavelli's thought, his anticlericalism. Neville associates republicanism with Protestantism and absolutism with Catholicism. To support this association, he offers an anachronistic Machiavelli – one of his own creation – who supports the Protestant Reformation.

Not as subtle as Neville in presenting and acting on his republican sympathies, Sidney was executed during the reign of Charles II for his alleged participation in the Rye House Plot. When trying Sidney for his life, the prosecution used portions of the accused's writings as a witness against him. In his life and in his writings, then, Sidney could not always dissemble his political allegiances.

He is subtle, though, in his own endorsement of Machiavelli, although he ultimately embraces openly an authentically Machiavellian teaching: the necessity of a republic designed for the accumulation of empire. What appears to induce this embrace is Sidney's zealous endorsement of republics. Republics do everything better than monarchies, he maintains, including waging war. The source he uses to corroborate this claim is Machiavelli's *Discourses*, which highlights both the necessity of war and the success of the Roman Republic at acquiring the empire. Having arrived at this juncture, Sidney reveals his devotion to Machiavelli's thought by doggedly following his logic that establishes Rome's superiority to other ancient and armed republics. He also appeals to another tenet of the *Discourses*, the necessity of punishing wrongdoers. He is in these respects an unreconstructed follower of Machiavelli, although he does not present himself in this manner. As a result, his commentators have failed to appreciate the depth of his allegiance to Machiavelli.

Sidney, however, applies the ferocious Machiavellian teaching in favor of stern punishments in the service of some liberal principles – in particular, the punishment of a monarch who infringes on the rights of the people to life, liberty, and property. He is a contractarian thinker who posits one contract that removes people from the prepolitical position and another that exists between the governor or governors and the people. The people, at any time, he declares, can withdraw their consent from the latter contract. Although Sidney helps to illustrate how Machiavellian vengeance and mass political participation can be brought to bear for liberal causes, ultimately his liberalism is equivocal because it stumbles on his Machiavellian embrace of war. He cannot apply his principle of consent universally, for example, because he endorses a conquering republic that subdues other states to its will. Moreover, he cannot allow the people to pursue their desire to acquire through peaceful endeavors, because, like Harrington, he would keep them armed and deployed.

As I have already suggested, Cato reaches the position that Sidney at times outlines but cannot fully sustain. Cato, rather than Sidney, reaches this destination because his liberalism is not equivocal: he eschews the Machiavellian embrace of war. Although he rejects this important and prominent theme of Machiavelli, his other Machiavellian themes are nuanced and robust. His politics reflects the Machiavellian analysis of the passions; it embraces competition and tumults but follows the pursuit of Machiavellian glory not into the martial but only into the political and commercial realms.

An examination of the thought of these English Machiavellians reveals that they draw on a surprising range of Machiavellian ideas. It is clear that each of the thinkers, in formulating his political thought, ventured to the source himself. Thus, it appears that the earlier ones, Nedham and Harrington, by invoking Machiavelli's authority in support of their causes (Harrington more often and more enthusiastically than Nedham), kept alive an attraction for Machiavelli for the thinkers who would be influenced by their writings. Thus, the later ones follow the example of the earlier in seeking guidance from Machiavelli's thought. Their uses of his thought become ever more nuanced and authentic, as can be seen particularly in the thought of Neville, Sidney, and Cato.

These Englishmen were not only writers but also often political actors – members of Parliament, plotters, and journalists jailed for their incendiary proclamations. They lived during tumultuous times and wrote in direct response to the political controversies of their day. In most cases, they intended to produce tracts in response to these controversies, not doctrines for the ages. Not thinkers of the caliber of Machiavelli or of Hobbes, they intended not to plumb for themselves the depths of human nature and of the origins and foundation of society. They were interested in such questions, however, and relied on those who did pursue such topics. These writers show how the various doctrines they used can be applied to specific political exigencies. They thereby show the resilience and adaptability of these doctrines.

The English Republicans and the Classical Republican Interpretation

This very political character of these thinkers has helped make them popular figures in the recent classical republican scholarship. That scholarship, though, offers a very different depiction of their thought and its sources than the one I offer here. Rather than depicting these English Machiavellians as formulators and promoters of liberalism, it portrays them as its dogged and hostile opponents. These English republicans do not welcome the new, on this alternative interpretation, but cling to the ancient past.

This erroneous depiction of the thinkers who drew on Machiavelli arises, I will demonstrate, largely from a fundamental misunderstanding of Machiavelli's thought that has been promulgated by the prominent historians of political thought, J. G. A. Pocock and Quentin Skinner. Each makes Machiavelli a central figure in the story each tells of the alternative to the modern, liberal conception of politics that flourished well after liberalism's advent. That alternative is ancient, community-centered, republican, and Machiavellian, they both argue. Because Machiavelli's thought was so influential, the thought of the ancients that he imbibed from his Renaissance surroundings he passed on to his readers in England, who, then, transmitted it to America.

As a result of their work, the adjective "Machiavellian" has become almost synonymous with "classical," "civic humanist," or even "Aristotelian." The pervasiveness of the understanding cannot be more effectively demonstrated than through the work of their critics. For example, Ronald Hamowy and Alan Craig Houston challenge elements of the classical republican scholarship by producing compelling interpretations of the thought of Cato and Sidney, respectively, which suggest a fundamental compatibility between these works and the writings of Locke – a conclusion with which my interpretation of these thinkers fully concurs. In offering this Lockean reading of their subjects, they both claim that Pocock, who labels both Sidney and Cato civic humanists, goes wrong by overlooking the modern elements of the writer each examines. Although Hamowy and Houston challenge Pocock with respect to the writer each treats, they themselves downplay the Machiavellian themes the writer also espouses. Their concurrent attention to liberalism and to the dismissal of Machiavelli's influence results, I believe, from an acceptance of Pocock's interpretation of Machiavelli as an adherent of classical political thought. If Sidney and Cato hold views compatible with those of Locke, Machiavelli cannot hold serious appeal for either of them, these two critics of the republican interpretation suggest. Therefore, paradoxically, these challengers to the classical republican interpretation actually demonstrate its pervasiveness.[31] In this way, we see the toll that the simplified

---

[31] Ronald Hamowy, "*Cato's Letters*, John Locke, and the Republican Paradigm," *History of Political Thought* 11 (1990): 273–94, and Alan Craig Houston, *Algernon Sidney and the*

view that Machiavelli's republicanism is always opposed to liberalism exacts on our historical understanding. It hinders scholars' abilities to assess the true nature of each by discouraging the identification of those places where they intermingle.

Despite the unsatisfactory character of the classical republican interpretations of Machiavelli's thought, and hence of the thought of those whom Machiavelli influenced, it is necessary to acknowledge the great benefits that have resulted from Pocock's and Skinner's reformulation of great swaths of intellectual history.[32] They have enriched our understanding of the depth and scope of Machiavelli's influence by establishing his impact on a myriad of later thinkers, thus bringing these other thinkers forward as subjects worthy of renewed and intensive scholarly scrutiny. Moreover, they rejuvenated, by deepening, fields of inquiry previously dominated by economic and materialist understandings of thought,[33] an understanding abetted in the field of American political history by a complacent understanding of liberalism, which assured its domination of American thought and society but did not search for its meaning in its original sources.[34] In addition, their suggestions that the republican tradition was the desirable alternative to Lockean liberalism challenged respondents to their interpretation to give a more nuanced attention to the classical texts of liberalism than had many scholars of previous generations. This new attention has helped to reveal the interest of the original liberal thinkers in the constitution of the self as well as in the individual's relation to the community.[35]

Skinner has to a certain extent helped to break down the strict dichotomy between republicanism and liberalism by significantly modifying the tradition he understands Machiavelli as conveying. In *Liberty before Liberalism*, which was developed from his Inaugural Lecture as Regius Professor of Modern History in the University of Cambridge in 1997, Skinner offers a "neo-roman" depiction of Machiavelli's influence on the very thinkers whom

Republican Heritage in England and America (Princeton: Princeton University Press, 1991), 5–8, 164–5.

[32] Daniel T. Rodgers, "Republicanism: The Career of a Concept," *Journal of American History* 79 (1992): 11–38, terms the impact of the republicanism on American history a Kuhnian paradigm shift.

[33] E.g., Charles Beard, *An Economic Interpretation of the Constitution* (1913; reprint, with a new introduction, New York: Macmillan, 1935); C. B. Macpherson, *The Political Theory of Possessive Individualism: Hobbes to Locke* (Oxford: Oxford University Press, 1962).

[34] Louis Hartz, *The Liberal Tradition in America: An Interpretation of American Political Thought since the Revolution* (New York: Harcourt, Brace, 1955).

[35] E.g., Peter Berkowitz, *Virtue and the Making of Modern Liberalism* (Princeton: Princeton University Press, 1999); Peter C. Myers, *Our Only Star and Compass: Locke and the Struggle for Political Rationality* (Lanham, Md.: Rowman & Littlefield, 1998); Nathan Tarcov, *Locke's Education for Liberty* (Chicago: University of Chicago Press, 1984); Michael P. Zuckert, *Launching Liberalism: On Lockean Political Philosophy* (Lawrence: University Press of Kansas, 2002).

I treat here: Nedham, Harrington, Neville, Sidney, and Trenchard.[36] Because
Skinner has over the years so modified his presentation of the tradition
Machiavelli transmits – from humanism[37] to classical republicanism that embraces negative liberty[38] to this neo-roman tradition – it is not clear whether
the interpretation I offer of these English Machiavellians is so much a stark
alternative to his most recent offering as it is a further step along the same
path. Nevertheless, a significant difference between our interpretations resides in the fact that Skinner still insists on linking Machiavelli, and hence
his influence, to classical antiquity.[39]

The neo-romans, maintains Skinner, share basic assumptions derived primarily from a Roman conception of law and from the Roman historians
Livy, Tacitus, and Sallust. Informed by these ancient sources, these thinkers
converge around an understanding of what it means for an individual to
live in freedom. According to Skinner, their thought repeatedly equates the
freedom of a state with that of an individual human being, likening a state
of civic unfreedom to personal slavery.[40] At one point Skinner summarizes
that the "main conclusion to which these writers are committed is thus that
it is only possible to enjoy civil liberty to the full if you live as the citizen of a

---

[36] Skinner, *Liberty before Liberalism*.

[37] Skinner's humanist depictions of Machiavelli can be found in *The Renaissance* and *Machiavelli*
(New York: Hill and Wang, 1981); reprint, *Machiavelli: A Very Short Introduction* (Oxford:
Oxford University Press, 2000). Page citations are to the reprint edition. In these particular
works, Skinner acknowledges his intention to work within the tradition of thought that
Hans Baron and Pocock had explicated, although Skinner indicates he supplements their
work by concentrating on the contributions of Roman, as opposed to Greek, thought (*The
Renaissance*, xiv and 156 and n.).

[38] Quentin Skinner, "Machiavelli on *Virtù* and the Maintenance of Liberty," in *Renaissance
Virtues*, vol. 2 of *Visions of Politics* (Cambridge: Cambridge University Press, 2002), 160–85,
reprint of "Machiavelli on the Maintenance of Liberty," *Politics* 18 (1983): 3–15; Quentin
Skinner, "The Idea of Negative Liberty: Machiavellian and Modern Perspectives," in *Re-
naissance Virtues*, 186–212, reprint of "The Idea of Negative Liberty: Philosophical in His-
torical Perspectives," in *Philosophy in History: Essays on the Historiography of Philosophy*, ed.
Richard Rorty, J. B. Schneewind, and Quentin Skinner (Cambridge: Cambridge University
Press, 1984), 193–221. Subsequent page references are to the reprint editions. Quentin Skin-
ner, "Paradoxes of Political Liberty," in *The Tanner Lectures on Human Values* 7, ed. Sterling
M. McMurrin (Salt Lake City: University of Utah Press), 227–50; Quentin Skinner, "The
Republican Ideal of Political Liberty," in Bock et al., *Machiavelli and Republicanism*; Quentin
Skinner, "Machiavelli's *Discorsi* and the Pre-humanist Origins of Republican Ideas," in Bock
et al., *Machiavelli and Republicanism*.

[39] Skinner does not offer a new interpretation of Machiavelli's thought to support his influence
on this neo-roman tradition but rather relies on his earlier interpretations (*Liberty before
Liberalism*, 10 and n. 29).

[40] E.g., Skinner, *Liberty before Liberalism*, 23, 45–6. Skinner draws heavily on Philip Pettit,
Republicanism: A Theory of Freedom and Government (Oxford: Oxford University Press,
1997).

free state."[41] This represents a considerably modified description from those that Skinner offered previously of the character of the classical thought that Machiavelli revived and transmitted.

Despite the facts that Skinner entitles the book *Liberty before Liberalism* and states "the theory of free states continued to be a thorn in the side of contractarian...theories of government until well into the eighteenth century,"[42] the book as a whole in many ways suggests – although far from proclaims – the compatibility between the ancient republican tradition and Lockean liberalism.[43] Further, breaking with his earlier claims regarding a Roman understanding of negative liberty associated with Machiavelli's articulation of classical republicanism, the tradition Skinner describes in this later book no longer makes virtue a necessary precondition for the preservation of liberty. In addition, in this book, he no longer associates liberty specifically with republics. Skinner reveals that virtue – and hence classical virtue – no longer plays a central role in the tradition Machiavelli transmits when he comments in a footnote on his statement that according to the neo-roman understanding both rulers and citizens must be equally subject to law. He specifies in the note that "[t]his is not to say that individual freedom according to these writers can in some sense be *equated* with virtue."[44] Liberty and virtue, then, are no longer equated in the tradition he understands Machiavelli as transmitting. He unhinges liberty and republics when he notes that "many of the writers I am considering actively prefer a system of mixed government in which there is a monarchical element together with an aristocratic senate and a democratic assembly to represent the citizens as a whole."[45] Republics, then, are no longer critical to the mix.

Locke, of course, endorses precisely such a type of government. This recognition suggests a point of compatibility between Skinner's neo-roman tradition and Lockean liberalism. The relation of Locke's thought with Skinner's neo-romans is much deeper, because Skinner, in fact, acknowledges in a footnote that Locke "espouse[s] the theory of liberty" that he associates with the Roman jurists and historians.[46] In the text itself, he explains that the neo-romans "assume that the freedom or liberty they are describing can be equated with – or, more precisely, spelled out as – the unconstrained

---

[41] Skinner, *Liberty before Liberalism*, 68.

[42] Ibid., 12.

[43] The real opponent of the neo-roman understanding appears to be William Paley (Skinner, *Liberty before Liberalism*, 77–82). See also Pincus's critique of Skinner's depiction of the neo-romans and of their differences with early liberals, in "Commercial Society and Defenders of the English Commonwealth," 706, 709 and n. 13, and 732–3 and n. 152.

[44] Skinner, *Liberty before Liberalism*, 74, n. 38.

[45] Ibid., 54.

[46] Ibid., 55, n. 177.

enjoyment of a number of specific rights."[47] He corroborates this claim with
evidence from Nedham, whom he quotes as declaring that "[n]ot only are
we endowed by God with a number of 'natural rights and liberties', but 'the
end of all government is (or ought to be) the good and ease of the people, in a
secure enjoyment of their rights, without pressure and oppression.'"[48] In this
way, Skinner's most recent treatment of Machiavelli's successors suggests –
but, as I said earlier, does not proclaim – that their thought is not fundamentally incompatible with liberalism. To this extent, Skinner's depiction of
Machiavelli's influence and my own cohere.

Nevertheless, Skinner still insists that the first debt these thinkers owe was
to the Roman understanding of liberty conveyed to them by the Roman historians.[49] He often prefers to attribute elements of their thought to antiquity,
when, in fact, a modern explanation is actually just as, if not more, plausible. For instance, he argues that the "disciples" of the ancient Roman writers
during the Renaissance follow Sallust, in particular, when they understand
the purpose of liberty as greatness.[50] Skinner, however, discerns that some
later thinkers in the neo-roman tradition express "a growing suspicion of
the ethics of glory and the pursuit of civic greatness." For Skinner, that hesitation too comes from Sallust, who also "laments" the greed that Rome's
empire fostered in its people. According to Skinner, these later thinkers "begin to place their main emphasis on the capacity of such regimes to secure
and promote the liberties of their own citizens."[51] To corroborate this point,
he refers in a footnote to Trenchard who "explicitly denounced the pursuit of conquest and military glory."[52] I too note the same hesitation in the
thought of Cato, but I link it not to an ambivalent Roman source but to
Cato's liberalism, which, I argue, he drew directly from Locke. In this work,
thus, Skinner still insists on specifying that Machiavelli and his successors
participate in a tradition of ancient political thought. In fact, he sees it as
"important to underline" the ancient character of their thought, given that
"recent commentators" "have argued for a sharp distinction between ancient
and modern republicanism."[53]

---

[47] Ibid., 18.

[48] Ibid., 20.

[49] For criticism of Skinner's depiction of this thought as classical generally and Roman specifically, see the reviews of the book by Paul Rahe, "Quentin Skinner's 'Third Way,'" *Review of
Politics* 62 (2000): 395–8, and Blair Worden, "Factory of the Revolution," *London Review
of Books* 20 (5 February 1998): 13–15.

[50] Skinner, *Liberty before Liberalism*, 61. Skinner also maintains at times that Machiavelli regards
the freedom to pursue their own ends as the ultimate purpose that free states render to their
citizens (Skinner, "Paradoxes of Political Liberty," 239–40, and Skinner, "Republican Ideal
of Political Liberty," 301–2).

[51] Skinner, *Liberty before Liberalism*, 64–5.

[52] Ibid., 65–6, n. 17.

[53] He names Paul Rahe in particular (Skinner, *Liberty before Liberalism*, 36, n. 113).

I, too, argue for that distinction. In order to make my case that a modern form of republicanism came to fruition in the thought of these writers of the English republican tradition, I first turn to its foundations in the writings of Machiavelli and Hobbes. After considering the foundations, I turn to the creators of the synthesis themselves: Nedham, Harrington, Neville, Sidney, and Cato.

PART I

THE FOUNDATIONS OF LIBERAL REPUBLICANISM

I

Machiavelli's Republicanism

The character of Machiavelli's republicanism comes most fully to light in his work *Discourses on the First Ten Books of Titus Livy*. His support of republics, then, is revealed in his treatment of Rome, which treatment, in turn, reveals much of the author himself; it presents a commentator delighting in Rome and its exploits. The Rome he embraces is marked by its dividedness, by its aggressiveness, and by its acquisitiveness. His is a republic that positively bristles with the energy emanating from the members of each class, the patricians and the plebeians, attempting to quench their unquenchable desires at the expense of the members of the other. With the desires of its population so highly keyed, Rome was an acquisitive dynamo because the safe outlet for these desires was the pursuit of empire.

As much as he admires Rome, he thinks he can improve on that ancient city. One sees the admirer actually recoil from his object of delight as he acknowledges that his esteemed republic eventually succumbed to tyranny. This recognition leads to others; he expresses hesitations with regard to the Roman Republic not only when it was in decline but also when it was seemingly at its most vigorous. Having ascertained the reasons for its collapse, Machiavelli charges that Rome did not have a sufficiently Machiavellian attitude toward its most ambitious men. Too respectful and, as a result, too permissive toward them, Rome was vulnerable to its great men's attempts to attain sole rule. And, in point of fact, the republic's collapse came when it allowed an extremely ambitious man to propel himself to tyranny by taking up the cause of the plebeians against the patricians.

Armed with this hindsight, Machiavelli makes it his enterprise to instruct "someone wish[ing] . . . to order a republic anew" (1.6.4).[1] Machiavelli's instruction – his plans for a republic even more enduring than historical Rome – combines the many admirable aspects of that republic with his own solution to the problem of its vulnerability to such ambitious men. His solution

---

[1] References to Machiavelli's *Discourses* in this chapter appear in the text.

can be encapsulated as an insistence on taking the dimmest possible view of any sort of ambition carrying even the slightest suggestion that it might be turned against the republic; he teaches the prospective founder that a republic cannot countenance any insolence toward its laws and that, as a result, it must maintain the utmost suspicion toward its leading men. It should act on that suspicion by punishing most harshly and, as a result, should be a fearful place. He clearly has learned from the Roman case, and he wishes to use that knowledge to correct its mistakes.[2] Of course, he teaches these lessons while insisting that a republic pursue military conquest and, hence, while unleashing the ambitions of the great on the battlefield and lauding their exploits there. He is not in the least afraid that such punishments taken against the great inside the republic will dampen their quest for honor outside of it. Honor seekers would seem to pursue their quarry anywhere they can.

Although his conquering republic must take particular care to channel the ambitions of the great, the desires of the people in such a republic also receive his attention. He insists on a republic that gives a prominent place to the people; he insists, in fact, on a democratic republic on the model of Rome. His concern both for the people's incorporation and for the degree to which a republic must placate their demands derives not from an interest in the self-development of the individual that might redound from political participation, or a belief in the justness of the people's cause, or an assertion of the equality among all human beings despite their social status. In his view, the people's participation is a necessary, but admittedly inconvenient, means to his end. Only a republic that allows the people some voice will be able to deploy an army large enough to conquer and maintain an empire. The people and their political participation are merely means to his end of war.

Each class in the city, the great and the people, offers Machiavelli an important component for the acquisitive republic he envisions, but each

---

[2] In highlighting Machiavelli's regard for the belligerent Roman Republic, my interpretation has much in common with those of J. Patrick Coby (*Machiavelli's Romans: Liberty and Greatness in the "Discourses on Livy"* [Lanham, Md.: Lexington Books, 1999]) and Mark Hulliung (*Citizen Machiavelli* [Princeton: Princeton University Press, 1983]). My interpretation differs from theirs, though, in understanding that, as much as Machiavelli admired Rome and hoped for a republic to imitate many prominent features of it, he also reveals both his dissatisfaction with it and the manner in which he would improve it. Its susceptibility to tyranny makes Machiavelli express at times what is almost contemptuousness, as we shall see. I have argued in another place (*Machiavelli's Three Romes: Religion, Human Liberty, and Politics Reformed* [DeKalb: Northern Illinois University Press, 1996]) that Machiavelli regards Rome's susceptibility to tyranny as related to the use it made of its pagan religion, a theme beyond my immediate purpose here. For a discussion of the mistakes Rome made before it was corrupt and the suggestion that Machiavelli understands that improvement on Rome's modes and orders should be sought, see Leo Strauss, *Thoughts on Machiavelli* (Chicago: University of Chicago Press, 1958), 114–20. See also Harvey C. Mansfield, *Machiavelli's Virtue* (Chicago: University of Chicago Press, 1996), 261–2.

also presents problems so severe that either class could subvert his very purpose – the establishment of a martial and democratic republic. The nobles possess the drive for honor and glory so necessary for a martial republic. Their love of dominion, though, can induce them to oppress the people, an oppression that would overturn his democratic republic. Moreover, those same passions in their most intense form could drive an individual to contend for tyranny – the most dangerous threat to his republic. The people present him with another set of assets and dangers. Their numbers furnish the body of his army. The members of this class love to acquire, but they also love security. When their love of security induces them to desert from his army, again his purposes are subverted. These threats emanating from each side keep Machiavelli in constant motion. He is on the side of the people when the nobles' oppression threatens, and he is on the side of the great when the people's defection looms. He is not, then, a principled supporter of either side but rather a dogged supporter of a martial republicanism.

Given that he is presumptuous enough to attempt to improve on Rome, the ancient practice he so admires, it is hardly surprising that he displays no particular allegiance to ancient philosophy. In fact, he has no respect whatsoever for the ancient philosophic understanding of the republican citizen and ruler as using and perfecting intellectual and moral virtue.[3] Machiavelli is far too interested in applying the human passions to his worldly enterprise of seeing human beings liberated "from a mode of life" that "seems to have rendered the world weak and given it in prey to criminal men, who can manage it securely, seeing that the collectivity of men, so as to go to paradise, think more of enduring their beatings than of avenging them" (2.2.2). He wishes to foster in the people of his time a relish for the prizes of this life rather than of the afterlife. With this end in view, he has no use for the excellence of the human soul, even as it was articulated by the ancient philosophers as opposed to the Christian thinkers.

Although he seeks to apply the human passions to worldly concerns, his citizen is certainly not a bourgeois. Although Machiavelli lauds the desire to acquire and upholds the desire of the people for security, he specifically intends for them not to achieve that end, for its attainment would necessitate the eradication of war. The acquisition Machiavelli seeks derives from war, not trade. He is too distracted by his promotion of war to be concerned with the rights or liberties of the individuals who serve in the republican armies he envisions.

The primary purpose of this chapter is to provide an exposition as faithfully as possible of Machiavelli's republicanism as it comes to light in his

---

[3] I outline my objections to Pocock's Aristotelian reading of the *Discourses* in Vickie B. Sullivan, "Machiavelli's Momentary 'Machiavellian Moment': A Reconsideration of Pocock's Treatment of the *Discourses,*" *Political Theory* 20 (1992): 309–18.

response to Rome in his *Discourses*. I also intend for it to serve the additional purpose of providing a foundation for the examination that is to follow of the use the English republicans made of Machiavelli's thought. In light of this purpose, this chapter serves as a point of reference when I turn to examine the themes that the English acolytes of Machiavelli explicitly embrace or reject, as well as salient themes of the Italian they silently disregard. In the process of responding to the Florentine in these ways, we will observe how these republicans transform Machiavellian themes for their own purposes, using elements of his thought – often for purposes of which he would likely disapprove – to construct a type of republicanism compatible with major tenets of liberalism.

Machiavelli's Rome and Its Pursuit of Empire

Machiavelli is a partisan of republics. He is a partisan of a particular type of republic – that is, of an aggressive, acquisitive republic. Before the exaltation of liberty, before the demonstration of public spiritedness, before the pursuit of the public good, Machiavelli judges the goodness of a republic by its ability to conquer in war. A republic worthy of his admiration may pursue these other goods or embody these other attributes, but they always serve his greater good of empire.[4] Given this criterion, he is a particular partisan of the ancient Roman Republic, declaring with not a small measure of satisfaction that "the Roman army . . . conquered the world" (3.36.2).

When baldly asserting the purpose of his admired republic, he simultaneously pinpoints the characteristic that distinguishes Rome from its republican rivals: "Rome had as its end empire and glory and not quiet" (2.9.1). By contrast, quiet is what, in his view, both the modern Venetian republic, which did not "employ the plebs in war," and the ancient Spartan republic, which did "not open the way to foreigners," pursued, and early in his *Discourses* he weighs the alternative that these two republics seem to present to his own devotion to a decidedly bellicose republicanism (1.6.3).

By refusing to employ either method that would have helped to assure a measure of domestic tranquillity, Rome chose the path of conquest abroad and tumults at home. These tumults were a result of the fact that Rome embraced the people, whether natives or foreigners, as the might of its armies, thus giving "the plebs strength and increase and infinite opportunities for tumult" (1.6.3). Tumults are indeed an inconvenience, he concedes, but

---

4 Hulliung, *Citizen Machiavelli*, 6; Mansfield, *Machiavelli's Virtue*, 16; Markus Fischer, *Well-Ordered License: On the Unity of Machiavelli's Thought* (Lanham, Md.: Lexington Books, 2000), 146.

he also insists that when one "examines well" "human things," one finds "that one inconvenience can never be suppressed without another's cropping up." With this consideration in mind, he compares the inconvenience of Rome's way with that of its rival republics: "[I]f you wish to make a people numerous and armed so as to be able to make a great empire, you make it of such a quality that you cannot then manage it in your mode; if you maintain it either small or unarmed so as to be able to manage it, then if you acquire dominion you cannot hold it or it becomes so cowardly that you are the prey of whoever assaults you" (1.6.3). He here casts his analysis of the comparative advantages of Rome in the form of advice to a potential founder who must choose between the good of world conquest combined with the inconvenience of domestic unrest or the good of domestic quiet combined with the inconvenience of a state unable to acquire without becoming perilously weak.

Machiavelli continues to make the case for Rome as if he were proffering to a prospective founder the choice between empire or maintenance: "If someone wished, therefore, to order a republic anew, he would have to examine whether he wished it to expand like Rome in dominion and in power or truly to remain within narrow limits." As he continues to weigh the inconvenience of a republic's inability to expand, however, the choice of Rome becomes even more evident. Because "acquisitions, founded on a weak republic, are its ruin altogether" (1.6.4), a quiet republic must avoid at all costs those circumstances that would lead to expansion, which means that it must avoid war entirely. War cannot help but lead such a state to its downfall, for war waged unsuccessfully by definition entails ruin, and war waged successfully, of course, entails the very expansion it is incapable of handling. He remarks that the cases of Sparta and Venice illustrate this latter outcome; these quiet republics were ruined by the rebellions of their conquered territories.

Because a quiet republic must completely shun war, Machiavelli inquires whether war can be avoided entirely. In pursuit of an answer, he reasons that a republic may choose not to make war, but others may decide to make war on it. Given this possibility, he proceeds to consider the reasons why another state would initiate such an attack: "one, to become master of it; the other, for fear lest it seize you." The second seems to permit of a solution: "If it stays within its limits, and it is seen by experience that there is no ambition in it, it will never occur that one will make war for fear of it." The first also seems to permit of a solution, although Machiavelli does not state that solution in terms quite so emphatic: "[F]or if it is difficult to capture it, as I presuppose,...it will happen rarely, or never, that one can make a plan to acquire it" (1.6.4).

As hopeful as these reflections seem, Machiavelli's further considerations show that he believes that one cannot rely on the possibility of avoiding war.

He declares:

> Without doubt I believe that if the thing could be held balanced in this mode, it would be the true political way of life and the true quiet of a city. But since all things of men are in motion and cannot stay steady, they must either rise or fall; and to many things that reason does not bring you, necessity brings you. So, when a republic that has been ordered so as to be capable of maintaining itself does not expand, and necessity leads it to expand, this would come to take away its foundations and make it come to ruin sooner. (1.6.4)

It would appear that because human things are in motion, "necessity" guarantees that war will come. It would appear that the passions of human beings propel this motion and this necessity. He states elsewhere in the *Discourses*, for example, that "human appetites are insatiable," and that "from nature [people] have the ability and the wish to desire all things" (2pr.3). In another place, he explains that "since [human] desire is always greater than the power of acquiring, the result is discontent with what one possesses and a lack of satisfaction with it. From this arises the variability of their fortune; for since some men desire to have more, and some fear to lose what has been acquired, they come to enmities and to war, from which arise the ruin of one province and the exaltation of another" (1.37.1).

It remains a question, though, from what direction the insatiability of human desires impacts a state and, hence, narrows its choices. Must a potential founder reject the pursuit of quiet because outsiders will desire to dominate a republic that evidences no ambition of its own; or because as much as a republic intends to disown armed acquisition, the allure of dominating other states is simply too powerful to resist? Machiavelli does not specify. Given his view of the passions, perhaps both explanations inform his conclusion. In any case, either explanation demands that a state be able to fight wars successfully and hence be capable of expanding. Seen in this light, then, foreign affairs dictate domestic arrangements. A state must embrace the inconvenience of a large and armed populace as well as the tumult that such a populace will necessarily engender.

Machiavelli, however, does not leave it at that. He invokes necessity from the opposite direction. If foreign relations demand an aggressive republic, so too do domestic considerations. Even if a state never had to go to war, the resulting peace would bring ruin from entirely domestic causes. He explains, "on the other hand, if heaven were so kind that it did not have to make war, from that would arise the idleness to make it either effeminate or divided; these two things together, or each by itself, would be the cause of its ruin" (1.6.4). Seen from this perspective, then, domestic relations determine an aggressive foreign policy. He reiterates this view much later in the *Discourses* when he declares that the "cause of the disunion of republics is usually idleness and peace; the cause of union is fear and war" (2.25.1). He embraces war because of its necessity both in countering foreign aggression and in permitting domestic control. Machiavelli emphatically teaches, then, the necessity and goodness of war, because ruin awaits, if a republic does not embrace it.[5] A republic must embrace the Roman way in order to avert a premature demise.[6] According to Machiavelli's logic, a founder has no choice between inconveniences: "I believe that it is necessary to follow the Roman order and not that of the other republics . . . and to tolerate the enmities that arise between the people and the Senate, taking them as an inconvenience necessary to arrive at Roman greatness" (1.6.4). His advice to a potential founder is that necessity, whether of foreign or domestic origin, dictates that a republic make empire its end.

Rome, in this respect, must be the model for anyone founding a republic. Indeed, so enamored is he with Rome's powers of acquisition that when discussing in his treatise on principalities how a prince should maintain

---

[5] See Rahe, *Republics Ancient and Modern*, 263, for a discussion of the significance of Machiavelli's rejection of Sparta and embrace of Rome as a rejection of Aristotle's view of politics. I consider the contrast between Machiavelli and Aristotle on war and peace in my discussion of the republicanism of Sidney, where I reach conclusions compatible with Rahe's. Skinner highlights Machiavelli's preference for an imperialistic republic in *Machiavelli*, 82–7, but does not draw the type of conclusion as does Rahe. Pocock, *Machiavellian Moment*, 199–204, however, points to Machiavelli's embrace of "an aggressive republic to dominate in a disordered world" as a manifestation of his ultimate reliance on Aristotle's view of citizenship.

[6] It is odd indeed that Machiavelli insists on embracing Rome and rejecting Sparta on the basis of longevity (acquisitive republics last longer than quiet ones), because Sparta lasted longer than did the republic he embraces here, a fact that he reports in 1.5. My interpretation explains Machiavelli's insistence here in maintaining Rome's superiority even to an extremely long-lived Spartan republic as an attempt to suggest that Rome, as a republic organized for empire, possessed a great deal of potential for an extremely long life that it left unrealized. As a result of that potential, he embraces Rome as a model for a new founder. His very embrace on this basis, though, also constitutes a tacit criticism of historical Rome for not fulfilling that very potential. As I argue, Machiavelli believes the Roman Republic collapsed as a result of Rome's incompetence in handling the corruption created by its most ambitious men. Coby notes the strangeness of Machiavelli's explanation for his choice of Rome, stating that his "case for Rome and against Sparta was never that convincing," but explains Machiavelli's preference for Rome anyway by his desire not for mere survival but for "survival in style, or greatness," a criterion that Sparta cannot fulfill (*Romans*, 261; cf. 37, 39, 44–7). While not denying Machiavelli's desire for greatness, I take more seriously than does Coby Machiavelli's explicit claims that the Roman pursuit of greatness confers greater potential for an extended life. Cf. Skinner's statement: "Since Rome preserved its freedom for more than four hundred years, it seems that its citizens must have correctly identified the most serious threats to their liberties, and gone on to evolve the right *ordini* for dealing with them" (*Machiavelli*, 77). Pocock offers a description of Machiavelli's preference for Rome in terms opposite to mine: "[N]ow we learn that the ideal of stability itself is not the only value to be pursued, since a republic may pursue empire at the sacrifice of its own longevity – a choice which involves a preference for a more popular form of government" (*Machiavellian Moment*, 197). In other words, on Pocock's view, Machiavelli prefers Rome because of the opportunity it affords to have the mass of people serve as soldiers, thus, perfecting their natures by "sacrificing particular goods to a universal end" (201). For this purpose, according to Pocock, Machiavelli is willing to sacrifice longevity.

conquered territories, he holds up the example of Rome, republican Rome: "[T]he Romans did in these cases what all wise princes should do."[7]

An Embrace of the People as the Ramification of a Martial Republic

The Rome that Machiavelli endorses was a democratic republic, one that welcomed large numbers of refugees into its midst, armed its people for war, and gave them a formal voice in governance through the institution of the tribunate. By using the people for so important an enterprise as war, Rome assured that they were at once demanding and impossible to disregard. Machiavelli terms Rome's attitude toward these multitudes the way of love. In admiring and advocating the way of Rome, Machiavelli engages in Rome's type of love himself, for, provoked by the derogatory views expressed by all the writers, he takes a stand on behalf of the people. As Rome rejected the ways of aristocratic republics, so Machiavelli rejects the ways of aristocratic writers. But his vaunted embrace of the people is merely an instrumental one. He needs the people to serve his end. Thus, Machiavelli loves the people in the same way that Rome loved its plebes, as soldiers.

As his *Discourses* opens, Machiavelli seems acutely aware that his embrace of the democratic republic of Rome, and hence of the multitude generally, will be particularly distasteful to some of his readers. Indeed, he offers what he thinks will be the objections to his embrace of those with aristocratic leanings. Someone might say, he points out, that "the modes [of Rome] were extraordinary and almost wild, to see the people together crying out against the Senate, the Senate against the people, running tumultuously through the streets, closing shops, the whole plebs leaving Rome – all of which things frighten whoever does no other than read of them." This description of Rome's domestic politics would hardly be a balm to the concerns of such a readership, if it is inclined in the first place to be as repelled by the people and the havoc they cause as Machiavelli seems to anticipate. He arrives, though, armed for the occasion with a response to the objections he ascribes to his prospective opponents: "I say that every city ought to have its modes with which the people can vent its ambition, and especially those cities that wish to avail themselves of the people in important things" (1.4.1). Greatness was the important thing for which Rome availed itself of the people, and the pursuit of this end, he teaches, was well worth what might be seen as its unpalatable consequences.

To achieve its end, Rome embraced the people, and Machiavelli explicitly terms its embrace love. He notes that "[t]hose who plan for a city to make a great empire should contrive with all industry to make it full of inhabitants, for without this abundance of men one will never succeed in making a city great." Again, greatness for Machiavelli clearly demands a

---

[7] Machiavelli, *Prince* 3.12.

vast empire, and such an empire, in turn, a large army. He specifies that a state can attract this population in two ways: "By love through keeping the ways open and secure for foreigners who plan to come to inhabit it so that everyone may inhabit it willingly; by force through undoing the neighboring cities and sending their inhabitants to inhabit your city" (2.3.1). Rome exemplifies both methods. To label Rome's stance toward foreigners as the way of love is disingenuous. Of course, as Machiavelli suggests, in certain cases refugees may have undertaken their migrations freely, in contrast to those many others when refugees were brought to Rome after their own cities had been destroyed by the city that was to embrace them. But even in such cases of "love," Rome welcomed such foreigners precisely for the purpose of war; Rome welcomed them for their ability to fight and their progeny's ability to fight. Rome's way of love, such as it was, was in service to force.

Machiavelli uses the occasion of these reflections on Rome's stance toward the people to underscore the Spartan deficiency he points to in 1.6. After describing the methods by which Lycurgus, Sparta's founder, undertook to assure that foreigners were unwelcome in that republic, he comments:

So a small republic cannot seize cities or kingdoms that are sounder or thicker than it. If, however, it seizes one, what happens is as with a tree that has a branch thicker than the stem: it supports it with labor, and every small wind breaks it. Thus it was seen to happen to Sparta, which had seized all the cities of Greece. No sooner did Thebes rebel than all the other cities rebelled, and the trunk alone remained without branches.

In contrast to the lamentable outcome of Sparta's policies, he again points to Rome, which welcomed various multitudes into its fold: "This could not happen to Rome since its stem was so thick it could easily support any branch whatever. Thus this mode of proceeding... made Rome great and very powerful" (2.3.1).[8]

---

[8] Maurizio Viroli uses evidence from the *Discourses* to support his claim that "Machiavelli's advocacy of military discipline and virtue certainly does not entail that his republicanism is inspired by a fascination for conquest and predation, as has been claimed." In support of his alternative view, he points out that Machiavelli supports the method of the Romans of making other peoples their partners in contrast to that of the Spartans and the Athenians, who made them their subjects, and declares that "the Roman method of expansion ... is not, at least in the way he presents it, predatory at all." What Viroli fails to mention, however, is Machiavelli's reason for favoring the Roman method; in Machiavelli's words, Rome's "partners came to subjugate themselves by their own labors and blood without perceiving it" (2.4.1). Moreover, later Machiavelli says with respect to Rome: "Nor could it use a greater deception in the beginning than taking the mode (discoursed of by us above) of making partners, for under this name it made them servile, as were the Latins and other peoples round about.... The Latins never perceived that they were altogether servile until they saw the Samnites given two defeats and constrained to an accord" (2.13.2). See also *Discourses* 2.2.2 for Machiavelli's consideration of the deleterious consequences of Rome's armed aggression: "[T]he

Just as Rome embraced the multitude, so too does Machiavelli. He makes himself the defender of the multitude, in which guise he takes an aggressive stance, declaring forthrightly in the chapter title of *Discourses* 1.58: "The Multitude Is Wiser and More Constant Than a Prince." In the body of the chapter he immediately explains the significance of this declaration: he "wish[es] to defend a thing that...has been accused by all the writers" (1.58.1). In the face of the aristocratic prejudices of the "writers," then, Machiavelli forthrightly declares his democratic leanings. His actual defense of the people in the body of the chapter, though, is far less dramatic than his proclamation of it in the heading of the chapter and its opening paragraph. It turns out that to a large extent his willingness to defend the people is based not on their claimed wisdom or constancy but rather on the considerations we have already examined. He reiterates that the people need to be embraced by a republic; they need to have a prominent role there, because they are the engine for armed expansion. When serving as this engine, Machiavelli is quite willing to celebrate the people. He does have serious objections to the aristocratic republics and their aristocratic advocates; he is a supporter of the people and is, as a result, a democratic writer. But he is a democratic writer only as long as the demos serves his end.

In the remainder of the opening paragraph Machiavelli continues to build the drama surrounding his case on behalf of the people by admitting that he knows not whether he undertakes "a hard task full of so much difficulty that it may suit me either to abandon it with shame or continue it with disapproval" (1.58.1). Having so intently promoted the significance of his claims on behalf of multitudes in the heading and first paragraph, his actual

Roman Empire, with its arms and its greatness, eliminated all republics and all civil ways of life."

Viroli also finds evidence of Machiavelli's more pacific views in his praise of the "Florentines' protective and benevolent policy towards Pistoia" as it occurs in 2.21. Again, he fails to mention an important piece of information. In 2.25, Machiavelli speaks of Rome using the "arts of peace" to "crush" a foe, and later in the same chapter, he reveals that Florence was using this same art for the same end in its dealings with Pistoia: "The city of Pistoia, as I said in another discourse and for another purpose, did not come under the republic of Florence by any art other than this. Since it was divided, with the Florentines favoring now one party and now the other, they led it, without disapproval from either the one or the other, to the limit where, tired of its tumultuous way of life, it came spontaneously to throw itself into the arms of Florence" (2.25.1). What Machiavelli is describing in these passages that Viroli uses to suggest that Machiavelli renounces conquest is not such a renunciation but rather conquest by fraudulent means. The result is the same as armed aggression, the subjugation of another city. See *Machiavelli* (Oxford: Oxford University Press, 1998), 139–40; see also 101–2. Cf. Maurizio Viroli, *From Politics to Reason of State: The Acquisition and Transformation of the Language of Politics, 1250–1600* (Cambridge: Cambridge University Press, 1992), 164: "The point that Machiavelli stresses again and again is that a city must be in a position to fight to protect its liberty, and that one must go to war in order to have peace. They should not, however, put at stake peace in order to have war." Viroli here refers to *The Art of War* to support this claim.

defense of the people cannot fail to disappoint, for he does not strike out to show that multitudes are wiser or more constant than princes, as the title would appear to promise, but rather that princes are equivalent to peoples. Rather than elevating peoples above the status of princes as promised, he chooses instead to lower princes to the level of peoples.

This change in strategy is evident from the opening of the second paragraph where he actually embarks on the substance of his defense: "I say, thus, that all men particularly, and especially princes, can be accused of that defect of which the writers accuse the multitude; for everyone who is not regulated by laws would make the same errors as the unshackled multitude." The conclusion of this paragraph reiterates this equivalence: "Therefore the nature of the multitude is no more to be faulted than that of princes, because all err equally when all can err without respect" (1.58.2). As a result, he accuses all, whether princes or peoples, without respect.

Later in the chapter he turns to consider the Roman people in particular, and becomes a much more venturesome advocate on their behalf: "Whoever considers the Roman people will see it to have been hostile for four hundred years to the kingly name and a lover of the glory and common good of its fatherland." This thought spurs him to offer strange endorsements of the people generally: "But as to prudence and stability, I say that a people is more prudent, more stable, and of better judgment than a prince. Not without cause may the voice of a people be likened to that of God." What moves him to make this remarkable statement is the reflection that "a universal opinion produce[s] marvelous effects in its forecasts, so that it appears to foresee its ill and its good by a hidden virtue" (1.58.3). What he means by this pronouncement is far from clear, because a people, even his exemplary Roman people, can be disastrously misguided as to what Machiavelli himself regards as its own good and evil. The tendency of the people – even the Roman people – to be misled is the very reason he makes such an effort in the *Discourses* to consider how the designs of deceptive potential tyrants can be thwarted. As we shall see, he believes it is the nature of the people to be tricked and easily misled.[9]

Machiavelli turns next to praising the people's judgment. "As to judging things," he claims, "if a people hears two orators who incline to different sides, when they are of equal virtue, very few times does one see it not take up the better opinion, and not persuaded of the truth that it hears" (1.58.3). In paying this compliment, Machiavelli begins to reveal the dependency of the people on their leaders; the people themselves do not ultimately render opinions; rather, they judge the worthiness of the opinions of others.

[9] Coby too expresses hesitations about Machiavelli's vaunted claims in this chapter. He shows, as do I in the subsequent section "War and the People's Demand for Security," that Machiavelli undermines his praise of the people's capacities by revealing elsewhere in the *Discourses* how the patricians repeatedly deceived the plebeians (*Romans*, 255–8). Coby does not emphasize, as I do, the grounds for Machiavelli's true embrace of the people.

He then proceeds to reveal the degree to which he regards peoples as being shaped by princes as he concludes this paragraph: "If princes are superior to peoples in ordering laws, forming civil lives, and ordering new statutes and orders, peoples are so much superior in maintaining things ordered that without doubt they attain the glory of those who order them" (1.58.3). Princes, not peoples, form the whole in which the many reside, giving the many their political lives by giving them their very purposes. Nonetheless, he certainly does seem to intend to compliment the people here. They maintain the creations of others.

He affirms the limited but nevertheless admirable abilities of the people, when in another context he says that it is necessary for a lone individual – a prince – to reform a badly corrupted state, insisting that such a demanding task as founding cannot be done "through the virtue of the collectivity that sustains good orders" (1.17.3). This statement declares that although the people are not capable of so glorious an enterprise as founding, they do possess a virtue essential to the founder; their virtue maintains his orders. That the extraordinary individual needs the many for the sake of glory is a key Machiavellian teaching, by which he attempts to teach a potential founder that the path to glory is to be found not in the establishment of a hereditary monarchy but rather in that of a republic: "[I]f one individual is capable of ordering, the thing itself is ordered to last long not if it remains on the shoulders of one individual but rather if it remains in the care of many and its maintenance stays with many" (1.9.2). For the sake of the longevity of his state, and hence of his own glory, a founder should institute a republic.

Of course, it is not merely the maintenance of republican institutions that should motivate a founder to look to the people. The people also assure that the orderer achieves his glory because republics, he insists, are better at empire building.[10] Machiavelli teaches prospective founders, as we know, that republics that embrace the people make the most successful conquerors. Elsewhere he even refuses to be awed by the conquest of the world effected by the monarchical succession of father and son; their accomplishment only induces him to marvel at the magnitude of the potential accomplishment of a well-ordered republic: "For it is seen that two virtuous princes in succession are sufficient to acquire the world, as were Philip of Macedon and Alexander the Great. A republic should do so much more, as through the mode of electing it has not only two in succession but infinite most virtuous princes who are successors" (1.20.1). Potential founders in search of glory should take note.

He corroborates this point regarding the ability of republics to conquer in his chapter devoted to his defense of the people: "Beyond this, one sees

---

[10] Of course, based on the logic of Machiavelli's argument in 1.6, longevity itself is dependent on empire.

that cities in which peoples are princes make exceeding increases in a very brief time, and much greater than those that have always been made under a prince, as did Rome after the expulsion of the kings" (1.58.3). He supports the people because of their role in conquest. Only two chapters after his conspicuous tribute to the people, he reveals his motivation for his support of their prominent role in a republic in particularly bald terms when acknowledging that eventually Rome allowed the lower class of men to stand for election to the consulate. He makes abundantly clear that, in his view, this relaxation of the city's practices was not in itself a good thing, but a necessary thing. In fact, he is willing to defend this particular practice of Rome only to the extent that it furthered the purpose of war. He states that this grant to the people "was conceded through necessity; and the necessity that was in Rome would be in every city that wished to produce the effects that Rome produced, as has been said another time; for men cannot be given trouble without a reward, nor can the hope of attaining the reward be taken away from them without danger." He continues that "the city that does not put its plebs to work in any glorious affair can treat it in its own mode, as is disputed elsewhere; the one that wishes to do what Rome did does not have to make this distinction." If a city does not use its people for war, it can treat them however it likes, he maintains. Machiavelli justifies the people's access to the highest offices only on the basis of the need to placate the people when a republic uses them for its – and the nobles' – glory. In support of his view, he refers twice to 1.6 where he makes his case for Rome on the basis of its ability to make war (1.60.1). He loves the people, as did Rome, because they can serve as soldiers.

In Machiavelli's view, then, the people are dependent on founders and their leaders for the institutions and laws under which they live; the founders and leaders who understand in which direction greatness lies are dependent on the people. Only the people rendered as soldiers can propel a republic to greatness, and hence assure the highest glory to its founder and to its subsequent leaders. This glory, though, comes with a price. If a republic is to use the people for this purpose, they must be given some outlet, a voice in their governance; as a result, one will have both tumults and a city of which it can be said that in some sense the people "are princes." It is necessary to embrace the people, to make them soldiers, and to weather such inconveniences. In speaking of the disarmed Rome that King Tullus inherited from King Numa, Machiavelli proclaims, "It is more true than any other truth that if where there are men there are no soldiers, it arises through a defect of the prince and not through any other defect, either of the site or of nature." It would appear appropriate to subject founders and leaders of unarmed republics to the same criticism, because he does, after all, offer King Tullus's conversion to the way of war as an example to "modern republics that lack their own soldiers for defense and offense" (1.21.1).

The Desires of Republican Peoples and Republican Princes

As has already become apparent, Machiavelli understands that princes, in a sense, populate republics, for he repeatedly refers to republican leaders as princes (e.g., 1.20.1 and 1.12.1). Princes are few and the people are many; princes desire to rule and to dominate, whereas the many desire property and security; princes seek to deceive the people, whereas the people are more often than not the victims of their deception. These groups only roughly correspond to the upper class and the lower class (patricians and plebeians), because nature does not always assure that individuals are born into the rank to which their passions and abilities suit them. Princes can be born among the people, and only a relatively small number of the upper class are ultimately moved by the rewards of honor, he suggests. Everyone's desires are infinite, he declares, but he finds the desire for property and security less threatening to a state than that for command and honor. This recognition further affirms his support for a democratic republic.

That Machiavelli does not regard the station of one's birth and one's fate in life as determinative of one's character is evident when considering the effect on humanity of the "free way of life" that reigned in ancient times. He notes that "larger peoples" were seen then and explains this phenomenon by asserting that an individual is likely to beget more children when one "does not fear that his patrimony will be taken away, and he knows not only that they are born free and not slaves, but that they can, through their virtue, become princes" (2.2.3). Rome's republican princes, who rose to prominence through talent and ambition, offer such an example of the goods of freedom. "Princes," then, can be born among the people, and Machiavelli, who though of humble station possesses the knowledge worthy of a prince, seems himself to be an example of this phenomenon.[11]

Despite his recognition that class does not necessarily determine one's passions and talents, he is more than willing to generalize with respect to each group. In *The Prince*, for example, he states that "in every city ... two diverse humors are found, which arises from this: that the people desire neither to be commanded nor oppressed by the great, and the great desire to command and oppress the people."[12] Early in the *Discourses*, he notes "that in every republic are two diverse humors, that of the people and that of the great" (1.4.1) and distinguishes between the two groups on the basis of their passions as he does in *The Prince*: "If one considers the end of the nobles

---

[11] See, for example, the dedicatory letter of *The Prince*, where Machiavelli explains that he should not be thought presumptuous because he endeavors to "give rules for the government of princes," because whereas the high (princes) know well the nature of the low (the people), the low know well the nature of the high. Of course, Machiavelli demonstrates that he knows well not only the nature of princes, but also the nature of the people and, hence, that he possesses knowledge characteristic of a prince.

[12] Machiavelli, *Prince* 9.39.

and of the ignobles, one will see great desire to dominate in the former, and in the latter only desire not to be dominated; and, in consequence, a greater will to live free, being less able to hope to usurp it than are the great" (1.5.2).[13] The many of a republic, then, pursue freedom because the opposite appears always ready to be foisted on them. The possibility that they might break from the domination of the nobles to dominate the upper class appears unlikely, if not impossible. He affirms the desirability of this continued conflict: "[A]ll the laws that are made in favor of freedom arise from their disunion" (1.4.1).

In a later chapter of the *Discourses*, he elaborates on this desire of the people for freedom, as well as on that of the great for domination, revealing, for instance, that the people pursue republican freedom as a means merely to escape oppression. As a result, a prince, well counseled by Machiavelli, could largely satisfy a people on this score: "If a prince wishes to win over a people that has been an enemy to him – speaking of those princes who have become tyrants over their fatherlands – I say that he should examine first what the people desires." The people, according to his analysis, desire two things: "one, to be avenged against those who are the cause that it is servile; the other, to recover its freedom" (1.16.5).

The content of this second desire, as exalted as it sounds here, is actually quite prosaic – so prosaic, in fact, that even a tyrant can satisfy it, if he understands the "causes . . . that make [peoples] desire to be free." In offering these causes, he differentiates between a "small part of them" who "desires to be free so as to command" and "all the others, who are infinite" and who "desire freedom so as to live secure."[14]

He elaborates on this desire to command by noting that "in all republics, ordered in whatever mode, never do even forty or fifty citizens reach the ranks of command." These few would appear to be the great precisely defined. By providing numbers for the members of this class significantly smaller

---

[13] According to Mansfield, for Machiavelli the distinction between the great and the people is "more fundamental" than that between republics and principalities (*Machiavelli's Virtue*, 24).

[14] In declaring that, in Machiavelli's view, "[w]e can never hope to live a free way of life unless we live under a republican regime," Skinner does not account for this passage of 1.16 of the *Discourses*, which suggests that a tyrant can provide the people with the purpose for which they desire liberty. Skinner does, however, use this particular chapter of the *Discourses* to delineate the ends that Machiavelli believes individuals should be free to pursue ("Idea of Negative Liberty," 199 and 197; see also "Machiavelli on *Virtù* and Maintenance of Liberty," 162–3). When Marcia Colish treats this passage, she refers only to a prince: Machiavelli notes that "since most people want freedom in order to live securely (*desiderando la libertà per vivere sicuri*), a prince can satisfy their desires by ruling according to laws that guarantee security" ("The Idea of Liberty in Machiavelli," *Journal of the History of Ideas* 32 [1971]: 337). Later, she declares that "there are circumstances under which all of these arrangements, with the exception of tyranny, are conducive to liberty" (345).

than was the patrician class in Rome,[15] he suggests that many members of its upper class were not motivated by the princely desire for command or domination. Because the number is so small, a "prince" can make himself "secure" against them "either by getting rid of them or by having them share in so many honors" (1.16.5). He offers similarly ruthless advice with regard to this group in *The Prince*, declaring that "against the great [a prince] can secure himself, as they are few."[16]

Those who compose the "infinite" do not seek command; these "others, to whom it is enough to live secure, are easily satisfied by making orders and laws in which universal security is included" (1.16.5). The people's desire for freedom, then, is so truncated in scope that it can be satisfied by a tyrant who provides for their security. Although not exalted, that desire for security is much less troublesome in a republic than is the great's desire for command. He emphasizes this point early in the *Discourses* when defending Rome's democratic character against supporters of the aristocratic Sparta and Venice. He pronounces against the great that "since they possess much, they are able to make an alteration with greater power and greater motion" and that "their incorrect and ambitious behavior inflames in the breasts of whoever does not possess the wish to possess so as to avenge themselves against them by despoiling them or to be able also themselves to enter into those riches and those honors that they see being used badly by others" (1.5.4). Their desires in conjunction with their greater ability to attain them can do a great deal of harm to a republic.

Machiavelli also makes it a point to disabuse the supporters of Venice and Sparta of the notion that the upper class is less rapacious because it can rest content with the greater amount of goods in its possession. He finds that tumults "are most often caused by him who possesses, because the fear of losing generates in him the same wishes that are in those who desire to acquire; for it does not appear to men that they possess securely what a man has unless he acquires something else new" (1.5.4). The desire to acquire burns in the hearts of all, and this recognition is quite in keeping with his declaration in *The Prince* that "it is a very natural and ordinary thing to desire to acquire."[17]

In contrast to the aristocratic supporters of Sparta and Venice, far from being repelled by displays of the people's desires, Machiavelli revels in them. No better example of his delight in the people's desire to acquire exists than

---

[15] Livy, for instance, relates that Romulus after founding Rome created a Senate of one hundred senators, whom he termed "patres," from which derived the term patricians applied to their descendants (*Ab urbe condita* 1.8.7; references to Livy's history are from the Loeb Classical Library edition [1967–84]). Given Machiavelli's manner of numbering the great, it would appear that not even a majority of the original patricians would he designate as the great, properly defined.

[16] Machiavelli, *Prince* 9.39.

[17] Ibid., 3.14.

his consideration of their reaction to Camillus's vow to dedicate to the god Apollo a tenth of the booty from the sack of Veii. The fulfillment of the vow became complicated when the "booty had come into the hands of the Roman plebs." In order to follow through on the vow, the Senate decreed that each soldier should give up a tenth of his own take. Their greed for acquisition simply would not countenance such a sacrifice on their part, and Machiavelli praises their reaction. He explains that "the plebs thought not of defrauding the edict in any part by giving less than it owed, but of freeing itself from it by showing open indignation." The soldiers were indignant at having to relinquish to a god a portion of their profits from war. The lesson he draws from this incident is that it "shows how much goodness and how much religion were in that people" (1.55.1). Of course, in showing just how much religion was in those people, it shows that the people's interest in property trumped their reverence for Apollo. Machiavelli actually terms this interest of the people their "goodness." In order to understand how for Machiavelli such behavior could be considered good, it is necessary only to reflect that these Roman plebeians were luxuriating in earthly goods generally and in the profits of war specifically; such a populace would seem inclined to fight other battles in pursuit of other such gains.

His discussion in *Discourses* 1.37 of the agrarian law, which would have distributed to the people a greater portion of conquered lands, furnishes additional information about the passions of both humors that amplifies his earlier presentation of them in the *Discourses* as well as in *The Prince*. Because in these other discussions he emphasizes the desire of the great to command and oppress, one is easily led to believe that all the members of this group burn for the preeminence that comes from the political honors that the city bestows on its leading men. He uses the reaction of the great to the people's demand for additional property, which was expressed in their fevered support for the agrarian law, to highlight the fact that in his estimation not all the members of the upper class are motivated primarily by the pursuit of honors. A review of the disputes over the passage of this law induces him to observe "how much more men" – including men from the patrician class – "esteem property than honors." He explains that "the Roman nobility always yielded honors to the plebs without extraordinary scandals, but when it came to property, so great was its obstinacy in defending it that the plebs had recourse to the extraordinary [means] . . . to vent its appetite" (1.37.3). Of course, the possession of some forms of property can be honorable, but Machiavelli does not acknowledge that possibility with his strict dichotomy between property and honor in this immediate context. That dichotomy suggests that the honor he here treats is that which derives from political command and preeminence. Many of the great simply do not care for political honor more than property. Their desire for property would appear to associate these members of the upper class with the people and their desires. After all, the desire for property in its most rudimentary form is much closer to what he designates as the people's primary desire for security, because property is necessary to satisfy the demands of daily life. Perhaps some of the great desire preeminence, dominance, and honor above all, but according to his analysis here, far from all do. This recognition, upon consideration, is entirely in keeping with his claim in *Discourses* 1.16 that only forty or fifty seek the ranks of command and, hence, would be dissatisfied with a prince's or tyrant's provision of "universal security." It would also appear to be another indication that, in his view, nature does not assign all individuals to their proper class. Many of the great by virtue of their desires – if not by virtue of the value of their property – are akin to the people.

Of course, in addition, the fact that the people accepted, and hence appeared to covet, the honors with which the great distracted them gives the people greater range of motivation than his other discussions would appear to assign to them; the people desire not only property but honor as well. With respect to the people's desires in this case, he observes that "it was not enough for the Roman plebs to secure itself against the nobles by the creation of the tribunes, to which desire it was constrained by necessity; for having obtained that, it began at once to engage in combat through ambition, and to wish to share honors and belongings with the nobility as the thing esteemed most by men." This particular observation seems to corroborate his view with regard to human passions generally – that is, that they are insatiable. Once the people of Rome believed themselves relatively secure, their desires expanded to encompass other goods such as property beyond their immediate needs, as well as political honors. As he says at the beginning of the chapter: "For whenever engaging in combat through necessity is taken from men they engage in combat through ambition, which is so powerful in human breasts that it never abandons them at whatever rank they rise to" (1.37.1). Perhaps another motivation for the people's desire for honors derives from the fact that they had seen the patricians using them badly, and thus their own desire for them was ignited (cf. 1.5.3).

Conversely, as we have already seen from his analysis of the actions of the patrician class in this chapter, many of its members had always found themselves in the very position that was so new to the plebeians; having satisfied their most basic needs they could contend either for additional property or for political honor. He has already shown us that in such circumstances most of the great pursued additional property and disdained honor, and it can be suspected that most of the people did the same when finding themselves in the new position of being able to choose between the two types of goods. Upon consideration, then, the individuals among the plebeians greedy for the new honors, which the patricians extended in order to distract them from their desire for patrician land, would appear to be nature's misplaced princes. Ultimately, he suggests that most of the great are motivated by the same passions as would be the people in similar circumstances.

War and the People's Demand for Security

The few long to oppress and the many long for security; when the few are driven by their princely natures to oppress the people, Machiavelli balances the scale by jumping to the side of the people. He cannot lend so much weight to the people's cause that they emerge victorious, however, because they pose their own threat to Machiavelli's republic. The people, on whom he explicitly relies to be the engine of acquisition, do not always want to fight. Of course, they will greedily accept war's plunder once won, but the dangers of battle conflict with their deepest desires for preservation and security – desires that because of their profundity and formative character are most difficult to deny.[18] Perhaps it is his very recognition of this difficulty that makes Machiavelli so eager to recount how the Roman plebeians grasped at war's spoils and hence seemingly rejoiced in war itself. Nevertheless, so aware is he of this difficulty that he depicts repeatedly in the *Discourses* the reluctance of the Roman people to fight. Their reluctance, in turn, fomented repeated conflicts between the Roman patricians and the plebeians. Whenever the people threatened to defect from Rome's cause, we find him supporting any palliations, prevarications, and constraints the patricians invented to induce them to submit once again to the cause of Rome. On the issue of the necessity of war, he is decidedly on the side of the great. Indeed, he goes so far as to support the patricians' endeavors to keep the highest ruling positions from falling to plebeians, as if war as the republic's enterprise would be threatened if the people actually exercised rule in this, his democratic republic. He takes evident delight in revealing, and hence he quite evidently supports, the manner in which the patricians tricked the plebeians, undermining the latter's efforts at subversion. Therefore, while making a show of befriending the people, Machiavelli displays the same hesitations as did Rome in allowing them to rule. Ultimately, his enthusiasm for the people and collaterally his support for democracy are limited by his promotion of war. Thus, he is not a principled supporter of either side in Rome's tumults. Rather than attempting to solve their disputes, he

[18] Skinner maintains that Machiavelli endorses negative liberty, that he believes that citizens should be allowed to pursue "whatever goals we may happen to set for ourselves" ("Paradoxes of Political Liberty," 240; "Republican Ideal," 302). In making this argument, Skinner does not consider how Machiavelli's pursuit of greatness may circumscribe the ability of individuals to attain their chosen ends, particularly the end of security. Indeed, Skinner maintains that Machiavelli regards the negative liberty of individuals as a more compelling goal than the state's pursuit of greatness: Machiavelli promises an "even greater gift [than 'civic greatness and wealth'] that free states are alone capable of bequeathing with any confidence to their citizens"; Machiavelli's promised gift is "personal liberty, understood in the ordinary sense to mean that each citizen remains free...to pursue his own chosen ends" (Skinner, "Paradoxes of Political Liberty," 239–40; "Republican Ideal," 301–2; cf. *Machiavelli*, 57 and 59).

endeavors to keep them alive and contentious – a necessity if a republic is to wage war.[19]

Machiavelli reveals very early in the *Discourses* the tensions that arose because of the opposing facts that the people furnished Rome's military might and that they occasionally defected from its campaign for empire. In praising the conflicts between the plebeians and the patricians as the source of Roman liberty, he points to the power that the plebeians wielded, observing that when the people "wished to obtain a law," sometimes "they refused to enroll their names to go to war, so that to placate them there was need to satisfy them in some part" (1.4.1). This, then, was quite a threat, and one that Rome had to avert. Just such a threat, for example, caused the patricians to grant the office of the tribunes to the people.[20]

The concession on the part of the patricians that established the tribunes, of course, did not alleviate this problem for the patricians, but actually intensified it by giving an official voice to this desire of the people. Machiavelli reports that "when the people saw one war after another arise, and that they could never rest, whereas they should have thought that it arose from the ambition of neighbors who wished to crush them, they thought it arose from the ambition of the nobles, who, since they were unable to punish the plebs when defended by the tribunate power inside Rome, wished to lead it outside Rome under the consuls so as to crush it where it did not have any aid" (1.39.2). Interestingly, Machiavelli does not say that the ambition of Rome's neighbors caused these wars, but rather that the people "should have thought" these wars arose from this cause. As we have seen, he maintains that war is a necessity on the basis not only of the competitive nature of the international realm but also of war's ability to quell domestic turmoil. Further, he indicates that the patricians acted on this latter understanding. For instance, during the people's agitation for an agrarian law, he notes that the patricians attempted to distract the plebeians "by leading an army out" (1.37.2).[21] Machiavelli's "should have thought" in *Discourses* 1.39 should not be taken to mean that he thinks the people or their leaders wrong in making this accusation; it does, however, reveal his belief that a republic should not permit them to act on their recognition.

Suspecting, then, that Rome's wars were a subterfuge through which the great could punish them and diminish their power, the people's leaders

---

[19] This procedure differs markedly from that of Aristotle, who in *The Politics* attempts to arbitrate the various claims of the oligarchic and democratic elements of the city in order to foster harmony and stability.

[20] According to Livy's account, the patricians wished to stem the people's riotous discontent over their treatment at the hands of the moneylenders by leading an army out of Rome "under the pretext that the Aequi had recommenced hostilities." So outraged were the people that they seceded from the city and occupied the Sacred Mount until they were granted the tribunes (2.32–3).

[21] Coby, *Romans*, 81.

determined that the patricians should no longer exercise supreme power. According to Machiavelli, the people thought that "it might be necessary either to remove the consuls or to regulate their power so that they did not have authority over the people either outside or at home." It was a tribune by the name of Terentillus who made the official proposal for a specific law that declared "that five men ought to be created to consider the power of the consuls and to limit it." This particular tribune was hoping to contain the power of the patricians, and the patricians were adamantly opposed to the Terentillan law, which "very much upset the nobility, since the majesty of the empire appeared to it to have altogether declined, so that there no longer remained any rank for the nobility in that republic" (1.39.2).

The patricians mustered their resources to counter this attack on their authority. They took several expedients to thwart Terentillus's specific proposal and to contain this general desire of the people to undermine their power. Machiavelli seems in every case to approve heartily of all of the patricians' efforts, no matter how duplicitous. In a chapter devoted to his praise of the use the Romans made of their religion, for example, he devotes a considerable portion of it to relating the tricks of the patricians in this particular exigency. Indeed, he points to these tricks as a particularly fine example of religion well used. After reporting in this chapter that "[v]ery many tumults had arisen in Rome" as a result of Terentillus's proposal, he notes that "[a]mong the first remedies that the nobility used against him was religion." In his first example of these recourses to religion as a means to combat the Terentillan law, he relates that the patricians "had the Sybilline books seen and made to respond that through civil sedition, dangers of losing its freedom hung over the city that year – a thing that, though exposed by the tribunes, nonetheless put such terror in the breasts of the plebs that it was cooled off" (1.13.2). Whereas in Livy's history the tribunes only charge that the patricians committed fraud, in Machiavelli's account of the incident they exposed actual fraud.[22] This fact suggests that, in Machiavelli's view, although the patricians' fakery was revealed, the people as a whole were so moved by religious fears that they succumbed to the patricians' desires anyway. He shows in this way how very susceptible the people were to manipulation.[23]

His other example in this chapter of how the patricians used religion to combat the Terentillan law is an intricate tale in which a particular senator induces the people to abide by an oath made to a deceased commander in order to get the plebs "to go out of Rome to go against the Volsci." The senator's intention in appealing to religion in this matter was to move the people to war so as "not to let the plebs rest or give it room to think about the Terentillan law," relates Machiavelli (1.13.2). Albeit after the proposal for the Terentillan law and thus after the people had lodged their complaint that

[22] Livy, *Ab urbe condita* 3.10.7–8.
[23] Sullivan, *Machiavelli's Three Romes*, 111–12.

Rome's wars arose from the ambition of the patricians, he nevertheless shows the patricians doing precisely what the people had suspected (cf. 1.39.2); the Roman upper class used war as a way to manage and control them; Rome's wars, then, did not always arise from the ambitions of its neighbors.[24]

Elsewhere in the *Discourses*, Machiavelli regales his readers with additional tales of how the patricians duplicitously maintained their authority against the challenge emanating from the tribunes. He states in *Discourses* 1.39 that "[t]he obstinacy of the tribunes was... so great that the consular name was eliminated" when the consuls were replaced by "tribunes with consular power" (1.39.2). Eight chapters later he returns to the subject to explain: "When the Roman people, as was said above, was disgusted with the consular name and wished for plebeian men to be able to be made consuls or for their authority to be diminished, the nobility, so as not to blemish the consular authority either with one thing or with the other, took a middle way and was content that four tribunes with consular power, who could be plebeians as well as nobles, be created" (1.47.1). The people accepted what they thought was a concession on the part of the great. It appeared, indeed, to be a significant one; it appeared to the people that the patricians were opening the city's highest offices to them.

In this place Machiavelli explains that the people advocated for these new offices and new privileges not only out of envy and suspicion of their social betters but also because they considered themselves worthy of them. They thought themselves worthy to occupy the highest positions of the city because it "appeared generally to the Roman plebs that it deserved the consulate because it had more part in the city, because it carried more danger in wars, because it was that which with its limbs kept Rome free and made it powerful" (1.47.1).[25] Interestingly, this claim of the people on their own behalf encapsulates Machiavelli's praise of them. He admires their bodily strength and numbers that made them capable of bearing the brunt of Rome's wars. This recognition moves him to be a partisan of the people and provides his motivations for defending them against the defamation of "all the writers" (1.58.1). Nevertheless, Machiavelli and the Roman people do not draw the same conclusion from this shared recognition. Unlike the people, Machiavelli does not posit that their greater part in war gives them a satisfactory claim to rule.

Initially at least, Machiavelli indicates that the people themselves came to recognize the inadequacies of their own men. Here, as in *Discourses* 1.58,

---

[24] This interpretation explains his claim in 2.25 that war results in a united republic. Of course, Rome's tumults would appear to make it anything but united, but now it appears that war was an instrument by which the patricians could contain the magnitude of the people's protestations, thus uniting the city to a certain degree.

[25] I have altered the translation of Mansfield and Tarcov by translating "le braccia" as limbs rather than arms (Niccolò Machiavelli, *Tutte le opere*, ed. Mario Martelli [Florence: Sansoni, 1971], 129).

his declared appreciation of the people's wisdom collapses into his relief at their willingness to live in accordance with the orders that the great have furnished them. This is not, however, his final view on the matter. He reveals with devilish delight that additional deceptions on the part of the patricians influenced the people's decision to decline the opportunity to elect their own men to office. Further, he recounts these maneuverings as if they are worthy of imitation by the nobles of any acquisitive republic who find themselves similarly besieged by a restive populace.

Noting that after the creation of the tribunes with consular power the people elected only patricians, he first attributes the results of the election to the fact that men may be "very much deceived in general things," such as the people's belief that their numbers and physical strength entitle them to rule, but "not so much in particulars." He explains that this rectitude in judgment with respect to particulars operated when the people considered particular candidates for office: "But as [the plebs] had to pass judgment on its men particularly, it recognized their weakness and judged that no one of them deserved that which the whole together appeared to it to deserve" (1.47.1). He appears here to offer sincere praise of the people's judgment, but the chapter concludes on an altogether different, but distinctly familiar, note. He says that it is not "superfluous to show, in the following chapter, the order that the Senate held to so as to deceive the people in its distributions [of offices]" (1.47.3). In this manner, he reveals that, in his view, the nobles had to "deceive" the people into electing only patricians to these offices.

The succeeding chapter reveals the precise nature of these deceptions of the Senate. He explains: "When the Senate feared that tribunes with consular power would be made of plebeian men, it held to one of two modes: either it had [the position] asked for by the most reputed men in Rome; or truly, through due degrees, it corrupted some vile and very ignoble plebeian who, mixed with the plebeians of better quality who ordinarily asked for it, also asked them for it." He attests that these methods had the desired effect on the electorate, claiming that the last tactic "made the plebs ashamed to give it," whereas "the first made" the people "ashamed to take it." He then concludes this very short chapter with the declaration that "[a]ll of this returns to the purpose of the preceding discourse, in which it is shown that the people does not deceive itself in particulars, even if it deceives itself in generalities" (1.48.1). But, of course, what he shows – and what he, in fact, admits to showing – is that the people have to be deceived into not being deceived with respect to particulars. _hm?_

His revelation of the machinations of the great in keeping the people from electing their own to this high office does not stop at this. Apparently, this particular expedient of the patricians did not always work; the good judgment of the people could not consistently be relied upon to accept the worthiest among the patricians and to reject the vilest of the plebeians. In the chapter devoted to the admirable ways in which the Romans made use of their religion, he points to a time when, "[a]fter the Roman people had created tribunes with consular power," these officers "were all plebeians except for one." It was necessary at this point for the patricians to use even more potent medicines to keep the ruling offices from being delivered to the people. The occasion for just such expedients presented itself "when plague and famine occurred that year and certain prodigies came." The "nobles used the opportunity in the next creation of tribunes to say that the gods were angry because Rome had used the majesty of its empire badly, and that there was no remedy for placating the gods other than to return the election of tribunes to its place." Again, this appeal to religious fear had its desired effect: "From this it arose that the plebs, terrified by this religion, created as tribunes all nobles" (1.13.1).[26]

In the third book of the *Discourses*, Machiavelli reveals that the wiles of the nobles allowed them not only to control the opinions of the people but also to infect the judgment of the people's leaders in the tribunate. He explains that the "power of the tribunes of the plebs in the city of Rome was great, and it was necessary . . . to place a check on the ambition of the nobility, which would have corrupted that republic a long time before it did corrupt itself." Nevertheless, in his opinion the tribunate presented a threat to Rome: "[T]he tribunate authority became insolent and formidable to the nobility and to all Rome" (3.11.1). He here shows again – but this time from the other side – his unwillingness to see either party gain a preponderance of power (cf. 1.37). To counter the "inconvenience" of an assertive tribunate, one that might have eventually become "harmful to Roman freedom," the nobles "always found among [the tribunes] someone who was either fearful or corruptible or a lover of the common good, so that they disposed him to oppose the will of the others, who wished to press forward some decision against the will of the Senate" (3.11.1). Even the tribunes, who were supposed to be the voice of the people, were, according to Machiavelli, often times puppets of the patricians.[27] Again, he emphasizes that this type of manipulation

---

[26] Machiavelli does concede in 1.60 that the Romans eventually opened the consulate itself to the plebeians. In this chapter, he explicitly praises Rome for electing men to office "without respect to age," finding it "a very harmful thing for the city not to be able to avail itself of [a young man] then, and for it to have to wait until that vigor of spirit and that readiness grow old with him." He offers no similar praise for its eventual decision to elect them without regard "to blood" (1.60.1). As shown earlier, he says in this chapter that eventually Rome had to make such concessions in order to maintain an army.

[27] In 1.51 of the *Discourses*, Machiavelli slyly questions the acuity of the tribunes. They apparently miss the real harm of the Senate's decision to offer pay to Rome's soldiers. Machiavelli reports that although the plebeians were so accepting of the grant that "Rome went upside down with joy," "the tribunes did their best to suppress this favor" by arguing that the plebeians would pay through their own wages through their taxes. The Senate was able to counter the tribunes' claims by making sure that the nobles were known to pay the greatest amount of tax. Thus, not only do the tribunes offer an argument that the Senate can so easily counter, but they miss the real burden of the decision. It made war an even greater burden

was necessary to maintain "Roman freedom." His understanding of Roman freedom is compatible with manipulation not only of the people but also of their leaders.[28]

Machiavelli makes a display out of asserting the wisdom of the people, but after this consideration their wisdom appears to be founded in the very gullibility that made them so vulnerable to the deceptions of the great. Not only do the people not always rule in the republic of Machiavelli, but they do not always grasp the grounds of their political life. According to Machiavelli's depiction, the Roman people were not full participants in the life of their republic,[29] which constantly demanded the people sacrifice their deepest desire by risking their lives for its glory. It is their achievement of this glory, though, that he believes makes the people worthy of admiration.

The Great and Their Desire to Oppress

Although Machiavelli displays such a keen appreciation of the tricks Rome's great played on the people, he is far from willing to cede complete control of a republic to the upper class. Although not all members of this class in Rome loved honor more than property, he acknowledges that many of Rome's patricians did burn with the ambition to distinguish themselves.

for the people, because with the pay the patricians could use the people in long sieges and lead them far away from Rome.

[28] See John P. McCormick, "Machiavellian Democracy: Controlling Elites with Ferocious Populism," *American Political Science Review* 95 (June 2001): 297–313, for a strong case for the opposite position, which maintains that Machiavelli regards the Roman people as playing not only an active but an efficacious role in the city's politics, and that he "resents, despises, and distrusts" Rome's nobles (298). As will become obvious in the subsequent sections of this chapter, I concur in this understanding of Machiavelli as highly suspicious of the ambition of the nobles when it is turned on the city itself. Nevertheless, I believe McCormick overstates both Machiavelli's dislike of the nobles and his support of the people. McCormick's interpretation of the *Discourses* concentrates primarily on the city's domestic life, thus largely abstracting from Machiavelli's concern for empire. Because empire is not part of the calculus, we do not get a full picture of Machiavelli's evaluation of either class. For example, Machiavelli holds in high regard the ambition of the great for honor won on the battlefield, and he supports a democratic republic not out of the decent concern to prevent the people from being oppressed at the hands of the nobility but rather because aristocratic domination could not put a popular army into service (*Discourses* 1.6, 2.3, and 1.60).

[29] Mansfield, *Machiavelli's Virtue*, 237. Fischer acknowledges that "the fact that Machiavelli's leaders manipulate the commons by various kinds of fraud" "*does* diminish the institutional quality of his republic, for this manipulation implies that power is exercised contrary to the laws and orders that ought to regulate it." Fischer concludes, however, that "Machiavelli ultimately believes in the ability of the commons to assert their interests against the tyrannical tendencies of the nobles to some extent." In Fischer's view, Machiavelli "makes it clear that Rome became a truly mixed regime when" they "forced the 'creation of the tribunes of the plebs' (D.I.2.7)" (Fischer, *Well-Ordered License*, 142–4). But, as we have seen, Machiavelli quite clearly shows the nobles exerting their will successfully even on the tribunes themselves.

In most instances, this intense ambition served the purposes of the martial republic by driving these ambitious individuals to amass victories over Rome's opponents. As he points out, the men of the ancient republic "esteem[ed]" "very much" "the honor of the world" and, in fact, "having placed the highest good in it, were ... ferocious in their actions" (2.2.2). Nevertheless, the intense desires of the great threaten the existence of a republic in two ways. The great as a class can act on their love for dominion and their general hatred of the people by overthrowing the people so completely that the populace cannot be used for the important enterprise of the prosecution of war; or the desire of a particular individual for preeminence and conquest can turn against the entire city in an attempt to establish a tyranny. Some of the city's ambitious men manifested the desire to have all other Romans bend to their will, and periodically one would emerge to threaten the republic in just this way. The most dangerous of threats occurred when an ambitious man assumed a benevolent veneer, beguiling the people by seemingly befriending them and making their cause his own; one need only recall that this is, in fact, the manner in which the Roman Republic collapsed to recognize the supreme danger of such an occurrence. The man who makes himself the people's champion in this way has the ulterior motive of attaining sole rule.

When the desires of the great as a class threaten the freedom of the people, Machiavelli is decidedly on the people's side. Indeed, he maintains that the people need to have a prominent role in a republic, as they did in Rome, in order to help contain the great's desire to oppress. So adamant is he in this view that even in the face of compelling evidence that the people's role in Rome led ultimately to its collapse, he still explicitly maintains his position. When discussing the people's advocacy for the agrarian law, he concedes that the contention so "inflamed so much hatred between the plebs and the Senate that they came to arms and to bloodshed, beyond every civil mode and custom"; that this fighting between the humors continued through "much bloodshed and changing of fortune"; and finally that "these humors were revived at the time of Caesar and Pompey – after Caesar had made himself head of Marius's party, and Pompey that of Sulla, in coming to grips Caesar was left on top." Machiavelli spells out the meaning of Caesar's victory when he continues that Caesar "was the first tyrant in Rome, such that never again was that city free" (1.37.2). He recognizes both the significance and power of these facts but forthrightly refuses to render a judgment that goes against the people: "[A]lthough the end of this Agrarian law appears not to conform to such a conclusion, I say that I do not, because of this, abandon such an opinion." He does not abandon his opinion in favor of the people because of what he identifies as the even more threatening passions and strength of the great: "For so great is the ambition of the great that it soon brings that city to its ruin if it is not beaten down in a city by various ways and various modes." The people served this function in Rome, and he adds that had they not, Rome would have been ruined even sooner: "[I]f the contention over the Agrarian law took three hundred years to make Rome servile, it would perhaps have been led into servitude much sooner if the plebs had not always checked the ambition of the nobles, both with this law and with its other appetites." As a result of these considerations, he maintains the validity of his earlier judgment "that the enmities in Rome between the Senate and the plebs kept Rome free by giving rise to laws in favor of freedom" (1.37.3).

Although he so steadfastly takes the side of the people when the great threaten to oppress, he cannot deny that because the people had so prominent a place in Rome, they were responsible for a critical vulnerability of that republic. They could throw their support to a single supremely ambitious individual. This is, in fact, what happened in the case of Caesar. By apparently renouncing the arrogance and hostility toward the people that typically mark the great, a potential tyrant could seek to elevate himself above his fellow citizens. He may appear benevolent in the eyes of the people, but his apparent kindness is merely the means by which he intends to satisfy his overweening ambition to rule; the people are the potential tyrant's avenue to the destruction of the republic. Rome failed because it allowed the ambition of one of its great to overwhelm it.

Machiavelli, then, displays extreme ambivalence toward the great. Their passions at once fuel Rome's acquisitions and threaten Rome's existence. He points to the dual nature of the supremely ambitious – to the benefits they confer and the extreme threat they pose – as well as the methods they use when he considers the case of Spurius Maelius, who was "very rich for those times" in the early republic. This Roman wished to use his wealth to gain the "favor" of the plebs for himself during a time of dearth and resolved to distribute grain "privately." Obviously, like the famous captains Rome produced, Spurius desired distinction and reputation, but he took a more direct and peaceful route of seeking to win the regard of the people by providing for their needs. The Roman Senate, Machiavelli notes, readily saw "the inconvenience that could arise from that liberality of his" and sought "to crush it before it could pick up more strength" by creating "a dictator over him and ha[ving] him killed." Machiavelli draws important lessons from the case of Spurius. The first concerns at once the necessity and the dangers of the great in a republic: "[A] republic without reputed citizens cannot stand, nor can it be governed well in any mode." Thus, he here asserts that a republic needs individuals who perform remarkable deeds for the sake of reputation; a republic needs the ambition of the greatest of the great. These ambitions create certain dilemmas, however: "On the other side, the reputation of citizens is the cause of the tyranny of republics" (3.28.1). This is, indeed, quite a downside.

Ultimately, Rome failed to contain the ambitions of its most ambitious citizens. Caesar's ultimate victory was prepared by the republic's laxness with regard to his predecessors; their limited successes paved the way for Caesar's tremendous success that was the Roman Republic's downfall.

Corruption's Role in the Establishment of Tyranny in Rome

Caesar won the prize of tyranny for which so many others had contended. Machiavelli names, for example, Appius Claudius, Spurius Maelius, and Spurius Cassius as earlier contenders for this prize. According to Machiavelli's analysis, however, the later republic was very different from the early republic in that it allowed aspiring tyrants a readier path to sole rule. Because he lived after "the corruption that the Marian parties had put in the people" (1.17.1), Caesar could use corruption to attain power in Rome. Given its decisive character, then, it is necessary to come to some understanding of what Machiavelli understands by corruption in the people. It appears to be the ability on the part of an ambitious man to gather a personal following, and also the willingness on the part of the people to compose that following.

At this juncture, in particular, the scholars who claim a classical republican heritage for Machiavelli find the Florentine calling for the austere republican virtue of the ancients, arguing that he demands from all citizens the self-renouncing virtues as a response to corruption.[30] His is a complicated response, but ultimately, it is not this. He does not expect the people to renounce their self-interested desires. Such a demand is neither necessary nor desirable, in his view. He intends to aim a republic's response more narrowly at the intense desires of a small number of the great; a republic must prevent them from attempting to serve their own ends by promising to serve the people's. Even when focusing on the harm this group can inflict, he asks these great men not to renounce their self-interested desires for renown; those desires are too valuable to his republic. Instead, he demands that a republic always channel those desires that are at once so valuable and so dangerous. As we shall see in subsequent sections, he uses another passion – fear – to produce that salutary result.

Machiavelli highlights the condition of Rome at Caesar's ascendancy in 1.17 of the *Discourses*, "Having Come to Freedom, a Corrupt People Can with the Greatest Difficulty Maintain Itself Free." He asks why, after the "Tarquins were expelled" from Rome, the city "could at once take and maintain its freedom," whereas after Caesar's death, the city could do neither. He responds with alacrity that this "difference of results in one and the same city arose from nothing other than that in the times of the Tarquins the Roman people was not yet corrupt, and in these last times it was very corrupt." Machiavelli goes on to explain that Rome's susceptibility to tyranny

[30] E.g., Pocock, *Machiavellian Moment*, 209; Skinner, *Renaissance*, 164–5; Skinner, *Machiavelli*, 64.

"arose from the corruption that the Marian parties had put in the people" with the result that Caesar as the "head" of this party "could so blind the multitude that it did not recognize the yoke that it was putting on its own neck" (1.17.1). In addition, he says elsewhere that Caesar took "a corrupt city" and "spoil[ed] it entirely" (1.10.6).

Although he suggests in this way the decisive importance of corruption, he has done very little to define it. We know only at this point that it is something put into the people that blinds them to the dire consequences of their support of a demagogue. In the remainder of the chapter he turns to consider how difficult such corruption is to eradicate once it has permeated a city. In explaining the source of this difficulty, he offers an indication of what he understands by corruption. By way of explanation, he says "such corruption and slight aptitude for free life arise from an inequality that is in that city." Corruption derives, then, from inequality. The nature of this inequality is so intractable that "if one wishes to make it equal, it is necessary to use the greatest extraordinary means, which few know or wish to use" (1.17.3).

In a chapter in which he justifies the Roman institution of the dictator, he offers further insight into what he understands as the character of that inequality that gives rise to corruption. In defending the dictatorship, Machiavelli sees fit to adduce the argument of "some writer" who blames this particular institution for being the "cause, in time, of the tyranny of Rome." According to Machiavelli, his unnamed scholarly opponent "cites the fact that the first tyrant in that city commanded it under the dictatorial title; he says that if it had not been for this, Caesar would not have been able to put an honest face on his tyranny under any public title." Here again, Machiavelli confronts us with the case of Caesar and his tyranny. Machiavelli counters by arguing that it is not authority dispensed through "public orders," or, most important, with a definite limit of duration, that is harmful to republican life, but rather authority that is taken in "extraordinary ways" (1.34.1). He further explains that conditions must be favorable to permit the seizing of such authority in such fashion: "[I]f a citizen wishes to be able to offend and to seize extraordinary authority for himself, he must have many qualities that in a noncorrupt republic he can never have." He then continues helpfully with a description of those qualities that distinguish a corrupt republic from a noncorrupt one: "[H]e needs to be very rich and to have very many adherents and partisans, which he cannot have where the laws are observed" (1.34.2). This is very important information; it helps to round out the portrait of the corruption that enabled Caesar to seize extraordinary power and, according to Machiavelli's analysis, to become "the first tyrant in Rome, such that never again was that city free" (1.37.2). An incorrupt republic is marked by the lack of any one man being outstandingly wealthy and having many adherents and partisans. Conversely, the elevation in a republic of such a man owing to his wealth and followers must be the content of that inequality that Machiavelli points to in *Discourses* 1.17 as being the distinguishing characteristic of corruption.

Machiavelli provides important information regarding the acquisition of such partisans in the same chapter in which he discusses Spurius Maelius, explaining in the continuation there that there are two ways of gaining a reputation in a city, "either" by "public or private" modes. He offers as an example of the public modes "when one individual by counseling well, by working better in the common benefit, acquires reputation." As this is an example of one of the ways in which the great may acquire the reputation they covet, it would appear that their work for the common benefit is a means to that reputation. The pursuit of their private desire in this way benefits the whole. He explains that "reputations, gained by these ways, are clear and simple, they will never be dangerous." By contrast, danger looms for a republic when men avail themselves of its opposite, the private way to reputation. He describes these "private ways" as "doing benefit to this and to that other private individual – by lending him money, marrying his daughters for him, defending him from the magistrates." His description of these methods then turns ominous when he states that such "private favors... make partisans to oneself and give spirit to whoever is so favored to be able to corrupt the public and to breach the laws" (3.28.1).[31] Here we see the beginnings of that inequality that defines corruption, which, in turn, makes tyranny possible.

Whereas a corrupt people will gladly exchange private favors for their freedom, an incorrupt people, Machiavelli suggests, may be unwilling to take the bait. Although his portrayal of the Roman people hardly emphasizes their perspicacity, an incorrupt people apparently will accede to the judgment of the Senate that the aspiring tyrant wishes them ill, as they did in the case of Spurius Maelius. For instance, he examines the case of Spurius Cassius, who proposed the first agrarian law in the early times of the republic. In considering how Rome countered the threat Spurius posed, Machiavelli describes Spurius as "an ambitious man," who "wished to take up extraordinary authority in Rome and to gain the plebs for himself by conferring on them many benefits." Spurius fails, though, in gaining the adherence of the plebeians because "the Fathers" "exposed" his "ambition," bringing him

---

[31] In *Discourses* 1.46 he offers another discussion of how "citizens who live ambitiously in a republic" proceed to gain power: "[T]hey acquire [friendships] in ways honest in appearance, either by helping with money or by defending them from the powerful. Because this appears virtuous, it easily deceives everyone, and because of this they offer no remedies against it, so that he, persevering without hindrance, becomes of such quality that private citizens have fear of him and the magistrates have respect for him. When he has ascended to this rank, and he has not already been prevented from greatness, he comes to be in a position where to try to strike him is most dangerous." See Niccolò Machiavelli, *Florentine Histories* 7.1, trans. Laura Banfield and Harvey C. Mansfield (Princeton: Princeton University Press, 1988), 276–7, for a similar discussion of these two methods of acquiring reputation.

"under so much suspicion that when he spoke to the people and offered to give them the money...they refused it altogether, since it appeared to them that Spurius wished to give them the price of their freedom" (3.8.1). This behavior of the Roman people was praiseworthy. In so readily following the judgment of the Senate, they replicate, in this instance, the type of behavior of the Roman people that he finds worthy of praise in 1.58; the people were prudent enough in this case to acquiesce in the judgment of their superiors.

He continues his discussion of Spurius by comparing the behavior of the Roman populace in this case to that of a corrupt one: "[I]f such a people had been corrupt, it would not have refused the said price, and it would have opened the way to tyranny that it closed" (3.8.1). In this instance the people turned down the immediate and easy goods that an ambitious man offered in order to preserve their republic. An incorrupt multitude in such circumstances acts differently from a corrupt one.

For the people to be incorrupt it is not necessary that they constantly perform self-deprecating acts that place their love of the fatherland before their self-interest. He makes this quite clear when speaking of the people's general motivations in his consideration of the threat Manlius Capitolinus posed. According to Machiavelli, out of envy for the honors of Camillus, Capitolinus developed "an ugly greed for rule" that induced him "to make tumults...against the Senate and against the laws of the fatherland." The people in this case withdrew their support to the aspirant, and "condemned him to death." Machiavelli comments with respect to this decision that "the people of Rome, very desirous of its own utility and a lover of things that went against the nobility, did very many favors to Manlius [Capitolinus]." Machiavelli says quite clearly here that people's incorruption is entirely compatible with their pursuit of their own benefit. In fact, this was precisely how the incorrupt Roman people behaved, in his view. The people in this case, though, abandoned their favorite when they "considered present dangers that depended on him much more than past merits, so much that with his death they freed themselves" (3.8.1). The people concluded, with the help of the nobles, that their interest lay not in continuing to follow Capitolinus but in having him executed.

One of the lessons that Machiavelli draws from his discussion here is that corruption is a work of time. "For the man can indeed begin to corrupt a people of a city with his modes and his wicked means, but for him it is impossible that the life of one individual be enough to corrupt it so that he himself can draw the fruit from it." Having had the good luck of being born after the civil wars, Caesar drew on the work of others. He inherited the party of Marius, which, in turn, had been given its impetus under the Gracchi, who revived the agrarian law that Spurius had proposed so very long before. Some ambitious men are simply unlucky; Capitolinus's only mistake was to have been born at the wrong time: Capitolinus "would have

been a rare and memorable man if he had been born in a corrupt city"
(3.8.2).

The Difficulties of Treating Corruption

Once corruption has made an inroad in a city, Machiavelli argues that it is
very difficult to uproot it. As difficult as the enterprise is, he refuses to call it
impossible. He himself perseveres in the face of so daunting a task by considering what Rome might have done to maintain itself "as the citizens little by
little became corrupt" (1.18.1). His response demands not that its citizens
pursue even more doggedly republican virtue, sacrificing their personal desires for the fatherland. On the contrary, he seems to expect and accept that
those who yearn most intensely for power will become ever more clever at
using the republic's laws for their own advantage. His response focuses on a
republic becoming ever more clever at forestalling their attempts. This, his
initial response to corruption, looks not to the citizens and their virtue, then,
but rather to institutional arrangements to forestall corruption. Ultimately,
it becomes obvious that the changes to the organization of a republic such a
response would require are so radical that they become almost indistinguish-
able from a new founding. This is a very demanding enterprise, indeed. The
gravity of allowing corruption an inroad is illustrated by the tyranny that
would be caused by resolute action taken too late. Given these difficulties,
it would be better to prevent corruption from gaining entry in a republic in
the first instance. Ultimately, he will propose to do precisely that by creating
a republic that punishes in a most frightening manner. This will be his ultimate response to corruption, a response made all the more palatable by the
difficulties of dealing with corruption once introduced.

In his chapter entitled "In What Mode a Free State, If There Is One,
Can Be Maintained in Corrupt Cities; or, If There Is Not, in What Mode
to Order It," he illustrates the manner in which Rome's "orders" became
inadequate as corruption spread. He cites in particular the way in which
the republic allowed citizens to nominate themselves as candidates for office
and to propose laws. These orders, Machiavelli says, were fine while the
city was not corrupt, but "became very pernicious in the corrupt city." With
respect to the way in which the Romans elected their officials, he explains
that after their city had extended its conquests to Africa, Asia, and Greece,
the Romans "became secure in their freedom." As a result, the people no
longer regarded "virtue" as the deciding factor "in bestowing the consulate"
but rather "favor." The virtue to which he here refers appears to be martial,
for he continues that the corrupt people of Rome "lift[ed] to that rank those
who knew better how to entertain men rather than those who knew better
how to conquer enemies" (1.18.3). Favor is precisely what Machiavelli says
Spurius Maelius the grain dealer sought when he distributed grain free to the
plebs (3.28.1), as well as what Appius Claudius sought when as a member of

the decemvirate he played court to the people in his quest to become tyrant of Rome (1.40.2). Apparently, when the city was corrupt, the people rewarded with election to office those unworthies who sought an easy popularity as a means of gratifying their ambition to rule. Machiavelli continues, though, that this particular problem became even worse, because "from those who had more favor, they descended to giving it to those who had more power" (1.18.3). In such instances, the people elected men not like Maelius, that is, those who sought popularity, but men who already had it. They elected men with power to high office; they elected men who apparently already had the power deriving from partisans and adherents that in Machiavelli's view are so dangerous to a republic that they signify its corruption.

Similarly, Rome's order that allowed any citizen to propose a law became harmful to the city "when the citizens have become bad," because "only the powerful" proposed laws with the intent not of furthering "the common freedom" but rather "their own power." Out of fear, no one spoke against their proposals. As a result, he concludes that "the people came to be either deceived or forced to decide its own ruin" (1.18.3). By considering how these specific orders of Rome were deficient, we have yet another rendition by Machiavelli's hand of Rome's corruption. The most ambitious were catering to the people in an attempt to amass power, and the people were either deceived or cowed into supporting their efforts.

He then turns to his analysis of how Rome might have kept itself free in the midst of such corruption to find that the Roman Republic should have changed its orders so that the ambitious could not so easily manipulate them for their own personal gain. As his two examples show, Rome failed in this regard. It should have become as clever at forestalling attempts at tyranny as the ambitious became at contriving them. "If Rome wished to maintain itself free in corruption, therefore, it was necessary that it should have made new orders, as in the course of its life it had made new laws" (1.18.4). It would appear, then, that when men attempted to use the manner of election and of proposing laws to further their designs against the commonwealth, the republic should have closed these avenues by no longer permitting its citizens to nominate themselves for office or to propose new laws. When the motivations of the people change, the republic too should change.

Changing orders, however, does not necessarily create a solution. The difficulty, as Machiavelli explains it, is that orders must be changed either gradually before their inadequacy is even evident or all at once when the need for change is evident even to the least perceptive. The first requires "someone prudent who sees this inconvenience from very far away and when it arises." This solution is not to be relied upon because, according to Machiavelli, so perceptive an individual may not "emerge in a city," and even if such a rare individual does emerge when needed, he will "never be able to persuade anyone else of what he himself understands." The other alternative, which demands that deficient orders be corrected "at a stroke" when the need for reform is obvious is similarly unlikely to offer remedy due to the sheer difficulty of the enterprise. The difficulty arises from the fact that ordinary methods are insufficient in such a situation, so "extraordinary" ones are required in their stead (1.18.4).

A further look at what these extraordinary means might entail and the type of individual capable of using them reveals that the radical change in orders necessary to maintain a republic in corruption looks very much like a refounding rather than maintenance strictly understood. Machiavelli points to "violence and arms" and observes that a unique individual would have to wield them, one capable of employing, in Machiavelli's estimation, "bad ways" for the good work of "the reordering of a city for a political way of life" (1.18.4). As rare as such an individual would be, ultimately he refuses to reject the possibility of a successful reformation of corrupt material. In fact, he points to Cleomenes who refounded the Spartan regime and Romulus who founded Rome as examples of individuals who meet his criteria of the employment of bad means for a good end; indeed, both had murders to their name, but they committed them, he insists, in order to be alone so as to accomplish their feats (1.18.5; see also 1.9). These examples underscore the magnitude of the reformation required for the maintenance of corrupt material – such maintenance is akin to a refounding or even a founding. Nevertheless, he still insists that such an outcome is possible. In a later chapter, *Discourses* 1.55, he goes so far as to describe in greater detail the violence that must be employed to order bad material, seemingly with a view to aiding whoever might undertake such an enterprise. The overcoming of corrupt material, he here suggests, is not so much a matter of inculcating virtue as it is of murder.[32]

The employment of such violent methods is fraught with danger. For example, Machiavelli highlights with the chilling example of Caesar's drive for tyranny precisely how dangerous it is to strike at a man who has already gained a great many partisans. Describing in general terms how "[m]any times a citizen is allowed to gather more strength than is reasonable, or one begins to corrupt a law that is the nerve and the life of a free way of life,"

---

[32] His discussion of the eradication of corruption in this later chapter of the *Discourses* seems aimed at the modern rather than the ancient world. For instance, he announces that France, Spain, and Italy are the "nations all together" responsible for "the corruption of the world" (1.55.3) and comments that their corruption is revealed by the large numbers of "gentlemen" there, "who live idly in abundance from the returns of their possessions without having any care either for cultivation or for other necessary trouble in living" and who often "command from a castle and have subjects who obey them" (1.55.4). Gentlemen of this sort seem to have been a product of the Middle Ages. Still he maintains that corruption of this type can be overcome: "[H]e who wishes to make a republic where there are very many gentleman cannot do it unless he first eliminates all of them." Such is the task of "a man who is rare in brain and authority" because "the greatness of the thing partly terrifies men, partly impedes them so that they fail in the first beginnings" (1.55.5).

he reiterates the difficulty of acting against corruption. By highlighting the allure this danger nonetheless holds, his elaboration here in this chapter adds a new dimension to that difficulty. He states that "[i]t is so much the more difficult to recognize these inconveniences when they arise as it appears more natural to men always to favor the beginning of things; and more than for anything else, such favor can be for works that appear to have some virtue in them and have been done by youths." The fact that the danger emanates from youth compounds the problem because "if in a republic one sees a noble youth arise who has an extraordinary virtue in him, all eyes of the citizens begin to turn toward him and agree in honoring him without any hesitation, so that if there is a bit of ambition in him, mixed with the favor that nature gives him and with this accident, he comes at once to a place where the citizens, when they become aware of their error, have few remedies to avoid it" (1.33.2). The two examples he names in this chapter, Cosimo de' Medici, who established the domination of the Medici in Florence, and Caesar, who established tyranny in Rome, help to underscore the insidiousness of the threat when it emanates from such beguiling sources.

When speaking of the case of Cosimo, Machiavelli explains that it was necessary for the Florentines not to make the error of "attempting to eliminate him," but ultimately and regrettably the republic made that very error, which eventuated in "the entire ruin of their state" (1.33.3). This outcome for the Florentines helps to illuminate the events that led to the establishment of tyranny in Rome. When speaking of Caesar in this chapter, Machiavelli says that the Romans began to fear him too late, but once they felt fear, it "made them think about remedies; and the remedies they made accelerated the ruin of their republic" (1.33.4). Although he fails to elaborate on the precise nature of the remedies the Romans attempted against Caesar's looming tyranny, it is quite clear in his view that the Romans made the same mistake the Florentines made: they attempted to eradicate tyranny from their city by attempting to kill the tyrant. Unlike the case in Florence, however, the Romans succeeded in carrying out the assassination. Despite this initial success, however, their conspiracy failed to expunge the tyranny Caesar established, as Machiavelli points out elsewhere (1.17.1). This discussion is, indeed, sobering, for he shows that resolute but late action against tyranny serves only to harden tyranny's grip on a city (see also 1.46). Given this prospect, Machiavelli advises a republic not to act at all but rather "to temporize" when the threat is so far advanced (1.33.2).

This chapter, then, adds an additional dimension to the danger posed by an attempt to overcome corruption already established in a city. When the aspiring tyrant is so very appealing, Machiavelli recommends the very un-Machiavellian course of temporizing. Such a course is likely only to delay tyranny's ultimate hold on the city; it will not of itself eliminate the threat. Machiavelli, though, has a much more Machiavellian way of dealing with the threat of tyranny and the corruption that ambitious men endeavor to introduce to a republic. As the next section argues, Machiavelli deems it unnecessary either to discern the precise moment of the onset of corruption or to strike at it once it has become entrenched. A resolute and unforgiving republic can prevent the onset of corruption entirely, he suggests.

Ingratitude, Punishment, and Machiavelli's Precautions against Corruption

Machiavelli offers an alternative prescription intended to make a republic invulnerable to corruption and, hence, to the dreams of tyranny that the most ambitious of its citizens harbor. It asks not that the republic run any of the dangers inherent in waiting until corruption has appeared. Instead of waiting to apply the remedy, Machiavelli would have the republic act early before the onset of corruption; instead of accepting the difficulties inherent in discerning the precise moment to instigate early change, Machiavelli would have the republic routinize preventive action, so that such measures would become a part of the very fabric of a republic, thus making the actual discernment of the symptoms of corruption superfluous.

Both his praise and criticism of Rome serve as guides to proper action. At times he describes the historical Rome taking measures that it did not actually take; the measures he ascribes to the city in these cases are actually his own. In this manner, his description replicates the actions he wishes Rome had taken or perhaps those that an improved republic of his own devising would take in similar circumstances. At other times, however, he concedes the failure of the historical Rome to act in the necessary way and criticizes his favored republic as a result. The remedy Machiavelli prescribes is punishment against the ambitious, applied often and spectacularly; it demands that a republic act against a beguiling youth before he can solidify his power. His prescription serves two purposes: at the same time that it applies capital punishment against one citizen, thus cutting down one who may have otherwise lived to contend for tyranny, it also frightens – and, hence, discourages – others who would certainly have contended for that prize in a less resolute republic. As unpalatable as this prescription is, he seems to have taken pains to prepare for its acceptance. It is certainly less difficult than a refounding and would appear to require fewer murders at any one time.

Machiavelli reveals his doctrine relatively early in the *Discourses*, although he continues to elaborate and examine its ramifications throughout the remainder of the work. He brings the teaching to light in his discussions of actions that might be construed as a republic's ill-tempered displays of ingratitude toward its great men.[33] The question of whether a republic had

---

[33] Machiavelli could be said to introduce this theme even earlier in the *Discourses*, in his discussion of accusations, in 1.7 and 8. He notes that one purpose of formal accusations in a republic is to provide "an outlet" by which the populace can "vent, in some mode against

displayed ingratitude would naturally arise when a republic responds to a grave wrong committed by a citizen who has in the past performed great services on its behalf. To punish severely the subsequent wrong of such a citizen could be viewed as ingratitude, and a republic that accepts the common understanding of ingratitude as a vice would eschew such action. Ultimately, Machiavelli disagrees with such an understanding, rebutting what he regards as a mistaken and pernicious understanding in two ways that are, in fact, contradictory: either by refusing to term ingratitude the punishment the republic dispenses in such cases or by admitting forthrightly that such punishment is indeed an example of ingratitude on the part of a republic but contending that ingratitude is nevertheless necessary for a republic's continued survival.

He first brings the topic of ingratitude to light when he considers a single incident that occurred when three Roman brothers fought three Alban brothers for the right of the homeland of the victors to subjugate that of the vanquished. The Romans claimed the prize when all the Alban brothers were killed in the fight, while a single Roman survived. On his return to his city, Rome's champion slew his sister when he found her grieving for the Alban brother to whom she had been betrothed. Machiavelli relates that Rome brought the murderer "to trial for his life, notwithstanding that his merits were so great and so fresh." On reflecting on the significance of this incident, he suggests that one who "considers it superficially" may find Rome's action to be "an example of popular ingratitude." Someone who "examines it better and inquires with better consideration what the orders of republics should be," however, would reach an altogether different conclusion. He suggests here that the city's indictment of the lawbreaker should not be construed as ingratitude. Further, he adds that such a reflective person would blame Rome "rather for having absolved him than for having wished to condemn him" (1.24.1). Of course, Machiavelli is one such reflective person, and he has just blamed the early Roman Republic for not punishing properly and hence for being too lenient with at least one of its great men. His discussion here at once exonerates Rome for bringing the hero to trial and criticizes it for not having been harsh enough in its punishment.

some citizen, those humors that grow up in cities." The example of such an outlet he provides is that of the tribunes compelling Coriolanus, who was, according to Machiavelli, an "enemy of the popular faction," to answer charges that he wished to "punish the plebs." Coriolanus is the embodiment of the great's desire to dominate the people, and, as we have seen, Machiavelli asserts that a democratic republic must restrain this desire to dominate on the part of the great. Nevertheless, manifestations of Coriolanus's form of ambition are easier to contain because they are devoid of the guile that defines the other form, which occurs when a prominent individual seeks sole rule by befriending the people. Machiavelli seems also to direct accusations against this latter, more insidious manifestation of the great's ambition in a way that prefigures his solution as it appears in later portions of the *Discourses*. He states here: "The first [purpose of accusations] is that for fear of being accused citizens do not attempt things against the state; and when attempting them, they are crushed instantly and without respect" (1.7.1).

Given his view of the outcome of this trial, it would appear that Machiavelli regards Rome as having failed to understand a republic's need to punish its outstanding men when they committed a wrong. This failure made Rome vulnerable to tremendous danger: "[N]o well-ordered republic ever cancels the demerits with the merits of its citizens" and that "[w]hen these orders are well observed, a city lives free for a long time; otherwise it will always come to ruin soon." He elaborates on this point by considering the passions of the ambitious man: "For if a citizen has done some outstanding work for the city, and on top of the reputation that this thing brings him, he has an audacity and confidence that he can do some work that is not good without fearing punishment, in a short time he will become so insolent that any civility will be dissolved" (1.24.1). To act in the harshest way possible against outstanding citizens who have transgressed – Machiavelli will not concede here that such action on the part of a republic constitutes ingratitude – is preferable to allowing a great man to become so insolent and audacious that he dares to make an attempt on the republic.

In a section closely following on this chapter and explicitly devoted to the topic of ingratitude, chapters 28–32 of the first book, he gradually embraces the view that rather than being a vice, ingratitude – actually using in this case the term conventionally understood as a vice – is a positive good for a republic. He ultimately urges the necessity of ingratitude in all such cases. In support of this final conclusion he reasons that "since a city that lives free has two ends – one to acquire, the other to maintain itself free – it must be that in one thing or the other it errs through too much love" (1.29.3). This, then, is his understanding: a republic risks the loss of its freedom when it is too loving toward its ambitious men. He also shows in this section that the opposite of love – that is, fear – will maintain a republic.

He confirms this view when he turns in the same chapter to the case of Caesar. It must be said, however, that the outcome of this particular case appears to suggest the opposite of what he has just concluded. It would appear in this instance that Rome erred through the overzealous application of fear and punishment, not love. Machiavelli himself would appear to attest to this fact, for as we already know, only four chapters later – in the chapter that immediately succeeds this section on ingratitude – he returns to the topic of the murderous action that members of the Roman Republic took against Caesar to deem their action an ill-advised move that brought their city all the more quickly to tyranny. He seems to anticipate such an objection and moves to clarify his meaning when he notes "nonetheless in a republic that is not corrupt they are the cause of great goods and make it live free, since men are kept better and less ambitious longer through fear of punishment" (1.29.3). Punishments are the key to the longevity of an incorrupt republic. Of course, the same fear-inducing punishments applied in a corrupt republic would produce ruin, not restoration. As the case of Caesar suggests, when a great man has acquired a significant train of partisans, assassination will likely result in martyrdom and thereby the perpetuation of his tyranny by others who "rul[e] under that name" (1.10.3). In accord with his conclusion in 1.33, temporizing is the safest tactic in corruption. The key, then, is to keep a republic incorrupt in the first instance.[34]

Machiavelli endorses the healthful properties of punishment and teaches the necessity of a republic's ingratitude, but historical Rome did not inflict the type of punishment he deems necessary: "The Romans, as we have discoursed of above, not only were less ungrateful than other republics but also were more merciful and more hesitant in the punishment of the captains of their armies than any other" (1.31.1). Knowing what we know, what would ordinarily appear to be praise is, in fact, harsh criticism.[35] He offers such criticism because a republic that is merciful with wrongdoers will embolden others to even greater insolence.[36]

Machiavelli's disappointment with Rome's failure to punish adequately, although certainly less pronounced, is also present in *Discourses* 3.1, where he gives his most extended consideration of his own precautions against corruption for which he makes extensive and impressive claims regarding their efficacy. Entitled "If One Wishes a Sect or a Republic to Live Long, It Is Necessary to Draw It Back Often toward Its Beginning," this chapter is a continuation of his treatment of corruption and how it might be stemmed. It is not so much about Rome but about what Rome might have been had it punished adequately; he claims that if Rome had availed itself of the

---

[34] Cf. Skinner, *Machiavelli*, 78.

[35] Coby recognizes Machiavelli's dissatisfaction with Rome in some respects and delineates how Machiavelli would improve on these missteps. In this context, he even notes Machiavelli's dissatisfaction with "the Roman practice of treating miscreants leniently" to reach the conclusion that in the Italian's view "grateful Rome was at fault for being too kind and just" (*Romans*, 202). Coby, however, fails to build on these recognitions, later claiming that "institutional remedies, plus the consequent disorder, soon returned Rome to the true way" after it had "veered from the true way" having "allowed" "its reputed citizens" "to use private favors to ascend to public power" (237). In contrast, my interpretation maintains that, in Machiavelli's view, there came a time when Rome failed to punish appropriately, and, as a result, never returned to that true way.

[36] He confirms his disappointment with Rome in its failure to punish harshly enough when later in 1.31 he considers two Roman captains, who, although not conspiring for tyranny, committed grave wrongs. Jealous of one another, one preferred defeat to condescending to request aid from the other, and that other preferred "the dishonor of his fatherland and the ruin of the army" to offering his aid to his colleague. Machiavelli comments that the "case [is] truly malevolent," and one could "draw not a good conjecture concerning the Roman republic if both had not been punished." His cool sarcasm when explaining Rome's reaction to these wrongdoers belies his disgust with the city on this issue: "It is true that whereas another republic would have punished them with the capital penalty, this one punished them with fines of money. This came about not because their sins did not merit greater punishment but because . . . the Romans in this case wished to maintain their ancient customs" (1.31.2). Just as obvious as Machiavelli's own endorsement of the punishment "another republic" would have inflicted on these malicious captains is his view of these particular customs of Rome that prevented these captains from being punished as they deserved.

precautions he himself concocts from his examination of its history, it need not have become corrupt.

He explains when introducing the topic that the goodness of a political entity at its founding becomes "corrupted, unless something intervenes to lead it back to the mark," so that without such intervention eventually the "body" dies (3.1.2). When speaking of republics specifically, he explains that these events that work such a revivifying effect can occur through internal and external causes. External causes, such as the near sacking of a city (as occurred to Rome when it was almost taken by the Gauls), serve to bring a republic back to its beginning because they overcome the complacency that develops when citizens feel secure. Although such external causes serve this good end, they are dangerous and unpredictable, being completely out of the control of the republic. It is better to rely on internal causes that occur "through the virtue of a man or through the virtue of an order." With respect to the latter, he furnishes the examples of "the tribunes of the plebs, the censors, and all the other laws that went against the ambition and the insolence of men," and explains that "[s]uch orders have need of being brought to life by the virtue of a citizen who rushes spiritedly to execute them against the power of those who transgress them." When he says execute in this context he means not merely to carry out but also to subject to the most extreme punishment. Among his examples of the latter are "the death . . . of Maelius the grain dealer" and "the death of the ten citizens" (3.1.3).[37] Such executions, even when they are not aimed at the worst of malefactors, work against the most dangerous manifestations of ambition and insolence.[38]

Not all the executions he speaks of here, however, resulted in the death penalty, and not all were applied against those who were aspiring for tyranny. In some cases, the executions of which Machiavelli speaks were carried out against promising young men, who in their youthful enthusiasm fought – and defeated – Rome's enemies when they had been ordered not to engage

---

[37] Such stern men rushed to "esequirli" (Machiavelli, *Opere*, 196). These examples, I believe, illuminate a statement regarding republics in 2.2.1 where he states that "it is not the particular good but the common good that makes cities great. And without doubt this common good is not observed if not in republics, since all that is for that purpose is executed, and although it may turn out to harm this or that private individual, those for whom the aforesaid does good are so many that they can go ahead with it against the disposition of the few crushed by it." Certainly, these men whom Machiavelli offers as sacrifices in 3.1 would qualify as the "few crushed" by the common good in a republic. See Harvey C. Mansfield, *Taming the Prince: The Ambivalence of Modern Executive Power* (New York: Free Press, 1989), 121–49, for a discussion of the implications of Machiavelli's use of the terms execute and executions.

[38] In concentrating on the rhetorical dimension of Machiavelli's writings, Kahn produces a striking analysis of the passage that contains Machiavelli's delineation of these executions: "Machiavelli suggests an analogy between Rome and the *Discourses*: just as Rome needs to be returned to its first principles by the drastic actions of a man of *virtù*, so the reader of the *Discourses* needs to be brought back to the mark by shocking examples" (Kahn, *Machiavellian Rhetoric*, 56).

in battle. For instance, "the execution of Papirius Cursor against his master of the cavalrymen Fabius" did not result in the death of Fabius. Having led and won a victory against the Samnites in the absence of the dictator and against the dictator's specific orders when the auspices were ambiguous, Fabius would have been put to death by Papirius as a result of this deed, if he had not escaped to Rome where he and his father appealed to the Senate and the tribunes. When the appeals of father and son elicited the sympathy of all, Papirius relented in his demands for the younger man's death.[39] By contrast, another such execution, "the death of the son of Manlius Torquatus," had a different outcome for the eager young man (3.1.3). Manlius Torquatus, when serving as consul in the field against the Latins, would not spare the life of his son, who killed his Latin challenger in a duel.[40]

Such terrifying actions carry great significance for Machiavelli, and he appears to hold the city in high esteem for providing such numerous instances of them. Nevertheless, he also reveals Rome's insufficiency on this score because the city he so admires did not always execute in the manner that he praises here – in the manner that he thinks necessary. For instance, the members of the decemvirate were not executed, as he suggests they were. He indicates that he is quite aware of this historical fact elsewhere in the work.[41] Given the tremendous effects he believes such executions have on a republic, clearly he thinks that Rome should have handled its treatment of the decemvirs in the way he indicates here.

He then explains how such executions can work to counter corruption. "Because they were excessive and notable, such things made men draw back toward the mark whenever one of them arose." He continues that "when they began to be more rare, they also began to give more space to men to corrupt themselves and to behave with greater danger and more tumult" (3.1.3). These executions, which belong in part to Machiavelli's imagination and which he imbues with so much significance, seem to be the alternative to the two methods that he offers in Discourses 1.18 of changing orders to circumvent the manner in which ambitious men learn to manipulate a republic's orders for their own nefarious ends. Again, he depicts the solutions of the earlier chapter as being either extremely difficult or extremely dangerous to put into effect. Now, rather than a republic needing to change orders as the ambitious become increasingly more arrogant, holding the power of the republic in ever greater contempt, the republic periodically cuts down

---

[39] Livy, Ab urbe condita 8.30–5. Whereas Machiavelli offers Papirius's execution as one of the events that reinvigorated Rome, Livy seems to take a dimmer view of the incident, referring in one place to the "madness" of the general (8.30.1–2).

[40] Livy, Ab urbe condita 8.7.

[41] Livy reports that Appius and one other member of the decemvirate killed themselves in prison and that the others went into exile (Ab urbe condita 3.58). Machiavelli indicates that he knows that Rome did not execute Appius when he notes, in accordance with Livy's history, that "before the day of the judgment [Appius] killed himself" (1.45.1).

one of the ambitious in order to foster fear and, hence, respect among the great for their republic. Machiavelli explains the need for a republic to recur periodically to this precaution:

[O]ne should not wish ten years at most to pass from one to another of such executions; for when this time is past, men begin to vary in their customs and to transgress the laws. Unless something arises by which punishment is brought back to their memory and fear is renewed in their spirits, soon so many delinquents join together that they can no longer be punished without danger. (3.1.3)

So powerful are the aspirations of the ambitious that they must consistently be hindered in their designs by so powerful an obstruction.

He goes on to equate the type of terror that such punishment instills in men to the type of terror that men had when the state was founded.[42] The terror that men felt at the founding, then, must be the reason that he can claim that "all the beginnings of sects, republics, and kingdoms must have some goodness in them" (3.1.2).[43] He uses this image to restate the potency of these executions, declaring that "as the memory of that beating is eliminated, men began to dare to try new things and to say evil; and so it is necessary to provide for it, drawing [the state] back toward its beginnings"

---

[42] Strauss, *Thoughts on Machiavelli*, 166–7, and Harvey C. Mansfield, *Machiavelli's New Modes and Orders: A Study of the "Discourses on Livy"* (Ithaca: Cornell University Press, 1979; reprint, Chicago: University of Chicago Press, 2001), 301–3; Rahe, *Republics Ancient and Modern*, 266. An important example of such a terrifying return to the beginning is "the death of the sons of Brutus," as he terms the incident in 3.1.3. His treatment of the incident, in which Brutus sentenced his sons to death for conspiring to bring back the Tarquins and then presided over their execution, blurs the distinction between a return to the beginning and a founding. Elsewhere he says that "a state that is free and that newly emerges comes to have partisan enemies and not partisan friends. If one wishes to remedy these inconveniences and the disorders" "there is no remedy more powerful, nor more valid, more secure, and more necessary, than to kill the sons of Brutus" (1.16.4; see also 1.16.3). This is what a republic must do at its inception, as is clear when Machiavelli's maxim of the necessity of killing the sons of Brutus furnishes the chapter title of 3.3: "[W]hoever makes a free state and does not kill the sons of Brutus, maintains himself for little time" (3.3.1). Cf. Fischer's "distinction between returns to the beginnings and a renewed founding" (*Well-Ordered License*, 142–3).

[43] Fischer helpfully points out that Machiavelli intends for these executions to be in accord with the laws of the republic, a fact that he proffers to counter the suggestions that he sees emanating from the works of Strauss and Mansfield and Tarcov that Machiavelli's republic amounts to an unlawful tyranny of its leading men (e.g., Mansfield and Tarcov, introduction to *Discourses*, xxiv and xxv) (Fischer, *Well-Ordered License*, 143 and n. 69). As my interpretation strives to show, Machiavelli expends a great deal of effort in preventing the tyrannical impulses of any of its leading men from becoming a tyranny in fact. In emphasizing republican lawfulness, Fischer's account, though, softens the harshness of the executions that recreates the fear of vulnerable human beings bereft of the security of laws and institutions (see the immediately preceding note). For additional treatments of tyranny and republicanism in Machiavelli's work, see Kahn, *Machiavellian Rhetoric*, who argues that Machiavelli's rhetorical strategy, as well as the substance of his thought, link tyranny and republicanism (especially at 35, 40, 45, 54, 58).

(3.1.3). In this way, Machiavelli even more forcefully equates this method of spectacular punishment with a founding or reordering of state, powerfully underscoring that this method could serve as the alternative to the two less desirable methods of reinvigorating a republic that he delineates in *Discourses* 1.18. If a state were consistently to avail itself of these periodic recourses to the founding fear, it would to be periodically rejuvenated. Could such rejuvenation prevent corruption altogether?

Harsh Captains and a Promise of a Perpetual Republic

If rejuvenation can prevent corruption, then perhaps a republic could defy the devastating effects of time altogether. This is precisely the claim Machiavelli eventually makes. He associates the defiance of corruption specifically with harsh captains, as exemplified by Manlius Torquatus. He so emphasizes the necessity of harshness, as well as the dangers of kindness, that it induces him to make an almost incredible claim: through the proper application of fear, a republic can be perpetual.

Machiavelli first broaches the possibility of a republic defying corruption altogether later in 3.1. In leading up to this claim, he explains that the "drawing back of republics toward their beginning arises also from the simple virtue of one man." He deems it necessary to point out that this method does not depend "on any law that stimulates you to any execution." Either surprised that executions are not employed in such cases or believing that he must underscore this fact for his reader, he adds that "nonetheless" men of this character "are of such reputation and so much example that good men desire to imitate them and the wicked are ashamed to hold to a life contrary to them" (3.1.3). He names six such Romans, and although all receive at least some mention elsewhere in the *Discourses*, none figure particularly prominently in the work.[44]

Thus, a republic has two methods of internal renewal at its disposal: terrifying executions and awesome displays of individual virtue. Apparently, these two methods must work together to maintain a republic, for immediately after providing examples of individuals of such high worth, he makes his claim for the efficacy of his prescription: "If the executions written above, together with these particular examples, had continued at least every ten years in that city, it follows of necessity that it would never have been corrupt" (3.1.3). Two things, in particular, must be noted about this statement. First, a state need not become corrupt. He here presents his solution to corruption. The primary way is to keep the ambitious chastened by spectacular executions and then to have individuals provide models for proper

---

44 He names "Horatius Coclus, Scaevola, Fabricius, the two Decii, [and] Regulus Attilius" (3.1.3).

behavior.[45] Finally, we have his full explication of the claim he makes so much earlier in the work that "men are kept better and less ambitious longer through fear of punishment" (1.29.3). Second, although a state may avoid corruption, Rome ultimately failed on this score. In fact, he points to this failure of his exemplary republic, observing that "as both of these two things began to diminish" in Rome, "corruptions began to multiply" (3.1.3). Rome became corrupt unnecessarily by permitting its ambitious men to become insolent. Apparently, only after having absorbed what was "written above," which includes, of course, Machiavelli's teaching regarding the necessity of executions of the ambitious, will a republic have hope of enduring.[46]

Although in 3.1 examples of virtue and terrifying executions combine to forestall corruption, later Machiavelli refers only to Manlius, an exemplary executioner, as the necessary ingredient for a republic's longevity.[47] This Roman's many remarkable deeds receive Machiavelli's admiring attentions throughout the *Discourses*.[48] In contrasting Manlius's harshness to the kindness of a benevolent captain, Machiavelli declares that "the proceeding of Manlius is more praiseworthy and less dangerous, because this mode is wholly in favor of the public and does not in any part have regard to private ambition." He justifies this claim by pointing out that such a captain, by "showing oneself always harsh to everyone and loving only the common good . . . cannot acquire partisans" (3.22.4). Here we have Machiavelli's familiar emphasis on the acquisition of devoted followers who wish to gain for themselves the beneficence of the one whom they elevate, but whose very existence furnishes the inequality that is the distinguishing feature of corruption. Manlius's personality repels rather than attracts such a following.

---

[45] As I suggest later, this latter method becomes overshadowed in Machiavelli's thought by the former.

[46] In commenting on *Discourses* 3.1, Coby states: "But even though [Machiavelli] has divined the secret to political immortality, he is, one supposes, none too hopeful of the result; for the two lists of virtuous Romans fail to show that Rome ever adhered to the schedule of decennial renewals" (*Romans*, 152). But Rome's failure may be his precise point. Having learned why the Roman Republic collapsed, he can instruct another how to avoid that same fate.

[47] In a later chapter Manlius actually appears to usurp the place of the Romans of simple virtue whom Machiavelli lists in 3.1. Whereas in 3.1.3 Machiavelli refers to Manlius as an executioner and to other men as those "who with their rare and virtuous examples produced in Rome almost the same effect that laws and orders produced," by contrast in 3.22.3 he describes Manlius as "one who with his *example* might renew the laws" and does not refer at all to the men who offered examples of virtue (emphasis added). Therefore, Manlius becomes an example by virtue of his role as executioner.

[48] Machiavelli treats the young Manlius's armed and effective threat against the tribune who had accused his father (1.11.1); his defeat of the champion of the Gauls from whose dead body he took the gold collar and so earned the appellation of Torquatus (3.34.2); his service as consul when he killed his son for fighting against orders, which both inspired the Roman army in its battle against the Latins (2.16.1) and brought the republic back to its beginning as one of Machiavelli's spectacular executions (3.1.1).

In this manner, Manlius would appear to make use of the public way to acquire reputation – as opposed to the private way, which attracts partisans (cf. 3.28.1). The private ambition, which Manlius apparently lacks, is the ambition that prompts an attempt at tyranny.

By contrast, the kind captain attracts the type of following that Manlius repels. This recognition induces Machiavelli to warn that the threat of tyranny hides behind an appealing appearance (see also 1.33). The "mode of proceeding" opposite to Manlius's, even if it promotes in the short term the same favorable outcome "to the public," must nevertheless produce "many doubts... as to the bad effects on freedom of a long command," "because of the particular goodwill that he acquires with the soldiers" (3.22.4). Machiavelli teaches that this particular way of love must be suspect. It has bad effects on freedom because it paves the way for tyranny.

In addition to the negative good of not posing such a threat to the continued existence of a republic, Machiavelli declares that the captain of a Manlian disposition benefits a republic in another way. To this end, Machiavelli points to the positive good – to the astounding good – that the Manlian way of proceeding offers through its complete vanquishing of the threat of corruption. He says with a measure of understatement, given his ultimate conclusion as to the worth of harsh captains, that Manlius's "extraordinary commands" "are useful in a republic because they return its orders toward their beginning and into its ancient virtue." By way of explanation he elaborates: "As we said above, if a republic were so happy that it often had one who with his example might renew the laws, and not only restrain it from running to ruin but pull it back, it would be perpetual" (3.22.3). This is an obvious reference to 3.1 where he speaks of executions and of the return to the beginning; it is not obvious, though, that this is the conclusion he actually offers in that chapter. Although he does say in that chapter that certain examples and executions could have combined to prevent Rome from ever being corrupt, he does not mention the word "perpetual" there. Only in the later chapter, 3.22, does he spell out the implications of the eradication of corruption in a republic to make the incredible claim that a republic could be perpetual.[49]

Machiavelli's answer to the problem of a republic's immortality would have to be effective against another threat to which acquisitive republics in particular are susceptible. Shortly after extending the promise of a perpetual

[49] Machiavelli's assertion of the possibility of a perpetual republic is far from dogmatic; five chapters earlier he says that "it is impossible to order a perpetual republic, because its ruin is caused through a thousand unexpected ways" (3.17.1). Nevertheless, he does hold out the possibility, and makes the possibility, in fact, his last word on the subject in the *Discourses*. Most important for my purposes here, he associates the means by which perpetuity is to be achieved with Manlius and punishment. For elaborations of Machiavelli's view of a perpetual republic, see Sullivan, *Machiavelli's Three Romes*, 156–7 and 174–6; Mansfield and Tarcov, introduction to *Discourses*, xli–xlii; Mansfield, *Machiavelli's Virtue*, 120–1.

republic, he notes that "two things were the cause of the dissolution of [the Roman] republic." The first, as we know, is "the contentions that arose from the Agrarian law," and the other is "the prolongation of commands." Of course, as Rome's conquests passed beyond Italy, its armies had to go further away to find new territories to conquer. As a result, it took longer to triumph over these new peoples. To meet this difficulty Rome extended the length of time generals could hold their command. Machiavelli points to two consequences deleterious to the republic deriving from this expedient: "one, that . . . they came to restrict reputation to a few; the other, that when a citizen remained commander of an army for a very long time, he would win it over to himself and make it partisan to him, for the army would in time forget the Senate and recognize that head." This result of Rome's command being concentrated in a threateningly powerful few directly contributed to its downfall in his view. "Because of this," he notes, "Sulla and Marius could find soldiers who would follow them against the public good; because of this, Caesar could seize the fatherland" (3.24.1).

He suggests, though, that this particular cause of Rome's downfall is remediable. At the beginning of this discussion, he proposes that the benefit of hindsight regarding Rome's downfall is helpful in overcoming both of these threats to a republic: "If these things had been known well from the beginning, and proper remedies produced for them, a free way of life would have been longer and perhaps quieter." As he concludes the chapter, he offers a possible way to counter, but not to overcome, the threats stemming from long commands: "[I]f the Romans had never prolonged magistracies and commands, if they would not have come so soon to so much power, and if their acquisitions had been later, they would have come later still to servitude" (3.24.1). He appears to have another answer, however – one that does not require a republic to contain its acquisitive impulses in this way. He certainly offers his spectacular punishments to counter the very type of arrogance displayed by the later generals, who used their wiles to turn their soldiers into their partisans. Surely, it was not merely the length of time in command that made their soldiers so devoted to them. Perhaps he intends his emphasis on punishment against the great to overcome the insolence to which long-serving captains are vulnerable.

If punishments appropriately applied by stern captains can offer a perpetual republic, then such punishments would have to be effective against the danger presented by long-serving captains. This solution would appear to be effective against the problem he points to when speaking of Valerius, the kind captain and Manlius's foil in 3.22. Machiavelli says that "because of the particular goodwill that [Valerius] acquires with the soldiers, many doubts resurge as to the bad effects on freedom of a long command" (3.22.4). Similar doubts apparently do not arise when those of Manlius's disposition have a long command; thus, captains of Manlius's disposition would provide a solution to the prolongation of commands.

In so emphasizing the need to provide punishment as the reward for in-solence and audacity – for ambition of the highest type – Machiavelli is oblivious to the concern that such a stance toward ambition may dampen it entirely and hence render the republic devoid of the good effects that derive from men's ambition for reputation (cf. 3.28.1). Apparently, in a republic of Rome's type, there will be no shortage of ambition, in his view. Such a republic must concern itself only with curbing it, not with fostering it. Of course, in a republic where men of Manlius's disposition were present, the ambitious could not become insolent, and, as a result, the public way would be more common as the route to reputation. This discussion suggests again the extent to which Manlius's disposition would strengthen a republic.

The deeds of Manlius and the disposition that could give rise to them are of the most vital importance to a republic, then. Given this importance, it is somewhat surprising that he does not demand a stern republican education that will teach young men to model themselves on Manlius's harshness. He does at one point in the *Discourses*, though, suggest that Manlius's harshness derived from the education he received from his family, as he observes that all the Manlii "were hard and obstinate" (3.46.1). Nevertheless, the Florentine seems not to believe that such an education widely applied could overcome the natural ambition of the great more generally. In a chapter devoted to the young patrician associates of Appius Claudius, the leading decemvir, Machiavelli marvels at "how easily men are corrupted and make themselves assume a contrary nature, however good and well brought up." He then urges that this recognition be used in politics: "If this is well examined, it will make legislators of republics and kingdoms more ready to check human appetites and to take away from them all hope of being able to err with impunity" (1.42.1). In the face of temptation, then, education is not efficacious for most individuals. As a result, he turns not to education[50] but to the remedy he has already prescribed: punishment. They may continue to err, but they will not be able to err with impunity.

Although a republic may not be able to nurture men with dispositions akin to Manlius, Machiavelli insists that such types be present in a republic. By exalting his character in such an extreme fashion, perhaps Machiavelli simply wishes to emphasize the abiding need for harshness and punishment. A republic that took Machiavelli's lesson seriously would be a less grateful and hence a more fearful place, one quick to take resolute action against any threat. He suggests that this would be the case when he adds that the kind captain is a threat not only to his country but also to himself, claiming that "in suspecting his mode of proceeding, his city is constrained to secure itself against him to his harm" (3.22.6). Machiavelli teaches that the lov-able captain lives in perpetual danger of coming under the suspicion of the

---

[50] Rahe, *Republics Ancient and Modern*, 266. Cf. Viroli, *Politics to Reason of State*, 159.

republic and hence of incurring its intense ingratitude, which takes the form of capital punishment.

Such suspicion and such readiness to act on it may characterize the republic Machiavelli envisions, but they do not characterize most republics, in his view. Indeed, he complains repeatedly in the *Discourses* of the unsuspecting character of republics, of their slowness in acting even when they do discern a threat, and hence of their vulnerability to tyranny. For instance, he maintains in his chapter on conspiracies that these very characteristics of republics embolden ambitious citizens to make attempts at tyranny, affirming there that "citizens can aspire to the principality by many means and many ways ... both because republics are slower than a prince, suspect less, and through this are less cautious and because they have more respect for their great citizens and through this the latter are bolder and more spirited in acting against them" (3.6.19). Moreover, in speaking of the necessity for an institution such as Rome's dictator, he says "the customary orders in republics have a slow motion ... their remedies are very dangerous when they have to remedy a thing that time does not wait for" (1.34.3). The institution of the dictator solved this problem only in part, for, as Machiavelli shows in 3.1, even with the addition of this institution specifically designed to enable the city to act with dispatch, Rome became less intent on acting on internal threats by punishing its most ambitious men and, as a result, became corrupt. Machiavelli envisions a republic that will not make such mistakes. In avoiding these mistakes it can make the best use of the ambition of the great precisely because that republic can contain their ambition within safe parameters by taking away their hope that they can err with impunity.

Machiavelli's Republic

This, then, is Machiavelli's republic. It celebrates the passions of its populace when they are applied to the acquisition of earthly goods. He knows that the people will seek security and the great will strive for rank and glory. These disparate ends will keep the two groups at odds, but a divided city, a city full of dissension and turmoil, does not in the least offend his sensibilities. He knows both that this contention is a necessity if a republic is to be an acquisitive one and that only an acquisitive republic can overcome the necessity that impinges from internal and external causes. He knows that in order to have such a republic, the people, as many people as a republic can embrace, must be soldiers. If they are to be used in such an enterprise, they must be given some effective defenses against the oppression of the great and, indeed, they must be allowed to participate to some extent in their regime.

In order to promote the common good, he has no intention of teaching the citizens to forgo their self-interested passions, the very passions that create this contention between the two parties. It is not that he denies that the common good can serve as the motivating concern of some individuals.

Indeed, as we have seen, Manlius Torquatus was distinguished in "loving only the common good" (3.22.4). In addition, one type of tribune – the respectable type – apparently pursued the common good; because such a tribune was "a lover of the common good," the patricians could motivate him to support their purposes and oppose the will of the other tribunes (3.11.1). And, of course, the "prudent" founder works not for himself but for "the common good" by renouncing the establishment of a hereditary succession and founding a republic (1.9.2). It must be said, however, that because republics are more resilient and better at acquiring, such a founder, by looking toward the common good in this way, would also be serving himself by assuring his enduring fame. A similar result occurs when the republic's leaders use the public mode by "working better in the common benefit" to acquire a reputation (3.28.1). Such regard for the common good, in Machiavelli's view, whether the public good or the individual good is the ultimate goal, is not so widely distributed among citizens as to be an effective means in controlling their behavior, however.

Moreover, as we have seen, the selfish passions of the citizens themselves can serve to promote the common good when they are kept in balance. And Machiavelli insists that they must be kept in balance. The most ambitious of the great pose a particularly virulent threat to the republic, because they can seek to overturn that balance in order to satisfy their passion to dominate all others by appearing to endeavor to satisfy the passions of the people. To counter this threat, Machiavelli mobilizes another passion, the passion of fear. Machiavelli intends to make his republic a most fearful place for those who would contemplate such an attempt at tyranny. He will sacrifice promising young men for the sake of reminding all of their own vulnerability and the strength and resoluteness of the republic in which they live.

Machiavelli shares with Hobbes, then, a reliance on the passions, and a particular confidence in the inculcation of fear that originates in the recognition of human vulnerability in relation to the power of the state. One might also be tempted to say that, again like Hobbes, Machiavelli takes the side of the people against the aristocrats. He does, after all, embrace the democratic republic of Rome. This democratic impulse of Machiavelli, however, has a limit, and that limit is war. Although Machiavelli's republicanism makes a display of celebrating the people, his celebration of them originates from his own pursuits, not from theirs. Unlike Hobbes, he does not take up the cause of the people against the aristocrats, whose cause is the pursuit of honor in martial undertakings.

2

Hobbes on Peace, the Passions, and Politics

In a Machiavellian spirit – and, indeed, with Machiavelli's own language – Hobbes proclaims "Force, and Fraud" "the two Cardinall vertues" (90).[1] As superlative as his praise of them is, however, it is definitely bounded, for he will recognize them as virtues, let alone the highest ones, only in the state of nature; they are, in fact, to be proscribed outside of the state of nature. After the state of nature is overturned, new virtues, ones that reject both aggression and competition, replace the old.

Machiavelli, by contrast, recognizes no such limit on these two so-called virtues. They are indispensable at all times for individuals who seek to rise in the world. In some sense, war is the fundamental condition not only among sovereign states but also among individuals. The Italian seems to have contemplated the possibility of the elimination of war, but he shuns that very possibility when he takes the side of Rome's patricians in their opposition to the plebeians who sought to be unchained from their city's wars. War is to be cultivated, in his view, and those most hungry for its honors must be embraced, despite the dangers such individuals present when they turn their aggressive instincts on the state itself.

---

[1] Page references to Hobbes's *Leviathan*, ed. Richard Tuck (Cambridge: Cambridge University Press, 1991), appear in the text in this chapter. Machiavelli praises Cesare Borgia for knowing how "to conquer either by force and fraud" (*Prince* 7.32). He also instructs a prince to be both powerful and cunning: "[O]ne needs to be a fox to recognize snares and a lion to frighten the wolves. Those who stay simply with the lion do not understand this. A prudent lord, therefore, cannot observe faith, nor should he, when such observance turns against him, and the causes that made him promise have been eliminated" (*Prince* 18.69). See also *Discourses* 2.13 for his insistence on the necessity of fraud: "I esteem it to be a very true thing that it rarely or never happens that men of small fortune come to great ranks without force and without fraud.... Nor do I believe that force alone is ever found to be enough, but fraud alone will be found to be quite enough" (2.13.1). Rahe, *Republics Ancient and Modern*, refers to Hobbes's use of this particular Machiavellian terminology, 982, n. 103.

Hobbes left no direct evidence that he knew Machiavelli's work. In fact, both Machiavelli and Hobbes could have been responding independently to Cicero's discussion in *De Officiis*

The battles that thrill Machiavelli repel Hobbes. And therein rests a great deal of the difference between the two thinkers. Having witnessed the Continent convulsed by the Thirty Years' War and England torn by civil war, Hobbes believes that such conflict is the greatest threat to human beings and that the condition of war can and should be superseded.[2] The highest pursuits of humankind, in the Englishman's view, are peace and improvement in human life, understood as a comfortable – even sensuously enthralling – existence that peace would foster. He attempts to expel war from the circle of civil society, and he would follow success on this front with the expulsion

1.13.41: "While wrong may be done, then, in either of two ways, that is, by force or by fraud, both are bestial: fraud seems to belong to the cunning fox, force to the lion; both are wholly unworthy of man, but fraud is the more contemptible" (Loeb Classical Library [1947], 45). Nevertheless, there are weighty reasons to suspect that Hobbes knew of the Florentine's work. According to Hobbes's contemporary, John Aubrey, Francis Bacon preferred Hobbes as his secretary because "he better liked Mr Hobbes's taking his thoughts, then any of the other [*sic*], because he understood what he wrote, which the others, not understanding, my Lord would many times have a hard taske to make sense of what they writt" (John Aubrey, *"Brief Lives," Chiefly of Contemporaries, Set down by John Aubrey, between the Years 1669 and 1696*, ed. Andrew Clark [Oxford: Clarendon Press, 1898], 1:331). Given both that Bacon considered Hobbes to have an unusual understanding of his work and that Bacon cited Machiavelli's works with approval, it would appear likely that Hobbes knew them as well. In addition, Machiavelli's works, excluding *The Prince*, appear in a catalog of books, written in Hobbes's hand, contained in the library of Hardwick Hall, home of the Cavendish family, whom Hobbes served (James Jay Hamilton, "Hobbes's Study and the Hardwick Library," *Journal of the History of Philosophy* 16 [1978]: 446–50). Richard Tuck (*Philosophy and Government: 1572–1651* [Cambridge: Cambridge University Press, 1993], 282) cites the same evidence in favor of Hobbes's knowledge of Machiavelli's thought.

Further, scholars have claimed that Hobbes authored three essays contained in *Horae Subsecivae*, a work published anonymously in 1620, one of which shows strong evidence of Machiavelli's influence (Thomas Hobbes, *Three Discourses: A Critical Modern Edition of Newly Identified Work of the Young Hobbes*, ed. Noel B. Reynolds and Arlene W. Saxonhouse [Chicago: University of Chicago Press, 1995]; for an interpretation of these essays that highlights Machiavelli's influence, see Saxonhouse, "Hobbes and the Beginnings of Modern Political Thought," in *Three Discourses*, 123–54). This claim of Hobbes's authorship has not been without controversy, however. See John C. Fortier, "Hobbes and 'A Discourse of Laws': The Perils of Wordprint Analysis," and the discussion that follows, John L. Hilton, Noel B. Reynolds, and Arlene W. Saxonhouse, "Hobbes and 'A Discourse of Laws': Response to Fortier," and Fortier, "Last Word," *Review of Politics* 59 (1997): 861–914. Rahe notes the fundamental impact of Machiavelli on Hobbes: Hobbes's "political thought presupposed Machiavelli's critique of moral reason and the moral imagination; it echoed the Florentine's denial that man is by nature a political or even a social animal" (*Republics Ancient and Modern*, 369; see also 366 and 976, n. 48).

[2] Hobbes sees very clearly how religious beliefs can foment war. This chapter focuses on Hobbes's response to conflict that arises primarily from the few who seek domination. My conclusion broaches an aspect of his approach to muting religious conflicts. It should be said, however, that he ultimately believes that the sovereign should decide all doctrinal issues. In effect, he attempts to remove the possibility of disagreement between or among various religious groups within a state, which would otherwise harbor the hope of imposing their views on the others.

of those virtues that make aggression possible. His virtues are those that encourage harmony among citizens.

Hobbes's antipathy to strife and war dictates a series of other positions that themselves serve as stark contrasts to corresponding elements of Machiavelli's thought. For instance, whereas Machiavelli smiles on the raucous public arena of Rome as a sign of that city's ability to muster an army large enough to wage aggressive war, Hobbes recoils from that ancient city's tumults. In fact, Hobbes denounces the ancient Roman Republic, which was marked by constant and, in his view, condemnable violations of the peace, both at home and abroad.

Although he abhors Rome with a particular keenness, republics less aggressive and less tumultuous also provoke his disapproval. He judges that all republics provide a public arena for those most covetous of honor to compete with their fellow claimants to distinction. There they slight, dishonor, and even attack each other. Hobbes endeavors to overcome this condition of strife within the state that republicanism fosters by promoting a monarchy; rule by one rather than many renders the political realm – the realm of contention – as small as possible. It appears that Hobbes is even more wary of the ambitious than is Machiavelli. After all, Machiavelli will allow them a republic in which to compete with each other but will keep them under control through the use of fear. Not one to stint on the generous use of fear himself, Hobbes takes away the republic and leaves only fear.

He also attempts to undercut the central assumption of those who seek self-promotion: the assumption that some human beings are inherently superior to others. In its stead, Hobbes assumes equality, and he makes the acceptance of his equality a necessary condition for the overcoming of the state of nature. To this end, he preaches that human beings are equal in the faculties of the body as well as of the mind.

In undertaking his case for the equality of mental faculties, he takes away the possibility that human beings can find in the intellect a haven from the passions. For Hobbes, all human beings are equal in being driven by their passions. In this, Hobbes endorses a view of human beings similar to Machiavelli's; individuals are all ceaselessly propelled by the desire to acquire, both thinkers agree. Hobbes, however, emphasizes the equality that derives from this understanding. The objects of the passions may differ, but people, understood as passionate creatures, do not.

Despite this overriding equality, Hobbes acknowledges that people can be divided into two different groups: those moved by the contentious passions and those moved by the amiable ones – those whose passions drive them to attempt to gain power over others and those whose passions induce them to seek peace. Hobbes replicates Machiavelli's formulation that although a few wish to dominate, most others do not.

From this common ground, Hobbes reaches conclusions very different from those Machiavelli draws. The difference results from Hobbes's fundamental opposition to war, whether civil or foreign. He therefore favors the pacific over the bellicose. Moreover, Hobbes's hatred of conflict fosters his wariness of the aristocrats, that is, Machiavelli's "great," who, driven by their pride, commit disruptive – even violent – deeds in order to demonstrate their superiority and maintain their honor. Hobbes praises the people as peaceful and censures the prideful as contentious.

Although Machiavelli makes a show of taking the side of the people against the few or the great, he intends for no such triumph of their desires as Hobbes envisions. The Florentine attempts to earn the democratic credentials he claims for himself by bringing the people into the political realm for the purpose of making war. Hobbes, by contrast, would expel everyone from the political realm – the people and the great alike – in order to prevent war. Although Hobbes is certainly no friend to a democratic form of government, his impulses are the more democratic. He is a friend of the people; he celebrates their passions and embraces their goals. Unlike Machiavelli, Hobbes makes the people's cause his own.

The Pursuit of Peace

No greater difference between Machiavelli and Hobbes can be located than in their views on war. Whereas in Machiavelli's eyes war is not only a necessity for a state but a positive good, in Hobbes's view it is an extreme evil to be shunned. Indeed, for Hobbes, the very purpose of government is to reduce – if not to eradicate – its threat. In addition to providing effective protection against war both by keeping the peace among its inhabitants and by offering defense against attacks from foreign states, his government will also avoid aggression toward other states. His state is not to seek uncertain gains from an armed citizenry but rather certain ones from a laboring population. If states were to embrace this Hobbesian lesson, the outbreak of war would become as rare as were those states foolish enough to hazard increase from so unprofitable an activity.

The very purpose of the creation of a government is, in Hobbes's view, to overcome war. Hobbes's thought, of course, contains a doctrine of the state of nature. His state of nature is a state of war, as he attests in one of his famous formulations: "[I]t is manifest, that during the time men live without a common Power to keep them all in awe, they are in that condition which is called Warre; and such a warre, as is of every man, against every man" (88). Life in this condition of war is miserable not only because it is one of continual fear of death, but it also fails to offer human beings any positive attraction to life: "[T]here is no place for Industry; because the fruit thereof is uncertain: and consequently no Culture of the Earth; no Navigation, nor use of the commodities that may be imported by Sea; no commodious Building; no Instruments of moving, and removing such things as require much force; no Knowledge of the face of the Earth; no account of Time; no Arts; no

Letters; no Society; and which is worst of all, continuall feare, and danger of violent death; And the life of man, solitary, poore, nasty, brutish, and short" (89). War is therefore the enemy of both the individual's life and society's continuance, and by being the enemy of society, it is also the enemy of the individual's enjoyment of life. "By *safety* one should understand not mere survival in any condition, but a happy life so far as that is possible. For men willingly entered commonwealths *which they had formed by design* . . . in order to be able to live as pleasantly as the human condition allows."[3] As inducement to accepting his teaching regarding peace, Hobbes tantalizes with the promise of the possibility of delight.

The preservation of life, which is threatened in war, furnishes Hobbes with his very definition of natural law. He defines a natural law as a "Precept, or generall Rule, found out by Reason, by which a man is forbidden to do, that, which is destructive of his life, or taketh away the means of preserving the same; and to omit, that, by which he thinketh it may be best preserved" (91). Thus, his general definition relates to the specific purpose of the preservation of life.[4] He reiterates the equation of peace and the natural law elsewhere when he declares that "the Lawes of Nature, dictating Peace, [are] a means of the conservation of men in multitudes" (109) and that "what is contrary to peace, is contrary to the law of nature."[5]

The specific laws he articulates under the heading of natural laws reflect this fundamental link between natural law and peace. Each one in some way looks to introducing and maintaining harmony among human beings whose day-to-day encounters are likely to create conflicts that always carry with them the possibility of outbreaks of violence. To this end, he announces that his first natural law enjoins everyone to *"endeavour Peace,"* but when one cannot secure it, one *"may seek, and use, all helps, and advantages of*

---

[3] Thomas Hobbes, *On the Citizen* [*De Cive*], ed. and trans. Richard Tuck and Michael Silverthorne (Cambridge: Cambridge University Press, 1998), 143–4.

[4] Many scholars have drawn a contrast between traditional natural-law teachings and the type of natural law Hobbes posits. See, e.g., Norberto Bobbio, *Thomas Hobbes and the Natural Law Tradition*, trans. Daniela Gobetti (Chicago: University of Chicago Press, 1993); Johann P. Sommerville, *Thomas Hobbes: Political Ideas in Historical Context* (New York: St. Martin's Press, 1992), 28–56, 74–9; Leo Strauss, *The Political Philosophy of Hobbes: Its Basis and Its Genesis*, trans. Elsa M. Sinclair (Chicago: University of Chicago Press, 1952), vii–ix, 15, 23–5; Richard Tuck, *Hobbes* (Oxford: Oxford University Press, 1989), 51–64, 102. Perhaps Bobbio's formulation of the distinction is most stark: "What has unleashed the most divergent discussions and has maddened critics, is that Hobbes has called these prudential rules 'natural laws.' But he has done so only to pay homage to tradition" (*Hobbes and the Natural Law Tradition*, 44). By contrast, Sommerville is rather ambivalent: "Hobbes altered the laws of nature in a vital respect, emptying them of any specifically moral as opposed to self-interested content. Provided these facts are recognised, it seems very much a matter of taste whether we style Hobbes a natural law theorist or not" (*Thomas Hobbes*, 79).

[5] Thomas Hobbes, *The Elements of Law Natural and Politic*, ed. J. C. A. Gaskin (Oxford: Oxford University Press, 1994), 92.

Warre." He explains that the "first branch" of his rule encapsulates the "Fundamentall Law of Nature" and that the second is "the summe of the Right of Nature; which is, *By all means we can, to defend our selves*" (92). Therefore, when the means of peace fails, another means – indeed, its very opposite – can follow. What is primary here for Hobbes is defense of life. Peace is a means, and not always the best means, to that end. This universal right to self-defense, as we will see later, makes the state of nature such an abomination.

His other laws of nature are intended to foster concord among human beings in their routine encounters with each other in civil society. For instance, his fifth natural law dictates "*That every man strive to accommodate himselfe to the rest,*" which Hobbes terms "COMPLEASANCE"; and his sixth demands "*That upon caution of the Future time, a man ought to pardon the offences past of them that repenting, desire it,*" which he terms "PARDON," and explains that it "is nothing but granting of Peace" (106). He asks that one be accommodating and forgiving. He encapsulates all of the natural laws in "one easie sum": "*Do not that to another, which thou wouldest not have done to thy selfe*" (109). Unlike the biblical injunction, "as you wish that men would do to you, do so to them,"[6] his injunction does not enjoin one to do to another the good that one would hope for oneself, but rather to refrain from doing the harm one would avoid for oneself. He asks not that one benefit others but only that one not provoke them.

The very purpose of the institution of a government, then, is the promotion of peace: "[T]he businesse of a Common-wealth is . . . to preserve the people in Peace at home, and defend them against forraign Invasion" (180). The state is a figurative fortress against civil war and a literal one in repelling foreign invaders; the state is to assure that if war is to come, it is to come from without and not from within its borders.

Hobbes supports the right of a state to wage such defensive wars, just as he upholds the right of an individual in the state of nature to make war when he or she cannot be assured of peace. The ability to wage war against foreigners, whom Hobbes understands as anyone not party to the covenant that establishes the state, is essential to the well being of the state. In support of this principle he justifies even preemptive, defensive wars. He declares that "it is lawfull by the originall Right of Nature to make warre" "against Enemies, whom the Common-wealth judgeth capable to do them hurt." Thus, although the contract that establishes the state works to expel war from the company of those who inhabit it, war persists outside of their state and can impinge on their security. In this way, the insecurity that is without can seep back into their midst. So potent a threat is this persistent state of war among sovereign states that he allows even innocent outsiders to suffer if, by their loss, the security of those within is fortified: "[T]he Infliction of what

---

[6] Luke 6.31. See also Matt. 7.12 RSV.

evill soever, on an Innocent man, that is not a Subject, if it be for the benefit of the Common-wealth, and without violation of any former Covenant, is no breach of the Law of Nature" (219).

Nonetheless, war of any sort derogates from Hobbes's purposes by threatening the lives of subjects and distracting society from discovering and distributing additional objects of delectation. At one point in *De Cive*, when discussing the manner in which states can undertake to enrich themselves, he broaches the possibility of a state seeking increase through war. He notes that in the past "great commonwealths, particularly *Rome* and *Athens*, at certain times so enlarged their country from the spoils of war, foreign tribute and the acquisition of territory by arms, that they did not impose taxes on the poorer citizens; in fact they actually distributed money and land to individuals." Even given this evidence in support of war as a means of garnering lucre, he rejects outright this method of acquisition: "But we should not take enrichment by these means into our calculations. For as a means of gain, military activity is like gambling; in most cases it reduces a person's property; very few succeed." Not willing to take the risk of armed aggression, he recommends only three ways to improve states, "*products of earth and water, hard work* and *thrift*" and renounces the fourth of "*military activity*," which "was once regarded as a gainful occupation."[7] If states in substantial numbers were to act on his recommendation, even defensive wars would become outmoded as fewer states sought increase in this way; as the numbers of aggressors diminished, so too would the number of defenders.

The example of martial and acquisitive Rome would appear in his mind to be likely to lead other states astray if the risks of its policy were not judiciously weighed. Elsewhere, however, he deems ancient republican Rome not merely a misleading example but a completely illegitimate one. He opens his epistle dedicatory to *De Cive* by pointing to the hypocrisy of Roman republicanism exemplified in Cato's declaration that "*Kings should be classed as predatory animals.*" He points to Rome's hypocrisy, reflected in this particular Roman's statement, by asking "*what sort of animal was the Roman People?*" He responds with the observation that "*the agency of citizens who took the names* Africanus, Asiaticus, Macedonicus, Achaicus *and so on from the nations they had robbed, that people plundered nearly all the world.*"[8] Because they were proud predators who feasted on the ravages of war, their example is to be shunned. In order to vanquish war, he must quell pride, because the proud – those who believe in their inherent superiority – are most likely to resort to violence to prove and to benefit from what they understand to be their preeminence. He counters human pride by his assertions of human equality.

---

[7] Hobbes, *Citizen*, 150.
[8] Ibid., 3.

Equality as Problem and Solution

The first inroad that human beings can make against war is to overturn the state of nature. People establish a commonwealth by transferring to an absolute sovereign their right to everything. Hobbes views equality as both the overriding problem in the state of nature and as the necessary egress from that deplorable condition. It is a problem because all possess a right to all things. To compound the problem, human beings are similar in that each holds the belief that he or she will likely be the victor in any confrontation over coveted items. As a result of the chaos they create, the freedom and equality that characterize the state of nature must be overturned. All are equally miserable without a sovereign authority, because all are equally vulnerable to violent death at the hands of others. No one, no matter what faculties he or she possesses, will necessarily be a winner in this competition. His dedication to his principle of equality must be explained, at least in part, by his claim that people who do not believe themselves equal will not enter into a contract. Belief in equality, then, is part of the solution to the chaos in nature. Once ensconced in civil society by virtue of the contract that abolishes the state of nature, all will be equally subjected to the law. Civil society overturns natural equality. The various inequalities found in civil society are the products of convention. Thus, the sovereign and, indeed, all masters do not owe their elevation over others to their natural superiority, he claims, but rather to a contract.

Human beings possess by nature complete equality of freedom and right, according to Hobbes. This momentous declaration means that human beings themselves are the creators of the political power that rules over them. They are its authors and they furnish it with their will – their will to preserve their lives. This notion contrasts sharply with Machiavelli's understanding that the founding or refounding of a state requires a single extraordinary individual. The actions of one, not many, create political power, in Machiavelli's view. He does specify, however, that the most prudent of founders should found a republic because that which rests with many will be better at maintaining and acquiring, and thus better at assuring the founder's posthumous glory.[9] By contrast, in Hobbes's view, the many should elevate one over them in order best to assure their preservation.

He describes the character of humanity's natural condition, for instance, in *The Elements of Law* as one in which "[e]very man by nature hath right to all things, that is to say, to do whatsoever he listeth to whom he listeth, to possess, use, and enjoy all things he will and can."[10] Far from being a doctrine of liberation, however, this declaration of equality in freedom and right issues in human bondage – bondage to fear. If one is equal to others in

---

[9] *Discourses* 1.9.2 and 1.58.3.
[10] Hobbes, *Elements*, 79.

possessing a right to all things, then all others possess the same. All possess even those things that are useful only if one can make oneself their sole owner, such as food, for example, or a habitation. Possession of any good can never be secure, because all others have a legitimate claim to it: "[T]here is . . . a right of every man to every thing, whereby one man invadeth with right, and another with right resisteth."[11] Conflict will, of course, result from such a condition of universal right to all things, and conflict, of course, raises the specter of violent death.

Hobbes spells out even more emphatically how this right imperils the likelihood of preservation: "[E]very man has a Right to every thing; even to one anothers body." As a result, one is justified in killing another. This right to the body of another is justified, because in his view, no one can be sure what the intentions of that other are. Absent laws and their execution, all are vulnerable. The survivor is the one who eliminates potential threats before they can do their damage. "And therefore, as long as this naturall Right of every man to every thing endureth, there can be no security to any man" (91). This type of equality, on Hobbes's understanding, is incompatible with human society.

He elaborates additional aspects of equality that exacerbate the chaos of the state of nature of his description. In addition to an equality of right to all things, a particular self-understanding of the actors who populate the state of nature serves to worsen their condition by increasing the likelihood of battle. Individuals tend to hold both their own qualities and capabilities in high regard and those of others in contempt (126). As a result of this pervasive attitude of individuals, they are confident of their success in violent engagements and, thus, are quick to enter into them. Hobbes describes them as possessing an "equality of hope in the attainment of [their] Ends." Emboldened by this confidence in their abilities, if another possesses some attractive good, another will be emboldened to endeavor to lay hold of it. Hobbes terms this cause of invasion "Competition," the first of three "principall causes of quarrell," "in the nature of man" (87–8). This first cause encourages people to come to blows over claims of possession.

Something of a paradox emanates from his discussion of equality here: everyone appears to believe he or she is superior, and thus, according to Hobbes's argument, people are alike – or equal – in cherishing the notion of their superiority. A belief in superiority produces a type of equality, a particularly noxious type. The individual's belief in his or her innate superiority results in an equality of hope, as Hobbes terms it. This pervasive hope that emanates from this pervasive belief in superiority encourages violence.

It is a fundamental facet of his project to transform an equality of belief in superiority to an acceptance of equality in vulnerability. He admits as much when he outlines one of the conditions for the contract that establishes

[11] Ibid., 80.

government: "If Nature therefore have made men equall; that equalitie is to be acknowledged: or if Nature have made men unequall; yet because men that think themselves equall, will not enter into conditions of Peace, but upon Equall termes, such equalitie must be admitted. And therefore for the ninth law of Nature, I put this, *That every man acknowledge other for his Equall by Nature*" (107). The success of his project requires that his assertions of equality win general approval. The rejection of this principle is simply unacceptable because those human beings who believe themselves to be naturally superior assume that, far from being harmed, they will thrive from a situation in which their strength and intelligence – their force and their fraud – are pitted against those who lack their natural gifts. The condition of nature, such individuals believe, works to their benefit, not their destruction.

Hobbes must, in fact, respond to the problem that Glaucon posits in Plato's *Republic*. According to Socrates' interlocutor, people by nature enjoy inflicting injustice on others but find it intolerable when others inflict it on them. When a significant number realize that they are more likely to be victims of injustice rather than its perpetrators, they "set down a compact among themselves neither to do injustice nor to suffer it." After this compact, they establish "their own laws and compacts and to name what the law commands lawful and just." Plato seems to have his character anticipate Hobbes's state of nature and the contract that overturns it.[12] Glaucon notes, however, that "[t]he man who is able to do it and is truly a man would never set down a compact with anyone not to do injustice and not to suffer it. He'd be mad."[13] This is the very problem – the problem of individuals who resist the compact because of their belief in their own superiority – that Hobbes attempts to solve with his various declarations of equality. He teaches that no such true man of Glaucon's description exists. Hobbes's teaching is intended to counter the view of many – if not of all – that they are so superior to the mass of human beings that they are more likely to win than lose in any confrontation. He must puncture their self-satisfaction and induce them to view themselves as vulnerable. Only when they accept this equality of vulnerability, will they enter into the contract that overturns the natural condition.

Hobbes bases his most dramatic and, hence, emphatic argument in favor of equality on the similarity of human bodies – all are vulnerable to violent death. As a result, the state of nature must be repugnant to all: "Nature hath made men so equall, in the faculties of body...; as that though there bee found one man sometimes manifestly stronger in body, or of quicker mind

---

[12] Hobbes, though, would not accept Glaucon's application of the term injustice to deeds committed in the state of nature, as the Englishman declares that both justice and injustice are a product of the contract.

[13] Plato, *Republic* 359a–b; quoted from *The Republic of Plato*, trans. Allan Bloom (New York: Basic Books, 1968), 37.

then another; yet when all is reckoned together, the difference between man, and man, is not so considerable, as that one man can thereupon claim to himselfe any benefit, to which another may not pretend, as well as he. For as to the strength of body, the weakest has strength enough to kill the strongest, either by secret machination, or by confederacy with others, that are in the same danger with himselfe" (86–7). Although Hobbes does acknowledge the difference of strength between individuals, he notes that that difference is not so considerable that any particular individual can with surety overcome all threats at all times. Any human being foolhardy enough not to recognize this equality in vulnerability risks his life – a steep wager, indeed.

Assertions of the Equality of Human Minds

Hobbes extends his claim for equality among human beings by claiming that the faculties of the mind are equally distributed among humankind. On this score, some of his assertions of equality take on the character of a debunking of cherished, but fallacious and deleterious, beliefs that one human being can be vastly superior to another. Hobbes's assertions of equality are intended to deflate vaunted estimates of any human being's abilities. Indeed, an important part of his project of teaching equality is to debunk any claims of an individual to authority based on innate superiority.

Hobbes punctures the general assumption that individual intelligence is unequally distributed with the statement that "as to the faculties of the mind, ... I find yet a greater equality amongst men, than that of strength." He acknowledges that his declaration is likely to meet with objection and parries that anticipated resistance with the following consideration: "That which may perhaps make such equality incredible, is but a vain conceipt of ones owne wisdome, which almost all men think they have in a greater degree, than the Vulgar" (87). Their vanity induces people to insist that equality cannot be the general rule because they and their friends must be distinguished from the rude multitude; sharp peaks, such as theirs, stand out from the vast plains of the topographical map of the distribution of intellects.

Hobbes explains that this universal vanity is a result of a common psychological phenomenon: "[M]en" "will hardly believe there be many so wise as themselves: For they see their own wit at hand, and other mens at a distance." Hobbes uses this fact of intellectual vanity to prove his conclusion regarding intellectual equality: "But this proveth rather that men are in that point equall, than unequall. For there is not ordinarily a greater signe of the equall distribution of any thing, than that every man is contented with his share" (87). Because there are no outcries regarding the unequal distribution of intelligence, there would appear to be no great dearths of the commodity.

He joins these arguments in favor of the equality of intellect with a demotion in the status of the faculty of prudence. Prudence, in his estimation, is not an innate capacity for good judgment. Because it is not such a capacity, its varying distribution among individuals cannot furnish a criterion of rank among them. He debunks prudence, in that it "is but Experience; which equall time, equally bestowes on all men, in those things they equally apply themselves unto" (87). He equates prudence with experience because he understands prudence to be the ability to predict an outcome of a set of circumstances from "some like action past, and the events thereof one after another." He notes that this ability to predict outcomes "is called *Foresight*, and *Prudence*, or *Providence*; and sometimes *Wisdome*." He adds somewhat irreverently that the "best Prophet naturally is the best guesser; and the best guesser, he that is most versed and studied in the matters he guesses at: for he hath most *Signes* to guesse by" (22). The only criterion Hobbes cites, then, for being prudent – indeed, wise – is that one have a significant amount of experience.

Given time, experience, of course, comes to everyone. "[T]he Experience of men equall in age, is not much unequall, as to the quantity," notes Hobbes in another context. He continues that the real difference in experience is to be found in the type of experience and points out that different people have experience in different types of activities. Because Hobbes understands prudence as experience, prudence is not necessarily readily transferable among various endeavors; it is not to be mistaken as a general acumen. The accumulation of experience in any activity, no matter how humble, is a valuable but limited asset because of the specificity of prudence. Those with experience in large, intricate, or magnificent endeavors are not necessarily qualified thereby for dealings in activities smaller, simpler, or more mundane. "A plain husband-man is more Prudent in affaires of his own house, then a Privy Counseller in the affaires of another man" (52–3).[14] There is an area in which a humble farmer is more qualified to rule than an august legislator. His teaching on prudence, therefore, buttresses his assertion of equality because it recognizes and recommends those who have hitherto been considered of lesser ability and significance.

An additional aspect of his discussion argues for the very wide dispersal of prudence. Prudence, as we know, is experience; experience, ultimately, is memory: "Much memory, or memory of many things, is called *Experience*." He defines memory, in turn, as "Sense" that "is fading, old, and past" (16). All human beings possess sense. Prudence, so defined, is certainly within the reach of all. It is no longer an exalted faculty. So very wide a distribution of any commodity necessarily robs it of its luster.

Of course, the faculty of prudence received a great deal of its luster from Aristotle's treatment of it in his *Ethics*. Hobbes responds to what he perceives as Aristotle's elevation of wisdom and prudence as rare and admirable

---

[14] Cf. Aristotle, *Nicomachean Ethics* 6.5.5: "Hence men like Pericles are deemed prudent, because they possess a faculty of discerning what things are good for themselves and for mankind" (Loeb Classical Library [1934], 339).

faculties, in part, by derisively pointing to the ancient's discussion of natural slavery in the *Politics* in order to dismiss Aristotle as a misguided elitist: "I know that *Aristotle* in the first booke of his Politiques, for a foundation of his doctrine, maketh men by Nature, some more worthy to Command, meaning the wiser sort (such as he thought himselfe to be for his Philosophy;) others to Serve, (meaning those that had strong bodies, but were not Philosophers as he)." Aristotle cannot be trusted, Hobbes implies, because he takes what he most values in himself and posits it as a particularly noble faculty that carries with it a most coveted privilege. Hobbes responds explicitly to the ancient's discussion by reiterating that master and servant are not established by nature but rather by convention; rule is always the result of contract. Hobbes then notes that Aristotle's elitism is disproved by human experience: "For there are very few so foolish, that had not rather governe themselves, than be governed by others" (107). Aristotle, according to Hobbes, is simply blinded by his own vanity.

His dismissal of Aristotle on this issue, though, represents something more than merely a difference in views on the issue of human equality. By debunking Aristotle's wisdom, Hobbes is helping people to accept the notion of equality by teaching them not to venerate the old authorities. On this score, Hobbes teaches by example. Aristotle had been a most esteemed philosophical authority for centuries, and the Englishman refuses to give the ancient pride of place. Although Hobbes's opposition to Aristotle's thought is well known, his boldness in assaulting such an authority is still arresting: "And I beleeve that scarce any thing can be more absurdly said in naturall Philosophy, than that which now is called *Aristotles Metaphysiques*; nor more repugnant to Government, than much of that hee hath said in his *Politiques*; nor more ignorantly, than a great part of his *Ethiques*" (461-2). By treating Aristotle so derisively he teaches people how to lower the high, how to tear down the peaks among humanity. Just as his debunking of prudence helps buttress his claims to equality, so too does his debunking of the elitist Aristotle.[15]

Equality and the Passions

A consideration of Hobbes's view of the passions provides additional evidence of Hobbes's demotion of the faculties of the mind, and thus his promotion of human equality. All human beings are slaves to their passions,

---

[15] Not one to foment political rebellion, Hobbes believes that an intellectual rebellion against Aristotle's thought can only serve to quell rebellion in politics. Aristotle's thought justifies political rebellion because it distinguishes between good and deviant regimes and thus teaches people to justify their dislike for a form of government by claiming a just cause, such as the overthrow of tyranny, for example. This very doctrine of just and unjust regimes is what Hobbes finds, in particular, so repugnant to government in Aristotle's *Politics* (*Leviathan*, 129-30). Thus, a blow struck against Aristotle is one struck for obedience to law.

and reason is merely a tool for their satisfaction, not a possible oasis from their insatiable demands. Having rejected the possibility of reason as a haven from the passions, he denies the very possibility of human happiness. The passions maintain all human beings in a constant state of agitation. On the basis of this understanding of the passions, he views human life as a constant struggle to acquire, in a manner akin to Machiavelli. Also, like Machiavelli, he understands that a distinction in the objects of the passions permits a fundamental distinction between types of people. He contrasts those who are buffeted by the passions that drive them to seek recognition, honor, and dominion with those who are moved by the passions that induce them to seek a means of commodious living. This divide replicates Machiavelli's distinction between the great and the people.[16] Hobbes insists that his distinction does not offer a noble and an ignoble, a higher and a lower. It is the passions that differ, not the inherent worth of the individual. Despite this avowal of equality between the two groups, his own sympathies are clearly with the people. He even suggests their moral superiority.[17]

When Hobbes observes human beings in all of their activities and conditions, in motion and in seeming rest, he sees nothing but constant agitation. There is simply no resting place for humankind. Within this constant striving he does, however, acknowledge a type of contentment: "*Continuall successe* in obtaining those things which a man from time to time desireth, that is to say, continuall prospering, is that men call FELICITY." He notes that such continual success in acquiring the successive objects of the desires cannot offer the possibility of complete fulfillment. Indeed, he specifies that "I mean the Felicity of this life. For there is no such thing as perpetuall Tanquillity of mind, while we live here; because Life it selfe is but Motion, and can never be without Desire, nor without Feare, no more than without Sense" (46). To satisfy one desire is to cause at least one other to emerge. He denies the very possibility of happiness.

So consuming is the pursuit of these objects of the passions that the faculties of the mind are completely harnessed to the task of attaining them. "For the Thoughts, are to the Desires, as Scouts, and Spies, to range abroad, and find the way to the things Desired: All Stedinesse of the minds motion, and all

---

[16] Although he does not link this division to Machiavelli, Neal Wood too discerns a fundamental divide between the two classes on the basis of the passions in Hobbes's thought: "While most, usually those of the lower classes, take pride in what they already possess and only wish to defend it, the seekers after glory are largely confined to the upper classes" ("Hobbes and the Crisis of the English Aristocracy," *History of Political Thought* 1 [1980]: 440).

[17] Rahe too notes that Hobbes's thought contains this Machiavellian division of humanity into two groups but, in contrast to my interpretation, argues that it ultimately points to "the aristocratic dimension" of Hobbes's thought (*Republics Ancient and Modern*, 380–1). My interpretation gives much more weight to what amounts to a challenge to Machiavelli's thought: Hobbes's promotion of the people's desires in order to counter the aristocratic promotion of war.

quicknesse of the same, proceeding from thence," declares Hobbes (53–4). Because quickness and resoluteness of thought derive from the passions, it comes as no surprise that reason is weak when standing against them: "[T]he Passions of men, are commonly more potent than their Reason" (131).

The mental faculties cannot provide happiness because they are in service to the passions, and the passions themselves can never be satisfied. By contrast, for Aristotle, the use of the highest mental faculties brings happiness. The ancient recommends philosophy, for example, to those who seek "the enjoyment that comes with pleasures unaccompanied by pains."[18] Hobbes, in fact, indicates that he directs his particular teaching regarding the passions and the impossibility of the attainment of happiness against the claims of just such an old-fashioned moralizer as he finds Aristotle to be: "[T]here is no such *Finis ultimus*, (utmost ayme,) nor *Summum Bonum*, (greatest Good,) as is spoken of in the Books of the old Morall Philosophers. Nor can a man any more live, whose Desires are at an end, than he, whose Senses and Imaginations are at a stand. Felicity is a continuall progresse of the desire, from one object to another" (69–70). Philosophy or reason, Hobbes retorts, cannot serve as a haven from the desires because these faculties serve the passions. Indeed, he defines philosophy as a type of reasoning able to produce such "*Effects, as humane life requireth*" (458). And human life itself is desire.

This perpetual onslaught of desires makes acquisition the only real activity of human beings. In order to acquire any type of good, in Hobbes's view, they need power. "The POWER *of a Man*, (to take it Universally,) is his present means, to obtain some future apparent Good" (62). As a result of the fact that power is what makes any acquisition possible, he characterizes human life as the relentless pursuit of power: "So that in the first place, I put for a generall inclination of all mankind, a perpetuall and restlesse desire of Power after power, that ceaseth onely in Death." He explains that this constant imperative to add power to power is not necessarily a sign that human beings are excessively greedy for superfluous acquisition: "And the cause of this, is not alwayes that a man hopes for a more intensive delight, than he has already attained to; or that he cannot be content with a moderate power: but because he cannot assure the power and means to live well, which he hath present, without the acquisition of more." It would seem that, in his view, the human condition demands such constant application of human exertion. In order merely to maintain what they have already acquired, they need to acquire more, and thus there is rest neither from the desires nor from the pursuit of acquisition in service to their satisfaction (70).

Hobbes seems to expose the same condition of humanity that Machiavelli describes. Indeed, when warning that the class in a city in possession of much can be the source of tumults to the same degree as the class that possesses little, Machiavelli makes the general observation that "it does not appear to

[18] Aristotle *Politics* 2.7, 1267a5–15.

men that they possess securely what a man has unless he acquires something else new."[19] Both Machiavelli and Hobbes understand that acquisition is the primary necessity and that the desire to acquire agitates all types of human beings perpetually.

Further, both Machiavelli and Hobbes depict two fundamental types of human beings in remarkably similar terms. In accord with Machiavelli's division of humanity into those who wish "to command" and those who wish "to live secure,"[20] Hobbes finds a fundamental divide between those who seek to elevate themselves over others and those who do not. The Englishman explains that "considering the great difference there is in men, from the diversity of their passions, how some are vainly glorious, and hope for precedency and superiority above their fellows, not only when they are equal in power, but also when they are inferior; we must needs acknowledge that it must necessarily follow, that those men who are moderate, and look for no more but equality of nature, shall be obnoxious to the force of others, that will attempt to subdue them."[21] As he says here, there is a great diversity in men, a diversity that arises from the diversity of the passions, but he points to only one fundamental division, that between those who seek superiority and those who do not. Those who are dissatisfied with equality will victimize those who are content with it.

This division among human types is fundamental to his thought. His political project, in fact, could even be said to be a response to this division. As we know, those who seek superiority resist a common authority, whereas those who do not seek preeminence welcome such an authority. One group loves war, the other peace. "Competition of Riches, Honour, Command, or other power enclineth to Contention, Enmity, and War: Because the way of one Competitor, to the attaining of his desire, is to kill, subdue, supplant, or repell the other." By stark contrast, "Desire of Ease, and sensuall Delight, disposeth men to obey a common Power" (70). Only when a state constrains the former type and nourishes the latter type will peace be assured.[22]

For the moment, though, it is necessary to consider how his assertion of these two human types relates to his teaching on equality. Hobbes, of course, is far from arguing that equality characterizes civil society, because all manner of conventional distinctions have overturned the natural equality that once reigned: "The inequallity that now is, has bin introduced by the Lawes civill" (107). He points, however, to another distinction among human

[19] Machiavelli, *Discourses* 1.5.4.
[20] Ibid., 1.16.5.
[21] Hobbes, *Elements*, 78.
[22] Deborah Baumgold, too, sees this divide as fundamental in Hobbes's thought, and she determines that "it was the ambition of the [political elites] for power that occupied his attention" ("Hobbes's Political Sensibility: The Menace of Political Ambition," in *Thomas Hobbes and Political Theory*, ed. Mary G. Dietz [Lawrence: University of Kansas Press, 1990], 75). She concludes that "it is finally institutionalized ambition that Hobbes feared" (85).

beings – the appreciable difference in the speed at which people think – that would appear to challenge his claim to the equal distribution of the faculties of the mind. He responds to this recognition by locating the source of the difference not in innate mental faculties but in the passions. In so doing, he is able to maintain his claim of human equality. The fact that some appear to reason – that is, to find the way to the achievement of their desires – more quickly than others is a product of the desires themselves, not of the unequal distribution of the faculties of the mind.

And first, those men whose ends are some sensual delight; and generally are addicted to ease, food, onerations and exonerations of the body, must of necessity thereby be the less delighted with those imaginations that conduce not to those ends, such as are imaginations of honour and glory, which . . . have respect to the future: for sensuality consisteth in the pleasure of the senses, which please only for the present, and taketh away the inclination to observe such things as conduce to honour; and consequently maketh men less curious, and less ambitious, whereby they less consider the way either to knowledge or to other power; in which two consisteth all the excellency of power cognitive. And this is it which men call DULNESS; and proceedeth from the appetite of sensual or bodily delight. And it may well be conjectured, that such passion hath its beginning from a grossness and difficulty of the motion of the spirits about the heart.[23]

In offering this explanation, he points to the familiar distinction between those who desire preeminence of some sort and those who desire ease and comfort. The urgency of the desires for distinction induce those who possess them to be quick and resourceful. Those who pursue not these ends are dull in the comparison.

In this manner, Hobbes acknowledges a difference in the quickness of thoughts, which he assiduously locates in a difference in the passions. This difference in the passions may itself arise from a physical difference, he proposes. This proposal may, in fact, suggest a natural difference among human beings, but, if such a difference exists, he locates it in the body, not in the mind. He thus continues to emphasize the equality of human minds.

In treating the same subject in the *Leviathan*, he similarly points to a physical cause for the difference of the passions but adds a circumstantial one in addition: "The causes of this difference of Witts, are in the Passions: and the difference of Passions, proceedeth partly from the different Constitution of the body, and partly from different Education" (53). Education can affect the character of the passions that move an individual, which, in turn, dictates how quickly or slowly one thinks. Presumably the members of the upper class are recipients of an education that encourages them to be honor seekers. As honor seekers, they think more quickly. The luck of circumstance, of course, dictates the extent to which one has the opportunity to acquire those passions that will improve one's wit. As it is a cause that lies outside of the

[23] Hobbes, *Elements*, 61.

control of the individual, those lacking in education cannot be deemed inherently inferior. Indeed, elsewhere he discusses how education can improve the mental faculties in a manner that actually emphasizes the equality that derives from birth: "There is no other act of mans mind, that I can remember, naturally planted in him, so, as to need no other thing, to the exercise of it, but to be born a man, and live with the use of his five Senses. Those other Faculties,... which seem proper to man onely, are acquired, and encreased by study and industry" (23).

Study and industry can produce something else; in combination, these elements can produce science. Science is "knowledge of Consequences" "attayned by Industry" (35). Much science produces a type of wisdom, just as does much experience. Whereas much experience produces the wisdom Hobbes terms prudence, much science produces that which he terms "sapience" (36).[24] Although he acknowledges the existence of such men of science, he goes out of his way to argue that those who lack this type of wisdom cannot be justly blamed. Science, he announces, is obtained through industry. Most cannot spare the leisure to be dedicated to its pursuit.[25] When he derives the laws of nature, he himself is engaging in "the Science of what is Good, and Evill, in the conversation, and Society of man-kind" (110). He undertakes to set out these laws for others, "whereof the most part are too busie in getting food" (109). He excuses others for not being devoted to science as is he, for their circumstances simply do not permit them the leisure.

Although he points to physical and circumstantial causes for differences in passions, he points out that the differences in wit to which they give rise cannot be understood as a moral distinction: "And therefore, a man who has no great Passion for any of these things;... though he may be so farre a good man, as to be free from giving offence; yet he cannot possibly have either a great Fancy, or much Judgement" (53). A man of dull wit can be a good man, pronounces Hobbes. Moreover, it may very well be the case that a man who seeks sensuous delights, and a quiet life by which to enjoy them, is more likely to be a good man than one who wishes to establish himself as superior. The latter will attempt, as we already know, to subdue others who are satisfied to live moderately and to accept equality. In preying so on others, they display their desire for superiority; in attempting to assert their superiority, they reject Hobbes's doctrine of equality; and, in rejecting equality, they reveal their pride. "Pride," declares Hobbes, is the failure to recognize every other man as one's "Equall by Nature" (107).

---

[24] For a discussion of the distinction between prudence and science in Hobbes's thought with a different emphasis, see Alan Ryan, "Hobbes's Political Philosophy," in The Cambridge Companion to Hobbes, ed. Tom Sorell (Cambridge: Cambridge University Press, 1996), 212–13.

[25] Much more blameable, in Hobbes's estimation, are those who possess leisure enough to attain scientific wisdom but instead follow the scholastics to engage in useless disputes.

Rejection of the Great and Their Passions

Those unwilling to embrace Hobbes's doctrine of equality contravene Hobbes's intention to tame human passions so as to promote stability and peace, and certainly the ranks of the aristocracy in England and in Europe generally were replete with such prideful individuals.[26] Because Europe's monarchies were supported by aristocratic families who were distinguished from the remainder of subjects by their social status, wealth, and education – if not by God's special grace – Hobbes's assertion of human equality challenged centuries of custom. Moreover, the members of these aristocratic families were skilled in the martial arts, having originally received their holdings of land in exchange for their military service to their king. The members of this exalted class had very much of which to be proud. Trained to seek honor on the battlefield, they are likely to advocate for war abroad; disposed to view themselves as superior in strength and resolve, they are likely to defend their honor vigorously, even violently, from insults and slights, and are, as a result, the source of disturbances within the realm. Their way of life, their passions, and their virtues are obstacles to Hobbes's goals of peace and stability.[27]

As much as the aristocratic few pose formidable obstacles to Hobbes's purposes, he does not so much attack them as a class as condemn proud individuals. Because these proud individuals are likely to be conscious of their status, wealth, and education, ready proponents of war, and eager for rule, Hobbes leaves no doubt from which class the most troublesome are drawn. Perhaps he cannot root out all ambition in human nature, but he certainly attempts to contain its ill effects. The first step Hobbes takes on this path to containment is to dispense both the blame and the praise that are due. He enumerates the problems the proud and contentious create. He then enshrines the milder desires and the pacific virtues that are most likely to be found among the people. He would like to see the people's morality and virtue become the touchstone for society. Genuine admiration for the

---

[26] "And who were more likely models for those 'children of pride' than the fiercely competitive and combative English landed gentlemen in their frenetic pursuit of honours, offices and riches in the first half of the seventeenth century?" (Wood, "Hobbes and Crisis of the Aristocracy," 437).

[27] Ryan, "Hobbes's Political Philosophy," 217; Strauss, *Political Philosophy of Hobbes*, 44–58 and 113–21. Wood examines the historical situation to argue that England's aristocracy was particularly troublesome during Hobbes's lifetime (Wood, "Hobbes and Crisis of the Aristocracy," 437–52). Cf. Keith Thomas, "The Social Origins of Hobbes's Political Thought," in *Hobbes Studies*, ed. K. C. Brown (Cambridge: Harvard University Press, 1965), 185–236, who claims to find some distinctly aristocratic elements in his thought and maintains that he was not opposed to the European aristocracy as such but rather merely to "the decaying relics of bastard feudalism," an attitude that was not itself "out of keeping with the mood of cultivated aristocratic society either before or after the Civil Wars" (192).

good that flows from an attachment to a quiet life can do much to counter the honor wrongly accorded the arrogant and belligerent.

Hobbes reveals the central place of pride in his project when in the *Leviathan* he refers to the passage of the Book of Job from which he derives the name of the work. "God," recounts Hobbes, "having set forth the great power of *Leviathan*, calleth him King of the Proud. *There is nothing, saith he, on earth, to be compared with him. He is made so as not to be afraid. Hee seeth every high thing below him; and is King of all the children of pride.*" Hobbes's "great power of [Man's] Governour" is similarly king of the proud (221).[28] In elevating an absolute sovereign endowed with the unlimited rights which had formerly belonged to the individuals who had inhabited the state of nature, Hobbes intends to subdue the pride that produces conflicts among citizens and war abroad.[29]

He must subdue pride in order to rule human beings. Hobbes announces both the difficulty and the necessity of this task in several ways. He enumerates "three principall causes of quarrell" "in the nature of man." One of these causes relates directly to pride and another indirectly. The first, as we know, he terms competition, which occurs when people contend over some prized possession. Competition occurs because people simply desire to acquire, but pride also plays a part here. People must be bold enough to enter into competition with another, and they are so emboldened when they believe themselves to be that other's superior. In addition, pride is directly responsible for the third cause for "quarrell," because, according to Hobbes, people fight "for trifles, as a word, a smile, a different opinion, and any other signe of undervalue, either direct in their Persons, or by reflexion in their Kindred, their Friends, their Nation, their Profession, or their Name" (88). They will fight to punish those who wound their pride.

---

[28] The fact that Hobbes terms his powerful sovereign in the *Leviathan* "King of the Proud" should serve at least to temper the claim of Gabriella Slomp that the pursuit of glory "loses its central place" in the later *Leviathan* as compared with *The Elements of Law* (*Thomas Hobbes and the Political Philosophy of Glory* [New York: St. Martin's Press, 2000], 91). Part of the evidence she marshals for this claim is that there is a prominent minority of "non-glory seekers" in the *Leviathan*. As she herself notes (e.g., 88), however, this group also appears prominently in *The Elements*. I concur with her claims that those who shun glory and are content with equality are not likely to be members of the aristocracy (89); that the pursuit of glory in Hobbes's view plays a "crucial destabilising role" in a state (51); and that the solution Hobbes seeks is a means by which "individuals can channel and direct their natural ambition to the benefit of the 'commodious living' of all, by developing industry, navigation, arts, cultivation of land, science, technology, trade, etc." (67). For an argument that members of the aristocracy may possess in particular the attributes of character that Hobbes prizes, see Michael Oakeshott, "The Moral Life in the Writings of Thomas Hobbes," in *Rationalism in Politics and Other Essays* (New York: Basic Books, 1962; reprint, with a foreword by Timothy Fuller, Indianapolis: Liberty Press, 1991), 339–50.

[29] Strauss, *Political Philosophy of Hobbes*, 11–13 and 111; Bobbio, *Hobbes and the Natural Law Tradition*, 40–1 and 97–8.

Those most likely to enter such conflicts to vindicate their honor – that is, the prideful – are moved by violent and uncontrollable passions. "Pride, subjecteth a man to Anger, the excesse whereof, is the Madnesse called RAGE, and FURY," he notes. "And thus it comes to passe that excessive desire of Revenge, when it becomes habituall, hurteth the organs, and becomes Rage.... Excessive opinion of a mans own selfe, for divine inspiration, for wisdome, learning, forme, and the like, becomes Distraction, and Giddinesse" (54). They can also be cruel in exerting their power over others. Hobbes warns that "there be some, that taking pleasure in contemplating their own power in the acts of conquest, which they pursue farther than their security requires" (88). The proud will also seek revenge. The hot blood bent on revenge will work a result to the general harm, he notes: "[T]he triumph of revenge, is vain glory: and whatsoever is vain, is against reason; and to hurt one another without reason, is contrary to that, which by supposition is every man's benefit, namely peace."[30] These are disagreeable characters, indeed.

Further, those who harbor the thought of their superiority are most likely to challenge the authority of the state in the commission of crimes: "Of the Passions that most frequently are the causes of Crime, one, is Vain-glory, or a foolish over-rating of their own worth.... From whence proceedeth a Presumption that the punishments ordained by the Lawes, and extended generally to all Subjects, ought not to be inflicted on them, with the same rigour they are inflicted on poore, obscure, and simple men, comprehended under the name of *Vulgar*" (205). Here Hobbes takes aim at their haughty arrogance. The laws, they believe, cannot apply to them, but rather to their inferiors – those who lack their status as rich and prominent persons.

They are also likely to foment violations of the peace both at home and abroad. He explains that "needy men, and hardy, not contented with their present condition; as also, all men that are ambitious of Military command, are enclined to continue the causes of warre; and to stirre up trouble and sedition: for there is no honour Military but by warre; nor any such hope to mend an ill game, as by causing a new shuffle" (70–1). Most eager for their own promotion, they will agitate for war that will destroy their country's bounty. Generally disrespectful of law, they will even attempt rebellion, if they find themselves denied the privileges of rule. Their so-called virtues, of which they are so proud, disrupt society and distract it from its real purpose, the maintenance of life and the promotion of comfort.

Hobbes sometimes even refuses to acknowledge the aristocratic virtues as virtues. His are those that conduce to peace; they are not the virtues of the aristocracy but rather of the people. In the *Leviathan*, he explicitly honors "*Justice, Gratitude, Modesty, Equity, Mercy*" as the means to peace, and hence, as virtues (111). Conspicuously absent from his enumeration of the virtues

---

[30] Hobbes, *Elements*, 91–2.

in the *Leviathan* is courage, for example.[31] Elsewhere in the work he terms courage a passion that "enclineth men to private Revenges, and sometimes to endeavour the unsetling of the Publique Peace" (483). Far from a virtue, then, courage is actually a vice, in Hobbes's view.[32] He justifies his rejection of the ancient catalog of the virtues and the elevation to virtues of alternative attributes with the thought that "the Writers of Morall Philosophie...not seeing wherein consisted their Goodnesse; nor that they come to be praised, as the meanes of peaceable, sociable, and comfortable living; place them in a mediocrity of passions" (111). His virtues do not conduce to noble acts that inspire awe and admiration in spectators as well as in those who merely hear or read of them, but neither do they produce cruelty and suffering. The spirit may not soar, but the body does not bleed. The moral philosophers who preceded Hobbes were too blinded by their own aristocratic prejudices to see the excellence of the virtues that conduce to peace.

The Eclipse of Politics and the Advent of Peace

The venue of the vainglorious is the political realm where they endeavor to glorify themselves in eloquent speeches and courageous deeds. His attempts at quelling pride do not stop at reciting the harm the virtues of the vainglorious create and the benefits that the simple but beneficial virtues of the people confer. He also endeavors to expel the pridefully contentious aristocrats from the political realm. Although he posits any type of sovereign – whether it be rule by one, a few, or all – as the necessary antidote to the state of nature, and hence of war, he finds the monarchical form of government most fitted to fulfill the very purpose of government, which is the preservation of human beings through the avoidance of war. Whereas the political realm is quite capacious in republics, it is much more confined in monarchies. He despises, in particular, the assemblies that characterize republics. There the opportunity abounds for the desires of the vain and ambitious to be ignited to the detriment of the state and the individuals who compose it. Because so many vie for superiority in republics, and hence so many become victims of their contests, life within one is more similar to life in the state of nature than is life in a monarchy. Hobbes could provide a better life for all, he believes, if he could cure those enamored of republics of their infatuation. To this end, he attempts to disabuse the admirers of the ancient republics of their notion

[31] Strauss, *Political Philosophy of Hobbes*, 50; cf. Bobbio, *Hobbes and the Natural Law Tradition*, 71.

[32] In *The Elements*, he declares that courage under the right circumstances could be considered a virtue: "Courage may be virtue, when the daring is extreme, if the cause be good; and extreme fear no vice when the danger is extreme." He also specifies in this place that "the habit of doing according to these and other laws of nature that tend to our preservation, is that we call VIRTUE" (98). It is not, then, the life-risking aspect of courage that Hobbes admires when he terms it a virtue but rather its life-preserving element.

that republican liberty is to be admired and pursued. In order to maintain civil concord and peace abroad, Hobbes would have the household eclipse the political realm.[33] Human life would be vastly improved if people were to abandon the battlefield and the assembly house and were simply to stay home.

Although he does not challenge the legitimacy of aristocracies or democracies, he does not recommend them. He makes no secret of his support of monarchy on the basis of its "Aptitude to produce the Peace, and Security of the people" (131). Those who favor republics – whether aristocratic or democratic – receive inspiration for their republicanism from the republics of antiquity. Far from admiring these ancient models, Hobbes denounces them. He finds that the love of ancient republicanism detracts from people's obedience to current monarchies:

And as to Rebellion in particular against Monarchy; one of the most frequent causes of it, is the Reading of the books of Policy, and Histories of the antient Greeks, and Romans; from which, young men, and all others that are unprovided of the Antidote of solid Reason, receiving a strong, and delightfull impression, of the great exploits of warre, atchieved by the Conductors of their Armies, receive withall a pleasing Idea, of all they have done besides; and imagine their great prosperity, not to have proceeded from the aemulation of particular men, but from the vertue of their popular forme of government: Not considering the frequent Seditions, and Civill warres, produced by the imperfection of their Policy. (225–6)

As he does here, of course, he attempts to produce a clearheaded understanding of these ancient polities by pointing to the wars and the civil discord they produced.

He also endeavors to disabuse people of their partiality to republicanism by challenging the republican notion of liberty as civic participation. No one has the freedom to disobey the law, Hobbes teaches, whether the person lives in a republic or an absolute monarchy. Hobbes declares that liberty consists not in participation in rule but rather in the silence of the laws. "In cases where the Soveraign has prescribed no rule, there the Subject hath the Liberty to do, or forbeare, according to his own discretion" (152). Thus, on this score, republican liberty would appear to be no different from monarchical liberty. Again, the ancient authors have harmed modern practice by teaching that the liberty that the ancients enshrined is true liberty: "And by reading of these Greek, and Latine Authors, men from their childhood have gotten a habit (under a falseshew of Liberty,) of favouring tumults, and of licentious controlling the actions of their Soveraigns; and again of controlling those controllers, with the effusion of so much blood; as I think I may truly say, there was never any thing so deerly bought, as these

---

[33] Rahe offers a similar formulation; see *Republics Ancient and Modern*, 389. Cf. Alan Ryan, "Hobbes and Individualism," in *Perspectives on Thomas Hobbes*, ed. G. A. J. Rogers and Alan Ryan (Oxford: Oxford University Press, 1988), 104–5.

Western parts have bought the learning of the Greek and Latine tongues" (150). Hobbes corrects such misconceptions by proclaiming that the freedom these partisans of antiquity admire is not the freedom of individual citizens within the commonwealth but the freedom of the commonwealth itself. "The *Athenians*, and *Romanes* were free; that is, free Common-wealths: not that any particular man had the Libertie to resist their own Representative; but that their Representative had the Libertie to resist, or invade other people" (149).[34]

He further castigates republican liberty in such a way that the liberty offered in monarchies not merely appears on a par with it but emerges as superior to it. He broaches this possibility by emphasizing the extent to which ambition and vainglory are rampant in republics. He stresses this characteristic of republics when exploring the attraction that some have for republican governance in order to reveal it for what it is – the particular attraction that the vainglorious have for self-promotion. He notes that "perhaps someone will say that the *popular state* is immensely preferable to *Monarchy*, because in that state, in which of course everyone manages public business, everyone has been given leave to publicly display his prudence[,] knowledge and eloquence in deliberations about matters of the greatest difficulty and importance."[35] He does not in the least admire the selfless devotion to the public good that civic participation connotes, because such participation is, in his estimation, utterly selfish. "There is no reason why anyone would not prefer to spend his time on his *private business* rather than on *public affairs*, except that he sees scope for his eloquence, to acquire a reputation for intelligence and good sense, and to return home and enjoy the triumph for his great achievements with friends, parents and wife." He intimates here what he ultimately discerns as the supreme significance of the household even to the most committed of public men. They contend in public in order to receive accolades at home. Even the fierce warrior Coriolanus fought in order to receive his mother's praises, Hobbes notes.[36]

Because men participate in political deliberations only to establish their superiority – "the most attractive of all things to all those who surpass others in such talents or seem to themselves to do so" – their counsels can do no political good.[37] He, of course, holds in contempt the fickle policy that results from the contentions and bad counsel endemic to republics, pointing to the embarrassments to which such policy can lead (131–2).

He notes that a monarchy does not offer subjects this opportunity to display their superiority: "[B]ut in *Monarchy* that road to winning praise and rank is blocked for most of the citizens." To which observation he

---

[34] Of course, Hobbes does not endorse the liberty to invade others.
[35] Hobbes, *Citizen*, 122.
[36] Ibid., 124–5.
[37] Ibid., 122.

responds with a facetious question: "What is a disadvantage, if this is not?" He launches his response with an eager "I will tell you," and proceeds to offer a litany of annoyances: "To see the proposal of a man whom we despise preferred to our own; to see our wisdom ignored before our eyes; to incur certain enmity in an uncertain struggle for empty glory; to hate and be hated because of differences of opinion . . . ; to reveal our plans and wishes when there is no need to and to get nothing by it; to neglect our private affairs."[38] A considerable disadvantage of political participation, in Hobbes's view, is the neglect of one's private affairs.

The private takes on even more significance in Hobbes's understanding of liberty, when one pursues his claim that liberty is found where the law is silent. He specifies that the "Liberty of a Subject, lyeth therefore only in those things, which in regulating their actions, the Soveraign hath praetermitted: such as is the Liberty to buy, and sell, and otherwise contract with one another; to choose their own aboad, their own diet, their own trade of life, and institute their children as they themselves think fit; & the like" (148). These are the areas of private life, not of the public, and, thus, liberty for Hobbes is found primarily in the private realm. If Hobbes can offer a Leviathan that is capable of truly subduing the kingdom of the proud, then people will quite literally stay home. They will pursue their desire for power after power through material acquisitions. They will educate their children. They will seek renown for their contributions to the arts and sciences – contributions that make life ever more pleasing.

In eclipsing the public realm, a monarchy nurtures and protects the private realm, and Hobbes finds the private realm to be the locus of liberty. A monarchy, then, actually can expand the realm of liberty, if it properly respects the private realm. By contrast, a republic cannot but fail to menace it, he observes. When so many vain and ambitious types populate the public realm, dangers loom even for individuals who themselves do not contend for political recognition and honor. By contrast, even under a particularly rapacious monarch, only those known to him will be vulnerable to his rapine, Hobbes claims. These turn out to be very few in number – only those courtiers who possess what the king "covets." All others are safe from his depredations. "In a *Monarchy* therefore anyone who is prepared to live quietly is free of danger, whatever the character of the ruler. Only the ambitious suffer." This is not the case in a republic, where there are "as many *Neros* as there are *Orators*." Because such numerous and ravenous orators come from the people, they know the people, and as a result, no one can be assured of escaping their predations, he claims. A secure private life cannot be attained "where there is *popular control*." The ravenous who dominate politics can, at any time, invade the household. Lack of personal ambition does

---

[38] Ibid.

not inoculate one against the unpleasant effects of this passion in a republic. Happily, according to Hobbes, the same cannot be said of a monarchy.[39]

Fear, Absolutism, and the Right of the Individual

On the one hand, Hobbes makes human beings subject to a most fearsome government, absolute in power and extensive in scope. On the other hand, although Hobbes is not a liberal himself, elements of his thought point in a liberal direction. Among such elements is his declaration that government must be understood as the instrument of the people themselves. They create it to satisfy their ends; not only its existence but its very decrees must be understood as expressions of their wills.[40] According to Hobbes, "in the act of our *Submission*, consisteth both our *Obligation*, and our *Liberty*; ... there being no Obligation on any man, which ariseth not from some Act of his own; for all men equally, are by Nature Free" (150). In this way, he understands the decrees of the sovereign as ultimately emanating from the people. Further, because human beings create a sovereign to satisfy their particular end, the preservation of their life, even subjects cannot relinquish the right to defend themselves. In articulating this right to preservation, Hobbes goes so far as to offer a limited right of resistance against the powers of the state. These notions could be readily transformed to support the claim that a liberal, as opposed to an absolute, government is the better means to his end.[41]

---

[39] Ibid., 120. In arguing for a fundamental change in Hobbes's thought between *The Elements* and *De Cive* on the one hand and *Leviathan* on the other on the subject of rhetoric, Skinner notes that Hobbes's attitude toward those who make use of the art changes in important ways. Whereas in the earlier works he declares that "trained orators" create dangers for a state by "rousing and 'stirring' the fickle populace," in the later he accuses instead "the hereditary nobility and those 'versed more in the acquisition of Wealth than of Knowledge'" for having this deleterious effect; and that whereas Hobbes "had previously attacked the selfish and destructive ambitions of trained orators, he now observes that eloquence is not merely one of the attributes for which men are most readily praised, but that it deserves to be regarded as honourable" (Quentin Skinner, *Reason and Rhetoric in the Philosophy of Hobbes* [Cambridge: Cambridge University Press, 1996], 357–8). Skinner identifies the important role rhetoric itself plays in Hobbes's later work as a means of effectively propounding his teaching, but even in this work, Hobbes would still severely restrict rhetoric's political role because he severely restricts the public realm. On this very point, see Skinner, *Reason and Rhetoric*, 343: "He continues to harbour many of his earlier anxieties about [rhetoric's] deceiving nature and its potentially pernicious effects on the proper conduct of public life. ... Later he focuses in particular on the dangers posed by rhetoricians in public assemblies."

[40] Pierre Manent, *An Intellectual History of Liberalism*, trans. Rebecca Balinski (Princeton: Princeton University Press, 1995), 26–7; Michael Oakeshott, "Introduction to *Leviathan*," in Oakeshott, *Rationalism and Politics*, 265.

[41] For discussions of Hobbes's thought as a precursor to liberalism, see Berkowitz, *Virtue and Modern Liberalism*, 35–6; Manent, *Intellectual History of Liberalism*, 31–2; Ryan, "Hobbes's Political Philosophy," 237; Tuck, *Hobbes*, 72–6. See also Sommerville, who deems "only partially correct" the notion that Hobbes "was an advocate of liberalism" (*Thomas Hobbes*, 103). Bobbio, who declares that Hobbes "was neither a liberal writer, nor a precursor of liberal

Hobbes leaves no doubt that the sovereign he endorses is a most fearful one. It is, after all, intended to keep all in awe. People have a natural tendency to chafe under any sort of rule. The sovereign needs absolute power to control their waywardness and to enforce their obedience.

Although their obedience is required to keep the chaos of nature at bay, once ensconced in the peaceful state of civil society, they come to resent that obedience. This resentment grows from their failure both to recognize the fact that "the estate of Man can never be without some incommodity or other" and to remember specifically "that the greatest [incommodity], that in any forme of Government can possibly happen to the people in generall, is scarce sensible, in respect of the miseries, and horrible calamities, that accompany a Civill Warre." These failures, Hobbes explains, derive from the engrossment in the self that the passions encourage: "For all men are by nature provided of notable multiplying glasses, (that is their Passions and Selfe-love,) through which, every little payment appeareth a great grievance." Hobbes, though, attempts to provide people with "those prospective glasses, (namely Morall and Civill Science,)" which will allow them "to see a farre off the miseries that hang over them, and cannot without such payments be avoyded" (128–9). The frightening details of civil war, which come into focus with the clearer vision his science furnishes, attest to the fact that as unpleasant as life in any monarchy can be, the state of nature is far worse. He hopes that the comparison that his clearer vision makes possible will produce a general satisfaction with the sovereign, as subjects are reminded of the miserable condition of nature, which will, in turn, generate obedience to the laws.

In addition, he hopes that people will be positively attracted to life in a society in which they are sheltered from war. He declares that "Desire of such things as are necessary to commodious living; and a Hope by their Industry to obtain them" "encline men to Peace" (90). He does not, however,

---

ideas," concedes that one finds "some features typical of liberalism in Hobbes's thought" (*Hobbes and the Natural Law Tradition*, 70). Strauss, *Political Philosophy of Hobbes*, 1, 121–2, 126, equates Hobbes's thought with bourgeois morality, and Macpherson contends both that Hobbes furnishes the foundation for liberal-democratic theory and that Hobbes's view of human beings as naturally competitive is actually a product of Hobbes's own historical immersion in a "possessive market society" (Macpherson, *Political Theory of Possessive Individualism*, 1–106; cf. Bobbio, *Hobbes and the Natural Law Tradition*, 71). Judith N. Shklar rejects the characterization of Hobbes as "the father of liberalism" because he did not advocate toleration ("Liberalism of Fear," in *Liberalism and the Moral Life*, ed. Nancy L. Rosenblum (Cambridge: Harvard University Press, 1989), 24; on the issue of toleration in Hobbes's thought, cf. Oakeshott, "Introduction to *Leviathan*," 282; Richard Tuck, "Hobbes and Locke on Toleration," in *Thomas Hobbes and Political Theory*, 153–71; and Ryan, "Hobbes's Political Philosophy," 234. Gordon J. Schochet challenges, on the basis of an analysis of Hobbes's presentation of political obligation, the notion that Hobbes's thought can be linked to liberalism ("Intending [Political] Obligation: Hobbes and the Voluntary Basis of Society," in *Thomas Hobbes and Political Theory*, 55–73).

ultimately rely on the desire for "commodious living" to restrain the unruly character of human beings. As he himself teaches, satisfaction cannot come from the achievement of the desires, because new desires always flare up to replace those that have been extinguished.

Therefore, the science that furnishes the proper perspective on monarchy, even when combined with the passion for commodious living, cannot assure obedience. He does place his firmest trust in a passion, however, and that "Passion to be reckoned upon," he declares, "is Fear" (99). "Feare of Death," of course, compels human beings to create a sovereign authority in the first instance (90). Once instituted, government itself wields the instrument to induce in its subjects this most reliable of all passions. "Lawes are of no power to protect them, without a Sword in the hands of a man, or men, to cause those laws to be put in execution" (147–8). After Hobbes provides his sovereign with a sword, fear works to enforce the law: "Of all Passions, that which enclineth men least to break the Lawes, is Fear. Nay, (excepting some generous natures,) it is the onely thing, (when there is apparence of profit, or pleasure by breaking the Lawes,) that makes men keep them" (206). Hobbes places his greatest faith, then, in fear. Although he portrays the ambitious as contending for something other than security, ultimately Hobbes's political project relies on the fact that most – if not all – will desire to avoid a violent death when confronted with its prospect. The power of all other passions fades when confronted by the vulnerability of the body, he suggests.[42]

Machiavelli shares with Hobbes this understanding that fear of punishment is the best motivator of human beings. The Florentine instructs a prince, for example, that "fear is held by a dread of punishment that never forsakes you."[43] But, even further, he teaches that a republic must be a most fearful place. He uses spectacular capital punishments for several purposes: to cut down potential tyrants, to demonstrate to other hopefuls the impossibility of achieving their fondest desire, and to foster in all an awe before the laws. Fearful punishment, in Machiavelli's mind, allows a republic to strive for perpetuity.

Although Hobbes shares in Machiavelli's endorsement of the effectiveness of fear, he is so repulsed by the ambitions of the great that if he had his way, he would not allow them a republic, a form of government that he regards as a mere playground for the ambitious. Because he does not endorse republics, he does not formulate a response to the threat of tyranny in them. He has, of course, no principled objection to tyranny, refusing even to acknowledge

---

[42] Manent points to the "bewitching" "moral ambiguity of ... Hobbes's vision": "[M]en defined explicitly as 'aristocrats' (struggling for power, honor, or prestige) behave at the decisive moment like 'bourgeois' (making certain that their security comes first)" (*Intellectual History of Liberalism*, 41).

[43] *Prince* 17.67.

the legitimacy of the term and denying the very distinction between good and bad regimes. In any case, he is not a partisan of republics in the manner of Machiavelli.

This divergence from their original point of unity seems to derive from a most significant disagreement, indeed: the desirability of war. Because Machiavelli not only countenances but encourages war, it is necessary for him to cherish the desires of the great. He cherishes the desires for honor and glory because their pursuit brings battlefield victories. He certainly would not consider expelling those individuals driven by such passions from the political arena as does Hobbes.

Similarly, although they agree on the degree to which human beings are captive to their passions, as well as on the fundamental divide between the two types of passions, their opposing views of war induce them to split on the extent to which a state should be the mechanism of their fulfillment. Machiavelli recognizes that it is sometimes expedient for a state to offer its members the opportunity to pursue their desires. He refuses, however, to make the desires of either the few or the many an inviolable principle. Concerns for the satisfaction of either group can be abandoned by a prince or republic the moment they become inconvenient. Indeed, the achievement of either group's desire would undermine the war-making capacity of the state in Machiavelli's view. Although there are important areas of agreement between Machiavelli and Hobbes, then, their opposed views of war prohibit them from attaining final concord.

Hobbes does, however, make one desire in particular an inviolable principle. It is the desire for life. Because the right to preserve one's life is the reason that individuals entered into government, they cannot renounce it. Hobbes's articulation of this right sometimes moves his thought in the direction of articulating a right of resistance to government. When people enter civil society they renounce their rights to all things except for the right to their body: "[N]o man in the Institution of Soveraign Power can be supposed to give away the Right of preserving his own body; for the safety whereof all Soveraignty was ordained" (202). The retention of this right requires that "If a man by the terrour of present death, be compelled to doe a fact against the Law, he is totally Excused; because no Law can oblige a man to abandon his own preservation." So adamant is Hobbes in the necessity of a right to self-defense that he reiterates it in the sentence that follows: "And supposing such a Law were obligatory; yet a man would reason thus, *If I doe it not, I die presently; if I doe it, I die afterwards; therefore by doing it, there is time of life gained*; Nature therefore compels him to the fact" (208; see also 206 on resisting an attacker). Although Hobbes demands obedience to law and contrives most compelling means to encourage it, he justifies the breaking of law when to observe it would threaten one's life. As much as obedience to law is one of his leading principles, he jettisons that very principle when it conflicts with his most cherished of all – preservation.

His dislike of war and his steadfast dedication to the principle of self-preservation seem to combine to encourage him to extend sympathy to the soldier frightened for his life. "When Armies fight, there is on one side, or both, a running away; yet when they do it not out of trechery, but fear, they are not esteemed to do it unjustly, but dishonourably. For the same reason, to avoyd battell, is not Injustice, but Cowardice." Thus, he exonerates flight in battle. No doubt, if this behavior were to become widespread, it could threaten the defense of the very government that protects the lives of its subjects, a fact that Hobbes does not fail to recognize. Even given this most dangerous of threats, he is willing to make allowances "for naturall timorousnesse" by allowing the subject to find an alternative method of satisfying his obligation to the state – for example, by furnishing a substitute soldier (151–2).

The same threat justifies, in Hobbes's mind, not only the breaking of law and the fleeing of battle but also active resistance to one who carries out the will of the sovereign in one particular circumstance. He declares that "though a man may Covenant thus, *Unlesse I do so, or so, kill me*; he cannot Covenant thus, *Unlesse I do so, or so, I will not resist you, when you come to kill me.*" The latter example is invalid because one can never forfeit the right to defend oneself against a threat to one's life. The hangman, as a result, is vulnerable to assault, and justly, too. In support of this point, he points to common practice of criminal justice: "And this is granted to be true by all men, in that they lead Criminals to Execution, and Prison, with armed men, notwithstanding that such Criminals have consented to the Law, by which they are condemned" (98). In this manner, Hobbes justifies resistance to the hangman, a minister of the sovereign, and thus resistance to the will of the sovereign power itself.[44]

Hobbes carries his exceptions to complete submission to an absolute civil authority no further. Only the direct threat of imminent death can warrant any resistance to law. Nevertheless, it is not difficult to see how others, who accept Hobbes's notion that government is a construct to satisfy human desires and to promote the general improvement of human life, would be tempted to create a wider sphere of inviolable rights around the individual. Hobbes himself complains that in the state of nature, others are likely to "deprive" an individual "not only of the fruit of his labour, but also of his life, or liberty" (87). Although the deprivation of labor and of liberty is worthy of complaint, he will not make their protection a right that can be enforced against the state – a state he has armed with an awesome power.

---

[44] Sommerville notes the distinctiveness of Hobbes's declaration: "If a criminal is justly sentenced to death, so the common view ran, then he is obliged meekly to accept his sentence. Hobbes was virtually alone in rejecting this idea. He claimed that criminals could resist all the way to the gallows . . ., for no one could forfeit the liberty of preserving himself" (*Thomas Hobbes*, 34).

This is a point that will not fail to elude Locke's observation: "It cannot be supposed that they should intend, had they a power so to do, to give to any one, or more, an *absolute Arbitrary Power* over their Persons and Estates, and put a force into the Magistrates hand to execute his unlimited Will arbitrarily upon them."[45] Locke responds to this danger by making the protection not only of life but also of liberty and property the reason for the creation of government and, hence, the purpose of government. In Locke's hands, they too become rights government cannot violate.

Before Locke could formulate this response, those with republican sympathies themselves articulate the notion that government is a human construct to protect the rights of individuals to life, liberty, and property. Being liberals, they find a way to protect individual rights; being republicans, they provide a political space; being liberal republicans, they use that public space for the vigilant protection of the private. This possibility will first come to sight in the thought of Nedham.

This liberal republican path is not the only one available from the ingredients that Machiavelli and Hobbes furnish, as the thought of James Harrington suggests. Unlike these liberal republicans, Harrington chooses to follow Machiavelli in the promotion of war. But he is Hobbesian in his fear of the tendency of the great to foment unrest in a state as a result of their intense desire to acquire. He believes that he can contain the nobility in domestic politics and unleash them in foreign conquests. By so doing, Harrington unleashes what Hobbes attempts to chain – that is, the passions that seek acquisition through war. At the same time, he chains what Hobbes attempts to unleash – that is, the passions that seek unlimited material acquisition through peaceful means and thereby produce commodious living.

---

[45] Locke, *Second Treatise*, para. 137.

PART II

THE FORMATION OF THE SYNTHESIS

3

Marchamont Nedham and the Beginnings of a Liberal Republicanism

Never mistaken as a man of principle, Marchamont Nedham is famous for his astonishingly rapid changes in alliances, writing at different times in support of Parliament, king, and Cromwell during the English Civil Wars and Interregnum. He began his career as a journalist in 1643 by writing for *Mercurius Britanicus*, a parliamentary newspaper. As a consequence of his use of the newspaper to disseminate his mocking humor, which he aimed directly at the king, he went to jail.[1] He then changed alliances just in time to be on the losing side, taking up the Royalist banner and editing *Mercurius Pragmaticus* beginning in 1647 and continuing through June of 1649, with a minor interruption in publication after the execution of Charles I. This episode ended with him again in jail, but this time his captors were the Parliamentarians. In order to win his freedom, he agreed to write a pamphlet supporting the fledgling government, and to edit a governmental newspaper.[2] He fulfilled the latter agreement when, the next year, he published *The Case of the Commonwealth of England, Stated*[3] and assumed the editorial duties

---

[1] For an account of these incidents, see Blair Worden, "'Wit in a Roundhead': The Dilemma of Marchamont Nedham," in *Political Culture and Cultural Politics in Early Modern England: Essays Presented to David Underdown*, ed. Susan D. Amussen and Mark A. Kishlansky (Manchester: Manchester University Press, 1995), 315–16; Philip A. Knachel, introduction to *The Case of the Commonwealth of England, Stated*, by Marchamont Nedham (Charlottesville: University Press of Virginia published for the Folger Shakespeare Library, 1969), xix–xx; and Joseph Frank, *Cromwell's Press Agent: A Critical Biography of Marchamont Nedham, 1620–1678* (Lanham, Md.: University Press of America, 1980), 26–8. For assessments of Nedham's journalistic career, see Paul Rahe, "An Inky Wretch: The Outrageous Genius of Marchamont Nedham," *National Interest* 70 (2002–3): 55–64, and Joad Raymond, "'A Mercury with a Winged Conscience': Marchamont Nedham, Monopoly and Censorship," *Media History* 4 (1998): 7–18.

[2] Frank, *Cromwell's Press Agent*, 74, and Knachel, introduction, xxiv.

[3] This title recalls that of an earlier work by Nedham, *The Case of the Kingdom Stated*, a pamphlet he wrote in May 1647. In it, he analyzes the interests of the king, the Presbyterians, the Independents, the City of London, and the Scottish. Most notably, he advises the king to make an alliance with the Independents, who, he argues, would be accepting of his prerogative

of *Mercurius Politicus*, a newspaper that John Milton[4] supervised for a time. His two treatises, *The Case of the Commonwealth* and *The Excellencie of a Free State*, would offer his editorials from this newspaper in a more coherent form.[5] During the Protectorate, he served Cromwell in the capacity of a spy.[6] Later, Nedham opposed the Restoration when it appeared a foregone conclusion, and finally fled to Holland.[7] He returned to England to laud the Restoration. Indeed, in the 1670s he was paid to become a propagandist for Charles II, opposing the beginnings of the Whig Party in England, and then, early in the next decade, Charles's lord treasurer, the earl of Danby, hired Nedham to attack in print the earl of Shaftesbury, one of the leaders of the Whigs, whom Nedham derided for his propensity to "shift principles like shirts."[8]

It should be clear enough that one does not turn to any of Nedham's writings to learn of his deeply held principles. Whether or not he believed what he wrote, however, his two treatises, *The Case of the Commonwealth* and *The Excellencie of a Free State*, are significant in the history of political thought. Indeed, John Adams devoted some of his energies to commenting on the latter work, which Adams said was widely known in America. Moreover, it was republished to provide republican inspiration during the French Revolution.[9]

(Marchamont Nedham, *The Case of the Kingdom Stated*, 2d ed. [London; 1647]. This pamphlet won the approval of the Royalists (Frank, *Cromwell's Press Agent*, 43).

[4] Because of Milton's supervisory role, scholars have wondered what, if anything, Milton contributed to the newspaper. J. Milton French ("Milton, Needham, and *Mercurius Politicus*," *Studies in Philology* 33 [1933]: 236–52) established the correspondence between *Mercurius Politicus* on the one hand and *The Case of the Commonwealth* and *The Excellencie of a Free State* on the other, thus proving Nedham's authorship and limiting the possible range of Milton's involvement. Elmer A. Beller ("Milton and *Mercurius Politicus*," *Huntington Library Quarterly* 5 [1941–2]: 479–87) went further than French by denying any possibility of Milton's contribution and endeavored to account for the issues of the newspaper that French left in question. H. Sylvia Anthony ("*Mercurius Politicus* under Milton," *Journal of the History of Ideas* 27 [1966]: 593–609) entered the debate to maintain that enough evidence did not exist to exclude Milton's direct involvement and to furnish some evidence in favor of it. See also Frank, *Cromwell's Press Agent*, 86–7. For an account of the friendship between Nedham and Milton, see Blair Worden, "Milton and Marchamont Nedham," in *Milton and Republicanism*, ed. David Armitage, Armand Himy, and Quentin Skinner (Cambridge: Cambridge University Press, 1995), 156–80.

[5] Roughly speaking, the earlier of Nedham's editorials correspond to *The Case of the Commonwealth* and the later to *The Excellencie of a Free State*.

[6] Frank, *Cromwell's Press Agent*, 107–10.

[7] For an account of the similiarity of the stands that Milton and Nedham took against the Restoration, which also attempts to counter the general understanding of Nedham as unprincipled, see Joad Raymond, "The Cracking of the Republican Spokes," *Prose Studies* 19 (1996): 255–74.

[8] Quoted from Knachel, introduction, xli–xlii. See also Frank, *Cromwell's Press Agent*, 154, and Worden, "'Wit in a Roundhead,'" 303.

[9] Perez Zagorin, *A History of Political Thought in the English Revolution* (London: Routledge & Kegan Paul, 1954; reprint, New York: Humanities Press, 1966), 124–5.

Most significantly for this study, these writings bring forward Machiavelli as a source for English republicanism, even before Harrington would do so famously with his *Oceana* in 1656.[10] Nedham uses Machiavelli in ways dissimilar from those of Harrington, as we will see in the following chapter. Nedham's republicanism values the people's participation in government and readily accepts boisterous contention between the rulers and the citizens – a feature of republics that Harrington never fails to condemn. Nedham's type of republicanism owes much to Machiavelli, himself an advocate of the people's participation in government, as evidenced by his admiration of the democratic and tumultuous republic of Rome. Unlike Machiavelli, however, Nedham sees this participation in service not so much of an aggressively militaristic republic but rather of the protection of the people's individual rights. In making the protection of people's rights the end, Nedham rejects the ancient conception of political association, expressed in Aristotle's view that a city should not only keep order but also improve the character of its citizens,[11] and instead he embraces something very close to the modern, liberal notion that politics is a means by which individuals attain security and comfort.

Nedham constructs this liberal notion by transforming elements of Hobbes's absolutist thought. In examining two of Nedham's works, *The Case of the Commonwealth of England, Stated* (first published in May of 1650 and revised with a new appendix in October of that year) and *The Excellencie of a Free State* (portions of which began appearing in *Mercurius Politicus* in February of 1651 but which was not published in book form until several years later), this chapter reveals Nedham's becoming ever more reliant on some of Hobbes's teachings. When the original version of *Case of the Commonwealth* appeared, he probably had not read Hobbes's writings; in the second edition, however, he included passages from Hobbes's *Elements of the Law* in his new appendix in support of obedience to the ruling power. In *Excellencie of a Free State*, he appeals to such Hobbesian themes as a contract that establishes political society and the rights of citizens. Precisely because Nedham takes the Hobbesian principle of the people's security so very seriously, he takes political expedients to provide for it that Hobbes's absolutism does not permit. Indeed, even when Nedham appears at his most republican (in *The Excellencie of a Free State*), he embraces Hobbes's teaching that politics originates in a contract but enlarges that contract to be in the service not only of life but also of liberty and property. Thus, although Nedham brings Machiavelli forward to serve the demands of English republicanism,

---

[10] Felix Raab, *The English Face of Machiavelli: A Changing Interpretation, 1500–1700* (London: Routledge & Kegan Paul, 1964), 160; Worden, "Milton and Nedham," 168; Rahe, "Inky Wretch," 60.

[11] Aristotle, *Politics* 3.9, 1279a31–1281a10, and my Introduction in this volume.

his Machiavelli is a Machiavelli transformed for liberal purposes.[12] By so transforming Machiavelli, Nedham anticipates in nascent form the synthesis of liberalism and Machiavellian republicanism that Trenchard and Gordon, writing as Cato, will propound in its perfected form at the beginning of the next century.

The Case of the Commonwealth and Its Relation to Hobbes

Nedham published his *Case of the Commonwealth of England, Stated* in May 1650 for the purpose of demonstrating that the Rump Parliament was a legitimate regime worthy of claiming the obedience of all Englishmen.[13] Political obligation was then a burning issue; at the beginning of that year, the government had expanded its requirement of the oath of "engagement" – a pledge of loyalty to the Commonwealth – to every adult male. In the October edition of his treatise, Nedham appends quotations from Hobbes's *Elements of the Law*, newly published in English and in England, to further his case for the necessity of obedience to the new regime.[14] The first part of Hobbes's *Elements, Human Nature*, received its English printing in February 1650 and the second, *De Corpore Politico*, in May 1650.[15] In fact, Hobbes's *De Corpore Politico* and the first edition of Nedham's *Case of the Commonwealth* were published the same week.[16] Later, from the fall of 1650 until that of

---

[12] Cf. Pocock, *Machiavellian Moment*, 382, where Pocock deems Nedham's work in *Mercurius Politicus* "the first sustained English exposition of republican democracy in classical and Machiavellian terms."

[13] Blair Worden, "Marchamont Nedham and the Beginnings of English Republicanism, 1649–1656," in Wootton, *Republicanism, Liberty, and Commercial Society*, 61.

[14] Frank, *Cromwell's Press Agent*, 85. The appendix also includes selections from *Defensio regia* by Claude de Saumaise (Claudius Salmasius), which Nedham puts to the same purpose as Hobbes's writing: embarrassing the Royalists. The thinker whom Nedham most often relies on in the first part of the work is Grotius, whom Nedham cites to corroborate his views on the necessity of the submission to those possessed of authority and on the fact that if one party breaks a covenant, then the other party is no longer obligated to obey it. Covenant looms large in the thought of Grotius, and, in fact, he is a type of contractarian thinker, who possesses a doctrine of individual rights. Nevertheless, Grotius differs significantly from Hobbes in maintaining the natural sociability of human beings, a position that keeps him within the broad orbit of Aristotle's thought. Indeed, his concern with the good of society trumps his concern with the individual's right to preservation (Richard Tuck, *Natural Rights Theories: Their Origin and Development* [Cambridge: Cambridge University Press, 1979], 79). On the place of natural sociability in Grotius's thought, see, e.g., Tuck, *Natural Rights Theories*, 59–60 and 72–3, and Zuckert, *Natural Rights and the New Republicanism*, 137–9 and 143. On Grotius's objection to Hobbes's state of nature, see Tuck, *Natural Rights Theories*, 81.

[15] Quentin Skinner, "Conquest and Consent: Thomas Hobbes and the Engagement Controversy," in *The Interregnum: The Quest for Settlement, 1646–1660*, ed. G. E. Aylmer (Hamden, Conn.: Archon Books, 1972), 94.

[16] Ibid., 95.

1651, Nedham reprinted portions of this treatise in his *Mercurius Politicus*, including the appendix containing quotations from Hobbes.[17] As scholars have noted, however, the journalistic form that the treatise later took is far less sophisticated than its original. In aiming for a broader audience, Nedham abandoned the scholarly trappings of *The Case of the Commonwealth*, such as the quotations in Latin and Greek, the citations of his sources, and many of the rather arcane historical examples.[18]

Hobbes's argument for the necessity of obedience to a ruling power is quite congenial to Nedham's purpose, and one can detect a certain amount of glee in Nedham's use of the argument of a philosopher associated with absolute monarchy to buttress his argument for the rule of Parliament. There is, however, something more of a Hobbesian strain in this work than merely an opportunistic attempt to wield an argument for absolute monarchy for the cause of the Commonwealth. Even before Nedham explicitly appeals in the appendix of his second edition to Hobbes's teachings, however, he uses concepts familiar from Hobbes's work, such as the importance of peace and security, within the body of *The Case of the Commonwealth*.[19] Before Nedham

---

[17] Numbers 31 (2–9 January 1651) through 34 (23–30 January 1651) of *Mercurius Politicus* essentially reproduce the part of the appendix of *The Case of the Commonwealth* devoted to Hobbes. For discussion of these issues, see Quentin Skinner, "The Ideological Context of Hobbes's Political Thought," *Historical Journal* 9 (1966): 311.

[18] Frank, *Cromwell's Press Agent*, 90–1, and Knachel, introduction, xxxvi.

[19] Skinner too notes the general similarity of Nedham's ideas on political obligation as expressed in the body of the text of *The Case of the Commonwealth* to those of Hobbes. He does not, however, ascribe that similarity to the influence of Hobbes's thought on Nedham, asserting instead that there is strong evidence that at the time Nedham originally wrote the work he had not read *De Cive*, which had been published abroad in Latin in 1642 and 1647 ("Conquest and Consent," 94). Skinner points to the Hobbesian tenor of *The Case of the Commonwealth*, as well as that of works of other English authors of the time, as evidence that Hobbes, rather than being the author of a strikingly original doctrine, was "contributing to existing traditions in political ideology" ("Ideological Context of Hobbes's Political Thought," 287). Not so clear, however, is whether Nedham had been exposed to Hobbes's thought indirectly either through the writings or conversation of those who had read *De Cive*. Skinner's enlightening depiction of Hobbes's warm reception by those English theorists who wrote in support of submission to the new government, including Nedham himself ("Ideological Context of Hobbes's Political Thought," 287, 303–5), suggests a conduit by which Nedham might have become acquainted with some of Hobbes's principles before he had composed the first edition of *The Case for the Commonwealth*. For example, in 1649 Anthony Ascham republished a work, originally published the previous year, in which he added references to Hobbes, having recently been exposed to *De Cive* (Skinner, "Conquest and Consent," 94–5). After referring to Hobbes's authority, Asham declares, for example, that "Security or Protection being here the chief end, it is suppos'd alwayes that we must contribute our obedience and riches so farre as may best conduce to the security both of our owne persons and estates, and of theirs also who command us, without which contributions, it were not called Society" (Anthony Ascham, *Of the Confusions and Revolutions of Governments [1649]*, ed. G. W. S. V. Rumble [Delmar, N.Y.: Scholars' Facsimiles & Reprints, 1975], 108–9).

had read Hobbes's work and appealed to his authority, then, he reveals that he shares some key concerns with this philosopher.

As the work opens, Nedham announces his attachment to republics by placing on its title page a quotation in Latin from Francesco Guicciardini that he later repeats in English. It runs: "[F]ree states are most pleasing to God because that in them more regard is had to the common good, more care for impartial distribution of justice to every man, and the minds of men are more inflamed with the love of glory and virtue and become much more zealous in the love of religion than in any other form of government whatsoever" (117).[20] Nedham's purpose is to vindicate the Commonwealth, and his tract thus begins with this appeal to the goodness of republics in general. Nedham knows, however, that such an appeal is not likely to win over the regime's opponents, and his purpose is to convince the unconvinced to obey the authority of the Rump Parliament.

He thus appends a note to the reader specifically addressed to those who hold "an opinion contrary to what is here written." He knows, he says, that he will be charged with "levity and inconstancy," because he was for a time himself opposed to the very ideas he himself posits in the work. His views subsequently changed, however, when he searched into the views of "those learned men who wrote before these times." Far removed from the issues that roil Englishmen of Nedham's day, they "were most likely to speak truth as being uninterested in our affairs and unconcerned in the controversy." Their impartial views convinced him, he avers (3).

Placing "*inter bruta animantia*" those who will reject his views as belonging to an unprincipled turncoat, he will not direct his appeals to them. In order, though, for his views to have as wide an appeal as possible among those who will actually weigh his arguments, he will address himself to the two types of people who inhabit the world: "the conscientious man and the worldling" (3–4). For the conscientious he will demonstrate the "justice of submission," which elsewhere he refers to as the "necessity and equity" of obedience (4 and 51), and for those less principled he will illustrate "the inconveniences and dangers that will follow" any opposition to a settlement. He admits that those of the former sort are unlikely to be convinced but expects "an abundance of proselytes," nevertheless, as "the greater part of the world being led more by appetites of convenience and commodity than the dictates of conscience." As a result, people can be more easily persuaded if they are told "what will be profitable and convenient for them to do than what they ought to do" (4). Nedham will show them that it is profitable and convenient for them to obey the government that reigns over them.

In so describing his rhetorical strategy, Nedham reveals a distinctively modern understanding of human nature. Human beings are led by their

---

[20] All references to *The Case of the Commonwealth* are from Knachel's edition; page references to this work in this section and the next appear in the text.

passions to accept a particular form of government; the passions – not the reason – of human beings are primary. This sentiment is familiar from Machiavelli, as well as from Hobbes. Nedham's statement here, however, reveals a particular compatibility between the understanding of Nedham and that of Hobbes, although Nedham had apparently not read any of Hobbes's writings at the time. In the *Leviathan*, for example, published the next year, Hobbes declares that "Desire of such things as are necessary to commodious living" "encline men to Peace" and hence to the submission to government.[21] On this understanding, government should be instrumental to the satisfaction of the passions; it appears that, at this point, Nedham may be inclining toward precisely that understanding.

Later, in the last chapter of the second part of the work, he supports a commonwealth by declaring that it is not "only a mere gallantry of spirit which incites men to the love of freedom; but experience tells us it is the most commodious and profitable way of government, conducing to the enlargement of a nation every way in wealth and dominion" (116). According to this comment, he bases his support of republicanism on the fact that it benefits the most people. It satisfies their desire for security and increase. Hobbes, of course, would not agree with Nedham's assessment of republican government. Nevertheless, Nedham reveals again a certain agreement between his own understanding and that of Hobbes, when he insists that government – any type of government – is a necessity. Without it there can be no "civil conversation" (30). Like Hobbes, then, Nedham views government as a necessity for promoting the essential ends of peace and security.

Nedham himself recognizes his agreement with Hobbes, however, when he makes use of Hobbes's theory in the appendix of the second edition of *The Case of the Commonwealth*. He cites approvingly, for instance, Hobbes's claims from *The Elements* that human beings put themselves under subjection to government in order to preserve themselves and to win their future security, and concludes from those declarations of submission that "since no security for life, limbs, and liberty (which is the end of all government) can now be had here by relinquishing our right of self-protection and giving it up to any other power beside the present, therefore it is very unreasonable in any man to put himself out of the protection of this power by opposing it" (136). In this way, Nedham uses Hobbes's words to corroborate his previous understanding of the importance of security: so important is it that it is the major – if not the exclusive – purpose of government.

The appendix reveals other aspects of Hobbes's thought that Nedham finds particularly attractive. Nedham appeals, for example, to Hobbes's claims that the sword of justice and that of defense must be in the same hands, that the sovereign establishes the common measure concerning such issues as property and what is to be held good and bad, and that there is

---

[21] Hobbes, *Leviathan*, 90.

no danger of damnation arising from the obedience to the sovereign's laws (136–8).

Nedham, though, transmits neither in the appendix nor in the body of his *Case of the Commonwealth* the Hobbesian doctrine – so familiar from *Leviathan* but also present in *De Cive* and *The Elements* – that, without government, human beings live in a state of nature that is a state of war, and that, in order to escape this most unsatisfactory condition, human beings can contract with themselves to establish an all-powerful sovereign. Nevertheless, Nedham will import this very doctrine into the text of his *Excellencie of a Free State*.

Nedham emphasizes, instead, in *The Case of the Commonwealth* that the sword is the instrument that creates governments. Hobbes too, of course, acknowledges that government can arise through compulsion, as well as through contract.[22] Nedham recognizes force as the only catalyst for its formulation, for instance, when tracing the origin of politics to the time after the Flood when the human population burgeoned and became more "vicious, being inclined to rapine [and] ambition." The then current way of organization in which the father of the family was the chief was no longer sufficient to control degenerate humanity: "[T]here was need of someone more potent than the rest that might restrain them by force." In response to this need, Nimrod became the first to wield "a new and arbitrary way of government." With this newfound power of the sword, he could "cut off by compulsion" those criminals who would not be curbed by "persuasion." Nedham concedes that later Nimrod abused this power over his subjects and as a result became the first tyrant, but nevertheless, the case of Nimrod establishes the origin of politics as such: "Thus you see the power of the sword to be the original of the first monarchy and indeed the first political form of government that ever was" (15). Politics, according to Nedham, begins violently in the need for protection.

Continuing to cite biblical history, as well as secular history ancient and modern, Nedham endeavors to show that "the sword [is] the only disposer and dispenser of titles to commonweals and kingdoms" (17). Indeed, the authority of Machiavelli is first adduced in this work in favor of this proposition. *The Prince* offers Nedham the example of Pope Alexander VI, who, "having a mind to make his son, Caesar Borgia, a prince in Italy, ... taught him how to make use of the French forces to build himself a fortune in Romania [*sic*]" (22).[23] Later, Nedham attempts to solidify his position further, with the maxim of the "Florentine Secretary": "[A]ll the prophets that were armed, prevailed; but those that were unarmed were too weak. And

---

[22] For example, in *De Corpore Politico* Hobbes declares that "there be two ways of erecting a body politic; one by arbitrary institution of many men assembled together ...; the other by compulsion" (*Elements*, 109).

[23] Nedham is referring here to chapter 11 of *The Prince*. Romania should read Romagna.

therefore it behooves all legislators to be so provided, that if the people will not be ruled, they may compel them by force" (35).[24] Once a ruler has emerged victorious through feats of war, Nedham declares that "private and particular persons have no right to question how those came by their power that are in authority over them. For if that were once admitted, there would be no end of disputes in the world touching titles" (31).

It almost goes without saying that Nedham's position, which both pays homage and acquiesces to the brutal forces of politics, is bolstered by the fact that the Rump Parliament was the sovereign power in England as a result of the capture and execution of King Charles I, although the royalist forces would not be destroyed until later in the year in which he writes. To the victor goes obedience, he declares, and the fact that Nedham writes in favor of the victorious side must make the theory he here propounds all the more palatable.

The only point at which Nedham softens his doctrine in this work occurs when he considers the question of the justice of the revolt against the king. If, as Nedham says, the obligation of the subject or citizen is only to obey and not to question the legitimacy of rule, how is it that Parliament came to question the legitimacy of the king? Is Parliament's sovereignty, then, illegitimate? Nedham responds:

I answer, there is a difference betwixt supreme power and the exercise of it. The controversy was not at first concerning his right of government, but the abuse of it by way of maladministration, in defense of which abuses he took arms; and so by the law of arms losing his right, as is proved before, the power descended to those that are now in possession, whose right we ought no more to question than at first we did his, their power deriving as natural a pedigree from heaven as his did and being as legally confirmed by the law of arms and nations as ever that was which he held from his predecessors. (47–8)

Charles, then, lost the kingship through arms, but Nedham concedes that the origin of "the controversy" was over Charles's maladministration of government. Thus, it seems that the sovereign power can be legitimately challenged when it abuses its power. This conclusion was, in fact, prefigured in Nedham's earlier discussion of the origin of political power in the rule of Nimrod. According to Nedham, the origin of Nimrod's political power was legitimate, but later, upon his abuse of that power, he became a tyrant (15). In this manner, Nedham here leaves open the possibility of just resistance to an ill-administered or tyrannical ruling power, a possibility that he seems to deny elsewhere when he repeatedly exhorts the people to obey the government – and a possibility that Hobbes, of course, categorically rejects.

[24] Nedham is here referring to chapter 6 of *The Prince*.

The Case of the Commonwealth in Its Machiavellian Aspects

In the second part, Nedham turns his attention from the conscientious to the more prevalent type, "the worldling." In order to get the attention of this type, Nedham turns to the designs of the Royalists, Scots, Presbyterians, and Levellers against the present government and proceeds first to show the "great improbability of effecting their designs" and then to delineate the "grand inconvenience which must needs follow" were their designs to succeed – a subject sure to capture the attention of the worldling. Later, in the last chapter he undertakes to demonstrate "the excellency of a free state or commonwealth as it is now established in England, and what happiness we may reap thereby" (51).

In this work's second part, aimed then at the pragmatic thinkers of the world, Nedham has much more frequent recourse to the authority of Machiavelli.[25] Thus, Nedham propounds both the thought of Hobbes and Machiavelli in this work. His Machiavelli is the republican Machiavelli of the *Discourses*. Nevertheless, his Machiavelli is considerably tamed, because it is the Hobbesian concern with the people's preservation and security that guides the application of Machiavellian principles. Specifically, although he ascribes the origin of government in this work to force – and hence, presumably, he must accept the likely possibility that one individual commands such force (as in the case of Nimrod) – he assiduously avoids elements of Machiavelli's thought that declare a single and powerful individual, capable of taking strong measures, is responsible for the establishment of republican rule. Moreover, he transforms Machiavelli's declarations in such a way as to claim him as an authority for the importance of the people's security.

Nedham appeals to Machiavelli's thought in the chapter devoted to his analysis of the designs of the royal party and the inconveniences that would result were its members to attain them. For instance, Nedham speculates here that if the prince were to regain his father's throne, it would have to be won through conquest. Because the new king will have gained his position through the sword, he would likely rule as an absolute king. "[H]e will be as absolute as was William the Conqueror, and we all must be in the same slavish condition as our forefathers," speculates Nedham (61). Even if this were not the case, the new king's followers would likely be advocates of

---

[25] As mentioned earlier, Nedham cites all of his sources less frequently in *Mercurius Politicus* – including Machiavelli – than in the source for these editorials, *The Case of the Commonwealth*. Anthony takes Nedham's reluctance to cite Machiavelli in *Mercurius Politicus* as evidence of Milton's taking an active role in supervising the newspaper. Noting that, although Milton was a student of Machiavelli, the poet is careful to disparage his thought when he cites him in his own writings, Antony suggests that Milton exerted his influence over Nedham's journalistic product by inducing him either to neglect to cite Machiavelli or to refer to his authority apologetically ("*Mercurius Politicus* under Milton," 599; cf. Knachel, introduction, xxxix).

tyranny. In Nedham's view, Machiavelli "speaks very aptly" to this situation when in his *Discourses* he notes

that a nation which hath cast off the yoke of tyranny or kingship, for in his language they are both the same thing, and newly obtained their liberty, must look to have all those for enemies that were familiars and retainers to the king or tyrant. Who, having lost their preferments, will never rest but seek all occasions to re-establish themselves upon the ruins of liberty and to aspire again onto a tyranny; that exercising an arbitrary power, they may take more sharp revenge against all those that dare but pretend to liberty. (62)[26]

Later in the same context, Nedham paraphrases *The Prince* as a warning to those who naively believe that the benefit of the throne will appease those who had previously been forced from power: "Machiavel adviseth never to trust them. For whosoever, saith he, thinks by new courtesies to take out of their minds the remembrance of old injuries, is extremely deceived" (66).[27] Thus, Nedham engages both the *Discourses* and *The Prince* to caution that, if the royal party is brought back to power, revenge may not come immediately, but it will come eventually and it will come bitterly.

In the third and last section of the second part, which constitutes the last chapter entitled "A Discourse of the Excellency of a Free State above a Kingly Government," though, Nedham comes to rely most heavily on Machiavelli's writings to help establish the "excellency of the present government" (111). In this chapter, Nedham's Machiavellian education, for example, is particularly evident. He quotes from Virgil and Dante for the only time in the work. It does not appear, however, that Nedham's wide reading of poetry is itself responsible for these learned references; both quotations appear in Machiavelli's works (118 and 127).[28] Machiavelli appears to provide Nedham with a literary education. His use of Machiavelli, however, is not unadulterated. He offers a softened, more Hobbesian Machiavelli – a Machiavelli who puts an emphasis on the people's security.

In this chapter, Nedham marvels that the people of England do not "prize this invaluable jewel of liberty which hath cost the Commonwealth so much blood and treasure" and turns to "the Florentine's subtile discourses upon Livy" for answers to the troubling puzzle (111). Nedham finds that his authority offers two answers. First, the people of England who have been bred

---

[26] Nedham is here referring to 1.16 of the *Discourses*.

[27] The passage refers to Cesare Borgia's mistake in believing that Pope Julius II would forget Borgia's past injuries to him, if only Borgia allowed him to become pope (*Prince* 7). Knachel misidentifies the passage as from chapter 5 of *The Prince*.

[28] On 118 Nedham quotes from Dante's *Purgatorio*, canto 7, lines 121–3. Knachel comments (n. 14) that Nedham probably copied this quotation from the Latin translation of the *Discourses*. Machiavelli quotes this passage from Dante in *Discourses* 1.11. On 127 Nedham quotes from the first book of the *Aeneid*, lines 563–64. Machiavelli offers this passage in chapter 17 of *The Prince*. In this case, Knachel does not note Machiavelli's use of this same passage.

and educated under a monarchy simply do not know any better. Machiavelli, after all, "compares such as have been educated under a monarchy or tyranny to those beasts which have been caged or cooped up all their lives in a den where they seem to live in as much pleasure as other beasts that are abroad, and if they be let loose, yet they will return in again because they know not how to value or use their liberty" (111–12).[29]

Nedham's second cause taken from Machiavelli's *Discourses* is "a general corruption and depravation of manners by luxurious courses when a nation is even swallowed up with riot and luxury; so that, being slaves to their own lusts, they become the more easily enslaved unto the lusts of another" (112). Although Nedham prefaces this discussion with the statement that he draws both reasons for the English insensitivity toward the benefits of republican liberty from Machiavelli's *Discourses*, he does not immediately produce any evidence from his source to bolster this claim. Instead, Nedham follows the rather Machiavellian method of examining the history of the Roman Republic, but he does so without any appeal to Machiavelli's presentation of the same history. In the earliest times of the republic, Nedham finds that the people were "zealous" for their liberty (112). Indeed, "when Rome was in its pure estate, virtue begat a desire of liberty, and this desire begat in them an extraordinary courage and resolution to defend it" (113). When, however, through the passage of time the Romans acquired soft manners and luxurious habits, they "lost that ancient virtue which purchased their liberty and an empire over the world." He then turns to a consideration of other peoples and finds that those who are "manly [and] have no acquaintance with luxurious diets and apparel" are more apt to live in liberty, while those who live in places where "civility hath degenerated into effeminacy" tend to be subject to "the will of imperious tyrants" (113). If it should happen that "virtuous spirits" should rise up against such tyranny, their enterprise usually fails as a result of general corruption, which causes their party to be "more superstitiously inclinable to adore the greatness of a tyrant than really affectionate to the worth of liberty" (113–14).

Finally, at this point Nedham provides the support from Machiavelli for this proposition that he had promised so much earlier: "For this cause it was that in elder time the people of Naples, Milan, and Florence lost their freedoms as they had gotten it" (114). Nedham's marginal note directs the reader to *Discourses* 1.17, where Machiavelli speaks of the lack of corruption at the time of the Tarquins, its pervasiveness during the time of the emperors, and the corruption of Milan and Naples that prevents these Italian cities from establishing their freedom.[30]

What Nedham fails to mention in this particular use of 1.17 of the *Discourses* is the point that Machiavelli emphasizes in that chapter: the necessity

---

[29] Nedham's marginal notes refer to *Discourses* 1.16–18.
[30] Machiavelli does not, like Nedham, put Florence in this category in this chapter.

of a single, great individual to take extreme measures if a corrupt people is to maintain its newly acquired freedom. Although the general point of Nedham's work is that whoever holds the power in the state – whether one or many – is the legitimate ruler of that state, and hence he is here willing to support sole rule in an abstract way, he seems not in the least attracted to Machiavelli's doctrine that republican rule must ultimately rest on the power of one. Of course, given the predominance of the Rump – the ascendancy of the Protectorate is still a matter for the future – it is hardly surprising that he shows no particular interest in this prominent aspect of Machiavelli's thought at the time he composes *The Case of the Commonwealth*. What this selective use of the *Discourses* shows is that Nedham's Machiavelli certainly is a republican, but one fitted out for the Englishman's own specific purposes. His willingness to use Machiavelli's thought selectively is hardly surprising, given his ability to manipulate his own views.

Not only does Nedham entirely neglect prominent but apparently unappealing facets of Machiavelli's thought, but he, in fact, is also willing to change significantly a passage he attributes to him. This particular treatment of Machiavelli's thought also occurs in the chapter devoted to the praise of free states. Nedham bolsters his point regarding the inability of hereditary succession to produce virtuous rulers by citing Machiavelli's authority. Nedham confidently reports: "Machiavell saith, not he that placeth a virtuous government in his own hands or family and governs well during his natural life, but he that establisheth a lasting form for the people's constant security is most to be commended" (118). Now Nedham's marginal notes refer to 2.11 of the *Discourses* as the source, and his modern editor endeavors to correct this citation, referring to 1.11 instead.[31] Neither chapter, in fact, contains a statement similar to the one Nedham claims to be reproducing.

The problem of finding the source for this quotation is that Machiavelli certainly did not put a premium on the people's security and, hence, did not single out as worthy of particular praise a founder who provided it.[32] Indeed, in the passage in the *Discourses* that most closely resembles the quotation that Nedham attributes to Machiavelli, the Florentine does not mention the

---

[31] The marginal note appears on 86 and reads "*Lib.de Rep. b.2.cap.11*" in Marchamont Nedham, *The Case of the Commonwealth* (London: E. Blackmore and R. Lowndes, 1650).

[32] Machiavelli did speak in *The Prince* of a ruler leaving the people largely alone, declaring that "he should inspire his citizens to follow their pursuits quietly, in trade and in agriculture and in every pursuit of men, so that one person does not fear to adorn his possessions for fear that they be taken away from him, and another to open up a trade for fear of taxes" (Machiavelli, *Prince* 21.91). Nevertheless, Machiavelli's overall concern in this context – and indeed in the work as a whole – is not with the people but with the prince; he offers this advice not out of any concern with the people's benefit but rather out of a concern with the prince's ability to remain in power, advising that the prince should not foster unnecessary hatred among his subjects. Nedham offers his supposed quotation from the alternative perspective, speaking exclusively out of an interest in the people's well-being.

people's security: "So a prudent orderer of a republic, who has the intent to
wish to help not himself but the common good, not for his own succession
but for the common fatherland, should contrive to have authority alone."[33]
There is certainly an element of commonality between the quotation from
Nedham and that from Machiavelli. Both assert that rulers should use their
position not to benefit their heirs but rather the common good, however
defined, in the case of Machiavelli, or the people's security, in the case of
Nedham. Beyond this similarity, however, are very important differences.

Nedham again omits Machiavelli's insistence that a founder or reformer
be alone. Machiavelli specifies that such a man should be alone so that he
may take the necessary measures – measures that could include murder –
to guarantee the success of his project.[34] Romulus, for example, was guilty
of precisely that crime, but Machiavelli exonerates him in the chapter from
which Nedham's quotation is apparently drawn. In that chapter the Italian
further specifies that if the founder's extraordinary methods are to have the
intended effect, he should contrive to have his creation rest on the many:
"[I]f one individual is capable of ordering, the thing itself is ordered to last
long not if it remains on the shoulders of one individual but rather if it
remains in the care of many and its maintenance stays with many."[35] The
obvious question becomes why would an orderer capable of such gruesome
deeds be willing to allow his creation, effected through his own effort and
travail, fall into the hands of many. The answer is to be found in part in the
above quotation and more fully elsewhere in the *Discourses*: only in this way
will the founder reap the greatest rewards for his endeavor. Only a republic,
and only a popular one at that, will assure him the glory that such an ambitious individual seeks because it will live longer and more vigorously.[36]
Again, Machiavelli's ultimate focus is on the rewards that will accrue to the
founder or ruler, not on the benefits that will accrue to the people.

In contrast, Nedham, as his "Machiavellian" quotation shows, is interested in the people's security. He shares this interest with Hobbes. Another glance at Hobbes's concern shows that Nedham has Hobbesified
Machiavelli's thought. According to Hobbes, it is the pursuit of "security" that drives people to submit to government.[37] So important is this end
for Hobbes that he maintains that the "duty" of the sovereign is to "procure" "the good of the people," which consists among other things in the

---

[33] Machiavelli, *Discourses* 1.9.2.

[34] As we will see in the next chapter, Harrington uses this passage from Machiavelli to explain the motivations of the fictional founder of the republic described in *Oceana*. Unlike
Nedham, Harrington recoils neither from the need for a founder to be alone nor from the
necessity that he take extraordinary measures. Harrington, however, does not specify that
such extraordinary measures include murder.

[35] Machiavelli, *Discourses* 1.9.2.

[36] E.g., ibid., 1.4–6 and 1.58.

[37] Hobbes, *Elements*, 111–12.

maintenance of internal peace and of defense against foreign powers.[38] Of course, Hobbes's sovereign is absolute, and there can be no earthly penalty for a sovereign who fails to fulfill this duty, but he sees fit to ascribe it to a sovereign, nevertheless. Nedham has made Hobbes's primary concern a primary one in Machiavelli's thought. In the process, Nedham has softened Machiavelli's thought. In so adopting Hobbes's concern with the security of the people, he seems to endeavor to protect them from the rule of one – a principle that did not so move Hobbes himself.

The Excellencie of a Free State and Nedham's Liberal Purposes

Nedham's next treatise *The Excellencie of a Free State*, like *The Case of the Commonwealth*, appeared in the pages of *Mercurius Politicus*. This treatise – for which Nedham had of all of his writings the greatest aspirations as a work of political thought[39] – was not published until 1656 as a book but made its first appearance in *Mercurius Politicus* as early as February 1651 and continued through August 1652.[40]

Although the concluding chapter of *The Case of the Commonwealth, Stated* is entitled "A Discourse of the Excellency of a Free State above a Kingly Government," it is not strictly true that Nedham's treatise *The Excellencie of a Free State* picks up where the previous one left off. This later effort is a much more radically republican work.[41] As a result, some of the purposes for which he had explicitly appealed to Hobbes in *The Case of the Commonwealth* – namely, the arguments that conclude that the people must necessarily obey the reigning power – have disappeared. Other elements of Hobbes's thought, however, appear in *The Excellencie of a Free State* that were absent in *The Case of the Commonwealth*; Nedham embraces in the later work the Hobbesian notion – a notion that would figure so prominently in later liberal thought – that politics begins in a contract that establishes civil society. Nedham, in fact, strikes out himself in this liberal direction by offering extensions of Hobbes's thought – extensions that Hobbes would not himself endorse. In *The Excellencie of a Free State* he declares that government should protect

---

[38] Ibid., 172.

[39] Worden, "Nedham and English Republicanism," 80.

[40] Most scholars agree that with *The Excellencie of a Free State* Nedham reversed the process of publication that he had used with *The Case of the Commonwealth*. Rather than extracting passages from his book to appear as editorials in *Mercurius Politicus*, as he did with *The Case of the Commonwealth*, Nedham collected editorials that had appeared earlier to form *The Excellencie of a Free State*. Antony, however, disagrees, making the case that *The Excellencie of a Free State*, although unpublished, was written before the editorials of 1651–2 ("*Mercurius Politicus* under Milton," 600–3).

[41] Worden notes that Nedham did not offer his strongest republican arguments in *Mercurius Politicus* until the destruction of the Royalist forces at the Battle of Worcester in September of 1651, although the last chapter of *The Case of the Commonwealth* does offer a vigorous defense of republican government ("Nedham and English Republicanism," 61–2).

individual rights to liberty and property in addition to life and that the people can and should withdraw their consent when government fails in that
protection. Thus, whereas in the second edition of *The Case of the Commonwealth* he used Hobbes's thought to argue for the obligation of obedience
to government, in *The Excellencie of a Free State* he uses its conceptions of
consent and rights to contravene the implications of that very argument. Not
just any ruling power is legitimate; the only government worthy of obedience
is a republican one.

The form of the work is clearly Machiavellian as it is modeled on the
Discourses on Livy in being a commentary on Roman republican history.
Rome is, in fact, his touchstone in this work; his purpose of determining
how liberty can be preserved, he maintains, is "best ... determine[d]" "by
observation out of Roman stories" (xiv–xv).[42] Not only those Roman stories but some of the lessons he draws from them are Machiavelli's. The purposes to which Nedham ultimately puts them, however, are different from
Machiavelli's, precisely because he puts the liberty of the people foremost,
and he understands that liberty as the protection of their rights. Thus, he
departs from Machiavellian orthodoxy by putting the people's security before their role as soldiers in the acquisition of an empire. Indeed, Nedham's
concern with the people's security, and his general favoring of the people
over the aristocracy in order to promote that security aligns him in this
respect with Hobbes. Nevertheless, Nedham's support of a republicanism
that endorses the people's vociferous participation belies a Machiavellian
spirit, even though that participation does not serve the Machiavellian end of
war. In Nedham's understanding, the people's vigorous participation allows
them to be the protectors of their own rights and liberty. Nedham marries
in this work Hobbes's concern with the people's security with Machiavelli's
republicanism.

Nedham's clear and unequivocal interest in *The Excellencie of a Free State* is
in that "inestimable jewel" – freedom. Although Nedham continually defines
freedom or liberty as the protection of individual rights to life and property,
in the preface of *The Excellencie of a Free State* he declares that it is "of more
worth than your estates, or your lives." Obviously, freedom cannot be in
service to these interests, if it is more valuable than they are. He then provides a list of five items in which freedom consists: "wholesome laws suited
to every man's state and condition"; "a due and easy course of administration" of "law and justice"; the "power of altering government and governors
upon occasion";[43] "an uninterrupted course of successive parliaments, or

---

[42] Page references to Marchamont Nedham, *The Excellencie of a Free State* (London, 1767),
appear in the text in this section and the following three.

[43] Nedham discusses the ability of a people to institute and to alter their government at 89; at
129 he places this abstract discussion in the context of England and the "late king's defaults
in government," which the people bore with "extraordinary patience" (128–30).

assemblies of the people"; and, finally, "a free election of members" to sit in those parliaments or assemblies. Having enumerated these constituent parts of freedom, Nedham declares that only when these conditions are satisfied will the people be "said to enjoy their rights, and to be truly stated in a condition of safety and freedom" (xiv). Freedom is a condition that emerges when one's rights are protected and, hence, when one is secure.[44] As a result, Nedham does not make it clear how freedom is more precious than one's property or estates; he nowhere argues or asserts that freedom serves an end higher than the maintenance of life or property.[45] His declaration that it is more important than either of these ends appears to be an unsubstantiated rhetorical flourish, an empty adornment for the introduction to his treatise. Thus, Nedham displays a modern, liberal conception of liberty, a conception readily apparent when he declares, as he did in *The Case of the Commonwealth*, that "experience assures" that freedom is "the most commodious and profitable way of government" (xxv).[46]

Moreover, like Hobbes, and the later Locke, Nedham insists that "the original and foundation of all just power and government is in the people" (34). The foundation ultimately rests in the people because politics itself is not natural; politics is a human construct that exists for the purpose of security. Politics, he explains, originates in a contract. In *The Excellencie of a Free State* Nedham recognizes what other writers call paternal government. He specifies that this form of government, which might also be termed natural because a father "ruled over his own children and descendants," existed until shortly after the flood when Nimrod introduced tyrannical government. Unlike his argument in *The Case of the Commonwealth*, he explicitly rejects the manner in which Nimrod's government came into being: He notes that "[n]either of these had . . . their original in or from the people, nor hath either of them any relation to that government which we intend in our position"; and, he continues, "[t]here is a government political, not grounded in nature, nor upon paternal right by natural generation; but founded upon the free

---

[44] Nedham's formulation is very close to the definition of freedom that Locke would later offer: "*Freedom of Men under Government*, is, to have a standing Rule to live by, common to every one of that Society, and made by the Legislative Power erected in it: A Liberty to follow my own Will in all things, where the Rule prescribed not; and not to be subject to the inconstant, uncertain, unknown, Arbitrary Will of another Man" (*Second Treatise*, para. 22).

[45] The passage from *The Case of the Commonwealth* (116) cited, earlier, and which Nedham repeats in *Mercurius Politicus* as well as in *The Excellencie*, seems to confirm this understanding: "Nor is it onely a meer gallantry of Spirit that excites men to the love of Freedom; but experience assures it to be the most commodious and profitable way of Government, conducing every way to the inlargement of a People in wealth and Dominion" (Marchamont Nedham, *Annales Reipublicæ Anglicanæ or A Relation of the Affairs and Designs by the Common-wealth of England, Scotland, and Ireland. With Intelligence from Forraigne Parts* by Mercurius Politicius [London: Thomas Newcomb, 1650–60], no. 68 [18–25 September 1651], 1079).

[46] Skinner notes Nedham's concern with the protection of life, liberty, and property (*Liberty before Liberalism*, 21, 67).

election, consent or mutual compact of men entering into a form of civil society.... [W]hen we speak here of government, we mean only the political, which is by consent or compact" (85–6).[47] Here Nedham clearly expresses the Hobbesian notion that neither government nor civil society is natural to human beings; rather, they construct both to serve their designs.

Because the people construct government for their ends, "the original and fountain of all just power and government is in the people." Nedham vehemently maintains that the only form of government that properly respects that just power is "free-state-government," consisting in the people's "successive representatives, or supreme assemblies, duly chosen." So enthusiastic is he in endorsing this form of government that he is willing to declare that it – an artifact individuals create to protect their rights – is "most natural, and only suitable to the reason of mankind." The other forms, which establish "a standing power" either "in the hands of a particular person, as a king; or of a set number of great ones, as in a senate" are the mere products of "artifical devices of great men, squared out only to serve the ends and interests of avarice, pride and ambition of a few, to a vassalizing of the community." He concludes, therefore: "The truth whereof appears so much the more, if we consider, that a consent and free election of the people, which is the most natural way and form of governing, hath no real effect in the other forms; but is either supplanted by craft or custom, or swallowed up by a pernicious pretence of right (in one or many) to govern, only by virtue of an hereditary succession" (34–5). Nedham sees a particular constitutional arrangement as essential to liberty's protection.[48] Indeed, he asserts that a representative republic is the only governmental form that fulfills his conditions of freedom.

Nedham's Explicit Repudiation of Machiavelli in *The Excellencie of a Free State*

Although in *The Excellencie of a Free State* Nedham clearly draws many of his "stories" of Rome from Machiavelli's *Discourses*, and although he shows no compunctions about referring to the Florentine repeatedly and favorably in his earlier treatise, in this later one he consistently treats Machiavelli as

---

[47] Whereas in *The Case of the Commonwealth* Nedham says that Nimrod's rule was political, he here refuses to accord Nimrod's government that designation.

[48] Nedham's *A True State of the Case of the Commonwealth* of February 1653/4 displays a keen interest in constitutional arrangements as it makes its case for the Instrument of Government, which established the Protectorate, consisting in a single executive, a parliament, and a council. Nedham is concerned with making the point in this pamphlet that the executive and legislative powers need to be in separate hands, and that in this "lies a grand Secret of Liberty and good Government" ([Exeter: The Rota, 1978], 10). Worden's identification of a passage in this work as deriving from an editorial in *Mercurius Politicus* helped in its attribution to Nedham (Blair Worden, *The Rump Parliament, 1648–1653* [Cambridge: Cambridge University Press, 1974], 362).

a source to be disputed. The only time that Nedham in this work explicitly refers to Machiavelli for corroboration, he does so in a rather embarrassed fashion. He attributes to Machiavelli the same radically transfigured quotation that appears in *The Case of the Commonwealth*. In this work, however, he introduces it with a disclaimer: "It was a noble saying, (though Machiavel's) 'Not he that placeth a virtuous government in his own hands or family; but he that establisheth a free and lasting form, for the people's constant security, is most to be commended'" (xxiv).[49] Such an apologetic reference to Machiavelli was, for some reason, not required in *The Case of the Commonwealth*.

Nedham does not cite Machiavelli again by name until, at the end of the work, he undertakes to refute him. Nedham devotes the book's last chapter to enumerating what he calls rules of policy and errors of government. His eighth and last error of policy is the "violation of faith, principles, promises, and engagements, upon every turn of time, and advantage" (163). For evidence of this error, he looks no further than Machiavelli's *Prince*: "I find it usually exprest in Machiavel, to be this, because the greatest part of the world being wicked, unjust, deceitful, full of treachery and circumvention, there is a necessity that those which are downright, and confine themselves to the strict rule of honesty, must ever look to be over-reached by the knavery of others" (163–4).[50]

Nedham then provides a quotation from chapter 15 of *The Prince*: "He which endeavours to approve himself an honest man to all parties, must of necessity miscarry among so many that are not honest." With apparent disgust, Nedham declares that such a doctrine is "fit only for the practice of Italy," and continues that the ancients "would have loathed" it. As evidence for this latter declaration, Nedham adduces the Romans who "did in all their actions detest it, reckoning plain honesty to have been the only policy, and the foundation of their greatness" (164). Nedham and Machiavelli seem to hold widely divergent views of the Romans. According to the Machiavelli of the *Discourses*, the foundation of Roman greatness was not plain honesty but rather fraud. In the chapter entitled "That One Comes from Base to Great Fortune More through Fraud Than through Force," Machiavelli explains how the Romans deceived those cities which it made its partners. Rome

[49] Worden suggests that Nedham's use of this quotation as it appeared in *Mercurius Politicus*, no. 69 (25 September–2 October 1651), is intended to influence Cromwell to renounce his power ("Harrington's *Oceana*: Origins and Aftermath 1651–1660," in *Republicanism, Liberty, and Commercial Society*, 120).

[50] When this passage appears in issue 112 (22–9 July 1652) of *Mercurius Politicus*, it mutes its criticism of Machiavelli by crediting him with "many noble Principles and observations upon record, in defense of the liberty of the people" (1753). Thus, his treatment of Machiavelli in *The Excellencie of a Free State* in this instance is even less hospitable than that which he accords him in *Mercurius Politicus*. Cf. note 25. See also Raab, *English Face of Machiavelli*, 160.

used its partners' arms to subdue other peoples further afield, and when by these means Rome had so increased its strength, its partners realized too late that they too had become servile.[51] Thus, whereas Nedham uses the Romans to prove the efficacy of honesty, Machiavelli uses them to prove the efficacy of fraud. Of course, a hallmark of Machiavelli's depiction of Rome also contravenes Nedham's point regarding the ancient Romans' honesty: the patricians' constant deception of the plebeians.

So that his readers will be better able to detect "the impious impostors" and "those jugglers" who use deceit to attain their ends,[52] Nedham quotes chapter 18 of "that unworthy book," The Prince (165–6). After having reproduced the entirety of the chapter in which Machiavelli maintains that princes cannot keep faith and that they should endeavor to emulate the characteristics of the lion and the fox, Nedham explains that Machiavelli's doctrine is "the old court Gospel," to which many "great ones" adhere. As a result, "it concerns the people to keep a strict hand and eye upon them all, and impose not overmuch or long confidence in any," so that they do not "suffer themselves to be deluded with colours, shadows, and mere pretences." Nedham concludes this denunciation of Machiavellian policy with the observation that, although Machiavelli thinks that the people are so simple as to fail to detect the deceit, the people must "make a narrow search ever into the men, and their pretences and necessities, whether they be feigned or not; and if they discover any deceit hath been used, then they deserve to be slaves, that will be deceived any longer" (171–2).

In opposing Machiavelli's teaching in The Prince, Nedham conveys an important Machiavellian teaching of the Discourses by maintaining that a republic should suspect all, even those who seem most worthy of admiration and rule. This will be a theme that, as we shall see, Nedham develops at great length and that, in fact, reveals his great debt to his Florentine teacher. Of course, Nedham differs from Machiavelli here in maintaining that the people themselves are capable of searching out the true characters of the most nefariously devious. That difference emanates from the differing status of the people in their thought. For Nedham, the people's participation serves more than the provision of fodder for war; he both displays the utmost concern for their safety and places a great deal of faith in their ability to secure it.

Given both his own mercenary tendencies and his demonstrated propensity to offer reason-of-state arguments, one might be inclined to dismiss Nedham's condemnation of "Machiavellian reason-of-state" as not credible.[53] Indeed, while condemning Machiavelli, he has managed to convey a great deal of his more disreputable doctrines. Nevertheless, whether sincere

[51] Machiavelli, Discourses 2.13.
[52] Raab notes that this is a faithful quotation from the Dacres translation of The Prince (English Face of Machiavelli, 160).
[53] Zagorin makes this argument, Political Thought in English Revolution, 125.

or not, Nedham's overt treatment of Machiavelli is hardly an endorsement; rather, it is a direct and pointed refutation. In this, his *Excellencie* differs significantly from his *Case of the Commonwealth*.

Nedham's More Subtle Divergence from Machiavelli in *The Excellencie of a Free State*

Despite this explicit rejection of the Machiavelli of *The Prince*, *The Excellencie of a Free State* seems on an initial inspection to be deeply indebted to the Machiavelli of the *Discourses*. Roman history offers Nedham, as it does Machiavelli, something of a primer for the construction and maintenance of a resilient republic. Nevertheless, just as when he undertook to determine whether Rome used fraud in attaining its greatness, the Englishman and the Florentine sometimes glean very different lessons from the same history. The Englishman consistently rejects Machiavelli's obsession with military expansion and his teaching regarding the type of republic that that obsession dictates.[54] Nedham incorporates Machiavelli's promotion of the people into his thought but rejects the people as a means to empire building; Nedham's regard for the people as something more than fodder for war produces significant differences in the character of their republicanism.

Like Machiavelli, however, Nedham refuses to take it for granted that a democratic republic is superior to an aristocratic republic as his work opens; rather, he sets out to establish that very point by weighing the advantages of both types of republics. In so doing, Nedham asks Machiavelli's question: "Where the Guard of Freedom May Be Settled More Securely, in the People or in the Great."[55] Given Nedham's concern with successive assemblies replacing standing powers, his phrasing of this question becomes: "Which is the safest way [to protect liberty]? whether by committing of it into the hands of a standing power, or by placing the guardianship in the hands of the people, in a constant succession of their supreme assemblies" (xiv). For both Machiavelli and Nedham, the answer to this question requires the examination of Roman history.

Nedham's examination of early Roman history leads him to conclude that, although the kings had been expelled from the city, the kingly power had not (xviii). Machiavelli had said the same in his *Discourses*,[56] although his meaning was rather different. Machiavelli had meant that after the

---

[54] Cf. Worden: "[I]n *Mercurius Politicus* in 1651–2 [when the editorials used for *The Excellencie* appeared], Nedham expounded the virtues of a free state or republic.... His editorials are a series of history lessons which imitate, both in form and in content, Machiavelli's *Discourses*" ("Milton and Nedham," 168).

[55] Chapter title to 1.5 of the *Discourses*. Zagorin too relates Nedham's question to this chapter of Machiavelli's *Discourses* but does not note how Nedham ultimately diverges from Machiavelli's reasoning (*Political Thought in English Revolution*, 125).

[56] Machiavelli makes the same point in *Discourses* 1.2.

establishment of the republic the kingly power resided in the two consuls who had replaced the kings. Machiavelli gives no indication that he disapproves of the power the republican consuls retained from the early kings. In contrast, Nedham does not concentrate on the consuls;[57] his concern instead is with the power of the Senate: "[T]he kingly power was retained with all art and subtilty, and shared under another notion among themselves, who were the great ones of the city" (xviii). In the Englishman's view, the Senate's power, which it used to oppress the people, had to be completely eradicated from Rome in order for the city to be free and prosperous.

Later, Rome corrected this defect with the establishment of the tribunes "and those conventions called assemblies of the people," which assured the people that "no laws could be imposed upon them without a consent first had in the people's assemblies" (xxii). His point, he summarizes, is that "not only the name of king, but the thing king (whether in the hands of one or of many) was plucked up root and branch, before ever the Romans could attain to a full establishment in their rights and freedoms" (xx).

In contrast, then, to Nedham's view, in Machiavelli's analysis the "thing king" is never extinguished in republican Rome, and Machiavelli approves of this power remaining rather cloaked but certainly powerful in a republic. Nedham's procedure here is certainly Machiavellian – he asks Machiavelli's question and he answers it by examining the history of ancient republican Rome – but the answer he provides does not replicate Machiavelli's because Nedham's predilections are far more democratic than Machiavelli's.

As different as *The Case of the Commonwealth* and *The Excellencie* are, Nedham's divergence from Machiavelli in both works seems to derive from the same interest – namely, his interest in the security and liberty of the people, which Machiavelli does not share. This conclusion becomes even more salient, when one compares their reasoning that drives both to respond that the people should be the guardians of liberty in a republic. Whereas Nedham does so out of a concern for liberty, Machiavelli does so out of an interest in empire.

In considering *Discourses* 1.5, for example, the chapter whose very title asks the question regarding where the guardianship of liberty should be placed, one finds that Machiavelli's overriding interest in empire drives his response in favor of the people. The chapter compares Venice and Sparta, both aristocratic republics where the guardianship rested with the nobles, to the more democratic Rome. Ultimately Machiavelli concludes:

In the end, he who subtly examines the whole will draw this conclusion from it: you are reasoning either about a republic that wishes to make an empire, such as Rome, or about one for whom it is enough to maintain itself. In the first case, it is necessary

[57] They play a slightly larger role in *Mercurius Politicus*; see, e.g., no. 72 (16–23 October 1651), 1142.

for it to do everything as did Rome; in the second, it can imitate Venice and Sparta, for the causes that will be told in the following chapter.[58]

Machiavelli's next chapter explains the necessity of empire simply; Sparta and Venice cannot, in his view, represent a viable choice for a thoughtful founder of a republic. The republic must pursue empire, and in order to do so, the republic must make its people its soldiers; in order to have such a citizen army, the republic must give its people a say in governance. Hence, the guardianship of liberty will rest with them, because it will be a democratic republic. The pursuit of empire guides Machiavelli's reasoning – a reasoning that prompts him to embrace his peculiar form of democratic republic.

By contrast, empire does not figure as one of Nedham's overarching concerns, a lodestar for all of his other principles. Indeed, this conclusion is prefigured to some extent in *The Case of the Commonwealth*, when, as we have seen, in replacing Machiavelli's concern with the greatness of an orderer of a republic with the security of the people, he implicitly renounces the martial glory that the Florentine holds out for the most successful republics and their founders. In this context in *The Excellencie*, this same conclusion becomes even clearer because, while Nedham follows Machiavelli in making the people the guard of liberty, he silently rejects Machiavelli's reasoning that the people must be in this position in order for the republic to make conquests. He does not even mention Rome's pursuit of empire in this particular discussion.

That is not to say that Nedham is a pacifist, that he nowhere uses republican success in acquiring territory through conquest as a weapon against standing powers, which he so despises. He does. Elsewhere in the work, he endorses empire when it serves his purpose, namely when it is one factor among many in the multiplication of the benefits to be derived from republican government. In the first chapter, for example, where Nedham lists fourteen reasons why the people are the best keepers of their own liberty, his seventh reason declares that in this form of government "the door of dignity stands open to all (without exception) that ascend thither by the steps of worth and virtue" (14). In support of this proposition, Nedham adduces the empire that Rome conquered after it had become more democratic: "[W]hen the state was made free indeed, and the people admitted into a share and interest of the government, as well as the great ones; then it was, and never till then, that their thoughts and power began to exceed the bounds of Italy, and aspire towards that prodigious empire" (15). Thus, the prospect of a democratic republic's acquisition of an empire is not even one of his fourteen points;[59] he uses it as a more minor point in support of another, more

---

[58] Machiavelli, *Discourses* 1.5.3.

[59] In *Mercurius Politicus*, Nedham offers over a period of several weeks fifteen reasons for the superiority of a republic rather than *The Excellencie*'s fourteen. The additional reason of *Mercurius Politicus* appears as the fourteenth and relates specifically to how republics handle

important one. Similarly, in support of his tenth reason, namely that "the people are ever indued with a more magnanimous, active, and noble temper of spirit, than under the grandeur of any standing power whatsoever" (25), he refers to military achievements, particularly those of the Romans, as well as to the vigor of the people in amassing their private fortunes (25–8).

He is also a supporter of a militia in a republic. In listing the errors of government and rules of policy in the last chapter, he makes the "sixth rule in practice" that of seeing "that the people be continually trained up in the exercise of arms, and the militia lodged only in the people's hands" (114). He offers Rome as a particularly fine example of the militia well used, when at the city's height "there was no difference, in order, between the citizen, the husbandman, and the soldier: for, he that was a citizen, or villager yesterday, became a soldier the next" (115–16). Nedham's praise of the militia mimics Machiavelli's in arguing that an armed people allowed for the people's greater stake in the republic; unlike Machiavelli, however, he uses the term "consent" to denote the character of the people's role in government (114). In further contrast to Machiavelli, Nedham here characterizes Rome's militia as being used against foreign powers only for defense (115).[60]

This recognition points to the important fact that Nedham is far from replicating Machiavelli's obsession with military acquisition. Rome's stunning conquests or England's future as a republican military powerhouse is not so prominent in his mind that it warrants constant discussion.[61] Nedham's

---

their empire: "because all new Acquisitions in this form, made by *Conquest* tend not only to the ease & benefit of the People Themselves, but also to the content of the conquer'd *Party*" (no. 90 [19–26 February 1652], 1425). For some reason, Nedham did not see fit to include this reason in *The Excellencie*.

[60] Pocock cites this sixth policy as it appears in *Mercurius Politicus* (no. 103 [20–7 May 1652], 1609–13) in support of his claim that Nedham offers "a democratic government [that] is to be based on the popular possession of arms and the rapid succession ... of the representatives and magistrates the people elect" (*Machiavellian Moment*, 382). In "The Historical Introduction" to *The Political Works of James Harrington*, ed. J. G. A. Pocock (Cambridge: Cambridge University Press, 1977), Pocock claims that "*Mercurius Politicus* turned ... to the delineation, in English terms, of a radical republicanism founded upon the Machiavellian concept of a *popolo armato*; an ideology not articulated in England before, whose presence in the government journal ranks the latter as a chief precursor of Harrington's *Oceana*" (34). Worden follows Pocock in arguing that Nedham is akin both to Harrington and Machiavelli in his embrace of an armed citizenry. See Worden, "James Harrington and *The Commonwealth of Oceana*," in Wootton, *Republicanism, Liberty, and Commercial Society*, 104, and "Harrington's *Oceana*," 111. In both of these instances, Worden refers to no. 103 of *Mercurius Politicus* to corroborate his point. Although Nedham does laud in this editorial Rome's militia and sees one as necessary for a republic, *Mercurius Politicus*'s concern with the militia is focused in this number. As a result, contrary to Pocock's claim in *The Machiavellian Moment*, the rapid succession of representatives is much more the basis of Nedham's republic than an armed people. As we see in the next section, the people participate primarily in Nedham's republic through election to the assembly and by their engagement with these representatives.

[61] In contrast, Worden compares Nedham with Machiavelli on this point, arguing that they both support a "commonwealth for expansion." In support of this proposition, Worden

hesitancy with regard to Machiavelli's imperialism will become even clearer later when we encounter the Italian's real English protégés on the subject of republics for increase: Harrington and Sidney. Nedham displays neither the jingoism of a Harrington when contemplating Englishmen's capacities for accumulating an empire, nor the lusty – indeed, covetous – admiration of a Sidney when describing Rome's conquests. In fact, whereas Nedham, as we know, refuses to follow the chain of Machiavelli's reasoning in *Discourses* 1.5–6, which ultimately forces the acceptance of the necessity of an empire, Sidney, as we will see, follows that chain most assiduously.[62]

Because Nedham's purpose is not the establishment of a republic for acquisition but rather the protection of the people's liberties, he need not be as respectful of the desires of the nobles that help to propel such acquisitions. The result is that he is even more forceful than is Machiavelli in condemning the nobles' imperious desires and lauding the people's more temperate ones. The passions of the nobles, in Nedham's view, serve only to threaten the people's security. The people, by contrast, "never think of usurping over other mens rights, but mind which way to preserve their own" (2) and "the people must needs be less luxurious than kings or the great ones, because they are bounded within a more lowly pitch of desire and imagination" (22). The members of the aristocracy are threatening precisely because their desires are so copious and so pressing.[63]

In his endorsement of the people as capable of maintaining a state's liberty, Nedham has recourse – without attribution – to some of the arguments contained in the very chapter of the *Discourses* in which Machiavelli declares

justly cites, among other passages, Nedham's justifications for his tenth reason cited earlier. In the version that appeared in *Mercurius Politicus*, Nedham cites "at present the valiant Swiss, the Hollanders, and also our own Nation; whose high atchievments may match any of the Ancients, since the extirpaion of Tyranny, and re-establishment of our Freedom in the hands of the People" (no. 85 [15–22 January 1652], 1352). (When this passage appears in *The Excellencie*, Nedham excises the passage that refers to the moderns surpassing the ancients.) Nevertheless, Worden, in making this argument, does not note how Nedham fails to follow Machiavelli in making territorial increase his guiding principle ("Nedham and English Republicanism," 71).

[62] Cf. Jonathan Scott, "The Rapture of Motion: James Harrington's Republicanism," in *Political Discourse in Early Modern Britain*, ed. Nicholas Phillipson and Quentin Skinner (Cambridge: Cambridge University Press, 1993), 146. Scott compares Nedham to Sidney on this basis, claiming that Nedham and Sidney were "two supreme Machiavellians, who understood and supported every hard decision taken before them by the master. The most important of these was the choice of vigour, of armed force and of the 'tumults' they would bring, at the expense of longevity and stability."

[63] Worden claims that it is Nedham's "social arguments" that make his republicanism distinctive. In support of this view, he cites Nedham's denunciations of the nobility that occur in *Mercurius Politicus*, no. 89 ("Nedham and English Republicanism," 64). The arguments of this issue did not appear in either *The Excellencie* or *The Case of the Commonwealth*. See Frank, *Cromwell's Press Agent*, 185. Pursuing this line of argument further, Worden doubts Nedham's criticism of the Levellers (Worden, "Nedham and English Republicanism," 66).

his own democratic leanings and, hence, his independence "from all the writers." Nedham provides as an example of the "people's constancy" the fact that the Roman people "continued constant irreconcileable enemies to all tyranny in general, and kingly power in particular" (78). This is a paraphrase of Machiavelli's statement that "[w]hoever considers the Roman people will see it to have been hostile for four hundred years to the kingly name and a lover of the glory and common good of its fatherland," made in support of his claims in favor of the people in this chapter.[64] Nedham also declares that "it is observable of this people, That in making their elections they could never be persuaded to chuse a known infamous, vitious, or unworthy fellow; so that they seldom or never erred in the choice of their tribunes and other officers" (79). He here paraphrases Machiavelli's statement that "the Roman people" "in so many hundreds of years, in so many choices of consuls and tribunes, it did not make four choices of which it might have to repent."[65] Unlike Machiavelli, Nedham nowhere revises this assertion of the people's wisdom by showing how the patricians duped the plebeians into electing men who would align themselves with the patrician interest by maintaining Rome's wars. One sees in this aspect of Nedham's thought the same deepening of Machiavelli's democratic leanings that one finds in Hobbes: because neither Hobbes nor Nedham advocate that war be a constant undertaking for a state, they need not oppose the people's achievement of their security; because war is not a necessity for them, they need not replicate Machiavelli's admiration of the great and their desires.

The Machiavellian Spirit of Nedham's Liberal Republic

Although both Nedham and Hobbes deepen Machiavelli's democratic leanings by providing for the people's security, the means by which they do so is starkly different: Hobbes insists on an absolute monarch, whereas Nedham insists on a representative assembly. Representatives are to serve the people's interests, and the people must keep a firm watch on their doings to assure that they do not forsake them. To this end, Nedham embraces salient aspects of Machiavelli's republicanism: the importance of accusations, the necessity of ingratitude and stern punishments, and the desirability of a raucous political realm, where individuals strive to satisfy their desires. Nedham embraces the spirit of Machiavelli's republicanism in order to provide for the people's security.

Nedham insists on blurring the distinction between the people themselves and their representatives. He clarifies that he is, in fact, combining these

---

[64] Machiavelli, *Discourses* 1.58.1 and 1.58.3. His chapter is entitled "The Multitude Is Wiser and More Constant Than a Prince." Interestingly, Nedham here fails to make reference to the Roman people as lovers of the glory of their fatherland.

[65] Machiavelli, *Discourses* 1.58.3.

terms, for instance, when he declares it an "undeniable rule, *that the people* (that is, such as shall be successively chosen to represent the people) *are the best keepers of their own liberties*" (2; emphasis in original). He specifies elsewhere that when he uses the term people, he means not "the confused promiscuous body of the people" (38). Nevertheless, one of the benefits of this form of government that Nedham touts is that "the door of dignity stands open to all (without exception) that ascend thither by the steps of worth and virtue" (14).

Moreover, the fact that he insists that the representatives hold their office by a short tenure guarantees that more new people will constantly be enabled to participate in government. Against objections that the neophytes who are conveyed into Parliament at every election have neither the experience nor the judgment to rule, he maintains that only a "few easy" faculties are required "such as common sense and reason," and hence, "the people's trustees are to continue, of right, no longer than meer necessity requires" (61–2).

These representatives, Nedham specifies, satisfy their own good, while serving that of the public. Due to the rapid succession in officeholders, the lawmaker will soon be among those who live under the laws. He explains that as a result "self-interest binds him to do nothing but what is just and equal; he himself being to reap the good or evil of what is done, as well as the meanest of the people" (12).[66] Moreover, the very reason why the people are so suited to govern is that they are best able to ascertain their own needs:

as the end of all government is (or ought to be) the good and ease of the people, in a secure enjoyment of their rights, without pressure and oppression: so questionless the people, who are most sensible of their own burthens, being once put into a capacity and freedom of acting, are the most likely to provide remedies for their own relief; they only know where the shoe wrings. (11)

At one place, Nedham speaks confidently of how in such a government the public and private interests meld unproblematically when the people elect those who appear eminent and devoted to freedom: "In such hands the guardianship of Liberty may be safely placed, because such men have made the public interest, and their own, all one; and therefore will neither betray, nor desert it, in prosperity or adversity" (130). He here uses Machiavelli's language to support representative government and the notion that its representatives will protect both their private and the public interest.

---

[66] J. W. A. Gunn characterizes Nedham as an interest theorist, who "purported to derive the public good from the citizens' understanding of their own interests." Gunn furnishes from *Mercurius Politicus* several examples of this reasoning (*Politics and the Public Interest in the Seventeenth Century* [London: Routledge & Kegan Paul; Toronto: University of Toronto Press, 1969], 33–5). See also Worden, "'Wit in a Roundhead,'" 317–19: "Like James Harrington,...[Nedham] sees the key to political health not in the elimination of private interest but in the harmonizing of private with public interest" (319).

Nedham is not so naive, however, as to insist that the public and private can always coexist so effortlessly, that all elected representatives will in every case find their country's good coextensive with their own. Nedham understands, just as does Machiavelli, that some individuals burn for the preeminence of tyranny. His insistence on rapid turnover in Parliament is meant also to combat the dangerous tendency that elected representatives have to form factions that could eventually lead to the overturning of the government in favor of a tyranny (5–8). Nedham makes sure that those who hold office simply do not have time for such nefarious designs: "[A]s motion in bodies natural, so succession in civil, is the grand preventive of corruption" (4).[67]

In further pursuing how representatives must be restrained, he even more clearly conveys his endorsement of Machiavellian teachings. Nedham demands not only that the most qualified among the people serve in the republic's assembly but also encourages the generality to remain on guard against the misuse of power on the part of their representatives. Like Machiavelli,[68] Nedham does not think that ingratitude on the part of a republic is necessarily always something to be condemned. Admittedly, the Englishman does, at times, admonish a republic to shun ingratitude: "[B]y all means [the people] should beware of ingratitude, and unhandsome returns" (134). Conversely, he is quite willing to transmit the other side of the argument, as when he states:

And though this accident [of condemning leaders who have provided past service to the state] in a free-state hath been objected by many, as a great defect; yet others again do highly commend the humour: For (say they) it is not only a good sign of a commonwealth's being in pure and perfect health, when the people are thus active, zealous, and jealous in the behalf of their liberties, that will permit no such growth of power as may endanger it; but it is also a convenient means to curb the ambition of its citizens, and make them contain within due bounds, when they see there is no presuming after inlargements, and accessions of powers and greatness, without incurring the danger and indignation of the people. (81–2)

One of those who say this is Machiavelli, of course. Although Nedham does not himself declare in favor of this view, he clearly displays admiration for a republic in which the people are so eager to maintain their liberty.[69]

Moreover, the people's ingratitude is often said to be most on display when they allow a previously worthy leader to be subjected to trial for

---

[67] This same principle will guide Harrington's constitutional arrangements.

[68] For Machiavelli's ultimate support of ingratitude in a republic, see 1.28–31 in the *Discourses* and my previous discussion in Chapter 1. In this set of chapters Machiavelli seems to praise gratitude and blame ingratitude, but he concludes by demonstrating why "too much love" displayed to a republic's leaders threatens the continued existence of the republic.

[69] Cato will be a vigorous supporter – in his own voice – of the people's vigilance against the misdeeds of rulers.

current abuses, and Nedham adamantly supports the people's right to accuse governmental officials of misdeeds in such a circumstance. He points out that standing powers can abuse the people with impunity because the people cannot accuse them. Similarly, even in free states, where the people lack the power of accusation, liberty is imperiled: the power of accusation "is a thing so essentially necessary for the preservation of a commonwealth, that there is no possibility of having persons kept accountable without it; and, by consequence, no security of life and estate, liberty and property" (72–3). In making his case for the necessity of accusations, Nedham reproduces – again without attribution – portions of Machiavelli's *Discourses*. In this instance, he replicates Machiavelli's argument in 1.7 and to that end adduces Machiavelli's own examples there: how the power to accuse Coriolanus saved Rome from harmful tumult, as well as how the lack of such power harmed Florence in the cases of both Francesco Valori and Piero Soderini (74–6). Nedham embraces Machiavelli's teaching that when leaders manifest a dangerous ambition, they must be accused and, if guilty, toppled from the republic's pinnacle of power; he simply is unwilling to acknowledge his agreement with Machiavelli on this issue.

At times, Nedham finds himself endorsing the same extreme sort of punishment as does Machiavelli. The Brutus who played the key role in overturning the rule of the Tarquins is very much one of Machiavelli's republican heroes. Nedham, however, finds reason to criticize him because he created "a mere shadow and pretence of liberty" in lodging the supreme power of the new state in the Senate, thus rendering the aristocracy an oppressive standing power (xvii). Despite his principled objection to the nature of Brutus's founding, Nedham shows a Machiavellian relish for his role as punisher of his own sons when they conspired against the new state: "[S]uch was the zeal of the Romans, for the preservation of their freedom, that they were all put to death without mercy; and, that all others in time to come, might be deprived of the least hope of being spared upon the like occasion, their own father was the man most forward to bring them to execution" (136–7).[70] When the protection of republican liberty is in the balance, Nedham displays an eagerness for Machiavellian expedients.

Because Nedham envisions the people's vigorous participation in a republic, it is likely a raucous place. To this end, he finds himself justifying tumults in a republic. He argues, for instance, that "there is not one precedent of tumults or sedition can be cited out of all stories . . . against the people's government; but it will appear likewise thereby, that the people were not in fault, but either drawn in, or provoked thereto, but the craft or injustice

---

[70] Machiavelli renders this deed of Brutus a maxim for the preservation of republican freedom: "[T]here is no remedy [for the problems facing a new and free state] more powerful, nor more valid, more secure, and more necessary, than to kill the sons of Brutus" (*Discourses* 1.16.4; on the importance of Brutus's deed, see also 3.1.3).

of such fair pretenders" who had "designs upon the public liberty" (68). Machiavelli, too, speaks in favor of Rome's tumults, going so far as to announce that "those who damn the tumults between the nobles and the plebs blame those things that were the first cause of keeping Rome free."[71] Nedham, too, identifies freedom as the by-product of Rome's tumults: "[B]y this means they came off always with good laws for their profit,... or else with an augmentation of their immunities, and privileges" (69).

Although this active, suspicious, and vengeful spirit of Nedham's republic is Machiavellian, its end is not. Machiavelli is concerned only with the preservation of the republic that necessitates aggrandizement; although he understands that the people will pursue the protection of their lives and property, he does not make that protection the imperative of government. The fact that Nedham has turned Machiavellian means to liberal concerns is nowhere more striking than when the Englishman declares that without the power of accusation there is "no security of life and estate, liberty and property" (72–3). Machiavelli shows how the passions of its citizens – including those of the people – could aggrandize the state. Nedham concludes from this demonstration that the people should be brought into political life, not for Machiavelli's purpose of winning great conquests and glory for their homeland, but for the purpose of protecting their own freedom, which Nedham understands to be the protection of their lives and estates.[72]

Nedham uses that liberal foundation, derived from what are extensions of Hobbes's teachings, to support an edifice, namely a republic, that Hobbes finds noxious to his ends of political order in the service of the preservation of life. Nedham expands Hobbes's right to life to include liberty and estates in an anticipation of Locke's doctrine that would appear later in the century. Nedham does more, however. He takes what will be Locke's concern with the protection of these rights and makes republicanism the means to that end.

---

[71] Machiavelli, *Discourses* 1.4.1.

[72] In his piece "Nedham and English Republicanism," Worden too underscores Nedham's emphasis on rights and consent and argues that he anticipates arguments that would become prominent later. Indeed, he puts Nedham with Sidney in the contractarian tradition (50 and 46). Following republican scholarship on Machiavelli, however, Worden emphasizes the incompatibility of this element of Nedham's thought with Machiavelli's, overlooking this point regarding Machiavelli's emphasis on how his version of republicanism requires citizens to act on their individual passions: "Alongside [Nedham's] espousal of a Machiavellian concept of virtue, a concept that modern terminology equates with 'positive liberty,' there runs a more conventional assertion of the claims of 'negative liberty.' Urging citizens to participate, on Machiavellian lines, in republican government, Nedham at the same time promises that republican government will leave them well alone" (69). Elsewhere, however, Worden overlooks this liberal side of Nedham: "Nedham's [republicanism] is uninhibited in its Machiavellian commitment to the primacy of the public sphere" ("Milton and Nedham," 171). Nevertheless, I do concur in Worden's assessment that Machiavelli neither had a theory of consent nor concerned himself with the security of individuals as opposed to the state ("Nedham and English Republicanism," 70).

With these republican means, Machiavelli's republicanism becomes crucial to the mix. This whole process results in Nedham introducing Machiavellian republicanism to liberal concerns while at the same time liberalizing Machiavelli. At the very beginning of English republicanism, then, one can descry the synthesis of liberalism and Machiavellian republicanism.

4

The Distinctive Modern Republicanism
of James Harrington

It is said that Thomas Hobbes, after considering James Harrington's *Oceana*, surmised that Henry Neville "had a finger in that pye." Even if Hobbes's conjecture that Neville was coauthor with Harrington is mistaken, Neville may, in fact, still be held partly responsible for Harrington's great work of political thought, though in an entirely different manner. According to John Aubrey, Harrington's contemporary and chronicler of the lives of prominent Englishmen, Neville encouraged Harrington to turn his literary aspirations from poetry to political discourse.[1] If true, Neville's advice helped produce a prolific political writer passionately dedicated to the establishment of a commonwealth in England.

Harrington published his great work *Oceana* in 1656 as a blueprint for the republican future he hoped to help usher into England, and between the occasion of the publication of his great work and the Restoration, Harrington attempted to make that future a reality by writing furiously to justify his model further and to defend it against its critics. In the process he collected a number of converts to his plan, who joined him in his efforts. The chaotic year of 1659 seemed to them to present an opportunity for the founding of that very republic. In July, Neville presented Parliament with "The Humble Petition of Divers Well Affected Persons," which contained Harringtonian ideas for the establishment of a new government, but his effort was rebuffed.[2] In the fall and winter of that year Harrington's famous Rota Club, which met in the evenings at a London coffeehouse, flourished. Attendees included Neville and John Wildman, as well as Aubrey himself.[3] According to Aubrey, their discussions were quite well attended ("[t]he room was every evening full as it could be cramm'd") and formal ("we had [very formally] a *ballotting-box*,

---

[1] Aubrey, *Brief Lives*, 1:289.
[2] Fink, *Classical Republicans*, 87, and Robbins, *Two Republican Tracts*, 10–11.
[3] Aubrey, *Brief Lives*, 1:289–91.

and balloted how things should be caried").[4] With George Monk's "comeing-in" in February 1660, "all these aierie modells vanished."[5] The Restoration brought not only the evaporation of their "aierie" dreams but also Harrington's imprisonment, first in the Tower and then in Portsey Castle. Although Harrington was eventually released, the effects of imprisonment lingered; Aubrey attributes Harrington's madness to this experience.[6]

Years earlier in 1647, this man who was held as a prisoner of the restored monarchy had befriended the captured father of Charles II. In that year Harrington was appointed a groom of the bedchamber to Charles I. Harrington acquired such an attachment to Charles that Aubrey reports both that Harrington was on the scaffold when the king went to his death and that he "oftentimes heard [Harrington] speake of king Charles I with the greatest zeale and passion imaginable, and that his death gave him so great griefe that he contracted a disease by it." Aubrey also reports that although the "king loved his company," he would not permit him to speak of a commonwealth in his presence.[7]

Despite Charles's injunction, Harrington is famous precisely for his discussion of commonwealths, particularly that which will rule Oceana, his lightly fictionalized version of England. In Harrington's republican conversation – that is, in *Oceana* and the later works that justified that work – he makes a point of declaring that his thought differs from that of all of his predecessors. Recently scholars have offered a depiction of him radically at odds with his own pronouncements. According to this interpretation, Harrington should be understood as a proselyte of ancient political thought, one who owes his greatest intellectual debt to the civic humanism of Aristotle.

In not heeding Harrington's own claims, the civic humanist interpretation of his thought mistakes his modern republicanism for an ancient variant. To be sure, he is partial to antiquity, primarily, as we shall see, because he links its political understanding to the promotion of republics. Nevertheless, this partiality does not make him a civic humanist, just as Machiavelli's promotion of republics does not make him a classical republican. Like Nedham, Harrington combines ingredients of Machiavelli and Hobbes, but Harrington's resulting mix is different from Nedham's concoction.[8] Harrington, like Nedham, uses the thought of Machiavelli

---

4 Ibid., 1:290.
5 Ibid., 1:291.
6 Ibid., 1:292.
7 Ibid., 1:288–9.
8 Worden claims that on many issues "Harrington travels where Nedham has pointed." While this is certainly true, particularly with regard to the importance each ascribes to rotation, nevertheless, I place greater emphasis on the importance of their differences. Harrington, for example, does not share Nedham's interest in rights, as we shall see. In addition, Nedham offends a Harringtonian sensibility by endorsing the assembly's, as well as the people's, protection of

and Hobbes to support republicanism, but, as a comparison with Nedham's thought helps reveal, Harrington's republic is not a modern, liberal version in which the spirit of Machiavelli is enlisted to protect individual liberty and rights. Instead, Harrington invokes Machiavelli's name by producing a militaristic republic but then ignores his predecessor's authority in his pursuit of a republicanism that does away with any type of civil upheaval by means of its emphasis on institutions. Harrington is confident that his republican institutions can neutralize conflict by balancing the interest of one group of citizens against that of another. Therefore, Harrington's is a manifestation of modern republicanism – a distinctive republicanism that surely borrows from many sources but, just as he claims, differs from all of its predecessors in fundamental ways.

Harrington as an Ancient

By highlighting the role of the author of *Oceana* in transmitting Machiavelli's thought from Italy to the shores of America, Pocock's account has made Harrington a major figure in modern intellectual history.[9] On Pocock's understanding, however, the Englishman is not so much a player in the development of modern thought as he is a dogged resistance fighter to its further encroachment on the territory of the ancients.

Before Pocock offered his pathbreaking interpretation, scholars commonly explicated Harrington's thought in light of a class analysis of his historical situation. The earlier approach clearly grows out of the emphasis that Harrington himself places on the connection between property and power. Not only does the amount of property a citizen holds determine the amount of his power; the distribution of property within a state determines the regime's ability to maintain power, he contends.[10] Pocock challenges such

those rights in a boisterous manner. See Worden, "Harrington and *Commonwealth of Oceana*," 98. In "*Oceana*: Origins and Aftermath," Worden suggests that *Oceana* may not be as original as it looks, because many of its ideas came from Nedham's editorials. Worden speculates that perhaps Harrington, in composing *Oceana*, worked with material that he had written earlier so that "we should think of Harrington working with editorials of *Mercurius Politicus* on his desk, or – who knows? – participating in discussions in which Nedham also took part" (114).

9 J. C. Davis, "Pocock's Harrington: Grace, Nature and Art in the Classical Republicanism of James Harrington," *Historical Journal* 24 (1981): 683.

10 J. G. A. Pocock, *The Ancient Constitution and the Feudal Law: A Study of English Historical Thought in the Seventeenth Century: A Reissue with a Retrospect* (Cambridge: Cambridge University Press, 1987), 128–9 and 131; R. H. Tawney, "Harrington's Interpretation of His Age," *Proceedings of the British Academy* 27 (1941): 199–223; Hugh Trevor-Roper, "The Gentry, 1540–1640," *Economic History Review Supplement*, no. 1 (1953): 1–55 ; Macpherson, *Possessive Individualism*, 160–93; Christopher Hill, "James Harrington and the People," in *Puritanism and Revolution: Studies in Interpretation of the English Revolution of the Seventeenth Century* (London: Mercury Books, 1962), 299–313.

interpretations by arguing that the author of *Oceana* is ultimately more interested in citizenship than property. "Harrington's economics and his politics were alike essentially Greek," Pocock maintains, "and...all he knew about English agrarian society was at the service of a fundamentally Aristotelian theory of citizenship."[11] On this understanding, Harrington learned this antique theory of citizenship from his master, Machiavelli. With these lessons in hand, the Englishman infused into his native land "a paradigmatic restatement of English political understanding in the language and worldview inherited through Machiavelli."[12] Pocock finds that the influence of Harrington's adaptation of Machiavelli's civic humanism was wide ranging as it helped to shape a distinctive form of thought among the English opposition thinkers of the seventeenth and eighteenth centuries, whom Pocock terms neo-Harringtonians.[13] These opposition thinkers, in turn, transmitted this style of thought to the American revolutionaries, who, in their struggle against English rule, sought for inspiration among the writings of the English opposition.[14] According to Pocock, then, Harrington is a key figure in the transmission of the civic humanism of antiquity to America, where it breathed its last gasp.

Contrary to Pocock's account, however, little of Harrington's thought derives from Aristotle. Ultimately, Harrington rejects Aristotle's politics because it relies too much on the moral virtue of the individual – particularly the virtue of moderation. Harrington believes that he has invented a regime that operates independently of the individual's moral virtue and hence is much more resilient than any regime that the ancients envisioned. In so doing, he explicitly rejects Aristotle and his theory of citizenship.[15]

---

[11] Pocock, "English Political Ideologies," 112.

[12] Pocock, "Historical Introduction," 15. Pocock specifies that Harrington expanded Machiavelli's notion of citizenship: to Machiavelli's insistence that a citizen must bear arms for his country, Harrington added that the possession of property was the foundation of arms ("Historical Introduction," 43, 54–5, and *Machiavellian Moment*, 386).

[13] Pocock, "English Political Ideologies," and "*Machiavellian Moment* Revisited," 63.

[14] Pocock, *Machiavellian Moment*, 515 and 528. See also Bailyn, *Ideological Origins*, 35; Wood, *Creation of American Republic*, 16.

[15] Pocock's depiction of Harrington as a civic humanist was preceded by Fink's characterization in *The Classical Republicans* of the thinker as a classical republican on the basis of his embrace of the goodness of the Polybian mixed regime. A number of scholars oppose the characterization of Harrington as an exponent of classical political thought. See e.g., Rahe, *Republics Ancient and Modern*, who argues that Harrington is a modern republican who rejects the Aristotelian premise that locates the foundation for political life in the human capacity for *logos* (410); Gary Remer, "James Harrington's New Deliberative Rhetoric: Reflection of an Anticlassical Republican," *History of Political Thought* 16 (1995): 532–57, who shows how Harrington creates a model of deliberative rhetoric that diverges significantly from the classical model, which in turn illustrates his rejection of the political life glorified in classical republicanism; Scott, "Rapture of Motion," who argues that Harrington undertakes to subvert classical republicanism – including what Scott understands as the civic humanism of Machiavelli – through a recourse to important elements of Hobbes's thought; Kathleen

Admittedly, Harrington often refers to Aristotle as an advocate of republics and explicitly aligns himself with the ancients on the basis of his own preference for republics. In *Oceana*, for instance, he contrasts the ancient political understanding to that of the modern by explaining that ancient prudence "is an art whereby a civil society of men is instituted and preserved upon the foundation of common right or interest, or (to follow Aristotle and Livy) it is the empire of laws and not of men," whereas modern prudence "is an art whereby some man, or some few men, subject a city or a nation, and rule it according unto his or their private interest" (8–9).[16] In his later explanatory work, *The Prerogative of Popular Government,* he declares simply that by "ancient prudence I understand the policy of a commonwealth, and by modern prudence that of king, lords and commons."[17] According to prominent declarations of his allegiances and sentiments, then, he is a partisan of the ancients in general and of Aristotle in particular. As we will see, however, he constructs a government that so depends on laws that he diverges from Aristotle, his guide on this very principle, who is unwilling, in contrast to Harrington, to dispense with the need for individual moral virtue.

Harrington also makes other declarations, often overlooked by the civic humanist interpreters of Harrington, that signify his desire to go beyond what he understands as the ancient conception of government. For instance, when undertaking to delineate the "goods of the mind," which turn out to be virtues, and the "goods of fortune," which he defines as riches, Harrington introduces his discussion somewhat cryptically: "To go mine own way, and yet to follow the ancients" (10).[18] This cryptic statement suggests that he

Toth, "Interpretation in Political Theory: The Case of Harrington," *Review of Politics* 37 (1975): 317–39, whose analysis refers to Pocock's work on Harrington before the publication of *Machiavellian Moment.* Despite the weight of these responses, the debate continues. J. C. Davis accepts the view of Harrington as a "subverter – rather than a transmitter – of the language of classical republicanism" ("Equality in an Unequal Commonwealth: James Harrington's Republicanism and the Meaning of Equality," in *Soldiers, Writers and Statesmen of the English Revolution,* ed. Ian Gentles, John Morrill, and Blair Worden [Cambridge: Cambridge University Press, 1998], 241), whereas Worden finds Pocock's interpretation more credible than that of his critics ("Harrington and *Commonwealth of Oceana,*" 106). I have criticized Pocock's interpretation of Harrington previously; see Vickie Sullivan, "The Civic Humanist Portrait of Machiavelli's English Successors," *History of Political Thought* 15 (1994): 76–87. The understanding of Harrington I express here grows out of this earlier piece.

[16] Page citations to *Oceana* are from James Harrington, *The Commonwealth of Oceana and A System of Politics,* ed. J. G. A. Pocock (Cambridge: Cambridge University Press, 1992), and are cited in the text. References to other of Harrington's works are cited in the notes and are from *Political Works.*

[17] Harrington, *The Prerogative of Popular Government,* in *Political Works,* 397.

[18] Rahe too notes this significant declaration of Harrington in his study but provides a slightly different, but complementary, explanation of its meaning (*Republics Ancient and Modern,* 410–11).

is both an independent explorer in the realm of political science and a follower of others. As we will see, it is precisely on the relation between riches and virtues that he explicitly diverges from Aristotle's teaching and initiates his own voyage away from the ancients. Harrington, then, while proclaiming his apprenticeship to the ancients, simultaneously and contradictorily announces his own mastership.

Harrington's *Oceana* is new and its creator a master because it has, in his own estimation, solved the problem of self-interest. When he turns to consider the "goods of the mind," he makes a statement condemning interest and praising virtue seemingly consistent with the civic humanist bent that Pocock ascribes to him: "Wherefore if we have anything of piety or of prudence, let us raise ourselves out of the mire of private interest unto the contemplation of virtue, and put an hand unto the removal of this evil from under the sun." In the discussion that this statement inaugurates, however, Harrington actually contemplates interest more than he does virtue. This examination of the "mire of private interest" is necessary because, as he explains in the continuation of the passage, no government is perfect unless it is secured from private interest (19). Harrington's proposal for rising from this mire to secure his government is hardly consistent with Pocock's delineation of civic humanism, however. Harrington believes he has secured his government against interest without relying on injunctions to embrace virtue precisely because virtue is not required. In this way, he departs significantly from Aristotle's understanding of political life.

Self-interest had hitherto been a formidable problem as a result of the perennial condition that "a man doth not look upon reason as it is right or wrong in itself, but as it makes for him or against him" (22).[19] Because of this human propensity, it is necessary to show how the "orders of a government as, like those of God in nature, shall be able to constrain this or that creature to shake off that inclination which is more peculiar unto it and take up that which regards the common good or interest, all this is to no more end than to persuade every man in a popular government not to carve himself of that which he desires most, but to be mannerly at the public table, and give the best from himself unto decency and the common interest" (22). He needs to find a way to convert self-interest into the public good.[20]

Harrington finds the secret to the imposition of such table manners, which is "the whole mystery of a commonwealth," in the behavior of "two silly girls" faced with a "cake yet undivided" between them. In order for each to secure the largest portion for herself, each girl will agree that one should divide the cake and the other should choose the piece she desires. "If this be

---

[19] Harrington's ultimate view of the relation between reason and the passions is very close to that of Hobbes. This correspondence between the two thinkers is treated in a subsequent section of this chapter.

[20] Zagorin, *Political Thought in English Revolution*, 138.

but once agreed upon, it is enough; for the divident dividing unequally loses, in regard that the other takes the better half; wherefore she divides equally, and so both have right" (22).

In applying this principle to the political realm, Harrington separates what he terms dividing and choosing, which, he announces, "in the language of a commonwealth, is debating and resolving" (24). Thus, he divides the republic's legislative function into two assemblies: a senate will do the dividing by engaging in debate and by offering its resolutions as proposals to the other assembly. This other assembly will then do the choosing by voting on the senate's proposals. This senate will be composed exclusively of those from the higher of the two property classifications and will represent the few whom Harrington regards as the "natural aristocracy" (170, 23). The assembly of the people, by contrast, will represent the many because it will comprise a majority of citizens drawn from the lower property classification. In this way, he has each assembly represent the interests of one of the two classes of citizens in the commonwealth. Harrington is explicit as to the character of the problem to which this is the solution. He declares: "The wisdom of the few may be the light of mankind, but the interest of the few is not the profit of mankind, nor of a commonwealth" (24). By this arrangement, though, he assures that his senate's wisdom cannot be used to further its own exclusive interest because it needs to gain the approval of the people as represented in their assembly.[21] The senate can gain this approval only if it does not slice itself a piece of the cake too large to gain the approval of the people.

In so separating these political functions of debate and result, or of dividing and choosing, Harrington delineates a means by which citizens satisfy their own needs and desires only in light of the needs and desires of others. As Harrington's "divident" divides the cake evenly in order to ensure herself the largest possible portion of the cake, so the senate will propose its laws to the people. There need be no appeal to virtue of any kind; the citizens' interests alone determine an equitable result – moderation in this case is clearly imposed from without.[22]

Another distinctive feature of Harrington's commonwealth is its agrarian law. Its importance to his orders for Oceana is evident in his adamant adherence to the principle that the manner in which the land of a particular realm is distributed determines the type of government that is most readily attainable for it. If a single person predominates in ownership of the nation's

---

[21] Cf. Worden, "Harrington and *Commonwealth of Oceana*," 98.
[22] Gunn makes a similar point (*Politics and Public Interest*, 116, 120, and 142). See also Toth's discussion of the cake, "Case of Harrington," 333. Cf. Pocock's treatment in "Historical Introduction," where he discusses "the greater good" that the girls attain by "having acted virtuously" (65, and see also 68). See also Worden's discussion of interest. He claims that Harrington is attempting to "accommodate Hobbes's skeptical insights into the functions of the passions and of instinct within the republican language of virtue and reason" ("Harrington and *Commonwealth of Oceana*," 91; see also 108).

land, then the state is most conducive to absolute monarchy; if the few, then the state is susceptible to mixed monarchy; and, if the whole people, then the state is capable of a commonwealth.

According to Harrington, the balance of property in England has undergone a significant change; since the reign of Henry VII, property has fallen from the hands of the nobility into those of the people.[23] As a result, the nation is now capable of sustaining the commonwealth of Harrington's creation, distinguished by its "fundamental laws" of "the agrarian" and "the ballot," which features a strict rotation in office (100–1). Rotation prescribes, for example, that members of Oceana's parliament serve three-year terms and must remain out of office for one term before they can be reelected. Voting in Oceana is characterized by an adaptation of the manner of voting in the Venetian republic that guarantees secrecy. Citizens drop pellets or balls into boxes so that "whatever a man's fortune be at the box, he neither knoweth whom to thank nor whom to challenge" (118).

In order to assure that the commonwealth of Oceana will not be overturned because the upper class comes to regain most of the land, Harrington offers an agrarian law that will provide for the breaking up of large estates by stipulating, among other provisions, that all sons, not simply the eldest, inherit land. He seeks to assure that whenever possible sons not inherit land that produces more than 2,000 pounds a year in revenue. The law also forbids anyone who possesses below that amount from acquiring land (except by inheritance that accords with the law) that will produce revenue that exceeds it (101). Of course, the imposition of such a measure would be sure to elicit opposition from the nobility, who already possess or stand to inherit larger properties.

When Harrington describes the manner in which Olphaus Megaletor, Archon and legislator of Oceana's commonwealth, propounds his new orders, the author has a young man of a noble family make a speech against the newly proposed agrarian law. The eldest of five brothers, Philautus faces the prospect that under the new law his expected inheritance of property worth 10,000 a year will be divided among his siblings so that each would possess the desired maximum, quite a significant reduction in Philautus's

---

[23] According to Harrington, what had determined England's future was the legislation promulgated during the reign of Henry VII, which undermined the feudal tenures. Henry had intended only to strengthen his own rule by weakening the power of the nobility, but his devices would have profound effects he had not foreseen: "[T]o establish his own safety he ... began to open those sluices that have since overwhelmed not the king only, but the throne." When the nobility lost its dependents, a formidable force was created; the people, who would not live "in a servile or indigent fashion," gained independence and land (54–5). This force, when compelled to act on its strength under Charles I, destroyed the remnants of the Gothic balance completely. Therefore, this shift in the ownership of land that began under the first Tudor king indicated to Harrington that England's future was republican rather than monarchical.

expectations. Harrington provides a comment on the young man's motivations for his opposition to the law by giving this character a name that means self-love in Greek. In his speech Philautus justifies himself by citing Aristotle's own opposition to an agrarian law in *The Politics*. Specifically, Philautus refers to Aristotle's discussion of the inadequacies of Phaleas of Chalcedon's proposal to remove factional conflict by leveling property. In offering an alternative to Phaleas's law, Aristotle prescribes labor and property for the necessary things for which people contend and "moderation" for the unnecessary.[24] For Aristotle, individual virtue is a prerequisite for political order.

Archon responds to Philautus that Aristotle is not "so good a commonwealthsman for deriding the invention of Phaleas" (106). Harrington's Archon speaks in direct opposition to Aristotle on this issue, and his response to the ancient ignores the virtue of moderation in dealing with the contention that arises over property. He can take this step and deride Aristotle on this issue because he finds the Aristotelian virtue of moderation superfluous. His republic operates without the moderation of the individuals who compose it. Moderation is imposed from without in the form of the republic's laws. He has devised an institutional means of assuring that the citizens of Oceana are mannerly at the public table.[25]

Despite Archon's explicit difference with Aristotle on the desirability of an agrarian law, he often suggests that, of all of his predecessors, Aristotle came closest to discovering the principle of the balance. In crediting Aristotle in this matter and attempting to draw an equivalence between them, Harrington actually helps to reveal the extent to which he diverges from Aristotle's thought. For instance, in *Oceana* when speaking of those who came closest to his understanding, he says "[y]ou have Aristotle full of it in divers places," and then attempts to corroborate this claim with a quotation from *The Politics*, in which he replaces Aristotle's formulation "greater in power" with his own "greater possessions" (14–15). Thus, Harrington gives the mistaken impression that Aristotle in this particular passage blames immoderate wealth for the change of regimes rather than immoderate power.[26]

In another of his works, *The Prerogative of Popular Government*, his method of transforming Aristotle's thought so as to corroborate his own is even more egregious. He notes there that if one replaces Aristotle's words "ἀρετή" and "δύναμις πολιτική" meaning virtue and political capacity, with the "words 'political balance', understood as I have stated the thing, it will give such a light unto the author as will go nearer... to deprive me of the honour of that invention." At this point, he proceeds to provide a passage

---

[24] Aristotle, *Politics* 2.7, especially 1267a2–10.
[25] Sullivan, "Civic Humanist Portrait," 85.
[26] Aristotle, *Politics* 5.3, 1302b15–20.

from Aristotle's *Politics*.[27] In it Aristotle discusses the possibility that one person or a number of persons in a city surpasses the virtue of the others,[28] but Harrington replaces the ancient's reference to virtue and to political capacity with references to the balance. So whereas in Aristotle's version a man is unequal in virtue, in Harrington's a man is unequal in his possession of property. In this way, he shows precisely the extent to which he would replace Aristotle's emphasis on virtue with his own on material considerations.[29]

Moreover, although in *Oceana* he retains Aristotle's distinction between good and deviant regimes, he changes the basis of the distinction. The deviant regimes – tyranny, oligarchy, and anarchy – are not those in which the ruler or rulers rule in their own interest, as in Aristotle's formulation,[30] but rulers who hold "the government not according unto the balance" and hence must use force to maintain their rule (12).[31] Again, Harrington replaces Aristotle's moral concerns with his own economic concerns.[32] So confident is he in the efficacy of the balance well maintained that he writes in another work that the "doctrine of the balance, not sufficiently discovered or heeded by ancient historians and politicians, is the cause why their writings are more dark, and their judgment less steady or clear, in the principles of government than otherwise they would have been."[33]

On the basis of these unique constitutional arrangements, he differentiates Oceana from all other regimes – "[s]o new a thing that neither ancient nor modern prudence can show any avowed example of the like" (65). It differs from ancient prudence largely by operating independently of its citizens' virtue. Surely, moderation is important to the regime, but individuals need not possess it, for it is imposed extrinsically.

On this understanding, his cryptic statement, discussed earlier, that he both follows the ancients and goes his own way, comes into clearer focus. "To go mine own way, and yet to follow the ancients, the principles of governments are twofold: internal, or the goods of the mind, and external, or the goods of fortune. The goods of the mind are natural or acquired virtues, as wisdom, prudence and courage, etc" (10). In his list of virtues, the ancient virtue of moderation is absent. Later Harrington broadens this list to include religion, but moderation is still missing (198). Surely, the members

---

[27] Harrington, *Prerogative of Popular Government*, 460–1.

[28] Aristotle, *Politics* 3.13, 1284a4–23.

[29] James Cotton cites this passage to show how Harrington borrowed from Aristotle. In doing so, he does not stop to consider how very far Harrington's changes in it drives him from Aristotle's thought ("James Harrington as Aristotelian," *Political Theory* 7 [1979]: 373).

[30] Aristotle, *Politics* 3.7, 1279a22–b10.

[31] See also Harrington, *The Rota*, in *Political Works*, 808.

[32] Pocock, *Machiavellian Moment*, 386–7; Rahe, "Antiquity Surpassed," 256–7. Raab and Worden make similar claims regarding Harrington's conception of corruption (Raab, *English Face of Machiavelli*, 208, and Worden, "Harrington and *Commonwealth of Oceana*," 100).

[33] Harrington, *A Note upon the Foregoing Eclogues*, in *Political Works*, 580.

of Oceana's senate require individual wisdom and prudence, and its soldiers courage, but none of its citizens needs possess moderation.[34] Harrington follows the ancients in praising virtue but differs from them in finding a way in which a regime can function without the virtue that Aristotle thought was critical both to the citizens' education and to a good regime: moderation.[35] Harrington certainly recognizes the degree to which the regime is independent of its citizenry's virtue, for after the orders of Oceana have been delineated, its founder proclaims: "[F]or as man is sinful, but yet the world is perfect, so may the citizen be sinful and yet the commonwealth be perfect" (218).[36] Harrington has, indeed, gone his own way, and found something not to be claimed by ancient prudence. As a result, Pocock's characterization of Harrington's republic as being "at the service of a fundamentally Aristotelian theory of citizenship" is untenable.[37]

Pocock, however, is not unaware of the manner in which individual virtue appears to be superfluous in Oceana. He explains that the "political individual depicted in Harrington's scheme is still the exponent of civic virtue presupposed – however skeptically – in all Florentine schemes of civic humanism, but we have already seen that Harrington emphasizes less the moral than the material bases of his personality."[38] Later he offers his

---

[34] Harrington indicates that he is aware of the significance of overlooking elements that others think are crucial when he refers to Machiavelli's conclusion that Livy dismisses the value of money in waging war because Livy does not list money among the necessary things (263; cf. Machiavelli, *Discourses* 2.10). Cotton too examines Harrington's treatment of Aristotle's discussion and concludes that Harrington puts more emphasis on "the importance of laws in the right ordering of the state" and less on training than does Aristotle, but he does not note this difference ("Harrington as Aristotelian," 374; cf. 377).

[35] Sullivan, "Civic Humanist Portrait," 85. In also disputing the view that Harrington was an Aristotelian, Rahe notes that nowhere does Harrington allude to the important Aristotelian claim, "which serves as the foundation for classical republicanism: that man is by nature a political animal endowed with a capacity for *lógos* enabling him to distinguish and make clear to others what is advantageous, just, and good" (*Republics Ancient and Modern*, 410). Rahe's perceptiveness in noting the absence of this claim in Harrington's thought must serve to challenge Pocock's explicit claim that Harrington's Englishman was a "*zōon politikon*" in the Aristotelian mold (Pocock, *Machiavellian Moment*, 386, and "Historical Introduction," 61).

[36] Wootton, "Republican Tradition," 15, and Remer, "Harrington's New Deliberative Rhetoric," 555–6.

[37] Pocock, "English Political Ideologies," 112.

[38] Pocock, *Machiavellian Moment*, 389. Pocock confirms the importance of these material bases when he says in the "Historical Introduction" that "the sole cause of corruption in government [is a] failure to adjust the distribution of power to property. Oceana having now a popular distribution of property, a popular government is the one thing necessary to ensure virtue in the people" (51). But he ultimately subordinates the material to citizenship. See, e.g., 55 and 61. In a more recent treatment of Harrington's thought, articulated in response to Scott's position that Oceana represents Harrington's abandonment of the participatory basis of citizenship, Pocock emphasizes the point that Harrington views the destruction of feudal tenures as "a motor of historical change" that will eventuate in a republic. Pocock

assurance that "Harrington is not unaware of that aspect...in which virtue appeared to have been mechanized and men fed into processes which made their behavior intelligent and disinterested whether they so intended it or not...but his dominant purpose is the release of personal virtue through civic participation."[39]

Harrington writes, though, of his dominant purpose. His purpose, as he states it, is to offer a perfect government, and his definition of perfection relates not to the release of personal virtue through civic participation but rather to the manner in which its citizens are constrained, and hence, its perpetuity secured: "[T]he perfection of government lieth upon such a libration in the frame of it, that no man or men, in or under it, can have the interest or, having the interest, can have the power to disturb it with sedition" (30–1).[40] Thus, Harrington presents Oceana as a model that aims at this mechanical perfection by so constricting the actions of its citizens. Release of any sort could be dangerous to its longevity and, hence, to its perfection.[41]

Machiavelli's Disciple

Not only does he declare himself to be partial to the ideas of Aristotle; Harrington loudly proclaims himself a follower of Machiavelli.[42] Harrington

then subordinates these material considerations not to citizenship, but to a "quasi-millennial *occasione* or *kairos*" (J. G. A. Pocock, "A Discourse of Sovereignty: Observations on the Works in Progress," in *Political Discourse in Early Modern Britain*, ed. Nicholas Phillipson and Quentin Skinner [Cambridge: Cambridge University Press, 1993], 403–4). Cf. Davis, "Pocock's Harrington," 687–94.

[39] Pocock, *Machiavellian Moment*, pp. 393–4. Cf. "Historical Introduction," where Pocock describes Harrington's commonwealth as "an association of virtues in which each must display the higher virtue of consenting to be balanced and limited by the others" (18).

[40] Scott, "Rapture of Motion," 147–8.

[41] The degree to which Harrington will countenance constraint on political actors is illustrated by an anecdote he relates elsewhere: "[A]t Rome I saw [a spectacle] which represented a kitchen, with all the proper utensils in use and action. The cooks were all cats and kitlings, set in such frames, so tied and so ordered, that the poor creatures could make no motion to get loose, but the same caused one to turn the spit, another to baste the meat, a third to skim the pot and a fourth to make green sauce." Harrington draws the following political lesson from this sight: "If the frame of your commonwealth be not such as causeth everyone to perform his certain function as necessarily as this did the cat to make green sauce, it is not right" (*A Discourse upon This Saying...*, in *Political Works*, 744). See Davis, "Pocock's Harrington," 696–7; Rahe, *Republics Ancient and Modern*, 412; Scott, "Rapture of Motion," 159–60; Sullivan, "Civic Humanist Portrait," 79–80.

[42] Worden deems Harrington "the most distinguished thinker of English Machiavellianism" ("Classical Republicanism and the Puritan Revolution," in *History and Imagination: Essays in Honor of H. R. Trevor-Roper*, ed. Hugh Lloyd-Jones, Valerie Pearl, and Blair Worden [New York: Holmes & Meier, 1981], 184). Here Worden defines Machiavellianism as follows: "Pointing back to Polybius, Machiavellianism propounded the cyclical view of history and examined the problem of the balanced constitution. Pointing back to Tacitus, it explored the techniques, and revelled in the fascination, of power" (183).

admires the Florentine as "the sole retriever of . . . ancient prudence" among the moderns and praises him as the "learned disciple" of the ancients (30 and 10). Because Harrington links ancient prudence to republican politics, he appears to align Machiavelli with the ancients on the basis of Machiavelli's advocacy of republicanism. Thus, as the only politician of the modern age, Machiavelli undertook to restore republicanism to its former glory after the fall of the Roman Empire and the invasions of the "Vandals, Huns, Lombards, Franks, [and] Saxons," who carried modern prudence – or what Harrington calls the "Gothic balance" with its kings and nobility – into the former lands of the Romans (46–7).

On some issues, Harrington surely is a follower of Machiavelli. But just as he is less an adherent of Aristotle than some of his proclamations in *Oceana* could lead one to believe, so upon examination he is less Machiavelli's disciple than an initial perusal of his own proclamations would suggest. What leads him to diverge from Machiavelli is precisely what induces his break from Aristotle: his belief that he alone has discovered the principles of a republic so resilient that it is perfect.

That said, however, on the issues on which he follows Machiavelli, he is very much an English Machiavellian. Indeed, unlike Nedham, who, as we have seen, refuses opportunities to follow Machiavelli's logic on such topics as the necessity of a lawgiver to have sole power and of a republic for increase, Harrington on these issues clings closely to the trail blazed by the Florentine. For instance, it turns out that in the story Harrington tells of the founding of Oceana, the writings of Machiavelli inspired Harrington's founder. Archon, growing disenchanted with the proceedings of the parliament that then ruled the land, turned to books for "diversion." He then happened upon Machiavelli's statement from the *Discourses*: "Thrice happy is that people which chances to have a man able to give them such a government at once, as without alteration may secure them of their liberties; seeing it is certain that Lacedaemon, in observing the laws of Lycurgus, continued about eight hundred years without any dangerous tumult or corruption" (66).[43] The glory that Lycurgus won as Sparta's legislator so agitated Archon that taking "so new and deep impression at these words of the much greater glory of Lycurgus that, being on this side assaulted with the emulation of his illustrious object, on the other with the misery of the nation . . . he was almost wholly deprived of his natural rest, until the debate he had within himself came to a firm resolution: that the greatest advantages of a commonwealth are, first, that the legislator should be one man, and secondly that the government should be made altogether, or at once" (66–7).[44]

---

[43] Harrington is quoting from Machiavelli, *Discourses* 1.2.1.

[44] Although Archon's desire for glory is certainly Machiavellian, his desire to imitate Lycurgus is less so. Machiavelli prefers Rome, whose institutions did not owe their origin to a single individual, to Lycurgus's Sparta.

In further explicating Archon's resolution to undertake by himself Oceana's reorganization, Harrington has recourse to another passage from Machiavelli's *Discourses*:

[I]t is certain, saith Machiavel, that a commonwealth is seldom or never well turned or constituted, except it have been the work of one man; for which cause a wise legislator, and one whose mind is firmly set not upon private but the public interest, not upon his posterity but upon his country, may justly endeavor to get the sovereign power into his own hands, nor shall any man that is master of reason blame such extraordinary means as in that case shall be necessary, the end proving no other than the constitution of a well-ordered commonwealth. The reason of this is demonstrable; for the ordinary means not failing, the commonwealth hath no need of a legislator, but the ordinary means failing, there is no recourse to be had but to such as are extraordinary. (67)

He has here paraphrased the very passage that Nedham had used in an expurgated form in both his *Case of the Commonwealth of England* and *Excellencie of a Free State*. In using this passage from *Discourses* 1.9, Nedham accepts the legislator's lack of concern with his succession as well as his dedication to his country, but makes reference neither to the necessity of being alone nor to that of taking extraordinary measures.[45]

In contrast, Harrington refuses to recoil from either facet of Machiavelli's thought that Nedham finds unworthy of citation. Harrington on these issues is very much a Machiavellian. He not only accepts but lauds the possibility that a single man will undertake to found a republic with a view to the greater glory of having founded a long-lived republic capable of vast enterprises. Although he does not revel in the crimes of Machiavelli's exemplar Romulus,[46] as does Machiavelli himself, Harrington is nevertheless willing to transmit the lesson that Machiavelli imparts through the example of Rome's founder: extraordinary times call for extraordinary actions, which will be forgiven after the founding. Of course, Harrington's use of this passage is an ill-disguised appeal to Cromwell to win by the same benevolent means the glory he awards his fictional Archon. Nevertheless, in making this appeal, he shows that he accepts Machiavelli's view. If the deed of founding a republic were to win them the glory of a Lycurgus, great men may be willing to forgo the benefit to their progeny that attends their establishment of a hereditary monarchy. In this manner, their republic would satisfy their own

---

[45] In the context of a discussion of Archon's decision to follow Machiavelli's injunction and to become founder of a commonwealth, Worden cites Nedham's use of the same passage in Machiavelli but does not note the significant changes Nedham makes when he "quoted" Machiavelli's "'noble saying'" (Worden, "*Oceana*: Origins and Aftermath," 120).

[46] Elsewhere he condemns Romulus's killing of Remus (*A System of Politics*, in *Political Works*, 853).

desire for glory and would benefit a great many others in addition. A republic ultimately rests on the profound passions of a great and solitary man.[47]

In addition to this Machiavellian element of his thought, Harrington accepts and adopts for his own use Machiavelli's distinction between republics for preservation and those for increase (e.g., 7, 217, 221).[48] Those for preservation, such as Sparta, are restrained by their orders from acquiring an empire. Harrington's Archon says of Sparta that, it "being made altogether for war and yet not for increase, her natural progress became her natural dissolution, and the building of her own victorious hand too heavy for her foundation; so she indeed fell by her own weight" (218–19). Those such as Rome and the new Oceana are constructed precisely to be able to acquire an empire and, thus, are not susceptible to Sparta's vulnerabilities. In this way, Harrington embraces Machiavelli's teaching in *Discourses* 1.6 that a state should be equipped not only to fight wars but to handle the acquisitions that accrue from them.

In so doing, Harrington follows Machiavelli's injunction to arm the people. With a nod to Machiavelli and a quotation from *Discourses* 1.6, Archon speaks of Venice's defect in failing both to allow the people to participate in governing and to arm them, warning that "[i]f you lay your commonwealth upon any other foundation than the people, you frustrate yourself of proper arms and so lose the empire of the world" (232). He provides against this eventuality by having most of the nation's young men eligible for participation in the nation's army (191–4). Those of the lower property classification will be the "foot" and those of the higher the "horse."

The militaristic character of his republic is evident in the fact that when the people vote for their various local and national officials, they participate in military dress and formation (90, 95, 97–8). In addition, he arrays the people's assembly in military discipline so that it resembles "a very noble regiment, or rather . . . two," consisting of the horse and foot (147). It is a militaristic republic built for increase.

Harrington makes no secret of his plans for his republic. The second paragraph of his introduction to *Oceana* states baldly that Oceana "is the most martial [country] in the whole world" (3). Later, his Archon brags that the people of Oceana have "shoulders [that] so universally and so exactly fit the corselet" (136). Finally, at the close of the work, he reveals in more

---

[47] Cf. Worden, "*Oceana*: Origins and Aftermath," 120.

[48] The distinction between the two types of republics is introduced in Machiavelli, *Discourses* 1.5.3: "In the end, he who subtly examines the whole will draw this conclusion from it: you are reasoning either about a republic that wishes to make an empire, such as Rome, or about one for whom it is enough to maintain itself. In the first case, it is necessary for it to do everything as did Rome; in the second, it can imitate Venice and Sparta, for the causes that will be told in the following chapter." Archon furnishes at 155–7 a long quotation from *Discourses* 1.6 that includes portions of 1.5.

detail his plans for his republic when his Archon explains that the orders of Oceana

are buds of empire, such as, with the blessing of God, may spread the arms of your commonwealth like an holy asylum unto the distressed world, and give the earth her sabbath of years or rest from her labours, under the shadow of your wings. It is upon this point where the writings of Machiavel, having for the rest excelled all other authors, come as far to excel themselves. (221)

Machiavelli, according to Harrington's Archon, is at his best when he writes of republics and their empires. Oceana will be the best of all previously known republics because its empire will span the oceans. Harrington has no less an aspiration for his envisioned republic than the "empire of the world" (228).[49]

Machiavelli's Opponent

Although Harrington manifestly follows Machiavelli's baldly aggressive republicanism, it is on the issue of how an acquisitive and long-lived republic can and should be organized that Harrington splits from Machiavelli. For all of his praise of Machiavelli, Harrington is also quite outspoken regarding this, his fundamental disagreement with him. Indeed, as a result of this disagreement, Archon announces both that he actually "erect[s] a commonwealth against the judgment of Machiavel" (155) and that Machiavelli, who is "the greatest artist in the modern world[,] giv[es] sentence against our commonwealth" (157).[50] The crux of the dispute derives from Machiavelli's claims in *Discourses* 1.6, the chapter in which the Florentine makes use of the distinction between republics for increase and those for preservation

[49] Archon assures his audience in one of his speeches that his commonwealth is capable of digesting the "whole earth" (220). Later in the same speech, he says that as Rome "held the empire of the world," so Oceana's organization is "intended to be capable at the least of the like" (227). Archon, though, characterizes such acquisition as the imposition of justice on the world (220–1). Oceana, it seems, will take on the responsibility of establishing republics in its conquests that are capable of them (229, 232). "[T]o ask whether it be lawful for a commonwealth to aspire unto the empire of the world is to ask whether it be lawful for her to do her duty, or to put the world into a better condition than it was before" (227). In *The Art of Lawgiving*, however, Harrington admits that arms are necessary to hold a province, and that even a republic may oppress its possessions: "[T]he possibility in a commonwealth of tyrannising over provinces is not to be cured; for be the commonwealth, or the prince, a state or a man after God's own heart, there is no way of holding a province but by arms" (*Political Works*, 691).

[50] Fink claims that Harrington "had no praises too high" for Machiavelli (*Classical Republicans*, 53) and fails to note any of Harrington's significant disputes with the Italian. Similarly, Zagorin describes Harrington's respect for Machiavelli as "unbounded" (*Political Thought in English Revolution*, 134). Raab, in contrast, is interested in finding the cause for Harrington's criticisms of Machiavelli and provides a quick survey of some of them (*English Face of Machiavelli*, 189–92).

in order to endorse those for increase. Although enthusiastically accepting Machiavelli's claim for the desirability of republics for increase and demand that such republics arm the people, Harrington repudiates Machiavelli's additional claim that, in so arming the people, a republic must accept as inevitable the resultant tumults. Archon founds a republic against Machiavelli's judgment because Oceana will not display any enmity between the many and the few, the people and the nobles, a feature so prominent in the Roman republic that Machiavelli endorses.[51]

Although Harrington, like Machiavelli, admires Rome for its acquisitions, he strongly disapproves of its tumults. According to Harrington's analysis, the greed of Rome's nobility caused the tumults, which, in turn, caused the republic's downfall: "[T]he nobility had almost eaten the people quite out of their lands...; whereupon the remedy being too late and too vehemently applied, that commonwealth was ruined" (37). He also blames, though, the feature of the Roman constitution that allowed the people such a large role in legislation. "Rome consisted of the senate proposing, the *concio* or people resolving and too often debating, which caused her storms" (29).[52] Harrington acknowledges, however, that the people fought for and needed that power of debate because the nobles were so ravenously imperious that they constantly attempted to deny the people even their power of resolving, which, in fact, they ultimately accomplished, according to Harrington's Archon (150–5, 139). Too greedy for property and power, the members of Rome's nobility were, according to Archon, "a distinct belly, such an one as took the meat indeed out of the people's mouths but, abhorring the agrarian, returning it not in the due and necessary nutrition of a commonwealth" (160–1).

According to Harrington, in embracing Rome's internal confusion and asserting that its tumults are the necessary price of empire, Machiavelli missed the balance. The nobility, a term that in Harrington's lexicon also includes the gentry (137), must be and, in fact, can be restrained by the constitution. "Machiavel hath missed it very narrowly and . . . dangerously; for not fully perceiving that if a commonwealth be galled by the gentry, it is by their overbalance" (15). Thus, Rome was tumultuous not because it was a commonwealth for increase, but rather because it was an unequal commonwealth (159).[53]

---

[51] Mansfield, *Taming the Prince*, 183–4, for Harrington's important divergences from Machiavelli, particularly with respect to the executive power in a republic.

[52] Archon declares: "[W]here there is a liquorishness in a popular assembly to debate, it proceedeth not from the constitution of the people, but of the commonwealth" (163).

[53] Arihiro Fukuda offers a different interpretation of this passage. The difference, I believe, grows out of our differing understandings of the role of the nobility in Machiavelli's thought. Fukuda suggests that Machiavelli's attitude toward "the political role of the nobility" can be expressed as "hostility" (*Sovereignty and the Sword: Harrington, Hobbes, and Mixed Government in the English Civil Wars* [Oxford: Clarendon Press, 1997], 16).

At points, Harrington concedes that Machiavelli articulated the problem to which he alone has been able to provide an answer. Archon nods thus to the Florentine before proceeding to furnish the solution: "There is not a more noble or useful question in the politics than that which is started by Machiavel: whether means were to be found whereby the enmity that was between the senate and the people of Rome might have been removed" (155).[54] Similarly, Harrington, both in his own name and in Archon's, uses passages from *Discourses* 1.55 to show how close Machiavelli came to the solution, while in actuality only apprehending the problem (15 and 137–8). In that chapter Machiavelli claims that anyone who attempts to establish in modern times a commonwealth where numerous gentlemen reside, who "live idly in abundance from the returns of their possessions without having any care either for cultivation or for other necessary trouble in living," will have to destroy them before his republican enterprise can be successful.[55] Although the balance was unseen by Machiavelli, this comment serves to confirm a portion of Harrington's own understanding. Of course, a republic cannot be established in such conditions. Such gentleman possess an overbalance that is so inimical to republics. It is unnecessary, though, to exterminate all gentlemen in order to maintain a republic, as Machiavelli suggests. What is required instead at the institution of a republic is precisely what Rome lacked – a strictly enforced "agrarian" and a "rotation" that guarantees the people the right to "resolve," to use Harrington's terms. If such a balance exists, then "a nobility or gentry in a popular government, not overbalancing it, is the very life and soul of it" (15). As a result of Harrington's discovery, Oceana, like Rome, will be a commonwealth for increase; but unlike Rome, it will be an equal, and hence a tranquil, commonwealth.[56]

Harrington portrays Machiavelli as examining closely the phenomenon of Rome, but failing to descry the real reason before his eyes for the contention between the patricians and plebeians (161). This is not quite an accurate depiction of Machiavelli's relation to that republic. It is not that Machiavelli

---

[54] Thus, according to the founder of Harrington's republic, Machiavelli's contribution to politics is his investigation of how the interests of the classes should be ordered. See John A. Wettergreen, "Note on the Intention of James Harrington's Political Art," *Interpretation* 2 (1971): 75–6. Wettergreen here contrasts Machiavelli's class analysis with the regime analysis. Although Pocock does not treat the Polybian classification of regimes and theory of the mixed regime to the extent that Fink does, Pocock does link Harrington to Polybius. See Pocock, *Machiavellian Moment*, 387; cf. 365. For a criticism of the use of the theory of mixed government as a means of grounding the antiquity of the thought of Machiavelli and Harrington, see Toth, "Case of Harrington," 323–31. See also Jesse R. Goodale, "J. G. A. Pocock's Neo-Harringtonians: A Reconsideration," *History of Political Thought* 1 (1980): 239–40.

[55] Machiavelli, *Discourses* 1.55.4.

[56] Sullivan, "Civic Humanist Portrait," 80–1. Scott mentions in passing Harrington's divergences from Machiavelli, but Scott's Machiavelli is a civic humanist ("Rapture of Motion," 158).

failed to see something that he would have accepted had he noticed it, for it is far from clear that Machiavelli would have accepted the eradication of Rome's tumults were such a thing possible. Machiavelli depicts the contention in Rome as desirable. Indeed, he claims that this very strife maintained Rome's liberty and asserts further that "if Rome wished to remove the causes of tumults, it removed too the causes of expansion."[57] Unlike Harrington, he celebrated the passions – both for property and power – that motivated it. As those passions roiled Rome, so they animated the glorious deeds of its martial men who won its enormous acquisitions.

Harrington and Machiavelli thus possess widely divergent views of the passions. In condoning the tumults, Machiavelli condones the resolute attachment to one's own that necessitates further acquisition, whether the desired goods are property or honor.[58] As for honor and glory specifically, he appears to wish to encourage his contemporaries to hunger for earthly rewards rather than heavenly ones.[59] Moreover, he much prefers the nobility of pagan times, whose desires helped propel Rome's territorial expansion, to the complacent gentlemen of his time whom he excoriates for doing nothing useful for life in 1.55 of the *Discourses*.

By contrast, Harrington condemns Rome's nobility and attempts to restrain the appetites of this class in his republic. As we have seen, he blames the Roman patricians for being too greedy for property. In addition, he criticizes the noble young man of Oceana who opposes his agrarian law by furnishing him with the name that translates into English as "self-love." Further, Archon makes the general statement that "the aristocracy is ravenous, and not the people" (180). Not only does he endeavor to curb its appetite for property, however, but also its appetite for glory. His rotation in magistracies and required vacations are meant to circumscribe the ability of ambitious individuals to gain preeminence. No single man will be able to rule alone for any period of time; even the office of dictator is to be occupied by a committee rather than by a single man. Moreover, he criticizes Machiavelli's expression of admiration for the Roman practice of distributing offices without respect to age.[60] According to Harrington, so dangerous was this practice that it was "no small step unto the ruin of the Roman liberty" because, "having tasted in their youth of the supreme honours, [they] had no greater in their age to hope for, but by perpetuating of the same in themselves, which came to blood, and ended in tyranny" (206). In this way, Harrington endeavors to close every possible entry for ambition in his commonwealth.[61]

---

[57] *Discourses* 1.6.3. See also 1.4.

[58] One does not feel secure in one's possessions "unless he acquires something else new" (ibid., 1.5.4).

[59] Ibid., 2.2.2.

[60] Ibid., 1.60.

[61] Sullivan, "Civic Humanist Portrait," 84.

Even Archon's ambition will not be an example fit for emulation. After completing the founding, he "abdicated the magistracy of Archon" so that "no manner of food might be left unto ambition" (245). Seeking to retire, Archon is called back again to rule as a precaution against the unsettled character of the nation. When Oceana's citizens offer him the extension of his rule, Harrington assures his readers that "the minds of men were firm in the opinion that he could be no seeker of himself in the way of earthly pomp and glory" (255). The citizens' understanding of Archon's motivation surely contradicts Harrington's depiction of the inspiration that led to Archon's undertaking of the legislation for Oceana.[62] Whereas his readers know better, having before them Harrington's own description of Archon's motivation, the citizens of Oceana, by contrast, believe that their founder was devoid of any desire for glory. As a result, his will be no model for ambitious members of future generations of Oceaners to follow in attempting to win preeminence.[63]

Thus, having armed his republic against the possibility of overweening ambition in its citizens, having discovered the fundamental political principle of the balance, and having armed his republic with the agrarian and rotation, he believes that he has constructed the perfect commonwealth – indeed, a commonwealth that is fitted to survive into eternity. On the issue of the eternal character of his republic, Harrington draws a stark distinction between his orders and those of Machiavelli. First, he has Archon unabashedly declare: "Look well unto it, my lords, for if there be a contradiction or inequality in your commonwealth, it must fall; but if it have neither of these, it hath no principle of mortality. Do not think me impudent; if this be truth, I should commit a gross indiscretion in concealing it." Then, he has Archon unabashedly challenge Machiavelli:

Sure I am that Machiavel is for the immortality of a commonwealth upon far weaker principles. "If a commonwealth," saith he, "were so happy as to be provided often with men that, when she is swerving from her principles, should reduce her unto her institution, she would be immortal." But a commonwealth, as we have demonstrated, swerveth not from her principles, but by and through her institution; if she brought no bias into the world with her, her course for any internal cause must be straight forward. (219)

Harrington has found another critical aspect in which he has surpassed Machiavelli.

---

[62] See the earlier section "Machiavelli's Disciple."

[63] Rahe detects the "element of subterfuge evident in Harrington's account of the Lord Archon's comportment" (*Republics Ancient and Modern*, 417). Worden, however, finds "[t]he joke" here not in the comparison between Archon's real motives and the perception of Oceana's citizens, but rather between Archon's motives and those of Cromwell ("*Oceana*: Origins and Aftermath," 121).

Archon is referring here to *Discourses* 3.22, where Machiavelli claims that if a republic were lucky enough to have an endless supply of men akin in character to Manlius, it would "be perpetual." To Machiavelli's thinking, such men, because of their severity, issue harsh commands and are, thus, incapable of accumulating the partisans so characteristic of a demagogue. Further, the example such men set would "not only restrain [the republic] from running to ruin but pull it back" toward its origin.[64] In speaking of a return to the republic's first principles, Machiavelli is himself referring to *Discourses* 3.1, where he discusses the necessity of such a return for a republic's longevity.

Machiavelli sees ambition as rampant in a successful republic. Of course, it is a dangerous thing, but it is also a necessary thing. Moreover, the young men who strain at sole rule present a danger to the continued existence of the republic, but their execution at the hands of a stern Manlius reinvigorates its orders by inducing fear in others. Thus, Machiavelli allows more scope for the ambitious to act on their desires, relying ultimately on fear to contain those who would threaten the life of his republic. Ambition cannot be superseded in Machiavelli's republic; it furnishes its very energy.

Of course, that is not the case in Harrington's *Oceana*, because he believes that he can at once use the nobility's passions on the battlefield but contain them completely in domestic politics. Having found perfection at its beginning, *Oceana* will not require recourse to the unpredictable and unsavory expedients Machiavelli recommends. This new understanding of ambition, however, allows us to come to grips with Harrington's peculiar treatment of ambition with respect to *Oceana*'s founder. On the one hand, Archon's desire to surpass the glory of Lycurgus drove him to found *Oceana*. In portraying Archon's pursuit of this magnificent enterprise, Harrington graciously nods to Machiavelli, going so far as to state that Machiavelli's writings inspired his legislator. On the other, such an ambitious individual as Archon founds a republic devoid of ambition for sole rule.[65] Such is the case because, given the character of Harrington's republic, an individual who possesses the magnitude of Archon's ambition is needed only once. Thus, once founded, his republic need not – indeed, should not – foster the greatest type of ambition, as does Machiavelli's. Archon is, quite simply, one of a kind. So as not to provoke others in *Oceana* to emulate Archon's glory, after the founding, official pronouncements never mention his desire for glory but only his selfless dedication to the good of his homeland (66; cf. 255). In

---

[64] Machiavelli, *Discourses* 3.22.3. Cf. Zagorin, *Political Thought in English Revolution*, 135 and n. 4, who overlooks this chapter in claiming that, unlike Harrington, Machiavelli "never entertained such a hope." See the discussion of these issues in Chapter 1.

[65] Davis too notes this "dilemma," but links it neither to Harrington's use of Machiavelli on the topic of the glory of founders nor to his ultimate departure from Machiavelli on the issue of a perpetual republic ("James Harrington's Republicanism," 229).

believing he has superseded ambition, Harrington believes he has superseded Machiavelli.

Harrington's Relation to Hobbes

In so disagreeing with Machiavelli on the issue of ambition, Harrington actually draws closer to Hobbes with whom he shares a fear of the grave consequences to a regime of such ambition.[66] Any rapprochement between Harrington and Hobbes on any issue is quite ironic given Harrington's strident denunciations of "Leviathan" in *Oceana*.[67] Whereas Harrington praises Machiavelli as the "only politician that hath gone about to retrieve" ancient prudence, he denounces Leviathan's attempt to destroy it (9). Clearly, Harrington disagrees with Hobbes's support of monarchical government. Nevertheless, given the effort he makes to praise so effusively Aristotle and Machiavelli, whom he believes he has surpassed, it seems fitting that he should embrace some important ideas of the thinker he so openly denounces.[68]

On the issue of ambition, Harrington is in hearty agreement with Hobbes's assessment of the problem but not with his judgment that a republican form of government will necessarily be wracked by the upheavals that that passion can engender. There are certainly additional points of correspondence between the thinkers who appear so different on the surface. Harrington is quite close to Hobbes's assessment of the relation between human passion and reason. For both Harrington and Hobbes, reason is in the service of the passions and does not have an independent status such that it can be counted on to guide the behavior of human beings.[69]

[66] Rahe, *Republics Ancient and Modern*, 414–18.

[67] Fukuda argues that in some ways Harrington should be understood as having learned from Hobbes – indeed, as being his "admirer" and "disciple." The subjects in which Fukuda finds this agreement are different, however, from those I outline later. See, for example, the discussion of fear and necessity (*Sovereignty and the Sword*, 4, 75–82).

[68] Others scholars have noted Harrington's deep debt to Hobbes's presentation of human nature: Gunn, *Politics and Public Interest*, 109–13, 129–30; Rahe, *Republics Ancient and Modern*, 410–26; Remer, "Harrington's New Deliberative Rhetoric," 548–55; John A. Wettergreen, "James Harrington's Liberal Republicanism," *Polity* 20 (1988): 679–82; Worden, "Harrington and *Commonwealth of Oceana*," 91. Scott emphasizes their similarity in their mutual desire for stability and argues that Harrington accepts Hobbes's metaphysics (Scott, "Rapture of Motion," 149, 151, 154–63). Earlier, Raab (*English Face of Machiavelli*, 196–8) and Zagorin (*Political Thought in English Revolution*, 134) had equated the two thinkers on their mutual desire for certainty in politics. Cf. James Cotton, "James Harrington and Thomas Hobbes," *Journal of the History of Ideas* 42 (1981): 407–21, who disputes Raab's characterization.

[69] Rahe, *Republics Ancient and Modern*, 411–12; Remer, "Harrington's New Deliberative Rhetoric," 553–5.

Despite these similarities, however, Harrington is not a strict Hobbesian. Harrington's support for a republic, no matter how it constrains and ritualizes the citizens' participation, produces important differences from Hobbes. Both from his people and nobles Harrington still demands a significant degree of dedication to his martial state in a manner completely foreign to Hobbes's monarchical system. Hobbes wishes to proscribe people from the realm of politics in order to foster peace.

As we know, Hobbes's very purpose is to furnish security and peace, and in service to that end he wishes to overcome the pride that can produce contention among individuals and war among nations. The very basis of Hobbes's politics challenges the pride that is nurtured by a belief in fundamental differences among human beings. Those who possess the ambition to distinguish themselves as superior are those who disturb the peace.

Hobbes and Harrington, then, both recognize the degree to which ambition can disturb a government to the extent that it threatens the civil peace.[70] On this basis, the two Englishmen join in turning away from Machiavelli's keen appreciation of those who strive above all for honor and glory. Nevertheless, they offer very different solutions to the problem of ambition. Harrington believes that his agrarian law, ballot, rotation, and division between debate and resolution can so tame the nobility that his republican government can be serene. Hobbes, of course, has a very different solution. In his monarchy, the private sphere entirely eclipses the public. The monarch and his or her advisers engage in politics, whereas the remainder of the nation is to tend to its own private affairs. He, thus, turns away from politics altogether in order both to quash those passions – the desire for glory and preeminence – that lead men astray toward war and civil war and to foster other passions that incline human beings to peace, namely "Feare of Death; Desire of such things as are necessary to commodious living; and a Hope by their Industry to obtain them."[71] Hobbes's desire for peace leads him away not only from the aristocratic ethic that favors honor above all but from politics itself. He instead embraces a teaching that promotes security and material comfort for individuals.

Harrington, however, cannot accept the elimination of the political because he constructs a republic for increase. The republican part of the equation requires, in particular, the desirable qualities that Harrington finds among his newly restrained nobility, and the imperial part requires a martial ethic that necessitates the continual intrusion of the public into the private sphere when citizens are called upon to bear arms for their country.[72]

---

[70] Rahe, *Republics Ancient and Modern*, 414 and 416–17.

[71] Hobbes, *Leviathan*, 90.

[72] Ultimately, I differ with Rahe's depiction of Harrington with respect to the degree to which he equates Harrington with Bacon and Hobbes in attempting to "channel" "energy away from the political arena into what [*Oceana*'s] author calls 'industry'" (*Republics Ancient and*

Moreover, in treating the nobility of Oceana, Harrington rejects Hobbes's notion of equality. Its members are, according to Harrington, simply superior to the others in the commonwealth and, on the basis of their inborn and acquired characteristics, more fit to rule. Indeed, rejecting Hobbes's rejection of the notion of ruling types by nature, Harrington insists that "a third" of men will be "wiser, or at least less foolish, than all the rest." This third composes "a natural aristocracy diffused by God throughout the whole body of mankind to this end and purpose [to guide the rest], and therefore such as the people have not only a natural but a positive obligation to make use of as their guides." These men are more fit to rule in a senate where the debate and the dividing occurs (23).

As members of the natural aristocracy, they owe their superior position not to "hereditary right" or to "the greatness of their estates only" but to their inherent intellectual superiority (23). Nevertheless, their property is important to the nurturing of their ruling qualities. Having imposed a minimum amount of property that members of the horse, the class eligible for election to the senate, must possess, Harrington attempts to guarantee that they have the leisure necessary to devote themselves to the study of political things and hence to become competent senators. In speaking of the nobles, Archon declares: "Ours of Oceana have nothing else but their education and their leisure for the public, furnished by their ease and competent riches, and their intrinsic value which, according as it comes to hold weight in the judgment or suffrage of the people, is their only way unto honour and preferment" (141). In lacking the financial resources of the nobility, the people of Oceana would not be free to engage in the work of the senate even if they were similarly wise: "Your mechanics, till they have first

Modern, 418). Rahe is quite right in discerning that "Harrington's distrust of man's love of preeminence" prevents Oceana from being "a repository of memory" (417) in which citizens' heroics are recounted. But neither is it a republic in which industriousness in the private realm is highlighted. Not commerce and trade, but Harrington's armies, his musters, and his idiosyncratically militaristic assemblies dominate *Oceana*. This view is confirmed in *Prerogative of Popular Government*, when Harrington explains that Oceana's "agrarian maketh a commonwealth for increase: the trade of a commonwealth for increase is arms; arms are not born by merchants, but by noblemen and gentlemen. The nobility therefore having these arms in their hands by which provinces are to be acquired, new provinces yield new estates" (*Political Works*, 471). Remer makes a parallel point when, through his examination of debate in Oceana, he concludes that although Harrington does not use a classical model of rhetoric, he does not dispense entirely with political rhetoric in the manner that Rahe claims. In this way, Remer, as do I, understands Harrington as still promoting the political realm – although one very different from the classical conception (Remer, "Harrington's New Deliberative Rhetoric," 542, 544–5). Pincus characterizes Harrington as a "classical republican" who "wanted to resurrect" "an agrarian and non-capitalist" "past" ("Commercial Society and Defenders of the English Commonwealth," 711–12). Although I concur with Pincus's characterization of Harrington's economics, his politics, as I argue, fails to qualify him as a classical thinker.

feathered their nests – like the fowls of the air, whose whole employment is to seek their food – are so busied in their private concernments that they have neither leisure to study the public, nor are safely to be trusted with it" (138).[73]

Its laudable natural and acquired endowments aside, the nobility, of course, is not to be trusted to ignore its own private interests and rule in the name of the common good without constraint. The mechanic people may be driven by self-interest to feather their nests, but in Harrington's view, as we have seen, the nobility wants so much more and will take it at the expense of the people: "[T]he aristocracy is ravenous, and not the people" (180). It cannot be so trusted because Harrington accepts Hobbes's understanding of the relation between reason and the passions. Hobbes writes that reason is subservient to the passions,[74] and Harrington concurs. In *Oceana*, for example, he quotes Hobbes without naming his source: "[A]s often as reason is against a man, so often will a man be against reason" (21).[75] Elsewhere, he is more forthcoming about his debt to Hobbes. He opposed "the politics of Mr Hobbes," he says, "to show him what he taught me," and as for his "treatises of human nature, and of liberty and necessity, they are the greatest of new lights, and those which I have followed and shall follow." Hobbes "is, and will in future ages be accounted, the best writer at this day in the world."[76]

Reason cannot, then, be counted on to guide Harrington's nobility; what is needed instead is external constraint. As we have seen, though, Harrington provides that constraint by having the people resolve on the resolutions of the senate, thus imposing moderation extrinsically. As a result of this mechanism, Harrington can claim that "the nobility, not over-balancing in dominion, is not dangerous but of necessary use in every commonwealth, provided that it be rightly ordered" (141).

Therefore, although the members of the senate are constrained – they are constrained to propose only what the people will accept – they are still a political body. As we have seen, Harrington expects them, as a result of

---

73 Pincus, "Commercial Society and Defenders of the English Commonwealth," 715–16, 728.

74 "For the Thoughts, are to the Desires, as Scouts, and Spies, to range abroad, and find the way to the things Desired" (Hobbes, *Leviathan*, 53). See Chapter 2.

75 Harrington quotes this passage from the Epistle Dedicatory of *The Elements of Law*, 19. Pocock says this statement has "a Hobbesian flavour," but does not provide the source (21, n. 20). For the relation between Hobbes and Harrington on this issue, see particularly Rahe, *Republics Ancient and Modern*, 411 and n. 69.

76 Harrington, *Prerogative of Popular Government* 1.7, in *Political Works*, 423. See also Matthew Wren, Harrington's critic and chosen opponent in the first book of *The Prerogative of Popular Government*, who asserts that Harrington "holds a correspondence with [Hobbes], and does silently swallow down such Notions as Mr. *Hobs* hath chewed for him" (*Consideration on Mr. Harrington's Common-wealth of Oceana: Restrained to the First Part of the Preliminaries* [London: Printed for Samuel Gellibrand, 1657], 41).

their leisure, to devote themselves to political activities.[77] Whereas Hobbes attempts to expunge aristocratic pride, one can easily see that Oceana's nobility, although not as oppressive as Rome's, will be prideful on the basis of its abilities, attainments, and status.

Similarly, members of both classes are to serve in the militia, and this must be viewed as an intrusion of the public into the private lives of individuals. Each year eligible men between the ages of eighteen and thirty have a one-in-five chance of serving in Oceana's army. It is ignoble to refuse this military service except for legitimate causes.[78] Indeed, those who refuse service without legitimate reason will be "deemed an helot or public servant" (195). Hobbes, by contrast, constructs a much larger private realm than does Harrington and is far from aghast regarding the "naturall timorousnesse" that induces men either to preserve their lives by fleeing the battlefield or to find substitutes to fill their places in the military rolls.[79]

Harrington's republic, then, intrudes on the private lives of individuals. As constricted as its republican life is, it still offers a public space. Although, as we have seen, he dispenses with the need for moderation in the individuals who compose his republic, he quite consciously retains the virtues of courage, as embodied in its soldiers, and of wisdom, as evinced by its senators: "[T]his commonwealth, being constituted more especially of two elements, arms and councils, driveth by a natural instinct at courage and wisdom" (205). Indeed, to nurture these virtues, Harrington introduces public education, which will be free for those who cannot afford to pay for it, and makes it a requirement for fathers who have more than one son to send their sons to this public school (191). Again, the contrast with Hobbes is instructive. In constructing a region around the individual in which sovereigns usually do not make laws, Hobbes identifies the ability "to institute their children as they themselves think fit."[80] Harrington's republic requires more dedication from its citizens than does Hobbes's state.

Nedham's and Harrington's Use of Hobbes and Machiavelli Compared

Despite important convergences between Hobbes and Harrington, then, the rapprochement is not perfect. The importance of their divergences is illustrated by means of a contrast between the elements of Hobbes's thought

[77] Clergy members, lawyers, and physicians will not serve in the senate (127, 136–7). They are exempted from service in the militia because of the demands of their education, and only men who have served in the "essays" are eligible for election to the senate (203, see also 191).

[78] Among those Harrington exempts from service are only sons and men studying for the professions mentioned in note 77.

[79] Hobbes, *Leviathan*, 151. Worden makes the same comparison ("Harrington and *Commonwealth of Oceana*," 104–5).

[80] Hobbes, *Leviathan*, 148.

that Nedham embraces, particularly in *The Excellencie of a Free State*, and
those that Harrington adopts. Specifically, Nedham embraces the doctrine
of rights in Hobbes's thought that Harrington rejects. Because Harrington
fails to select those elements compatible with a liberal understanding, which
Nedham finds so appealing, he cannot expand on them in the way that the
journalist does. Thus, Harrington does not take the liberal path to which
Hobbes's thought can lead. As a result, Nedham's early anticipation of a
liberal, participatory republicanism, in which the liberty and rights of individuals are primary and in which they participate in their republic to protect
them, is absent in Harrington's *Oceana*. Moreover, in a manner reminiscent of Hobbes, Nedham takes the side of the people against the elites. In
this crusade, Nedham shows up both Machiavelli, who proclaims himself
the people's defender, and Harrington, who follows Machiavelli's somewhat
cloaked but nevertheless palpable contemptuousness toward the people's political acumen. Nedham's advocacy of the people's capacities, although of a
Hobbesian cast, must be distinguished from Hobbes's as a result of its direct
application to republican politics.

When one assesses Harrington's debt to Hobbes, it is necessary to note
that his thought contains neither a state of nature[81] nor a doctrine of rights in
which such reasoning can culminate. Unlike Hobbes, he does not make the
preservation of the life of the individual central, and, unlike Nedham, he does
not make security primary such that it, or the right to life, can easily expand
to include liberty and property,[82] as we watched it doing in the transition

---

[81] Wettergreen argues on the basis of a poem that Harrington sent to Aubrey that Harrington
does have a state of nature. He concedes, however, that Harrington does not mention it in
any of his political works. If the poem is Harrington's and if he does believe that such a
state existed, such a state is very far from providing the basis of his politics. See Wettergreen,
"Harrington's Liberal Republicanism," 668–73, and Aubrey, *Brief Lives*, 294. At the beginning of his *A System of Politics*, Harrington seems to broach a notion of a state of nature:
"A people is either under a state of civil government, or in a state of civil war; or neither
under a state of civil government, nor in a state of civil war." The latter alternative sounds
very much like a state of nature, but when he clarifies his meaning it turns out that he is not
suggesting the existence of a state of nature. He explains later that such a "privation" of government exists when the ruler or rulers assume power against the balance. These situations
correspond to his deviant forms of government: tyranny, oligarchy and anarchy (*System of
Politics*, 834, 836–7).

[82] At one point in *Oceana*, when speaking of the importance of not excluding any party from
governance, Harrington uses language that mimics the common concern of liberals: "Men
that have equal possessions and the same security of their estates and of their liberties that
you have, have the same cause with you to defend" (62). Nevertheless, this is a formulation
rarely found in his thought, and thus does not guide it. Moreover, even here he points to
his overarching concern: the defense of the commonwealth. See Worden, "Harrington and
Commonwealth of Oceana," 105–6, where he refers to this passage. Worden states, though,
that Harrington "is not interested, or is barely interested, in rights. Political life is not, for
him, a conflict between the power of that state and the liberty of the individual. There is no

from Nedham's *Case of the Commonwealth of England* to his *Excellencie of a Free State*.

Still enamored of the martial glory of the historical republics of antiquity, Harrington clings to Machiavelli's vision of a republic for increase to a much greater extent than does Nedham. Because he endorses the virtue of courage, which he seeks to foster in his state, Harrington is quite willing to put the lives of citizens at risk in displaying that attribute on the battlefield for the purpose of acquiring additional territory for his state. His thought simply does not lend itself to the liberal concern that makes the desire for "commodious living" the basis for political life. Like Machiavelli, Harrington has fallen under the thrall of antiquity in this respect – a tendency that Hobbes regarded as a foible to be chastised mercilessly.[83]

Just as that tendency does not make Machiavelli an ancient, it does not make Harrington one. Harrington is a modern in that he founds his government squarely on the desires of the people who compose it. We have said the same about Machiavelli. Harrington – like Machiavelli and unlike Nedham – however, refuses to transform those desires into rights. Although both Machiavelli and Harrington are moderns, neither are liberals.

As we have seen, Harrington's republic, in direct opposition to Machiavelli's, is to channel and constrain those desires so they do not disturb the tranquillity of his republic. He is much more weary of the desires than is Machiavelli, who can be said to revel in them. Harrington is so confident that he has succeeded in disarming the desires that can bring down governments that he claims his republic is immortal.

Merely by endorsing republican government, of course, Harrington, like Nedham, rejects the fundamental tenet of Hobbes's politics. In their respective preferences for republican government, there are, however, fundamental differences between these two English republicans, particularly concerning the abilities of the people and the manner in which they can and should participate in a republic. Whereas Nedham promotes the capacities of the people, Harrington is decidedly less enthusiastic about the people's ability to participate fully in governance. On this issue, in fact, Harrington sides with Machiavelli as Nedham moves away from the Florentine in a manner that brings him closer to Hobbes's assertion of fundamental human equality.

What participation there is in Oceana among the people is ritualized and severely constrained. The greatest amount of participation among the people occurs when they bear arms for their republic. Indeed, Harrington borrows a page from Machiavelli's book in attempting to convince the people that their role in government is actually much larger than it is. Similarly, Harrington

'state' in Harrington's thinking, only a 'commonwealth' whose 'liberty' becomes inseparable from the 'liberty' of its citizens" (105).

[83] Hobbes, *Leviathan*, 225–6.

undertakes to dupe the people into believing that the government that Archon creates is in large measure their own creation. To this end, Archon designates a committee of noblemen to hear any suggestions for the "fabric of the commonwealth." Harrington explains that this expedient is intended to make the people, "who were neither safely to be admitted unto, nor conveniently to be excluded from the framing of their commonwealth ... verily believe when it came forth that it was no other than that whereof they themselves had been the makers" (70).[84] When elected to the assembly of the people, the people are to participate in legislation by either accepting or rejecting the propositions of the senate, but they are primarily intended to bear arms for their republic. Harrington sides, then, with Machiavelli against Hobbes on the degree to which fundamental differences among classes affect politics.

In opening up the participatory character of his republic, Nedham simultaneously acts on Hobbes's notion of equality. He adopts the perspective of the people that Hobbes embraced but makes that perspective new by giving it a decidedly republican cast. For Nedham, the people are not merely window dressing in the actual workings of the commonwealth. Real debate is to occur in the assemblies of the people that Nedham so heartily endorses – a thought that could only horrify Harrington. Nedham wishes also to foster the vigilance required to protect the people's rights and liberties – a goal (but certainly not the means) that has a rudimentary basis in the thought of Hobbes. As Nedham says in *The Excellencie of a Free State*: "[W]hen the people are thus active, zealous, and jealous in the behalf of their liberties, [they] will permit no such growth of power as may endanger it."[85] The people have a real role to play in governance.

Having brought the people into the public realm for the purpose of protecting their rights and liberties, Nedham stakes out his own territory, different in critical ways from Harrington, Hobbes, and Machiavelli. Nevertheless, as we saw in the previous chapter, Nedham follows in the spirit of Machiavelli. After all, it was Machiavelli who so loudly claimed that he supported the people and the creation of a democratic republic. Nedham, however, is much more willing to act on the claim that Machiavelli put forth than either Machiavelli himself or Harrington, Machiavelli's declared disciple.

Harrington, then, will simply not follow Machiavelli's spirit and Hobbes's declared sentiments in the direction that Nedham leads. Nevertheless, there is something modern about Harrington. Indeed, he is an early but prime exemplar of the modern impulse to neutralize conflict by having institutions

---

[84] Rahe refers to this "subterfuge" on the part of Archon. Rahe does not relate this action to Machiavelli and argues that it reveals the extent to which Harrington believed "that consent is the sole source of political legitimacy" (*Republics Ancient and Modern*, 417–18).

[85] Nedham, *Excellencie of a Free State*, 81.

channel interests so that they are checked against other interests. He lacks, however, the liberal spirit that Nedham evinces. He also lacks the hearty appreciation of the passions, evident in Machiavelli, and in some of the English republicans who would follow Machiavelli more scrupulously on this issue. In some ways, the true synthesis of liberalism and Machiavellianism will not be born until the later English republicans have reacted against this very influential one of their number.

5

Henry Neville's Proposal for a Republic under the Form of Monarchy

Before the Restoration, Henry Neville had been an active republican. He was first elected to Parliament in April 1649, only a few months after the execution of Charles I, and was elected to serve on the Council of State in 1651.[1] At that time he was "a favourite of Oliver [Cromwell]," but when Neville saw that the general "gaped after the government by a single person, he left him."[2] So far was Neville from being a favorite of Cromwell at this point that, when Cromwell expelled the Rump Parliament in April 1653, he included Neville among the members whom he criticized.[3] Neville was back in Parliament immediately before the Restoration and brought forward for consideration "The Humble Petition," which offered a proposal for an English republic modeled on Harrington's Oceana.[4]

That futile petition was far from Neville's only association with Harrington, of course. In addition to Aubrey's report that Hobbes credited him with having helped Harrington compose Oceana,[5] Aubrey claims that he helped Harrington to win converts to his cause: Harrington's and "H. Nevill's smart discourses and inculcations, dayly at coffee-houses, made

---

[1] Robbins, *Two Republican Tracts*, 6–7.

[2] Anthony à Wood, *Athenae Oxonienses, An Exact History of all the Writers and Bishops who Have Had Their Education in the University of Oxford*, s.v. Henry Nevill, 3d ed. (London, 1820), 4:410.

[3] Worden, "*Oceana*: Origins and Aftermath," 117.

[4] Robbins, *Two Republican Tracts*, 10–12. For a discussion of Neville's efforts on behalf of Harringtonian ideas in parliamentary debate in 1659, see Worden, "*Oceana*: Origins and Aftermath," 126–36, and Blair Worden, "Republicanism and the Restoration, 1660–83," in Wootton, *Republicanism, Liberty, and Commercial Society*, 145. For a further discussion of Neville's manner of pursuing the establishment of a republic immediately before the Restoration, see Nicholas von Maltzahn, "Henry Neville and the Art of the Possible: A Republican *Letter Sent to General Monk* (1660)," *Seventeenth Century* 7 (1992): 41–52.

[5] Aubrey, *Brief Lives*, 1:289, and my comments in Chapter 4.

many proselytes."[6] A friend to Harrington to the last, he "never forsooke him to his dyeing day."[7]

After the Restoration, Neville was careful to keep a low profile, at least for a time. Jailed in 1663 under suspicion of conspiracy, he traveled to Italy after his release.[8] He published *Plato Redivivus: Or, A Dialogue Concerning Government* in 1681.[9] The work, in the form of a dialogue, offers a proposal for the reform of England's monarchy. Its title may pay homage to Plato, but it is Machiavelli whom it terms "divine" (e.g., 81, 92, 126).[10] Neville certainly seems to have been a long-standing devotee of Machiavelli: he is probably the translator of the collected works of the Florentine that appeared in England in 1675 and the author of the spurious letter appended to it, purporting to be from Machiavelli's own hand, which offers a defense of himself against the accusations of favoring tyranny, atheism, and republicanism.[11] In *Plato Redivivus*, Machiavelli's problem of how to reform a government hangs over the dialogue, and Neville, like Machiavelli before him, affirms the difficulty of identifying and correcting grave political problems before it is too late (76). Ultimately, in offering timely reform, Neville draws inspiration from a facet of Machiavelli's *Discourses* that other English republicans sympathetic to Machiavelli's thought leave untouched: subtle reform is sometimes preferable to obvious and spectacular reform. Neville does not seek a solution to misgovernment in the extreme remedies of Machiavelli, as Sidney and Cato later will. Thus, although Neville is in some ways a more vocal adherent of Machiavelli – evident, for instance, when he unabashedly calls his Italian predecessor divine – in other ways he is a quieter Machiavellian than they, owing to his own subtle solution to England's misgovernment.

Although he draws from Machiavelli in these ways, he also uses prominent features of Harrington's thought. The content of his analysis of England's

---

[6] Ibid., 1:289.

[7] Ibid., 1:293. See also the purported transcript of Harrington's interrogation when he was imprisoned in the Tower of London, where Harrington says that he knows Neville "Very well," and that Neville made a practice of visiting him at home every evening (Harrington, *The Examination of James Harrington*, in *Political Works*, in 857).

[8] Robbins, *Two Republican Tracts*, 12–13.

[9] Fink says that it was published in 1681 in order to "influence" Charles's last Parliament, which was to meet at Oxford (*Classical Republicans*, 129). Robbins claims that despite the date on its title page, the work was published the previous year before the parliamentary session that began in October 1680 and went into an expanded edition the next year in time for the Parliament that met at Oxford (*Eighteenth-Century Commonwealthman*, 33).

[10] I cite Caroline Robbin's edition of *Plato Redivivus* in *Two Republican Tracts*, and the page references to that edition will appear in the text of this chapter. Worden refers to *Plato Redivivus* as "that classic of Machiavellian literature" ("Classical Republicanism and Puritan Revolution," 184).

[11] For Neville as author of the letter and preface and as translator of Machiavelli's works, see Raab, *English Face of Machiavelli*, 267–72.

ills and his proposed solution derive in many ways directly from *Oceana*. But even in this recourse to the thought of his friend, Neville seeks a quiet revolution, because the Harringtonian elements of his thought, like the Machiavellian ones, rest on a new foundation – a liberal foundation. Neville, like Nedham in *The Excellencie of a Free State*, accepts Hobbes's account of the origins of politics and thus makes politics serve the satisfaction of the desires. Although closely following Harrington in some important respects, then, he is one of those republicans who draws away from Harrington by putting less constraints on the play of the passions. Neville crafts a version of Harringtonian republicanism that rests on a more liberal foundation.

The Setting of the Dialogues and the Human Setting

The dangers of disease endemic both to the human body and the body politic cast a pall over the setting of Neville's *Plato Redivivus*. The illness of a visitor from the Venetian republic, who had been enjoying the hospitality of an English Gentleman in London for nearly three months, is the event that brings the three unnamed interlocutors together, on three consecutive days, for the dialogues that compose Neville's work. Having been in the country on business for nearly three weeks, the Englishman by chance hears of the illness of his guest, whom he had left in London. He hurries to the bedside of his guest to find that the Noble Venetian had called for the services of an eminent English physician, who is ministering to his new patient on the Englishman's return.[12]

The patient is so much recovered before the Englishman's arrival that he is eager to engage his physician in a discussion of political matters; the Doctor reports that the patient had asked him "to give ... some account of our affairs here, and the turbulency of our present state." The Doctor further relates that he had told his patient that he should address his inquiry to his host, "whose parts and studies have fitted him for such an employment." It is odd, indeed, that, having spent so much time in the company of his host, the Venetian should address his political concerns to one whom he had known for a considerably shorter time – and much of that time presumably in a condition ill-suited for establishing an intimacy beyond that of a doctor and his patient. The patient, though, even before he had the benefit of the Doctor's medical skill had known both of the Doctor and of the Doctor's

---

[12] Many scholars have attempted to identify the character of the Doctor. Walter Moyle claimed to have been informed that the Doctor was a representation of William Harvey. Because the Doctor reveals himself to be an exponent for the exclusion of James from the succession, Fink maintains that he is a representation of John Locke (*Classical Republicans*, 130n.). As Robbins points out, however, at this time Locke did not have major writings to his credit as the Doctor in the dialogue is said to have (Robbins, *Two Republican Tracts*, 71 and n.). Thomas Hollis believed that the Doctor was a representation of Richard Lower (Raab, *English Face of Machiavelli*, 218–19n.), and Robbins concurs.

acquaintance with his host. He acknowledges, in fact, that he had intended to have his host introduce him to the Doctor (75).[13]

Perhaps he had desired that introduction in order to address to the Doctor his question regarding England's distemper. Such a desire on the part of the Venetian would not seem to be misplaced given that the Englishman himself notes that the Doctor is "very well known to be as skilful in the nature and distemper of the body politic, as the whole nation confesses you to be in the concerns of the natural" (75). Each of the Englishmen, then, asserts that the other is capable of addressing the Venetian's political concerns. With a view to addressing those concerns, the Englishman declares: "But let us leave the contest who shall inform this gentleman, lest we spend the time we should do it in unprofitably, and let each of us take his part; for if one speak all, it will look like a studied discourse fitted for the press, and not a familiar dialogue" (76). Despite this expressed wish of the Englishman Gentleman, who is clearly Neville's mouthpiece, it turns out that he does most of the speaking. Although the Doctor can understand Italian, he cannot speak it. In addition, the Venetian has difficulty understanding the Doctor's pronunciation of Latin. As a result of these difficulties, it is necessary for the Englishman to address the Venetian's concerns at length in Italian. Presumably, the considerably shorter remarks of the Doctor would be spoken in a Latin scarcely recognizable to the Venetian.[14] Moreover, as the dialogues unfold, it becomes apparent that the Englishman has given England's distress a great deal of thought: he has not only a diagnosis but a proposed cure. The Doctor takes as keen an interest in the responses of his English friend as does the Venetian, as evidenced by the many questions he addresses to his countryman. As the work progresses, the Doctor becomes as a much a pupil of the Gentleman as is the Venetian.

Although the Noble Venetian's distemper has been cured, the remainder of the work addresses the question whether England's can be similarly healed. In posing this question of England's political health, Neville's dialogues clearly draw an equation between the human body and the body politic. Such an equation could suggest that Neville embraces an organic view of the polity, a view that would suggest that human beings are fitted by nature to live

---

[13] In his description of the setting, Skinner claims that the Noble Venetian "has come to England in search of medical advice" (*Liberty before Liberalism*, 24–5). That is not at all clear from the work. Although the Noble Venetian does say that he had intended before his sudden illness to seek the acquaintance of the Doctor, he does not say that he sought medical advice in England or even from the Doctor whose acquaintance he wished to make. Indeed, he says that before the onset of his sudden illness he had no intention of becoming the object of the doctor's care (73–4). Moreover, the Argument of the work specifically says that the Venetian came to England when, finding himself out of employment in France where one of his relatives served as ambassador, he "resolved to divert himself, by visiting some part of the world he had never seen" (71).

[14] Of course, Neville presents the entirety of the dialogue in English.

in harmony with each other in a political setting; nature has provided a hierarchy among human beings that corresponds to the hierarchy found within political society. Whereas some are suited by nature to be ruled, others are fitted to rule. Whatever their natural endowments, all must subordinate themselves to the good of the whole, just as the various parts of the human organism are subordinated to maintaining its continued life. The part, or the individual, is of less dignity and importance than that of the whole.

It would be a mistake to take Neville's equation between the human and the body politic this far. The English Gentleman makes clear when he touches on the human setting and the origin of politics that he does not subscribe to the organic view of the polity. Indeed, he possesses an individualistic understanding of the relation between the state and its citizens; the state is in no way a natural entity but rather a human artifact created for the purpose of satisfying basic human needs. Like Nedham, Neville has been schooled in the Hobbesian teaching regarding the origins of political society and the relation between the state and the individual.[15] Specifically, Neville embraces the doctrine that declares that, before the establishment of government, human beings lived in a state of nature and that human beings establish government to alleviate the dangers of that hostile original condition.

The Englishman of Neville's dialogue begins his description of the origin of government by declaring that he will "take for granted, that which all the politicians conclude: which is, that necessity made the first government." He proceeds to explain how necessity impelled its creation: "For every man by the first law of nature (which is common to us and brutes) had, like beasts in a pasture, right to everything; and there being no property, each individual, if he were the stronger, might seize whatever any other had possessed himself of before, which made a state of perpetual war." Thus, Neville embraces Hobbes's conception of a state of nature that collapses into a state of a war of all against all. The Englishman continues: "To remedy which, and the fear that nothing should be long enjoyed by any particular person, (neither was any man's life in safety,) every man consented to be debarred of that universal right to all things; and confine himself to a quiet and secure enjoyment of such a part, as should be allotted him." In this manner property came into existence, and in order to protect this newly created property "it was necessary to consent to laws, and a government; to put them in execution" (85). Thus, Neville imports into his *Plato Redivivus* Hobbes's doctrine that

---

[15] Skinner does not claim that Nedham possesses an organic view of the polity but rather that he makes use of "ancient metaphor of the body politic." Skinner continues that the "principal way in which [the neo–roman] writers [such as Neville] pursue this metaphor is by examining the sense in which natural and political bodies are alike capable of possessing and forfeiting their liberty" and that Neville of all of the neo–romans "makes the most systematic use of the traditional imagery" (*Liberty before Liberalism*, 24–5).

individuals consent to government in order to escape a state of war and thus to satisfy their desires that arise from their basic needs.

The Englishman states that he does not know which type of government was first, but that whatever type it was, it is beyond dispute that "it was made by the persuasion and mediation of some wise and virtuous person, and consented to by the whole number." Government, then, is not made "for the exaltation and greatness of the person or persons appointed to govern," because "it seems very improbable, not to say impossible, that a vast number of people should ever be brought to consent to put themselves under the power of others, but for the ends above-said, and so lose their liberty without advantaging themselves in any thing" (85).

This point illustrates that Neville is concerned, as Locke will be later, with the inconveniences people must endure not only in the state of nature but also under an absolute sovereign. Neville's understanding of the purpose of politics is liberal. Hobbes, by contrast, was concerned above all with the dreadful consequences of life in the state of nature; life under a sovereign – no matter how absolute – could not approach in horror the life that one led in the state of nature that was also a state of war. Nevertheless, Neville follows Hobbes's lead in a decisive respect. Neville's admiration for republican antiquity and his proposals for modifying England's restored monarchy in the direction of a republic are premised on an individualistic understanding of the place of politics in human life; politics is to serve the needs and desires of individuals. For this understanding, Neville is indebted to Hobbes.

England's Distemper and Neville's Cure

While the short first dialogue is devoted primarily to pleasantries and pre-liminaries, such as the decision of what language to use, the dialogue of the second day proceeds directly to the question at hand. Indeed, it opens with the Noble Venetian posing his question to his host that he had originally directed to the Doctor during his host's absence: "Then, sir, my first request to you is, that you will vouchsafe to acquaint me for what reasons this nation, which has ever been esteemed (and very justly) one of the most considerable people of the world; and made the best figure both in peace, treaties, war and trade; is now of so small regard, and signifies so little abroad?" (79).

The Englishman has an answer as well as a solution at hand. The recent civil wars and the continued unrest of the country derive from a change in the ownership of property: "[F]or want of providence and policy in former kings, who could not foresee the danger afar off, entails have been suffered to be cut off; and so two parts in ten of all those vast estates, as well manors as demesnes, by the luxury and folly of the owners, have been within these two hundred years purchased by the lesser gentry and the commons; which has been so far from advantaging the crown, that it has made the country scarce governable by monarchy" (88). Neville's analysis, thus, accepts both

Harrington's dictum that "Dominion is founded in property" (89) and his historical analysis that declares that the distribution of property in England makes the country especially suited to republican rule.

In embracing Harrington's dictum in the early 1680s, Neville must face a political situation wholly unexpected to Harrington when he authored *Oceana*: this change in the ownership of property has not brought forth a stable commonwealth in England but has issued in the reestablishment of the monarchy. Although the monarchy has been restored, it is far from healthy precisely because of this ownership of property, as Neville maintains through the Englishman: "[T]he property of the peers, and church . . . have inherited likewise, according to the course of nature, their power: but being kept from it by the established government . . . so that for want of outward orders and provisions, the people are kept from the exercise of that power, which is fallen to them by the law of nature" (145). The current arrangement, which keeps formal power from the people who have a great deal of strength as a result of their possession of the land, has issued in misgovernment and is ultimately untenable. The Englishman states:

The consequence is: that the natural part of our government, which is power, is by means of property in the hands of the people; whilst the artificial part, or the parchment in which the form of government is written, remains the frame. Now art is a very good servant and help to nature, but very weak and inconsiderable, when she opposes her, and fights with her; it would be a very uneven contest between parchment and power. This alone is the cause of all the disorder you heard of, and now see in England. (133–4)

As a result of the people's power, the king fears for his own power and ultimately for his crown; the people, in their turn, fear that the king intends to establish arbitrary rule (172). The most evident symptom of this disease is that "every parliament seems a perfect state of war." When the people contend "very justly and very honourably" "for their right," "the court sends them packing," without the necessary laws being passed (145).

The third day's discussion treats the Englishman's solution to the problem. He broaches the issue of the outcome of the current state of affairs by declaring there exist only two possible solutions to England's malaise: either "[T]he king [must] have a great deal more power, or a great deal less" (172). The Doctor responds to this observation of the Englishman by saying "I begin to smell what you would be nibbling at; the pretence which some had before his majesty's Restoration, of a commonwealth, or democracy" (173). The Englishman denies that this is his intention, affirming "I abhor the thoughts of wishing, much less endeavouring, any such thing, during the circumstances we are now in: that is, under oaths of obedience to a lawful king" (173).

Although Neville does not foresee the need to depose the king in the name of a commonwealth that will rest on the de facto distribution of power in the state, he does envision a severe restriction of the king's power. Specifically, he discerns four areas in which the powers of the king "hinder the execution of our laws, and prevent by consequence our happiness and settlement": foreign affairs; raising military forces; nomination and appointment; and the dispensation of the public revenues (185–6). He proposes that these powers be delegated to four committees elected by the parliament. After the initial election of the complete complement of officers to serve on the committees, the term of office of one-third of the membership of each committee would expire yearly. The term of office, then, is to be three years, and he specifies that after a member serves this term, he may not be elected to serve on that, or any other, committee for a period of three years. In this manner, Neville accepts the principle of rotation exemplified by the Venetian republic that Harrington admires and adopts for Oceana.[16] Neville specifies that these measures will prevent any member from becoming either insolent to or corrupted by his king. After stating the latter concern, however, Neville insists that the king would not have the means under this model to corrupt these officeholders in any case (187).

Neville allows the king to retain his privy council, to which he can appoint anyone he desires as long as his choice is not a member of one of the four committees. Neville allows the king and his privy council to "meddle" in matters "of merchants, plantations, charters, and other matters to which the regal power extends" (188). What Neville's proposal does is to insure that the most important executive powers of the state will be wielded by committees elected in Parliament.[17] He specifies that either the king himself or a representative of his choosing shall preside over each committee, but that the decisions of each committee will be rendered by majority vote. The king's wishes, if they diverge from those of the majority of each committee, are superfluous. The king will be a figurehead for a republican regime.[18]

---

[16] For a discussion of the Venetian and Harringtonian character of the various institutional features of the Englishman's proposal, see Fink, *Classical Republicans*, 130–3.

[17] H. T. Dickinson, *Liberty and Property: Political Ideology in Eighteenth-Century Britain* (New York: Holmes and Meier, 1977), 111.

[18] Fink too understands Neville as a cloaked republican and his proposal as essentially a republican one (*Classical Republicans*, 134–5). Indeed, Fink likens the king's power after the introduction of the four councils to that of the doge of the Venetian republic (130). In keeping with this general thesis, Fink portrays Neville as a classical republican, neglecting those important elements of Neville's thought that link him to liberalism, and hence to modernity. In contrast, although linking Neville to antiquity, Pocock does not emphasize the republican implications of this proposal. He argues that unlike Harrington, who views the Ancient Constitution as an "anarchic wrestling-match," Neville holds it in high esteem for its harmony and provision of liberty for the commons as well as the baronage (*Machiavellian Moment*, 417, and "Historical Introduction," 134). This distinction, for Pocock, is emblematic of the distinction between Harrington, who dismisses the past, and those neo-Harringtonians who embrace it ("English Political Ideologies," 135). The implication is that Neville's regard for the past prevents him from envisioning a republican future. Goodale challenges Pocock's

Therefore, Neville's plan will introduce a republic that hides under the form of a monarchy.[19] According to the Englishman, this radical diminution of the king's power will be instituted with the king's blessing. To the Venetian's quite reasonable objection that the king will not accept any plan that weakens his power, the Englishman responds: "But because you ask me how we would persuade the king to this? I answer; by the parliament's humbly remonstrating to his majesty, that it is his own interest, preservation, quiet and true greatness, to put an end to the distractions of his subjects" (177–8). The Englishman's general response to the objection of the king's unwillingness to accept any change is that Charles cannot ignore the wishes of his people and continue to rule by force indefinitely; the people's strength, deriving from their property, would not permit this unsettled condition to continue.

Neville's Debt to Harrington

As the previous section makes abundantly clear, Neville is deeply indebted to Harrington for his understanding of the relation between property and political power, and hence for his understanding of England's political predicament. Given the restoration of the monarchy in 1660, Neville is not willing to proclaim as loudly as Harrington that England's future is republican; nevertheless, he accepts Harrington's analysis of the change in the distribution of property that makes the unchecked power of the king in England ultimately unstable. Indeed, *Plato Redivivus* acknowledges Neville's debt to Harrington quite early. A note appended to the beginning of the work, purporting to be from the publisher,[20] provides a history of how this anonymous work came into the hands of its eventual publisher and of his initial concerns about publishing it.

---

claim that Neville saw the change in property ownership that began under Henry VII "as destructive," "and wanted to return the present government, as much as possible, to the principles of an ancient constitution" by arguing that "Neville's proposed monarchy was little more than a Harringtonian republic with a king attached" ("Pocock's Neo-Harringtonians," 243; cf. Pocock, "Historical Introduction," 135). See also Worden's discussion in "Republicanism and the Restoration," 148: "For if Neville ostensibly regrets the breakdown of the ancient constitution and of the medieval polity, no more than Harrington does he think them recoverable."

[19] Many critics of *Plato Redivivus* did not find Neville's republican sympathies difficult to uncover. For instance, Thomas Goddard calls its author a "Republican Dæmon" in the note to the reader in his *Plato's Demon: Or, the State-Physician Unmaskt; Being a Discourse in Answer to a Book call'd Plato Redivivus* (London: H. Hills Jun. for Walter Keeilby, 1684). See also Fink, *Classical Republicans*, 134–5.

[20] Robbins seems to accept this note as actually coming from the pen of Neville's publisher (*Eighteenth-Century Commonwealthman*, 33–4). Pocock ("Historical Introduction," 11) and Worden ("Harrington and 'The Commonwealth of Oceana,'" 116) express some doubt.

Upon first perusing the work, the publisher fears that because "a considerable part of this treatise being a repetition of a great many principles and positions out of *Oceana*, the author would be discredited for borrowing from another and the sale of the book hindered" (68). The publisher relates that he consulted a knowledgeable friend on this point who, after having read the treatise in question, assured him that his fear was unfounded. Even before *Oceana* itself was published, other tracts were published that contained the same principles, and this fact did not derogate from Harrington's achievement in that work. The publisher's friend then proceeds to draw a distinction between Harrington and the author of the anonymous work: "*Oceana* was written (it being thought lawful so to do in those times) to evince out of these principles, that England was not capable of any other government than a democracy; and this author out of the same maxims or aphorisms of politics, endeavors to prove, that they may be applied naturally and fitly to the redressing and supporting one of the best monarchies in the world, which is that of England" (69). This difference between Harrington and Neville, though, can be understood as one of mere circumstance. A consideration of the Englishman's proposals in the dialogue reveals that Neville goes very far in favoring a republic when living under a monarchy.

Neville mimics Harrington's political thought in other ways. For example, he places much more emphasis on the material than on the moral causes of corruption. Thus, by sacrificing the necessity of individual moral restraint to the concern with the distribution of property in a state, Neville distinguishes his teaching from Aristotle's. In reflecting on why so many absolute monarchies have arisen in the world, Neville's Englishman supposes that the "ancient principalities" arose as corruptions "of better governments, which must necessarily cause a depravation in manners." Although he merely offers a conjecture on this point, when it comes to considering from what cause that depravation of manners arose, he is absolutely definitive: "[N]othing is more certain than that politic defects breed moral ones." As we already know, these political defects arise from the misallocation of property. From these defects arise a general "debauchery of manners" that blind the citizens to the public good, so that it becomes easier for "some bold aspiring person, to affect empire" (87). As a result of this understanding, Neville does not focus relentlessly on the need for individuals to sacrifice for the common good; instead, if the government of the state is in accord with the distribution of property, then such moral considerations take care of themselves.

He acknowledges that this understanding of politics induces him to "presume to differ from Aristotle." What Aristotle calls the corruptions of aristocracy or democracy, for example, Neville insists on calling merely the "extremes." He will not call them corruptions because "they do not proceed from the alteration of property, which is the only corruptor of politics" (101). Thus, Neville refuses to call corruption what is corruption for Aristotle – namely, those governments in which the rulers look to their own good rather than to the common good.[21] Thus, Neville not only accepts what is Harrington's crucial departure from Aristotle, but he is quite forthright in acknowledging that departure.[22]

The Englishman's definition of democracy, which he claims is best exemplified by the Roman Republic, also betrays Harrington's influence on Neville's thought. He declares that this form of government "does consist of three fundamental orders; the senate proposing, the people resolving, and the magistrates executing" (92). This distinction between proposing and resolving is, of course, the political equivalent of dividing and choosing that Harrington installs in his *Oceana* by dividing these functions between the senate and the assembly of the people. Thus, the definition of democracy that the Englishman provides is one that he borrows from Harrington.

Further, the Englishman's definition of anarchy also reveals a debt to Harrington: "An anarchy then is when the people not contented with their share in the administration of the government, (which is the right of approving, or disapproving of laws...) will take upon themselves the office of the senate too, in managing subordinate matters of state, proposing laws

---

[21] Aristotle, *Politics* 3.7, 1279a22–1279b10. Although both Harrington and Neville, in contesting the basis of Aristotle's distinction between good and deviant regimes, emphasize the ownership of property in contrast to the ancient's moral considerations, the details of their explanations are different. Harrington says that the deviant regimes are illegitimate because they use force, as they rule against the balance of property in the state. By contrast, Neville seems to concede that the deviant regimes rule for their own personal advantages, as in Aristotle's description, but claims, against Aristotle's understanding, that this cannot be termed corruption, as corruption only proceeds from material considerations. On Harrington, see Chapter 4.

[22] One of the identifying concerns of Pocock's neo-Harringtonians is a concern with corruption, which is in his view a "civic and republican" and "classical" concept (*Machiavellian Moment*, 407, 420). The term is used by Pocock's neo-Harringtonians to denote an attempt on the part of the executive branch to influence members of the legislative through patronage, pensions, and places, and in its full development such corruption is not merely "an infringement of the sphere of legislative action" but an attempt "to bring the individual members, as well as the corporate body, of the legislature into dependence upon the executive, a dependence which must be termed corruption since it existed where independence should obtain" (*Machiavellian Moment*, 420). Pocock concedes that Harrington's thought lacks such a theory of corruption (e.g., 409, 417) and that it did not play a prominent part in Neville's (419). Despite these concessions he still links both thinkers to his classical exposition of corruption: the concept of corruption "owed much to Harrington" (407); Harrington's "republican and Machiavellian language of which he was the chief English exponent was the appropriate vehicle for expounding a theory of corruption" (417; see also "Historical Introduction," 136); and, "if Neville himself has no highly developed theory of corruption, he has provided the historical context in which one might be situated" (*Machiavellian Moment*, 419). In attempting to link Neville to his classical conception of corruption, Pocock does not confront what Neville says is his departure from Aristotle on this topic. For a criticism of Pocock's exposition of the neo-Harringtonians generally, see Zuckert, *Natural Rights and the New Republicanism*, 166–83.

originally, and assuming debate in the market-place, making their orators their leaders" (101). Thus, Neville accepts Harrington's distinction between debate and result and shares his old friend's wariness regarding the people's assumption of debate.

Neville's further commentary on republican Rome, namely his discussion of its agrarian law and its military strength, serves to illustrate additional debts to Harrington. With respect to the agrarian law, the Englishman recounts that at their founding the Romans "omitted... to provide for the fixing of property" (96). As a result of this omission, the patricians began to amass more land than was healthy for a republic. A tribune by the name of Licinius Stolo proposed an agrarian law, which the Romans did not, of course, strictly observe, and this lapse inevitably brought about the republic's decline (96–7). In the midst of the republic's death throes, the brothers Gracchi, whom the Englishman terms "illustrious persons," attempted to rectify this defect, but they died martyrs to the cause of "preserv[ing] and restor[ing] their commonwealth" (99–100). Clearly, Neville views the collapse of the Roman Republic through distinctly Harringtonian lenses.

Moreover, like Harrington, Neville displays a Machiavellian admiration for the military might of the Romans. When discoursing on Rome as the exemplification of a democracy properly understood, the Englishman comments: "This government is much more powerful than aristocracy; because the latter cannot arm the people, for fear they should seize upon the government; and therefore are fain to make use of none but strangers and mercenaries for soldiers: which, as the divine Machiavel says, has hindered your commonwealth of Venice from mounting up to heaven" (92). Although, as we noted earlier, Neville assigns the cause of the people's political prominence in Rome to their holding of a significant amount of property, he does not overlook that distinctive feature of Rome that Machiavelli, as well as Harrington following him, highlights: Rome's armed populace. For the Florentine, it was this factor, not the people's ownership of property, that accounts for the people's political power in that city. Neville, in embracing Machiavelli's point, offers a less than hospitable comment on the homeland of his guest for making use of mercenaries in its wars. This disparagement of Venice suggests that Neville regards Rome's military greatness as a worthy goal in the modern world.

Harrington certainly does. Indeed, Harrington envisions England making such conquests that it will be the Rome of the modern world. Unlike Harrington, however, Neville makes no pleas for England to follow Rome's example by adding to its dominions, no bellicose assertions that Englishmen best fit the corselet.[23] Similarly, Neville differs from Harrington in not demanding that an agrarian law be instituted in England. Thus, although Neville loyally

[23] Cf. Robbins, *Eighteenth-Century Commonwealthman*, 40.

follows Harrington's analysis of Roman history, neither Rome's greatness nor its defects are as alive for him as they are for Harrington.[24]

As a result, Neville does not undertake to remake the life of the average Englishman in the way Harrington does. He seeks neither to constrict the play of passions of individuals nor to have the government stake as large a claim in their lives as does his friend. An agrarian law will not impose any barrier to an individual's acquisition of land in England, although, as we have seen, he accepts Harrington's analysis of the relation between ownership of land and political power. Moreover, in the context of the Englishman's discussion of the application of the agrarian law in Rome, he says that it is "not...dangerous to a city to have their people rich" as long as they do not hold enough land so as to make others dependent on them (99). This statement provides a stark contrast to Harrington, who is decidedly wary of the passions that might lead people to acquire such fortunes. His Archon, for example, declares that "covetousness is the root of all evil."[25] As for the claim that the government is to have over their private lives, Neville specifies neither that they will be eligible every year for service in the militia nor that they will assemble periodically in military formation to vote for their representatives. Moreover, Neville's thought contains nothing similar to Harrington's railings against ambition. He does not laud ambition, as does Machiavelli, but neither does he appear to fear it to such an extent that he deems it necessary to dampen it at every turn. Apparently, not thinking the passions present a threat, he does not attempt to constrain them preemptively. Neville's difference from Harrington on the passions complements his other significant difference from Harrington: his acceptance of Hobbes's claims that before the advent of government, human beings lived in a state of nature, which was a state of war, and that people consent to be governed so as to satisfy their most basic needs and desires.

Neville's Regard for Machiavelli

A more approving epithet than the one that Neville applies to Machiavelli is difficult to imagine. Of course, the application of the term "divine" to the writer who had widely been decried as a devil reveals more than a trace of Neville's rather wicked sense of humor.[26] However, it also makes manifest

---

[24] Cf. Worden, "Republicanism and the Restoration," 150.

[25] Harrington, *Oceana*, 111.

[26] Neville displays that sense of humor in other of his works, particularly *The Isle of Pines* and *A Parliament of Ladies*. The former relates the adventures of the surviving passengers (one man [George Pine] and four women) from a ship bound for the East Indies who were marooned on an uninhabited island after a severe storm. The result of this shipwreck is that by the four women Mr. Pines produces forty-seven children. Almost a hundred years after the shipwreck, the population of the Isle of Pines is said to be ten or twelve thousand. The

a political principle to which the Englishman is vehemently attached. He understands himself as sharing Machiavelli's view of divine matters – or, more strictly speaking, of the members of the clergy, who, in Neville's view, merit the execrative term more than does the Florentine. Indeed, it just might be the case that Neville rewards the Florentine with the godly appellation of "the divine Machiavel" because Machiavelli criticizes these avaricious corrupters of politics. Neville, who was himself accused of impiety in Richard Cromwell's Parliament because of his alleged declaration that he preferred Cicero to the Bible,[27] must have felt that he had found a kindred spirit in Machiavelli, who was subject to similar charges.

Such sympathy does Neville have for Machiavelli that he writes in the Florentine's name in a letter that purports to be Machiavelli's own effort to vindicate himself. This letter is appended to the beginning of Neville's own English translation of the works of Machiavelli, which appeared in 1675. Declaring Machiavelli to be "one of the greatest Wits, and profoundest Judgments that ever liv'd amongst the Moderns,"[28] he writes in the advertisement to the reader that "I did yet think that it was fit to say something in a Preface to vindicate our Author from those Slanders which Priests, and other byast Pens have laid upon him."[29] He continues that he abandoned this intention, however, when he discovered Machiavelli's own effort. The letter he attributes to Machiavelli is clearly a hoax.[30] It is dated 1 April 1537 – ten years after Machiavelli's death. Thus, it reveals to its readers not Machiavelli's mind but Neville's. By writing in Machiavelli's name,

---

latter work is a satire that describes how the women of ancient Rome, believing erroneously that the Senate had decreed that each man may marry two women, established their own parliament to decree that each woman could have two husbands. During their deliberations, they pass other laws for their pleasure and delight. Robbins describes it as "a very bawdy piece," which makes "free with the reputations of prominent women on the roundhead side" (*Two Republican Tracts*, 6).

[27] Robbins, *Two Republican Tracts*, 8–9; Worden, *Roundhead Reputations*, 61.

[28] I have referred to two versions of the letter: the first is contained in *The Works of the Famous Nicholas Machiavel, Citizen and Secretary of Florence* (London, 1680), and the second is *A True Copy of a Letter Written by N. Machiavill, in Defence of Himself, and his Religion* (London, 1691). Because the earlier version does not have page numbers on the note to the reader or on the letter itself, I have quoted from the later edition for ease of reference. Robbins notes that this letter was published in an enlarged form in 1689 and 1691 and speculates that the additions were the work of another hand (*Two Republican Tracts*, 15). I have not, however, quoted or cited any passage that does not appear in the earlier version. In the passages to which I refer there are minor differences in spelling, punctuation, and capitalization between the two editions.

[29] Neville, *Letter Written by N. Machiavill*, 4, 3. At one point in *Plato Redivivus* the Englishman voices the same concern: "Do not you know that Machiavel, the best and most honest of all the modern politicians, has suffered sufficiently by means of priests, and other ignorant persons?" (168). Robbins attributes the translation to Neville and terms it the first collection of Machiavelli's works in English (Robbins, *Two Republican Tracts*, 15).

[30] Robbins, *Two Republican Tracts*, 15.

Neville offers a means by which to assess his understanding of his Italian predecessor.[31]

Neville's Machiavelli responds to three charges leveled against him and his writings: first, that he possesses "great affection to the Democratical Government, even so much as to undervalue that of Monarchy in respect of it"; second, that his writings "vent very great impieties, slighting and vilifying the Church, as Author of all the Misgovernment in the World, and by such contempt make way for Atheism and Profaneness"; and finally, that his *Prince* in particular describes to "Monarchs all the execrable Villanies that can be invented, and instruct[s] them how to break Faith, and so to Oppress and Enslave their Subjects."[32] The fact that the first and third charges are contradictory, evincing completely different motives and purposes, is not lost on the author of this apologia: "[M]y Accusers . . . make me first exhort and teach Subjects to throw off their Princes, and then to instruct Monarchs how to Enslave and Oppress them."[33]

By far the greatest portion of the letter is devoted to answering the central charge – that of Machiavelli's impiety. That disproportionate length is required because Neville's Machiavelli, rather than taking a defensive posture, actually amplifies the charges against the church that appear in Machiavelli's authentic political writings. In expanding those charges, Neville takes the opportunity to render his version of the Florentine an adherent of the Reformation. Indeed, of greater longevity than the real Machiavelli, Neville's Machiavelli writes approvingly of Luther and Calvin.[34] By so depicting Machiavelli, Neville attempts to make his subject more palatable to his English Protestant audience – perhaps in the hopes of inducing other Englishmen to embrace Machiavelli as "divine."

Neville would essentially repeat the charges that his Machiavelli levels against the church in *Plato Redivivus* through the arguments of the Englishman. Indeed, when touching on the usurpation that brought the priests to the power they exercise "over the persons and consciences of men," the Englishman of *Plato Redivivus* refers to the "incomparable Machiavel" and "his posthumous Letter, printed lately in our language with the translation of his works" (155).

---

[31] Mark Goldie terms this letter "Neville's own encapsulation of Harringtonianism" ("The Civil Religion of James Harrington," in *Languages of Political Theory in Early-Modern Europe*, ed. Anthony Pagden [Cambridge: Cambridge University Press, 1987], 221). For Goldie, Harrington attempts to make Christianity a civil religion by reconciling "the Graeco-Roman *polis* with the Hebraic and Christian Apocalyptic" (209). The creation of that Christian civil religion, for Harrington, requires the overthrow of the "papal tyranny" (210). Thus, Neville's attack on the political power of the priests in Machiavelli's letter and later in *Plato Redivivus* illustrates Neville's debt to Harrington on this theme, according to Goldie.

[32] Neville, *Letter Written by N. Machiavill*, 8–9.

[33] Ibid., 29.

[34] Ibid., 23, 28.

In broaching the charge of impiety, Neville's Machiavelli admits that he has attacked the church: "I do not deny but that I have very frequently, in my Writings, laid the blame upon the Church of *Rome*; not only for all the Misgovernment of Christendom, but even for the depravation, and almost total Destruction of Christian Religion it self in this Province." Having conceded these points, however, the letter writer maintains that his charges do not teach "Men Impiety" or tend toward "Atheism." On the contrary, he avers that "I do firmly Believe the Christian Profession to be the only true Religion now in the World."[35]

In criticizing the church, he begins by subjecting the "Bishops of *Rome*" to his censure for "their insatiable Ambition and Avarice." After commenting on selected passages from the New Testament, in a manner akin, he claims, to his commentary on Livy's history of Rome, he finds no scriptural support for the power that the popes wield.[36] Worst of all, their power led to the "most hellish of all the Innovations brought in by the Popes" – the introduction of the clergy. Neville's Machiavelli explains that the members of the clergy

are a sort of Men, under pretence of ministering to the People in Holy things, set apart, and separated from the rest of Mankind (from whom they have a very distinct, and a very opposite interest) by a Humane Ceremony call'd by a Divine Name, *viz.* Ordination; these, wherever they are found (with the whole body of the Monks, and Fryers, who are called the Regular Clergy) make a Band which may be called the *Janizaries* of the Papacy; these have been the Causers of all the Solicisms and Immoralities in Government, and of all the Impieties and Abominations in Religion, and by consequence of all the Disorder, Villany, and Corruption we suffer under in this detestable Age.[37]

The members of the clergy are exempt from "all Secular Jurisdiction," but they themselves exercise decisive influence over secular rulers through their power over these rulers' religious consciences.[38] Just as there is no basis for the power of the popes in Scripture, so there is no basis for the power of the clergy, although the clergy exercises "an Empire so destructive to Christian Religion, and so pernicious to the Interests of Men."[39] "The word Clergy is a term wholly unknown to the Scriptures, otherwise than in this sense" of "the whole *Jewish* Nation," or in the New Testament in the sense of "the true Believers, who are also called the Elect."[40] Ordination as it is practiced by the church is similarly a sham. In the scriptures it signifies no more than a decree of an assembly of the faithful, "but is particularly used for an Election of any into the Ministry" – a ministry vastly different in its humility and lack

---

[35] Ibid., 16.
[36] Ibid., 18–23.
[37] Ibid., 23.
[38] Ibid., 24.
[39] Ibid., 25.
[40] Ibid., 26.

of political power from the one found in modern European countries. In concluding his vindication of himself on this point, Neville's Machiavelli explains: "From these words, Church, Clergy, Ordination, Pastor... you see what Conclusions these Men have deduced, and how immense a Structure they have raised upon so little a Foundation, and how easily it will fall to the ground, when God shall inspire Christian Princes and States to redeem his Truths, and... to bring back again into the World, the true Original Christian Faith, with the Apostolical Churches, Pastors, and Ordination, so consistent with Moral Vertue, and Integrity."[41]

Neville's Englishman expresses precisely the same sentiments. In front of his Venetian guest, a professed Catholic, he says "I could wish there had never been any" clergy. He explains this potentially insulting statement by claiming that "the purity of Christian religion, as also the good and orderly government of the world, had been much better provided for without them; as it was in the apostolical time, when we hear nothing of clergy" (115). The anticlericalism of Neville's Englishman, like that of Neville's Machiavelli, objects to the fact that the clergy exercise a dominion over human beings: "[T]he empire which the ecclesiastics pretend to over the consciences and persons of men, and the exemption from all secular power" is "a cheat and usurpation" (119). Similarly, the Englishman denounces ordination that purports "to metamorphose a poor lay-idiot, into a heavenly creature: notwithstanding that we find in them the same human nature, and the same necessities of it, to which they were subject before such transformation" (118). In terms strikingly similar to the sham Machiavelli, the Englishman explains that scripture does not support the rite of ordination or the formation of a church distinct from civil authority (116–18).

That similarity of arguments should be no shock given the fact that Neville is the author of the opinions of both the Florentine and the Englishman. That similarity is nevertheless important; it reveals what Neville finds so attractive in the thought of Machiavelli. Of course, whereas the anticlericalism of Neville's Englishman risks only insulting the Catholic visitor from Venice, that of the authentic Machiavelli risked much more; given his place and time, the Italian's views were both shocking and dangerous, while those expressed by Neville, who writes in England after the Reformation, were commonplace. Despite the differences in their respective rhetorical situations, Neville can extrapolate from the anticlericalism of Machiavelli's authentic writings to find a thinker who embraces his own views. Thus Neville's understanding of Machiavelli permits Neville to view the Florentine as sympathetic to Protestantism, just as is the Englishman. The core of Neville's Machiavellianism, then, might be said to reside in the vehement anticlericalism of the Florentine with which the Englishman identifies.

[41] Ibid., 27.

Neville and Neville's Machiavelli on Republicanism

A very important second layer surrounds the core of Neville's attraction to Machiavelli. That second layer is Machiavelli's republicanism, and these two strata, it must be said, are closely related. Catholicism, according to the Englishman, supports monarchy, whereas Protestantism supports republicanism. Thus, he notes that "popery might have suited well enough with our old constitution; yet as to the present estate which inclines to popularity, it would be wholly as inconsistent with it" (155). Nevertheless, both Neville's republicanism and his understanding of Machiavelli's republicanism are somewhat equivocal. Neville is, and he understands Machiavelli to be, willing to make accommodations with the rule of one. As we will see, the recognition of this fact leads to the ultimate Machiavellianism of the Englishman's proposal for the four councils to limit the king's power.

The Machiavelli who speaks in Neville's letter admits that he is a republican but insists that he is a temperate one. He defends himself against the charge of advocating republican government by pointing to his measured procedure in the *Discourses*, the work that his critics point to as evincing his republican bias. He protests that he merely followed "the Order of my Author, without ever taking upon me to argue problematically, much less to decide which of these two Governments is the best."[42] Despite this restraint, however, he concedes that his sympathies lie with republics. What if the accusation against him regarding his preference for republics were true, he asks. His personal sympathies in favor of republics must be accepted as natural when it is remembered, as he reminds his reader, he had been born in and employed by a city that "did owe all Wealth and Greatness, and all property to" a republic. "If I had not very designedly avoided all dogmaticalness in my Observations," he continues, ". . . I might easily have concluded from the Premises I lay down, that a Democracy founded upon good Orders, is the best and most excellent Government."[43] Moreover, he later sees fit to warn princes that "some Monarchies have been wholly subverted, and changed into Democracies, by the Tyranny of their Princes,"[44] and thus Neville's Machiavelli can be seen as giving Charles II of England a warning regarding the possible consequences of ruling by force against the wishes of the people and Parliament. Thus, Neville makes his Machiavelli acknowledge that his principles are republican but protest that he is no agitator.

The spurious letter goes on to reveal that it was Machiavelli's intention in the *Discourses* to show that "Humane Nature it self obtained amongst the *Romans*, did proceed naturally from their Government, and was but a plain effect and consequence of the perfection of their Commonwealth."

---

[42] Ibid., 9.
[43] Ibid., 10.
[44] Ibid., 13.

Indeed, Neville's Machiavelli marvels at the "Integrity, and purity of Manners, that scorning of Riches and Life it self, when the Publick was concerned" displayed by the citizens of republican Rome.[45] In this manner, Neville's Machiavelli reveals himself to be more of a classical republican than Neville himself. Although taking the liberty of extending Machiavelli's life, Neville did not go so far as to claim that his Machiavelli was actually familiar with the thought of Harrington. Therefore, it cannot be expected that his Machiavelli is familiar with the doctrine that such moral effects as the care the Romans manifested for the public good and the purity of their manners derive from the distribution of property in the state – principles that Neville himself espouses through the Englishman of *Plato Redivivus*.

The republican sympathies of Neville's Machiavelli surface again in this spurious letter when he turns to the last charge against which he defends himself. *The Prince*, he maintains, neither recommends tyrannical government nor intends to teach unscrupulous men how to establish that form of rule. That work, he reveals, is merely a "Satyr against them, and a true Character of them." Of the rulers who populate this work, he says "[i]f I have been a little too punctual in designing these Monsters, and drawn them to the Life in all their Lineaments, and Colours, I hope Mankind will know them, the better to avoid them." On this point, he cautions that he did not intend to impugn great princes such as the kings of France or England, for instance, but rather those "Vermine" that have arisen from the corruption of Italy.[46] Moreover, one should not turn to *The Prince* to know his mind, but rather to the *Discourses*, where he was "a little more serious" than he was in "this Book of the Prince."[47]

Despite these decided republican sympathies, Neville's Machiavelli avers that "the animating of private Men, either directly or indirectly, to disobey, much less to shake off any Government, how despotical soever, was never in my thoughts or Writings."[48] Moreover, rebellion defined as the design to overthrow the reigning government whether overtly or covertly is "the greatest Crime that can be committed amongst Men." Nevertheless, it is a crime that will never be eradicated as long as "Princes tyrannize" and, "by Inslaving and Oppressing their Subjects, make Magistracy, which was intended for the Benefit of Mankind, prove a Plague and destruction to

[45] Ibid., 10.

[46] Ibid., 30.

[47] Ibid., 31. This understanding of *The Prince* is very much akin to that which Spinoza expresses, who wishes to ascribe to Machiavelli the "good design" in writing *The Prince* of "show[ing] how cautious a free multitude should be of entrusting its welfare absolutely to one man." This intention on Machiavelli's part is plausible, according to Spinoza, because "that most farseeing man" "was favourable to liberty, for the maintenance of which he has besides given the most wholesome advice" (*Political Treatise* 5.7, in *The Chief Works of Benedict de Spinoza*, trans. R. H. M. Elwes, 2 vols. [London: George Bell and Sons, 1891], 1:315).

[48] Neville, *Letter Written by N. Machiavill*, 11.

it." "[I]t is impossible," he continues, "that Humane Nature . . . can support
with patience and submission the greatest Cruelty and Injustice, whenever
either the Weakness of their Princes, the Unanimity of the People, or any
other favourable accident, shall give them reasonable hopes to mend their
Condition, and provide better for their own interest by Insurrection."[49] In
this way, the letter's author actually justifies rebellion against princes, as well
as explaining why it will remain a constant in the human condition.

For this reason, it seems, Neville's fictitious Machiavelli can, at the end of
his letter, justify his actions against the Medici during the siege of Florence
in 1530, when the Medici struggled to regain the city of which they had
lost control in 1527. This long-lived Machiavelli admits that in this instance
he "did break the Confines of my Neutrality, and not only Acted as I was
commanded barely, but rouz'd my self, . . . Acting as a Soldier . . . at the Age of
above Sixty." The battle having been lost, however, Machiavelli praises the
new Medici leader of Florence, "the Most Excellent *Seigneur Cosimo*," who
came to power in 1537.[50] Like, Neville himself, Neville's Machiavelli, having
once been a participant in a republican government and making no secret
of his continued admiration of such governments, displays his willingness to
accommodate himself to the rule of one when the battle has been lost.[51]

Neville, it so happens, was a friend of the descendant of the Medici whom
Machiavelli praises. The Englishman met the heir to the Grand Duchy of
Tuscany, Cosimo, during his travels in Italy after the Restoration in England.
When the heir visited England in 1669, Neville hosted Cosimo and traveled
with him.[52] They remained correspondents years after Cosimo became the
grand duke in 1670.[53] Moreover, the advertisement to the reader praises

---

[49] Ibid., 12–13.
[50] Ibid., 34.
[51] Neville, in the advertisement to the reader, does seem to question tacitly Machiavelli's loyalty
to this new prince by claiming that someone named Machiavelli participated in a rebellion
shortly after this letter was penned: "*[W]e find, in the story of those times, that in the Month
of* August *following, in the same Year 1537 this* Nicòlo Machiavelli *(except there were another
of that Name) was committed Prisoner to the* Bargello, *amongst those who were taken in Arms
against* Cosimo, *at the Castle of* Montemurli; *notwithstanding all his Compliments in this Letter
to that Prince, and profest Allegiance to him*" (Neville, *Letter Written by N. Machiavill*, 4–5).
Neville then muses that the passion to restore liberty to one's country has affected other
great men, such as Brutus and Cassius. Given that the whole letter is a creation of Neville's
imagination, this detail, even though he finds reason to question the true identity of the
participant, must serve to undermine the dedication of Neville's Machiavelli to Cosimo.
[52] Robbins, *Two Republican Tracts*, 13.
[53] Raab, *English Face of Machiavelli*, 271. Raab, in fact, speculates that Neville created the ruse
of the letter as a means to flatter Cosimo. According to Raab, Neville's choice of 1537 was
no accident. It was the year that the members of the younger branch of the Medici assumed
their rule of Florence, when Cosimo I became duke of Florence. Thus, according to Raab's
scenario, Neville pays his friend a compliment by having the republican Machiavelli praise
his ancestor. This may very well be the case. Nevertheless, Raab does not account for – let
alone mention – the fact that Neville suggests that his Machiavelli may have rebelled against

the entire younger branch of the Medici, members of which ruled Florence as dukes and became the grand dukes of Tuscany in 1570. Neville declares that "there was never any Succession of Princes since the World began, in which all the Royal Vertues, and other Qualities necessary to those who Rule over Men, were more eminently perspicuous, than in every individual of this Line."[54] Neville's friend is given his due, when the advertisement points to his particular "Prudence, Magnanimity, Charity, Liberality, and above all, the Humanity, Courtesie and Affability."[55] Neville is not so vehement a republican that he shuns the very prospect of complimenting sole rulers, whether sincerely or not. The Machiavelli of his creation shares this nondogmatic quality with him.

The Machiavellian Quality of the Englishman's Proposal

The Englishman of *Plato Redivivus* consistently shies away from any hint of overt disloyalty to Charles II. Similarly, he shies away from the violent and spectacular in Machiavelli. Nevertheless, his slyly subtle proposal for England's future finds a source in the authentic writings of Machiavelli.

The Englishman's preference for subtlety is evident in the fact that he would have been happy to overlook the controversy surrounding the Protestant duke of Monmouth when discoursing on England's political situation. The Doctor, however, is adamant that Monmouth's claim to the throne not be overlooked, given the works that are published in support of his claim to the throne and the "great and honourable persons" who "frequent him in private, and countenance him in public" (164). The Doctor having made this case for the duke's consideration, the Englishman responds with a note of exasperation, "I see I must be more tedious than I intended" (165). The tedium of the Englishman's explanation of why Monmouth is unlikely to succeed to the throne with or without the king's consent does not deter the Doctor from pursuing the possibility that the people will nevertheless make Monmouth their cause for rebellion (169). Unlike certain other political thinkers of the time, notably Sidney, who was executed for his alleged involvement in the Rye House Plot to kill Charles and his brother James, Neville displays no enthusiasm for the possibilities represented by Monmouth. Neville seeks a more subtle revolution.[56]

Sidney and Cato, as the following chapters show, have a particular penchant for the violent and vengeful in Machiavelli. These thinkers betray an

---

his prince in the months following this letter. See my note 51. Perhaps Neville, like the Machiavelli of his creation, would be similarly moved by a worthy opportunity for rebellion against princely rule.

54 Neville, *Letter Written by N. Machiavill*, 5.

55 Ibid., 6.

56 "Yet if [Neville] insists on peaceful means, his ends are revolutionary" (Worden, "Republicanism and the Restoration," 151).

attraction to Machiavelli's discussion in 3.1 of the *Discourses* of the salutary effects of spectacular executions, and seek to apply that chapter's lessons to their situation in England. Such affinity for this aspect of Machiavelli's thought is completely absent in *Plato Redivivus*. In seeking his subtle revolution, however, Neville emphasizes an element of Machiavelli's thought that Sidney and Cato ignore.

As we have seen, when the Doctor imputes to the Englishman the desire to restore a commonwealth to England, the Englishman denies it, citing their oaths of obedience to Charles. There appear to be considerations in Neville's mind other than his oath of obedience; he is keenly aware of the dangers of speaking too candidly in a monarchy.[57] He has the publisher say, for example, in the note to the reader that "talking of state-affairs in a monarchy must needs be more offensive, than it was in the democracy where Plato lived" (69).[58] In this way, Neville intimates just how careful he has to be even in speaking through his English Gentleman about contemporary political matters. Although his criticism of the church entails no dangers, his criticism of his king certainly does.

After having delineated his plans for the four councils, the Venetian schooled in the ways of republics asks whether it would not be better, "now you are upon so great alterations, to make an annual elective senate; or at least one wherein the members should be but for life, and not hereditary?" The Englishman objects to this suggestion: "By no means, sir; the less change the better: and in this case, the metaphysical maxim is more true than in any, viz. nothing should be multiplied unnecessarily: for great alterations fright men, and puzzle them; and there is no need of it in this case" (192). Neville's Englishman is careful to keep the outward forms of the monarchy.

At this point of the work, its editor inserts a note referring the reader to chapter 1.25 of Machiavelli's *Discourses*. In that chapter Machiavelli treats the change from the kingship to the republic in Rome. Machiavelli writes approvingly of the fact that the Romans who founded the republic retained certain ceremonial and religious forms from the kingship so that the people would not be dissatisfied with their new way of life and thus not "desire the return of the kings." Anyone who wishes to maintain an innovation in a state, he insists, "is under the necessity of retaining at least the shadow of its ancient modes so that it may not appear to the peoples to have changed its order even if in fact the new orders are altogether alien to the past ones." His admonition arises from his observation that "the generality of men feed on what appears as much as on what is."[59]

---

[57] Raab, *English Face of Machiavelli*, 218.
[58] Neville was imprisoned on charges of conspiracy in 1663 (Robbins, *Two Republican Tracts*, 12).
[59] Machiavelli, *Discourses* 1.25.1.

Clearly, Neville is aware of this principle, because Neville's Englishman refers to this very facet of Roman history in the second day's dialogue. When speaking of the change from the rule of a king to that of a republic, the Englishman says that the leaders of the new republic "chose an officer that was to perform the king's function, in certain sacrifices which Numa appointed to be performed by the king; lest the people should think their religion was changed" (103). When it comes to his own proposals for England, he strictly adheres to Machiavelli's advice, being careful not to frighten and puzzle the people. He resists the appearance of profound political change by having the king retain the throne. Nevertheless, the change is, in fact, profound because the councils elected by Parliament wield the king's former power. In this manner, his Englishman endeavors to introduce a free way of life, without changing the outward form of the monarchy. Neville's proposal for England endeavors to "suppress an ancient way of life in a city and to turn it to a new and free way of life," because Neville knows, at Machiavelli's instruction, that "since the new things alter the minds of men, you should contrive that those alterations retain as much of the ancient as possible."[60]

Therefore, the political proposal that Neville offers in *Plato Redivivus* is Machiavellian – but that Machiavellianism is one of a certain character. Neville abandons the spectacular in Machiavelli for the subtle.[61] Surely, this abandonment is very much in the spirit of the thinker who, while admiring force, praises the deviousness of the fox and advises that important ends could sometimes be achieved only through fraud.[62] Neville puts this subtlety to use in the service of republicanism. This use of Machiavelli is particularly appropriate given that Neville understands Machiavelli to be a committed republican, but, as his spurious letter maintains, Neville's Machiavelli is not a dogmatic one. Rather, his Machiavelli, like Neville himself, is willing to make accommodations with monarchy. In shunning dogmatism, and in being willing to make accommodations, each gains for himself more latitude to further a republican agenda.

It is certainly fair to ask what could be more Machiavellian than such cunning deception. Nevertheless, in taking this Machiavellian path, Neville abandons another. Machiavelli often speaks of a great man who takes the most extreme, and hence overt, actions to reform or found a state.[63] Machiavelli emboldens prospective reformers and founders to the cause by assuring them that the bloody deeds that their formidable task demands will

---

[60] Ibid.

[61] Worden likens this Machiavellian strategy of *Plato Redivivus* to Neville's parliamentary strategy in 1659 on behalf of Harrington's republican ideas ("*Oceana*: Origins and Aftermath," 131).

[62] Machiavelli, *Prince* 18, and *Discourses* 2.13.

[63] Machiavelli, *Discourses* 1.9, 10, 17, 18, 55.

be more than forgiven at its successful completion; the prize of everlasting glory attends their founding of a republic.[64]

In Neville's version of England's republican future, not only is force absent at its institution, but so too is the great man who will take sole power to institute these changes and receive the reward of glory. This is quite a change from Harrington, who transmits the Machiavellian doctrine that a founding must be orchestrated by one man whose extraordinary measures to that end must be excused. Although Neville's English predecessor diverges from Machiavelli in being so wary of the dangerous effects of glory in his Oceana, Harrington does bow to Machiavelli in assuring that Oceana's founder was crowned with glory, both during and after his death. It is Machiavelli's dictum, after all, that the greatest human types seek this greatest of all rewards. Thus, Harrington holds out the award of Megaletor's glory to Cromwell, whom he hoped would be moved by his depiction of it to institute Harrington's republic in reality.

Of course, one might say that in *Plato Redivivus* the character of the Englishman who in the dialogue proposes the reformation of the constitution and Neville himself who stands behind his character are to be the founders of England's new institutions. Nevertheless, even if they can be understood to be founders in this way, Neville takes measures to assure neither his character nor the character's creator will receive the reward of glory. First, the manner in which the Englishman offers the proposal will mute his authorship, and thereby Neville's, of England's new constitution. The Englishman would have the Parliament offer this proposal to the king during its next meeting. In making the proffer, Parliament would be its author and, in so being, might make significant changes in the Englishman's original conception. Second, the very notion of an individual founder contravenes the spirit of this innovation. It is to be muted change that is not to draw attention to itself so as not to "fright men, and puzzle them" (192). The very character of the change Neville proposes derogates from anyone's particular glory.

As we have seen, Neville seeks a subtle revolution. In the revolution he would seek to foment,[65] he severely restricts the prerogative of England's king. His revolution conceived more broadly will do something more, however. He transforms the very basis of government when he accepts and transcribes into his work Hobbes's doctrine that government is a human artifact created for the purpose of remedying the state of war in the state of nature and serving the desires of human beings for safety and security. Government,

---

[64] "And truly, if a prince seeks the glory of the world, he ought to desire to possess a corrupt city – not to spoil it entirely as did Caesar but to reorder it as did Romulus. And truly the heavens cannot give to men a greater opportunity for glory, nor can men desire any greater" (1.10.6). Romulus achieved this glory despite murdering both his brother and his colleague in rule (1.9.2).

[65] Ultimately, the Englishman is not optimistic about the possibility of reform: "I believe that we are not ripe yet for any great reform" (196).

he claims, rests on consent. In this manner, Neville imports a central tenet of liberalism into his understanding not only of England's history but also that of all governments. Neville, as is his way, moves in a very subtle fashion away from Harrington, his friend and mentor. In the process, Neville prepares for another subtle revolution, one that blends Machiavellian republicanism with liberalism.

6

Algernon Sidney as Anticipator of Locke and Secret Admirer of Machiavelli

In his *Discourses Concerning Government*, Sidney undertakes to vindicate human liberty against the claims of Robert Filmer, whose *Patriarcha* maintains that nature and God dictate human dependency. Human beings, in Filmer's view, are born subject to a rigidly hierarchial chain of command that passes upward from the father, to the king, and finally to God. On the way to his repudiation of the Filmerian divine right of kings, Sidney produced the diffuse *Discourses*, which, among many other topics, considers the corrupting influence of monarchy, the unreasonable character of inheritance as a claim to rule, and the vigor of republics.

Liberty, it becomes increasingly clear as his *Discourses* progresses, is best guaranteed through a republic.[1] He acted on that belief throughout his life, although it has been said that his commitment to republicanism was "intermittent and inconsistent."[2] He fought on the side of Parliament and was wounded in battle at Marston Moor in 1644. He entered Parliament in 1646, where he somewhat surprisingly – given the glee he will later manifest in his *Discourses* when contemplating the punishment of wayward monarchs – opposed the execution of Charles I. He came to work closely with a group of republicans in Parliament, among whom was Henry Neville, whose family had shared friendships and alliances with his own that went back for generations. He actively supported England's efforts in the Anglo-Dutch war, which broke out in the middle of 1652, and he joined the Council of State later that same year. So actively did he encourage the English republic to pursue the war that Blair Worden suggests that his deep-seated republicanism

---

[1] Jonathan Scott claims that the "practical intention [of the *Discourses Concerning Government*] was to argue for insurrection. In this role, the *Discourses* was to provide what may be the only explicit defence of rebellion, both the word and the thing, in seventeenth-century English political thought" (*Algernon Sidney and the Restoration Crisis, 1677–1683* [Cambridge: Cambridge University Press, 1991], 203).

[2] Houston, *Algernon Sidney*, 15.

dates from this period.[3] He denounced Cromwell's dissolution of the Rump Parliament and his Protectorate. After the Restoration he was an exile in Europe for seventeen years, living primarily in Italy, Holland, and France. He alternatively encouraged the Dutch and French to help orchestrate an invasion of England in hopes of establishing a republic there. He returned to England in 1677, and became active in the resistance to Charles II. He failed in his attempts to be reelected to Parliament. During this time, in order to advance his republican cause he took payments from the French ambassador to England; France at this time was providing money both to Charles II and his opposition in hopes of keeping England divided.[4]

Ultimately executed in 1683 for his purported involvement in the Rye House Plot, Sidney was both theorist and hero for the American founders. Both roles, intellectual forebear and heroic martyr, are closely intertwined in his reception in America,[5] as well they should be, since the prosecution used his ideas as espoused in his then unpublished *Discourses Concerning Government* as the second witness necessary for conviction for treason under English law. Surely, the ability of the English Whigs to apotheosize Sidney's memory derives from the manner of his death, but there is also evidence – particularly in America – for an appreciation of Sidney's theory unencumbered by the memory of his death.[6]

There can be no more striking evidence of that appreciation than when Thomas Jefferson took the occasion of the selection of the curriculum for

---

[3] Blair Worden, "The Commonwealth Kidney of Algernon Sidney," *Journal of British Studies* 24 (January 1985): 7.

[4] For accounts and interpretations of these incidents, see Houston, *Algernon Sidney*, 48–9, and Scott, *Restoration Crisis*, 108–13. See also Peter Karsten, *Patriot-Heroes in England and America: Political Symbolism and Changing Values over Three Centuries* (Madison: University of Wisconsin Press, 1978), 44–6, for reactions in England and America to the revelation in 1771 that Sidney was the recipient of these bribes.

[5] Houston makes this point: "Had Sidney not been a martyr, it is unlikely the *Discourses* would have been as widely read in eighteenth-century America; had he not written the *Discourses*, on the other hand, it is unlikely his death would have received the attention it did" (*Algernon Sidney*, 235). For considerations of Sidney's impact in America, see Caroline Robbins, "Algernon Sidney's *Discourses Concerning Government*: Textbook of Revolution," *William and Mary Quarterly*, 3d ser., 4 (1947): 267–96, and Karsten, *Patriot-Heroes*, 38–44. Bailyn declares, "above all, [the American Revolutionary writers] referred to the doctrines of Algernon Sidney, that 'martyr to civil liberty' whose *Discourses Concerning Government* (1698) became, in Robbins' phrase, a 'textbook of revolution' in America" (Bailyn, *Ideological Origins*, 34–5).

[6] Sidney's *Discourses Concerning Government* was a common holding of colonial libraries. The source for colonial holdings is H. Trevor Colbourn's accounting of public and private library holdings and book sellers' lists in *The Lamp of Experience: Whig History and the Intellectual Origins of the American Revolution* (Chapel Hill: University of North Carolina Press, 1965), 199–232. On the basis of Colbourn's research, Karsten proclaims, "After Trenchard's and Gordon's contemporaneous *Cato's Letters* and Locke's *Two Treatises on Government*, Sidney's *Discourses* were the most popular of all works on political science in the colonies" (*Patriot-Heroes*, 34).

the university that he had founded to identify the sources from which he believed the American principles of government had derived. The minutes of the 4 March 1825 meeting of the board of visitors for the University of Virginia report the following resolution: "[I]t is the opinion of this Board that as to the general principles of liberty and the rights of man, in nature and in society, the doctrines of Locke, in his 'Essay concerning the true original extent and end of civil government,' and of Sidney in his 'Discourses on government,' may be considered as those generally approved by our fellow citizens of this, and the United States."⁷ The board acted on this declaration by enjoining its scholars to imbibe the prescribed dose of American liberty directly from its sources in the thought of these two Englishmen.

Jefferson's statement helps to underscore the unsatisfactory character of the republican scholarship on English and American political thought of the seventeenth and eighteenth centuries. First, it asserts the importance of the thought of Locke in informing the principles of the American regime, a notion denied by the republican interpretation of the American Revolution. Second, it links the political thought of Locke and of Sidney, a link that this scholarship has difficulty countenancing; liberalism is largely incompatible with republicanism, or so says this scholarship.⁸ Jefferson, thus, identifies something for which this scholarship cannot account: Sidney's thought offers both prominent anticipations of Locke's liberalism,⁹ as well as deeply held republican sentiments, largely derived from Machiavelli, as I will show in this chapter.

In fact, Sidney is much more Machiavellian than scholars have hitherto recognized. Specifically, he embraces two of Machiavelli's conclusions from the *Discourses on Livy*: the superiority of warlike Romulus to the peace-loving Numa and the superiority of bellicose Rome to all other republics. Like Machiavelli, Sidney does not embrace these conclusions without a great

---

⁷ Thomas Jefferson, *Writings* (New York: Library of America, 1984), 479.

⁸ Although Sidney does not figure prominently in Pocock's *Machiavellian Moment*, Pocock does secure a place for him in the classical tradition that opposed Locke (J. G. A. Pocock, "Virtue and Commerce in the Eighteenth Century," *Journal of Interdisciplinary History* 3 [1972]: 127). Scott, who defines classical republicanism as "combining Aristotelian political forms with the Polybian idea of balance...and the republicanism of Machiavelli's *Discourses*," challenges Pocock by arguing that Sidney is a better representative of this classical tradition than Harrington, the English thinker who figures so prominently in Pocock's depiction and whom Scott depicts as a Hobbesian (Jonathan Scott, *Algernon Sidney and the English Republic, 1623–1677* [Cambridge: Cambridge University Press, 1988], 15, and "Rapture of Motion"). For Skinner's treatment of Sidney as a participant in the neo–roman tradition, see *Liberty before Liberalism*, 12, 23, 26, 38. Elsewhere, Scott does point to the manner in which Sidney's thought coincides with Locke's (e.g, Scott, *Restoration Crisis*, 208, 211). Wootton, too, notes a similarity between Sidney's thought and that of Locke (David Wootton, introduction to *Political Writings of John Locke* [New York: Mentor, 1993], 14–15).

⁹ This aspect of his thought links him, of course, to Nedham, who earlier offers some of the same anticipations (Worden, "Republicanism and Restoration," 153, 158–9).

deal of travail, subjecting initial conclusions to fundamental revision.[10] In the end, Sidney shows, as does Machiavelli, that his readers' judgment must accept the necessity – indeed, the desirability – of war. These conclusions, in turn, force Sidney to break with the philosophical authority of Aristotle, to whom he often refers and whom he clearly follows early in his *Discourses* when he offers the dictum that "*homo est animal rationale*" (1.18.60; see also 1.16.51).[11] In effect, in the course of his *Discourses*, Sidney moves from espousing the highly respectable republicanism of Aristotle to the belligerent republicanism of Machiavelli. Whereas Aristotle's republicanism endeavors to cultivate the reason of its citizens, Machiavelli's endeavors to unleash their passions.

Despite relying on Machiavelli's political teachings, Sidney seems to attempt to distance himself from Machiavelli. As a consideration of Sidney's use of the Machiavellian principle that endorses a periodic return to first principles through the spectacular punishment of overweening leaders will show, Sidney finds reason to dispute his teacher's conclusions even when compelled to acknowledge Machiavelli's tutelage. This dispute notwithstanding, Sidney applies, with a relish that surpasses even Machiavelli's, this particular lesson of his mentor. Although Sidney gleefully endorses the necessity of ferocity in punishing wrongdoers, he applies that Machiavellian ferocity to a liberal purpose, that of punishing a despotic ruler's encroachment on the life, liberty, and property of citizens.

Thus, Sidney in important ways anticipates the political thinking of John Locke. He, like Locke, utilizes the Hobbesian understanding that government rests on the consent of those who seek to alleviate the difficulties of the prepolitical condition by entering into society. Both use this notion to show that government is constructed for the express purpose of providing security, and both assert, very much unlike the Hobbesian understanding, that governments that fail in providing that security can be changed.

In this way, an examination of Sidney's thought helps to reveal that the classical republican depiction of the stark distance between Machiavellian republicanism and liberalism is overdrawn, because he is himself close both to Machiavelli, the alleged patron of classical republicanism, and to Locke, the advocate for liberal individualism. Thus, Sidney's thought suggests how Machiavelli's republicanism and Lockean liberalism might be compatible.

In Sidney's thought, however, that ultimate compatibility between the two strains of thought remains at the level of a suggestion. Because Sidney is such

---

[10] Lee Ward ("Rhetoric and Natural Rights in Algernon Sidney's *Discourses Concerning Government*," *Interpretation* 28 [Winter 2000–1]: 119–45) describes a somewhat different, but nevertheless complementary, movement in Sidney's argument in the *Discourses*.

[11] Quotations from Sidney are derived from *Discourses Concerning Government*, ed. Thomas G. West (Indianapolis: Liberty Classics, 1990). References to chapter, section, and page numbers appear in the text.

an enthusiastic acolyte of Machiavelli's belligerent republicanism, a tension remains in his thought between his liberalism and his Machiavellianism. Although he ultimately bases his politics on the attempt to satisfy human passions, as does the liberal, he chooses violent means to arrive at that end. As a result, although his understanding of the purpose of politics promises security, he cannot act on that promise to the extent that Locke does. Whereas Sidney promotes the people's security against the tyrannical inclinations of leaders, as does Locke, he fails to make an attempt at shielding the people from the loss of life and property that war brings, as Locke surely does not. Thus, Sidney's thought helps to illustrate the degree to which Machiavelli's imperialism must be tamed before the synthesis of republicanism and liberalism can be achieved.

Sidney's Sly Use of Machiavelli

Although scholars have frequently noted a Machiavellian element in his admiration for republics,[12] they have not fully explored the extent to which Sidney follows Machiavelli in both method and substance when not explicitly referring to the Florentine. The lack of attention to important passages that do not announce themselves as Machiavellian on the part of those interested in Sidney's Machiavellian origins is far from surprising, given that Sidney appears to wish to obscure the source for his ruminations. It is certainly easy to dismiss Sidney's *Discourses* as too maddeningly convoluted to contain a method; nonetheless, Sidney seems to maintain a consistent approach with respect to his use of Machiavelli: he is careful not to reveal early in the work his allegiance to this thinker. In so doing, his *Discourses* contains two seemingly contradictory purposes: first, to mimic the manner

---

[12] Fink, *Classical Republicans*, 155–8; Raab, *English Face of Machiavelli*, 221–3; Scott, *English Republic*, 13, 15, 17–18, 30–3; Scott, *Restoration Crisis*, 350, 354, 357–8; Ward, "Rhetoric and Natural Rights in Sidney," 130–3; Thomas G. West, foreword to *Discourses Concerning Government*, xxii; Neal Wood, "The Value of Asocial Sociability: Contributions of Machiavelli, Sidney and Montesquieu," in *Machiavelli and the Nature of Political Thought*, ed. Martin Fleisher (New York: Atheneum, 1972), 292–8; Worden, *Roundhead Reputations*, 140; Worden, "Commonwealth Kidney," 18–19; Worden, "Classical Republicanism and Puritan Revolution," 188. Scott and Ward are the scholars who examine in an extended fashion Sidney's reliance on Machiavelli's thought (for Scott, see particularly *Restoration Crisis*, 235–7). My understanding of Sidney's use of Machiavelli is similar to that of Ward. In contrast, Houston denies that Machiavelli exerted an important influence on Sidney (*Algernon Sidney*, 164–65). Houston, though, draws many similarities between Locke and Sidney, and argues, in a manner compatible with my thesis that republicanism is not an antiliberal doctrine (e.g., 4, n. 6; 225). This view notwithstanding, his acceptance of the republican interpretation of Machiavelli's thought (e.g., 217–18, 173) that implies a strict opposition between Machiavellianism and Lockeanism perhaps blinds him both to the possibility that in many ways Sidney borrows from Machiavelli and to the ultimate compatibility between Locke and Machiavelli on some critical issues.

in which his Florentine master presents important arguments; and, second, to appear to maintain a respectable distance from that very master. Despite Sidney's best efforts, however, the very rhetoric that he uses to distance himself from Machiavelli, when carefully examined, actually ties the Englishman more closely to Machiavelli; Sidney's rhetorical style is thoroughly Machiavellian.[13]

Sidney reveals his knowledge of Machiavelli's *Prince* early in the first chapter of his *Discourses* when he proclaims, " '[T]is an eternal truth, that a weak or wicked prince can never have a wise council, nor receive any benefit by one that is imposed upon him, unless they have a power of acting without him, which would render the government in effect aristocratical" (1.3.14). He is

---

[13] Worden's book *Roundhead Reputations* suggests a possible explanation for Sidney's apparently devious rhetorical strategy: another, who was both sympathetic to Machiavelli and practiced in rhetorical deception, later edited Sidney's original work. Worden finds that the "men who published [Edmund] Ludlow's *Memoirs* also produced, at the same time, Sidney's *Discourses Concerning Government*" (13). With respect to Ludlow's *Memoirs*, published in 1698–9, Worden offers compelling evidence that John Toland edited the manuscript and largely rewrote it (95–121). With respect to Sidney's *Discourses*, published in 1698, he suggests that Toland not only wrote its introduction, but in preparing Sidney's manuscript for publication, Toland might also have forged parts of it (13). See particularly his discussion of the first sentence of both texts (101). Ultimately, however, Worden concludes that Toland, "who took so many liberties with Ludlow's text," "is unlikely to have done so on anything like the same scale" with Sidney's manuscript for the *Discourses*, and that "[w]e probably have, in the *Discourses*, more or less the text Sidney wrote" (131–2). One particularly interesting aspect of Worden's claim for Toland's editorship of the *Discourses* is that Toland is the known author of *Tetradymus*. In the second part of that work, entitled "Clidophorus, or Of the Exoteric and Esoteric Philosophy," Toland argues that ancient and modern authors alike have hidden their true meanings for the sake of self-preservation. The rhetoric of the *Discourses* that obscures Sidney's reliance on Machiavelli's teachings is strikingly akin to the type of dissimulating writing that Toland describes in this work. The question that arises from this recognition is whether Toland might be responsible both for the deep reliance on Machiavelli's teachings in the *Discourses* as it has come down to us and for the attempt to obscure the depth of that reliance. A comparison of the *Discourses* with Sidney's *Court Maxims*, written in the mid-1660s but not discovered until 1976, and for which Sidney was almost certainly solely responsible, seems to support Toland's responsibility for the later work. In this earlier work, Sidney also makes use of Machiavelli's thought, but his attitude toward it is very different; he regards the Florentine largely as the reason-of-state thinker of *The Prince*, whose inspiration for devious court politics he decries. In addition, the manuscript does not support military acquisition to the extent of Sidney's *Discourses*. See, for example, Algernon Sidney, *Court Maxims*, ed. Hans W. Blom, Eco Haitsma Mulier, and Ronald Janse (Cambridge: Cambridge University Press, 1996), 15–16; on this point, see Scott, *English Republic*, 191. The work is also noticeably more religious. These differences buttress the claim, as Worden recognizes, that Toland may have played a significant role in editing the *Discourses* (*Roundhead Reputations*, 144). Indeed, Worden finds that Toland's most significant change in Ludlow's manuscript was to turn a deeply religious thinker into a secular figure. In the context of this evidence, Worden muses, "Toland's hand, though it can be guessed at, cannot be proved" (144). Given this uncertainty regarding the authorship of the *Discourses*, I will refer to its author as Sidney.

clearly borrowing from chapter 23 of *The Prince* where Machiavelli broaches this issue of a deficient prince being advised by an astute subordinate:

For this is a general rule that never fails: that a prince who is not wise by himself cannot be counseled well, unless indeed by chance he should submit himself to one person alone to govern him in everything, who is a very prudent man. In this case he could well be, but it would not last long because that governor would in a short time take away his state.[14]

Sidney agrees with Machiavelli's conclusion that the existence of so clever an adviser will transform the character of the state. Moreover, Sidney is as convinced as Machiavelli is of the veracity of this maxim. Sidney's "eternal truth" is a clear echo of Machiavelli's "general rule that never fails."

Much later in the *Discourses* Sidney returns to the same issue. This time he credits Machiavelli with the idea, but disagrees with it: "[T]ho it were not impossible (as Machiavelli says it is) for a weak prince to receive any benefit from a good council, we may certainly conclude, that a people can never expect any good council chosen by one who is weak or vicious" (3.16.404–5). Sidney's very different uses of the same passage from *The Prince* show that he is willing to attribute an idea to Machiavelli when he disagrees with it explicitly, but unwilling to do so when he agrees with the Florentine; he adheres to this strategy consistently throughout the entirety of the work. His Machiavellianism is muted. Nevertheless, Sidney's rhetorical style reveals its author to be quite Machiavellian.

Embracing the Machiavellian Necessity of War

Sidney becomes much more Machiavellian in the second chapter of his *Discourses*, when he examines in detail another Machiavellian topic – the necessity of war. He borrows not only the matter of Machiavelli's arguments but also the manner of their presentation and does not bother to cite his source. The matter of Machiavelli's arguments, which Sidney ultimately embraces, teaches that the passions of human beings demand that states must always maintain a posture of war. War, in turn, dictates that a state that is to persevere in such a hostile environment must cultivate the passions – not the reason – of it citizens.

Sidney's acceptance of this key Machiavellian teaching occurs as he defends the martial honor of republican Rome against Filmer's castigation of republican governance. Against Filmer's claim that "Rome began her empire under kings, and did perfect it under emperors,"[15] Sidney avers: "The Glory, Virtue, and Power of the Romans began and ended with their Liberty"

---

[14] Machiavelli, *Prince* 23.95.
[15] Robert Filmer, *Patriarcha and Other Writings*, ed. Johann P. Sommerville (Cambridge: Cambridge University Press, 1991), 26.

(chapter heading, 2.12). The opening chapters of Machiavelli's *Discourses on Livy*, specifically 1.4–6, furnish Sidney with the materials necessary to launch this particular attack against Filmer. Sidney, like Machiavelli, praises Rome because of its capacity to make war.

As we know, Machiavelli concedes that Rome was a tumultuous place, particularly in comparison to the tranquil republics of Sparta and Venice. He defends Rome, at least initially, by claiming that if a republic chooses to expand, then "it is necessary to order it like Rome and make a place for tumults and universal dissensions, as best one can; for without a great number of men, and well armed, a republic can never grow, or, if it grows, maintain itself," as Machiavelli explains in 1.6 of his *Discourses*.[16]

No sooner does Machiavelli offer this choice between expansion and domestic harmony than he rescinds his offer; in the very same chapter he proceeds to explain that a republic has no choice but to seek armed expansion:

[A]ll things of men are in motion and cannot stay steady, they must either rise or fall; and to many things that reason does not bring you, necessity brings you. So when a republic that has been ordered so as to be capable of maintaining itself does not expand, and necessity leads it to expand, this would come to take away its foundation and make it come to ruin sooner.

Others will attack it. Either it loses, if it is not properly armed, or it wins, if it is. If it wins, it needs to be able to digest its winnings. To digest such acquisitions, it needs to be a republic that embraces the people. His final embrace of Rome rests on the recognition that its way is the only way for a state to persevere in a necessarily hostile environment: "I believe that it is necessary to follow the Roman order and not that of the other republics."[17]

Sidney, in two distinct discussions in his second chapter, eagerly subscribes to Machiavelli's reasoning concerning the necessity of a republic imitating the Roman Republic's ability to make war and to digest its winnings. In this, Sidney must be distinguished from Nedham who, as we have seen, also uses for his own purposes these same chapters of Machiavelli's *Discourses*. Although Nedham eagerly accepts the Florentine's endorsement, which occurs in these chapters, of a republic that bases itself on the people, he steadfastly ignores the ultimate point of Machiavelli's discussions – that is, that a democratic republic is preferable to an aristocratic one precisely because the former is better at accumulating and holding an empire. Sidney displays no such hesitations, adopting a Machiavellian pose from the start by defending the unsavory aspects of the bellicose city precisely because they foster its ability to make war.[18] He also insists, like Machiavelli, that war is an

---

[16] Machiavelli, *Discourses* 1.6.4.
[17] Ibid.
[18] Worden, too, discerns Sidney's kinship to Machiavelli on this point, but rather than distinguishing Sidney from Nedham on their respective use of Machiavelli, he draws an equivalence between them ("Republicanism and Restoration," 168–9).

inextricable part of the human condition and that, as a result, a state must organize itself to wage it. In his second treatment of the same theme Sidney compares Rome with Sparta, and rejects Sparta on the same grounds that lead Machiavelli to eschew it.

Sidney's first discussion begins when he entitles section 14 of the second chapter, "No Sedition was hurtful to Rome, till through their Prosperity some men gained a Power above the Laws" (2.14.153). Sidney is just as unwilling as Machiavelli to condemn the seditions that occurred early in the republic's history. At the conclusion of this first discussion, Sidney also defends civil tumult because of its utility in making war:

After the expulsion of the kings, the power was chiefly in the nobility, who had been leaders of the people; but it was necessary to humble them, when they began to presume too much upon the advantages of their birth; and the city could never have been great, unless the plebeians who were the body of it, and the main strength of their armies, had been admitted to a participation of honours.... Rome that was constituted for war, and sought its grandeur by that means, could never have arriv'd to any considerable height, if the people had not been exercised in arms, and their spirits raised to delight in conquests, and willing to expose themselves to the greatest fatigues and dangers to accomplish them. (2.17.170)

In furnishing that summary of Roman history, Sidney follows Machiavelli who proclaims in 1.4 of the *Discourses* that "every city ought to have its modes with which the people can vent its ambition, and especially those cities that wish to avail themselves of the people in important things."[19] Of course, the important thing for which Rome used its people was war.

In imitation of Machiavelli, Sidney forges his own winding trail that leads to his final embrace of the necessity of war to a state. Initially, however, the Englishman is willing to consider peace a possibility: "Peace is desirable by a state that is constituted for it, who contenting themselves with their own territories, have no desires of enlarging them" (2.15.158). Thus, Sidney replicates Machiavelli's preliminary statement in 1.6 of the *Discourses* that if a city "stays within its limits, and it is seen by experience that there is no ambition in it,"[20] then the city can turn its attention to domestic pursuits.

As we have seen, however, Machiavelli rejects this possibility as inconsistent with the way of the world. So too will Sidney. In the continuation of the passage quoted previously, Sidney casts doubt on the pacific alternative he has just posed: "Or perhaps it might simply deserve praise, if mankind were so framed, that a people intending hurt to none, could preserve themselves; but the world being so far of another temper, that no nation can be safe without valour and strength, those governments only deserve to be commended,

[19] Machiavelli, *Discourses* 1.4.1.
[20] Ibid., 1.6.4.

which by discipline and exercise increase both, and the Roman above all, that excelled in both" (2.15.158–59). Owing to the passions of human beings, the world is in flux; a state must be prepared to meet the consequences of that flux.[21]

In his second discussion of Rome's war-making capacity in sections 21–23 of the second chapter, Sidney restates this notion even more emphatically. Merely the titles of these sections reveal the progression of his argument. The title of section 21 proclaims that "Mixed and Popular Governments preserve Peace, and manage Wars, better than Absolute Monarchies" (2.21.195). Whereas Sidney is decidedly in favor of republics, he here expresses a degree of impartiality on the question of whether a republic should pursue war or peace. The title of 23, the last of this group of sections, however, abandons that element of impartiality: "That is the best Government, which best provides for War" (2.23.209).

In section 22, "Commonwealths seek Peace or War according to the Variety of their Constitutions," Sidney provides the groundwork for the conclusion he will articulate in the following section by distinguishing among three varieties of republics: those which "have been principally constituted for war"; those which "have as much delighted in peace"; and those which "having taken the middle, and (as some think) the best way, have so moderated their love to peace, as not to suffer the spirits of the people to fall, but kept them in a perpetual readiness to make war when there was occasion" (2.22.202). It is clear which republics Sidney designates as pacific. He names Venice, Florence, Genoa, and Lucca as being among those cities that "aimed at trade" to such a degree that they had to use mercenaries when they went to war. He names both Rome and Sparta among those cities that "seem to have intended nothing but the just preservation of liberty at home, and making war abroad." Although he specifies this similarity between these two ancient cities, later in the section he draws the distinction between them: "[S]ome of those that intended war desir'd to enlarge their territories by conquest; others only to preserve their own, and to live with freedom and safety upon them" (203). Rome is of the first sort, and Sparta is of the second. Thus, Sparta, according to Sidney, adopted "the middle ... way" that some thinkers prefer (203–4).

Machiavelli explicitly shuns Sparta, as we have seen. Indeed, in concluding 1.6, Machiavelli uses the term "middle way" when treating those republics that hope to avoid incursion while they shun expansion: "[S]ince one cannot, as I believe, balance this thing, nor maintain this middle way exactly, in ordering a republic there is need to think of the more honorable part and to order it so that if indeed necessity brings it to expand, it can conserve what it has seized."[22] Machiavelli thus rejects the "middle way" of Sparta.

---

[21] Scott also recognizes the importance to Sidney of 1.6 of Machiavelli's *Discourses on Livy* (*Restoration Crisis*, 237).

[22] Machiavelli, *Discourses* 1.6.4.

Sidney not only borrows Machiavelli's association of Sparta with "the middle way," but he ultimately rejects that "middle way" on Machiavellian grounds. He reveals those grounds only gradually, however. For eight hundred years the Spartans remained free,[23] Sidney explains, but when "they were brought by prosperity to affect the principality of Greece, and to undertake such wars as could not be carried on without money, and greater numbers of men than a small city was able to furnish... [they] fell into such straits as were never recovered" (2.22.204). Machiavelli and Sidney agree that Sparta's constitution could not sustain an empire, but whereas Machiavelli implies that expansion was a necessity simply, Sidney here suggests that Sparta's decision to expand was freely chosen. The implication is that if Sparta had not abandoned its long-standing defensive stance it might have persisted for an even longer period of time. Therefore, Sidney's favorable disposition toward Sparta itself persists as he resists making a decision between Sparta and Rome in this section.

In section 23, the last of this particular discussion, Sidney renders a decision between the two republics and decides in favor of Rome. His judgment comes to light when he discusses the best form of government: "[T]hat government is evidently the best, which, not relying upon what it does at first enjoy, seeks to increase the number, strength, and riches of the people; and by the best discipline to bring the power so improved into such order as may be of most use to the publick" (2.23.209). The power that Sidney seeks for his best government will be garnered through offensive forays: "[W]hen a people multiplies (as they will always do in a good climate under a good government) such an enlargement of territory as is necessary for their subsistence can be acquired only by war" (210).[24] A state must seek such increase because "[i]f it do not grow, it must pine and perish; for in this world nothing is permanent; that which does not grow better will grow worse" (209). Sidney adheres to Machiavelli's view that "all things of men are in motion and cannot stay steady, they must either rise or fall."[25] Sparta made the mistake of seeking stasis in a world that will not permit it. As a result, Sidney rejects the view that Sparta's middle way exemplifies the best form of government. Thus, according to Sidney's Machiavellian ruminations, Roman aggression is the only alternative. Sidney presents a view of the human situation that demands human preparedness against necessity. Necessity itself dictates the type of political life a state must cultivate. Rather than being organized with a view to peace, a state must be organized with a view to wars of aggrandizement.[26]

---

[23] It appears that Sidney imports Machiavelli's exaggeration of Sparta's longevity into his text. See Machiavelli, *Discourses* 1.2.6.

[24] Cf. West's statement in the foreword to *Discourses Concerning Government*: "[U]nlike Machiavelli, Sidney qualifies his imperialism with the requirement that a war of acquisition be a just war, carried on for a just cause and by just means" (xxii).

[25] Machiavelli, *Discourses* 1.6.4.

[26] Cf. Sidney, *Court Maxims*, 15–16.

A Machiavellian Turn to War and Rejection of Aristotle

Sidney's analysis of the comparative merits of Rome's first two kings, Romulus and Numa, corroborates his reliance on both Machiavelli's analysis of the necessity of war and of the effects that necessity will have on the domestic purposes of a state. Romulus was a warlike king and Numa a peace-loving one. Again, Sidney borrows liberally from Machiavelli's discussions without attribution. And just as he did when considering martial Rome's superiority to republics less belligerent, he closely follows Machiavelli's rhetorical style that reconsiders initial statements and subjects them to fundamental revision. In this case, both thinkers begin by praising the peaceful king, only to reject him as dangerously weak in order to embrace the lover of war. A consideration of Sidney's ultimate embrace of Romulus and rejection of Numa, whom Sidney terms an unarmed philosopher, reveals his ultimate rejection of Aristotle's teaching concerning politics and war.

When both Sidney and Machiavelli consider the relative merits of Rome's first two kings, they offer initial statements highly favorable to Numa, which they later revise to such a degree that they actually repudiate Numa's example. In castigating Romulus and glorifying Numa in the first chapter, Sidney appears to offer an evaluation diametrically opposed to Machiavelli's final conclusion. This appearance is intensified by the fact that Sidney's final verdict does not appear until much later in the work. In this later discussion, though, he follows Machiavelli's ultimate conclusion by declaring that Numa's pursuit of peace weakened Rome.

Machiavelli first considers Numa in 1.11 of the *Discourses* and expresses unqualified admiration for him. According to Machiavelli's résumé of early Roman history, Numa introduced a new religion into the city. As a result of his innovation, Rome owed its later good fortune to Numa. Machiavelli judges that "if one had to dispute over which prince Rome was more obligated to, Romulus or Numa, I believe rather that Numa would obtain the first rank."[27]

When Sidney discusses the first two kings of Rome in the first chapter of his *Discourses*, he too expresses a clear preference for Numa. Because Sidney is interested here in establishing that the first kings of Rome were chosen through consent, he speculates that Romulus must have gained his rule through consent because "one man could not force a multitude of fierce and valiant men" to submit to his rule. Although Sidney favors Romulus with such a mild description of the manner of his ascent to power, Sidney finds the character of his rule problematic: "[W]hen he aimed at more authority than [the Romans] were willing to allow, they slew him" (1.16.48).

Numa succeeded Romulus, and Sidney highlights the reason for the successor's appointment. The Romans "fetched Numa from among the Sabines:

[27] Machiavelli, *Discourses* 1.11.2.

He was not their father, nor heir to their father, but a stranger; not a con-queror, but an unarmed philosopher" (1.16.48). Whereas Sidney considers Romulus to be an usurper of the rightful power of the Roman people, he praises Numa as a philosopher.

Even aside from the fact that Sidney mimics Machiavelli's initial pref-erence for Numa over Romulus, there is a Machiavellian undertone in Sidney's treatment of the issue. Sidney appears to draw the term "un-armed philosopher" from chapter 6 of *The Prince*, where Machiavelli dis-cusses the difficulties inherent in introducing "new orders and modes," and makes a distinction between prophets who are armed and those who are not. Because the adherents of the old ways are opposed to the new, and because the dedication of "those who might benefit from the new or-ders" will inevitably slacken, the potential founder must find a method of sustaining the resoluteness of his followers. Force is the method that Machiavelli recommends: "[I]t arises that all the armed prophets conquered and the unarmed ones were ruined."[28] Rather than using the term "un-armed prophet," Sidney uses the term, "unarmed philosopher." At this point, Sidney appears to admire Numa's peaceful and philosophical ways against Machiavelli's advice. Indeed, in the very chapter from which Sidney appears to draw his terms, Machiavelli offers additional warnings about the perils of lacking arms.

Despite his early approval of Rome's second king, Sidney reassesses the value of Numa to Rome in the second chapter of his work. His reassessment follows precisely Machiavelli's own in 1.19 of the *Discourses*, where the Florentine reconsiders his earlier praise of Numa's peaceableness. In that later chapter Machiavelli emphasizes the danger that Numa's nature posed to the fledgling city: "Those princes are weak who do not rely on war." Only chance prevented Rome's collapse, for if Numa's successor had been similarly weak, Rome's future would have been threatened: "[S]urely one can estimate that if Rome had chanced upon a man for its third king who did not know how to give it back its reputation with arms, it would never, or only with the greatest difficulty, have been able to stand on its feet later or to produce the effects it produced."[29]

Sidney rejects Numa for precisely the same reason and in language re-markably similar to Machiavelli's:

Peace therefore may be good in its season, and was so in Numa's reign; yet two or three such kings would have encouraged some active neighbours to put an end to that aspiring city.... But the discipline that best agreed with the temper and designs of a warlike people, being renew'd by his brave successors, the dangers were put on their enemies. (2.15.159)

---

[28] Machiavelli, *Prince* 6.23-4.
[29] Machiavelli, *Discourses* 1.19.2-4.

Thus, Sidney shuns his own unarmed philosopher. Without attribution, he borrows Machiavelli's analysis of the threat that Numa posed to Rome, for the statement that two or three kings of Numa's character would have ruined Rome is not to be found in Livy's history, the common source for Machiavelli's and Sidney's accounts of the early history of Rome.[30] Indeed, contrary to the analyses of Sidney and Machiavelli, Livy suggests that Numa's reign actually improved Rome's security against its hostile neighbors as when he suggests that the other cities were reluctant to attack a nation so dedicated to the worship of the gods.[31] Sidney's Machiavellianism here is undeclared but quite faithful nonetheless. Moreover, Sidney reproduces not only Machiavelli's content but his method of argumentation, which reconsiders and revises previous statements.[32] Nevertheless, if a reader were to accept the conclusion of Sidney's first chapter as definitive and fail to compare the conclusions of his two treatments of Numa in his work with those of Machiavelli in the *Discourses*, the Machiavellian form and content of Sidney's argument would remain undetected.

Sidney's ultimate embrace of Machiavelli's reasoning concerning the indispensability of Romulus and the threatening character of Numa carries significant ramifications for his ultimate stand on Aristotle's teaching. Sidney repudiates Aristotle's subordination of war to peace as well as his injunction that politics should aim at cultivating the higher faculties of human beings. Sidney begins the *Discourses* reciting Aristotelian dicta that stress the reasonable nature of human beings. In the transition from the first to the second chapter, however, he moves from an Aristotelian emphasis on reason, which allows him to embrace unarmed philosophers such as Numa, to a Machiavellian emphasis on force, which necessitates that he promote armed rulers who rouse the people's spirits for war.

Of course, because Aristotle lived before the military achievements of republican Rome, he did not comment on them, but he knew Sparta's constitution well. Although Aristotle maintains in his *Politics* that Sparta is one of the best states that has existed, he finds important deficiencies in its constitution. Whereas Sidney and Machiavelli suggest that Sparta is not warlike enough, Aristotle locates its critical flaw in the fact that the Spartan regime is too focused on war.[33] The Spartan regime aims at inculcating warlike virtue in its citizens with a view to dominating others.[34] According to Aristotle, because the city exists for the sake of living well, the highest purposes of

---

[30] See Livy's discussion of Numa's reign, *Ab urbe condita* 1.18–21.

[31] Ibid., 1.21.

[32] Cf. John Toland, *Tetradymus* (London, 1720), 85: "Nor are we to wonder any longer, that *the same men do not always seem to say the same things on the same subjects, which* problem can onely be solv'd by the distinction of *the External and Internal Doctrine.*"

[33] See also Rahe, *Republics Ancient and Modern*, 262–3, for a discussion of the implications of Machiavelli's choice of Rome over Sparta.

[34] Aristotle, *Politics* 2.9, 1271b1–10 and 7.14–15, 1333a30–1334b5.

the city are to be found in the highest faculties of human beings, specifically those required for participation in politics or philosophy. Both activities require the leisure that peace affords. In contrast to the view expressed by Machiavelli and Sidney that the best organized city is organized for war, Aristotle maintains that "war must be for the sake of peace."[35] Because the Spartan regime promoted war and the martial virtue of courage to such a high degree, the Spartans did not know how to be at leisure. The Spartans, in Aristotle's view, were incapable of pursuing the activities of peace and hence the true purposes of the city.

In supporting leisure, Aristotle promotes the highest rational faculties of human beings. Conversely, in highlighting the passions of human beings, Machiavelli and Sidney conclude that states cannot seek the leisure that nurtures these rational faculties. The passions of human beings dictate a predatory posture for a state; the passions fuel not only the aggressiveness of neighboring states but also that of one's own state as prosperity promotes the desire of citizens for more – a desire that can only be satisfied by aggression against others.

As a result, reason can no longer occupy as prominent a place in the state as Sidney originally seemed to advocate.[36] In the first chapter, Sidney expresses admiration for those who "lived private lives, as Plato, Socrates, Epictetus, and others, made it their business to abate men's lusts, by shewing the folly of seeking vain honours, useless riches, or unsatisfying pleasures" (1.19.67). In the second, Sidney establishes the need for constant military adventure and praises the Romans for having the people's "spirits raised to delight in conquests" (2.16.170). Given this need, one must wonder whether a state can afford to exalt those who teach through precept and example that the desires for riches and honor should be curbed. For this reason, Sidney has no choice but to reject the example of Numa, the "unarmed philosopher."[37]

More Than Machiavellian Bloodthirstiness

Sidney demonstrates both the thoroughly Machiavellian character of his thought and his reluctance to associate himself with Machiavelli in yet another way. He borrows from Machiavelli's *Discourses* the idea of the necessity to reduce a state to its first principles, an idea that reappears throughout Sidney's work. On this topic Sidney uncharacteristically credits Machiavelli, and this fact very likely accounts for the willingness of some scholars to identify Sidney's thought with Machiavelli's. Nevertheless, Sidney, characteristically, still refuses to acknowledge his full debt to Machiavelli. Indeed,

[35] Ibid., 7.14, 1333a35.
[36] West discerns no such diminution of Sidney's attachment to Aristotle's pronouncement (foreword to *Discourses Concerning Government*, xxv).
[37] Cf. Worden, "Republicanism and Restoration," 174.

in one place he even wonders how deeply Machiavelli is committed to his own principle. Sidney is able to quibble with Machiavelli in this way because he seems not to grasp the full meaning of Machiavelli's injunction. Sidney mistakenly reports that it is a mere endorsement of returning a state to its original laws and traditions, ignoring Machiavelli's harsher enjoinder to reintroduce to the state the type of fear that existed at its founding. According to Machiavelli, citizens will eventually become insolent enough to dare to break the laws, "[u]nless something arises by which punishment is brought back to their memory and fear is renewed in their spirits."[38] Elsewhere, however, when Sidney does not explicitly refer to Machiavelli, he shows that he not only grasps, but readily accepts this additional and harsher meaning of Machiavelli.

Sidney explicitly refers to this Machiavellian principle when, after reflecting that the products of human hands are imperfect and that even natural bodies are in need of "medicines and other occasional helps," he concludes that states require the same remedial action. "Some men observing this, have proposed a necessity of reducing every state once in an age or two, to the integrity of its first principle" (3.25.462). Although Sidney suggests that a number of men makes such a claim, he points to Machiavelli's *Discourses* as the preeminent source for this notion.[39]

Sidney thus adheres to Machiavelli's idea of the necessity of continuous renovation for a state, but he objects that Machiavelli does not go far enough: "[Those who propose this as a necessity] ought to have examined, whether that principle be good or evil, or so good that nothing can be added to it, which none ever was; and this being so, those who will admit of no change would render errors perpetual, and depriving mankind of the benefits of wisdom, industry, experience, and right use of reason, oblige all to continue in the miserable barbarity of their ancestors" (3.25.462). It is fine to renovate, but while one is at it, Sidney advises, one ought to examine the very foundation of the state. If the foundation is wanting, Sidney recommends not a renovation but rather an entirely new edifice; one should not unthinkingly adhere to inadequate principles.

Sidney's advocacy of thorough innovation is linked to his promotion of the necessity of progress. Against Filmer, who maintains that any deviation from God's original provision for humankind represents a decline, Sidney insists that people should not be beholden to their ancestors to the extent that they perpetually replicate ancient foibles and misunderstandings. He is fond of saying that people are no more bound to follow the ways of their ancestors than they are "obliged . . . to live upon acorns, or inhabit hollow trees, because their fathers did it when they had no better dwellings, and found

---

[38] Machiavelli, *Discourses* 3.1.3.
[39] Although Sidney refers to the second book of Machiavelli's *Discourses*, the discussion is actually found in the first chapter of the third book.

no better nourishment in the uncultivated world" (2.8.122).[40] Although he eagerly appeals to the authority of history and Scripture when it serves his point, he baldly states that recourse to such authority is wrongheaded: "We are not therefore so much to inquire after that which is most ancient, as that which is best, and most conducing to the good ends to which it was directed" (3.25.460).[41] The corollary of Sidney's emphasis on the necessity of human activity in the service of progress is an understanding of nature as radically defective.

Machiavelli would certainly not deny this conclusion of Sidney, and, in fact, the dispute Sidney initiates with Machiavelli obscures their fundamental agreement on the need for innovation. In initiating this dispute, Sidney not only overlooks Machiavelli's endorsement of harsh punishment as a means of returning a state to its beginning, but he neglects other important aspects of Machiavelli's thought that support Sidney's conclusion regarding the necessity of human activity generally and of the renovation of states specifically. After all, Machiavelli is adamant that human beings rouse themselves from the languor that derives from the view that "worldly things are so governed by fortune and by God, that men cannot correct them with their prudence, indeed that they have no remedy at all; and on account of this they might judge that one need not sweat much over things but let oneself be governed by chance."[42] Like Sidney's, Machiavelli's view of the imperfection of the human situation colors his view of politics. Machiavelli prefers Rome, whose founding was incomplete and which required such important later additions as the tribunate and the censors, to Sparta, whose founding was completed at a single stroke by Lycurgus. Although Machiavelli prefers incomplete Rome in part because it was better able to respond to the exigencies that arose to threaten it, he is not reluctant to criticize his model city for not making changes radical enough. He states, for example, that Rome held "steady the orders of the state, which in corruption were no longer good" and notes that "the laws that were renewed were no longer enough to keep men good." He continues that such changes in the laws "would indeed have helped if the orders had been changed together with the innovation in laws."[43] According to Machiavelli, the Romans should have changed not only their laws but also their orders. In Machiavelli's lexicon a change in "orders" denotes

---

[40] Gordon J. Schochet, *Patriarchalism in Political Thought: The Authoritarian Family and Political Speculation and Attitudes Especially in Seventeenth-Century England* (New York: Basic Books, 1975), 195.

[41] James Conniff maintains that Sidney argues both from the position that history should be conceived as degeneration from a perfect beginning and that history should be understood as progress ("Reason and History in Early Whig Thought: The Case of Algernon Sidney," *Journal of the History of Ideas* 43 [1982]: 399, 411–14).

[42] Machiavelli, *Prince* 25.98.

[43] Machiavelli, *Discourses* 1.18.2.

a thoroughgoing innovation equivalent to a new founding.[44] Machiavelli notes the consequences of this failure to innovate: the republic fell. Thus, Machiavelli initiates a criticism of the Romans for not transforming their foundation, a criticism entirely in keeping with Sidney's concern.[45]

Thus, while using Machiavelli's terminology, Sidney attempts to distinguish himself from his source, but the difference between them is superficial rather than substantial. Moreover, Sidney obscures the true meaning, and hence the harshness, of Machiavelli's injunction to restore a state. Machiavelli's injunction does not merely mean, as Sidney suggests, that the state return to the way things were when the state was young but, more precisely, return to the fear that preceded and accompanied the founding of that state. Because states are vulnerable to corruption as a result of the complacency of human beings, it is necessary therefore to reawaken them with a return to the fear that is coeval with the original founding. Prominent among the incidents that, in Machiavelli's view, instill such fear, are the execution of those who attempted to overturn the state or of young men who, eager for the fray, merely disobeyed military orders. "Because they were excessive and notable," explains Machiavelli, "such things made men draw back toward the mark whenever one of them arose."[46] Machiavelli's return to first principles brings with it frighteningly bloody spectacles.

The excessiveness of Machiavelli's own discussion of the necessity of excessive actions clearly does not repel Sidney. Both before and after he has explicitly referred to and criticized Machiavelli's notion of the need for a return to first principles, Sidney uses that notion for his own purposes without attribution, unabashedly endorsing Machiavelli's thesis on the necessity

---

44 Machiavelli's treatment in chapter 6 of *The Prince* of the "prophets" who introduced "new modes and orders" suggests the radical nature of a change in orders.

45 Raab accepts at face value Sidney's suggestion that he differs from Machiavelli because whereas the Englishman is willing to renovate, the Italian is not (*English Face of Machiavelli*, 222). Raab goes on to distinguish Sidney's use of a return to first principles from that of Machiavelli on the basis of Machiavelli's continued reliance on the "essential pessimism" of the Polybian conception of cycles (*English Face of Machiavelli*, 222). Houston, like Raab, equates Machiavelli with Polybius on this issue. In arguing that Sidney's ideas owe little to Machiavelli, Houston acknowledges that Sidney uses Machiavelli's language concerning the necessity of a return to first principles. Nevertheless, Houston maintains that this facet of Sidney's thought is not Machiavellian: "Sidney's vision of returning a government to its 'first principles' had little more to do with Machiavelli's concept of *rinnovazione* than a similarity of words" (*Algernon Sidney*, 218). In making this judgment, Houston relies erroneously on Fink's interpretation that equates Machiavelli with Polybius, in which for Machiavelli "all change was movement away from the perfect form of a mixed republic" (217–18). Worden too differs with Houston on this issue ("Republicanism and Restoration," 160 and n. 61). For Machiavelli's rejection of Polybian pessimism, see *Discourses* 3.22. Scott, by contrast, understands Machiavelli as endorsing the necessity of change and Sidney as following the Italian master on this point (*Restoration Crisis*, 233–4; see also *English Republic*, 16) and sometimes surpassing him (*English Republic*, 30–5).

46 Machiavelli, *Discourses* 3.1.3.

of "reduc[ing] [states] to their first principles" (2.30.302; see also 2.31.306, 2.13.150, 3.41.550). Moreover, apparently guided by Machiavelli's provision of the list of Rome's salutary executions, Sidney advocates harsh punishments against those who disregard the laws of the state. He clearly grasps the harshness of Machiavelli's teaching – the very harshness he ignores when he attributes the idea to Machiavelli. "If injustice therefore be evil, and injuries forbidden, they are also to be punished; and the law instituted for their prevention, must necessarily intend the avenging of such as cannot be prevented" (2.24.219).

He also follows the Machiavelli of *Discourses* 3.1 in approving of the action that Rome took against Scipio. A commander who had taken Spain and vanquished the great Carthaginian general Hannibal in the battle at Zama, Scipio was awarded the honorific title of Africanus. Despite his unsurpassed military record, the Romans prosecuted him for a number of crimes, among which was embezzlement of funds captured from Rome's enemies. Livy suggests that those who supported the prosecution were motivated not so much by the belief that he had committed the crimes of which he was accused but by the fear that Scipio had grown too great to live under republican laws.[47] Like Machiavelli, Sidney sides with Scipio's accusers: "Scipio being the first Roman that thus disdained the power of law, I do not know whether the prejudice brought upon the city by so dangerous an example, did not outweigh all the services he had done" (2.18.179).[48] Sidney understands and endorses the spirit in which Machiavelli offers his teaching.

Machiavelli seems to recommend his stern regimen with a view to republics in particular, because he draws his examples of such salutary punishment from the history of the Roman Republic. He is particularly concerned with using such punishment as a means of stemming a republic's slide toward tyranny.[49] But as 3.1 comes to a close, he turns his attention to monarchies and broaches a far less violent method of performing "executions" in the context of a discussion of the French monarchy. He praises the French system not only because the laws and orders restrain the king but because the parlements assure that the laws and orders are observed. He comments that laws and orders "are renewed" whenever the Parlement of Paris "makes an execution against a prince of that kingdom and when it condemns the king in its verdicts."[50]

The example of Scipio aside, Sidney expends his real ire not on the insolent young men of a republic, as does Machiavelli, but on wayward monarchs. When it comes to the prospect of punishing kings, Sidney actually surpasses

---

[47] Livy, *Ab urbe condita* 38.40–46.
[48] For Machiavelli's discussion of the threat that Scipio posed to Rome, see *Discourses* 1.29.
[49] See Chapter 1.
[50] Machiavelli, *Discourses* 3.1.5

Machiavelli's ferocity directed at those who threaten tyranny in a republic. Sidney follows his source to the extent that he offers reflections akin to those of Machiavelli on the necessity of institutions that restrain the king. In speaking of the need to have kings observe the fundamental laws of the state, Sidney states: "Nothing is more essential and fundamental in the constitutions of kingdoms, than that diets, parliaments, and assemblies of estates should see this perform'd" (2.30.296). But Sidney is not content merely with the benign "executions" against a king that Machiavelli recommends. Sidney says later that "it may well fall out, that the magistrate who will not follow the directive power of the law, may fall under the coercive, and then the fear is turned upon him, with this aggravation, that it is not only actual, but just." Moreover, he observes, not without a degree of satisfaction, the grisly facts that "many emperors and kings of the greatest nations in the world...have been so utterly deprived of all power, that they have been imprisoned, deposed, confined to monasteries, kill'd, drawn through the streets, cut in pieces, thrown into rivers, and indeed suffer'd all that could be suffer'd by the vilest slaves" (3.11.382). In contemplating the violence to which a king may be subject, Sidney bests Machiavelli in bloodthirstiness. Such an action taken against a king must, of course, qualify as a circumstance in which the state is reduced to its first principles. At this point, it becomes evident why Sidney stresses the need for a people to reconsider the foundational principles of the state. It is precisely at such a juncture that a people may well decide to alter the basis of the state by changing a monarchy to a republic.

Sidney's Contractarianism and Its Relation to Liberalism

The people's punishment of a malevolent monarch is justified in Sidney's understanding because a contract exists between all ruling magistrates and those whom they rule. "The Contracts made between Magistrates, and the Nations that created them, were real, solemn, and obligatory," he announces in a chapter title (2.32.309). The people always remain the judges of that contract between themselves and their governors: "And as for the peoples being judges in their own case, it is plain, they ought to be the only judges, because it is their own, and only concerns themselves" (2.32.316).[51] Thus, according to Sidney, all government, including monarchy, rests on the consent of the governed. The people, then, are the judges of their reigning king and can withdraw their consent at any time. When the monarch, established for the people's benefit, acts contrary to that purpose, the people have a right

---

[51] This passage is quoted from that part of the *Discourses* that was seized upon Sidney's arrest and was read at his trial. It is reconstructed from what appears to be have been a transcript of the trial. See West's editor's note, *Discourses Concerning Government*, 312, n. 7.

to punish his malfeasance.[52] In these cases, then, the people are justified in expending Machiavellian ire in punishing their offending ruler.

Thus, all governments in Sidney's view rest on consent. This notion of a king's power resting on consent by virtue of a contract between the people and the king was not unusual at the time.[53] Although Sidney lavishes a great deal of attention in the *Discourses* on this type of contract, at other times he broaches the existence of another contract – one that rather than instituting a particular government establishes civil society itself, thus bringing human beings out of the state of nature.[54] The former type of contractarianism – the type that establishes a particular form of government – implies neither an understanding of the asociability of human beings nor that of the artificiality of all government, whereas the latter certainly does. This latter conception of contract is more philosophical, finds prominent expression in Hobbes's thought, and was to become a staple in liberal thought.[55] That Sidney makes use of this contract that establishes a unity out of previously disassociated individuals is evident, for example, when he declares in passing that "a people is, by mutual compact, joined together in a civil society" (2.5.102).

Moreover, as we have seen, he possesses a vivid conception of the prepolitical condition: it is populated by human beings who reside in hollow trees and derive their sustenance from a diet of acorns (e.g., 1.6.22–3; 2.8.122;

---

[52] In speaking of Sidney's conception of the contract, Worden comments that it is "so radical that 'contract' (his word) hardly seems the right term for a one-sided bargain that leaves kings permanently subject to the whims of the sovereign people" ("Commonwealth Kidney," 16).

[53] J. P. Sommerville, *Politics and Ideology in England, 1603–1640* (London: Longman, 1986), e.g., 11, 57–85.

[54] Conniff too notes Sidney's appeal to these two types of contract ("Case of Sidney," 405 and n. 28).

[55] Harro Höpfl and Martyn P. Thompson, "The History of Contract as a Motif in Political Thought," *American Historical Review* 84 (1979): 919–44, distinguish between these two types of contracts: "constitutional contractarianism" and "philosophical contractarianism." "The history of contractualism subsequent to Hobbes is, indeed, in part a record of the adaptations and modifications of the language Hobbes consolidated. This language spoke of 'natural right,' 'natural liberty,' 'natural equality,' 'condition of nature,' 'covenant,' and 'sovereignty' – best described as the language of philosophical contractarianism, because the theoretical ambitions and the aimed-for generality of thought of those who employed it tended to be greater than that of the alternative language, best described as constitutional contractarianism. This second language set covenant within the terminological context of 'fundamental law,' 'fundamental rights' or 'liberties,' 'original contract,' and 'ancient' or 'fundamental constitution.' In constitutional contractarianism particular positive laws and the institutional inheritance of specific polities were most relevant and important, rather than universal propositions about all men and all polities" (941). Zuckert also argues for the distinctiveness of the Lockean conception of the contract that ultimately derives from Hobbes. Although he agrees with many of Höpfl and Thompson's findings, he disagrees with their claim that the alternative to Lockean contractarianism was entirely unphilosophical. See Zuckert, *Natural Rights and the New Republicanism*, particularly 64–5, 116–18.

3.7.358).[56] This condition is not to be endured because, as Sidney observes, "No one man or family is able to provide that which is requisite for their convenience or security, whilst everyone has an equal right to everything, and none acknowledges a superior to determine the controversies, that upon such occasions must continually arise, and will probably be so many and great, that mankind cannot bear them" (1.10.30). On the unsatisfactory character of this condition, he also comments:

> The fierce barbarity of a loose multitude, bound by no law, and regulated by no discipline, is wholly repugnant to [the good of ourselves]: Whilst every man fears his neighbour, and has no other defence than his own strength, he must live in that perpetual anxiety which is equally contrary to that happiness, and that sedate temper of mind which is required for the search of it. The first step towards the cure of this pestilent evil, is for many to join in one body, that everyone may be protected by the united force of all; and the various talents that men possess, may by good discipline be rendered useful to the whole. (2.1.83)

This state sounds strikingly reminiscent of Hobbes's state of war. It is certainly possible that he had Hobbes's depictions in mind when writing the preceding passage. Indeed, despite the fact that he does not apply Hobbes's terminology to his descriptions of this condition, he displays his awareness of Hobbes's characterization of the state of nature, when, in another context he refers to "that which Hobbes calls *bellum omnium contra omnes*" (1.17.55).

Although the condition of human beings before the advent of civil society is so unpleasant as to induce human beings to construct civil society, that original state of freedom provides a standard, in Sidney's view, by which to judge all governments that civil society subsequently establishes. At this point, Sidney's thought bears a striking resemblance to that of Locke. Specifically, both Sidney and Locke argue that this state of nature was characterized by equality and human freedom. In this, both thinkers differ fundamentally from Hobbes,[57] who sternly maintains that the state of nature, which is the state of war, is fit only to be shunned. Although Sidney almost certainly did not know Locke's *Two Treatises*,[58] Locke would later encounter Sidney's

---

[56] Sidney does not use the term "state of nature." See also Houston's discussion of Sidney's "anti-Aristotelian portrayal of the state of nature" (*Algernon Sidney*, 119).

[57] Ward too identifies the manner in which Sidney both borrows from and transforms Hobbes's teaching. He points to Spinoza's work as a means of explicating Sidney's departure from Hobbes and as a possible source of influence on Sidney ("Rhetoric and Natural Rights in Sidney," 133–8).

[58] Sidney's *Discourses* and Locke's *Two Treatises* were almost certainly composed during the same period, but it is highly unlikely that Sidney knew of Locke's manuscript given Locke's secrecy regarding it. The *Two Treatises* was published in 1690. See Peter Laslett, introduction to Locke, *Two Treatises*, 25–66. Of course, because Sidney's *Discourses* was not published until 1698, it could well be the case that the editor of the *Discourses* is responsible for these

Discourses. Locke attests to the compatibility between his own ideas and those of Sidney when he included *Discourses Concerning Government* among those works he recommended for their treatment of the theoretical side of politics.[59]

For Locke, the equality that reigns in the state of nature is characterized by the fact that no one is ordained by nature to rule or command anyone else: "there being nothing more evident, than that Creatures of the same species and rank promiscuously born to all the same advantages of Nature, and the use of the same faculties, should also be equal one amongst another without Subordination or Subjection."[60] As a result, "only his own Consent" can "put him into subjection to any Earthly Power."[61] In terms remarkably similar, Sidney endorses the same basis for fundamental equality among human beings: "[N]o man could be subject to another: that this equality of right and exemption from the domination of any other is called liberty: that he who enjoys it cannot be deprived of it, unless by his own consent, or by force" (2.31.304).

According to both Sidney and Locke, before the people decide to contract to leave the prepolitical condition, they are at liberty. Human beings are "naturally in" "a *State of perfect Freedom*," according to Locke, "to order their Actions, and dispose of their Possessions, and Persons as they think fit, within the bounds of the Law of Nature, without asking leave, or depending upon the Will of any other Man."[62] In society, freedom for Locke is characterized by being under a legislative power established by consent.[63] Similarly, Sidney understands that human beings are naturally at liberty and must consent to the limitation of that natural liberty: "[M]an is naturally free; that he cannot justly be deprived of that liberty without cause, and that he doth not resign it, or any part of it, unless it be in consideration of a greater good, which he proposes to himself" (1.2.8). In another place, Sidney seems to posit something very close to a Lockean right to liberty: "[E]quality of right and exemption from the domination of any other is called liberty: that he who enjoys it cannot be deprived of it, unless by his own consent, or by force" (2.31.304).[64]

---

themes that seem to anticipate Locke's *Second Treatise*. Worden points to Toland as that editor; see *Roundhead Reputations*, 100–2 and 131–2.

[59] Höpfl and Thompson, "Contract as a Motif in Political Thought," 941. West recognizes some important points of agreement between Sidney and Locke but does not draw that comparison as fully as he might, claiming instead that "Sidney's republicanism still adheres to a view of life that is recognizably at home within the ancient and medieval tradition of political philosophy" (foreword to *Discourses Concerning Government*, xxiv–xxv).

[60] Locke, *Second Treatise*, para. 4.

[61] Ibid., para. 119.

[62] Ibid., para. 22: "The *Liberty of Man, in Society*, is to be under no other Legislative Power, but that established, by consent, in the Common-wealth."

[63] Ibid., para. 22.

[64] Cf. Houston, *Algernon Sidney*, 110–14.

Sidney's exemption from the rule of another that characterizes the prepolitical condition remains to inform the political condition that supersedes it because that right to rule oneself can only be alienated through consent. As we have seen, a ruler can only be a ruler with explicit consent of the ruled: "[T]he right of magistrates do essentially depend upon the consent of those they govern" (2.6.108). At one point, he describes the power of the individual quite emphatically: "[E]very man is a king till he divest himself of his right, in consideration of something that he thinks better for him" (1.7.25). Further, Sidney will not accept tacit consent: " 'Tis not therefore the bare sufferance of a government when a disgust is declared, nor a silent submission when the power of opposing is wanting, that can imply an assent, or election, and create a right; but an explicit act of approbation, when men have ability and courage to resist or deny" (2.6.108–9). In this way, the two contracts merge somewhat in his thought. Not only do the equality and liberty that reign in the prepolitical condition necessitate that individuals consent to become a part of civil society, but they must consent to any and all governments raised above them.

Locke does not go that far. In contrast to Sidney, Locke speaks not of a contract that binds the ruler and the people. Rather in Locke's thought, individuals contract among themselves to initiate civil society, and then the majority binds the minority in its determination of what type of government is best to secure their safety and security. Particularly concerned that a government be established in order to combat the inconveniences of nature, Locke emphasizes that it is necessary that the will of the majority predominate: "[I]t is necessary the Body should move that way whither the greater force carries it, which is the *consent of the majority*: or else it is impossible it should act or continue one Body, *one Community*."[65] Sidney, in contrast, seems too concerned with vindicating the liberty of individuals and their claims against a monarch to be bothered with the problem of guaranteeing that a government be instituted in the first instance.

Despite this difference, however, Sidney and Locke offer strikingly similar reasons for the establishment of civil society. According to Locke, the reason why individuals unite to form society is for the "mutual *Preservation* of their Lives, Liberties, and Estates, which I call by the general Name, *Property*. The great and *chief end* therefore, of Mens uniting into Commonwealths, and putting themselves under Government, *is the Preservation of their Property*."[66] It must be admitted that, at least initially, Sidney, in considering the purpose of government, offers formulations that are closer to those of Aristotle than to those of Locke. In the first section of the first chapter, he praises, for example, men who founded commonwealths and who understood "the end for which men enter'd into societies" and who, as a result, "endeavoured

---

[65] Locke, *Second Treatise*, para. 96.
[66] Ibid., para. 123–4.

to make men better, wiser and happier" (1.1.6). Aristotle, as we have seen, explicitly denies that political life can begin in a contract because its end surpasses that which any contract could secure. The purpose of government for the ancient is not merely to guarantee security but to make the citizens good and just.[67] Later, in his long work, however, Sidney ends up sounding very much like Locke when speaking of the purposes of government. He declares, for example, that "if the safety of nations be the end for which governments are instituted, such as take upon them to govern, by what title soever, are by the law of nature bound to procure it; and in order to this, to preserve the lives, lands, liberties and goods of every one of their subjects" (3.16.405). So critical is government's protection of what we now understand as Lockean rights to Sidney that he announces that a king who finds it "grievous" "to preserve the liberties, lives, and estates of his subjects, and to govern according to their laws" should "resign the crown" (3.17.416).

Therefore, Sidney shares with Locke the acceptance of the important Hobbesian premise that society begins in a contract among individuals, which implies that society is artificial and that human beings are not first and foremost political beings. They become political beings only in order to satisfy their basic needs. As the creation of discrete individuals, then, government must furnish the good for which it is created: security. Sidney and Locke define security in broader terms than does Hobbes; they understand security to be the protection of life, liberty, and property. Both use the pre-political condition as a means to understand the purpose of government and to evaluate its success in fulfilling that purpose.

Resistance and Sidney's Machiavellian Vigilance and Vengeance

A government created specifically for the purpose of protecting life, liberty, and property may not simply fail in that purpose through feebleness and inability but may also actively undertake to undermine the people's security by intentionally threatening their lives, infringing their liberty, and seizing their property. To meet this exigency, Locke posits a right of resistance. In delineating this right, he specifies that the citizens who act to protect themselves in such a situation are not rebels because they merely resist those who are properly termed rebels – those who "bring back again the state of War" by the "*endeavour to take away, and destroy the Property of the People,* or to reduce them to Slavery under Arbitrary Power."[68]

Similarly, Sidney insists in the section heading of 3.36 that "The general revolt of a Nation cannot be called a Rebellion." In the body of the section he explains that the Latin *rebellare* means to renew a war, and thus the word is not applicable to a citizen body that was never at war with its

---

[67] Aristotle, *Politics* 3.9, 1280b10–14, and see my discussion of these points in the Introduction.
[68] Locke, *Second Treatise*, para. 226, 222.

governors: "The whole body therefore of a nation cannot be tied to any other obedience than is consistent with the common good, according to their own judgment: and having never been subdued or brought to terms of peace with their magistrates, they cannot be said to revolt or rebel against them to whom they owe no more than seems good to themselves, and who are nothing of or by themselves, more than other men" (3.36.519).

The difference visible here between the teachings of Sidney and Locke on the right of resistance is negligible: whereas Locke speaks of a return to war, Sidney does not.[69] This difference derives from the fact that Locke's writings contain a more fully elaborated state of nature, which, according to his precise specification, devolves into a state of war before human beings will endeavor to seek refuge in civil society. Perhaps the more fundamental difference between them on the subject of resistance resides in the pleasure, which we have already witnessed, that Sidney derives from the contemplation of the punishment that an errant monarch would receive at the hands of his vengeful subjects.

At this point in Sidney's *Discourses*, elements of Machiavelli's thought marry important principles of liberalism. As we know, Sidney, in a Machiavellian fashion, endorses punishment for those rulers or aspirants to rule who step beyond the bounds. So interested is he in establishing the right of the people to overturn an unsatisfactory government and to punish wayward rulers – particularly kings – that he countenances the political upheaval necessary to right the rulers' wrongs. The endorsement of tumults is a distinctive and fundamental facet of Machiavelli's republicanism. On this specific point, he even acknowledges Machiavelli: "Civil war in Machiavelli's account is a disease, but tyranny is the death of a state" (3.40.545). Thus, in declaring that tyranny is worse than civil war, Sidney implies that for Machiavelli civil war may be an appropriate means of eradicating tyranny.

This is certainly the case in Sidney's own thought. In a section of the second chapter entitled "Civil Tumults and Wars are not the greatest Evils that befall Nations," he declares that "'Tis ill that men should kill one another in seditions, tumults and wars; but 'tis worse to bring nations to such misery, weakness and baseness, as to have neither strength nor courage to contend for anything" (2.26.259). Elsewhere he acknowledges that "[i]t may seem strange to some that I mention seditions, tumults, and wars, upon just occasions; but I can find no reason to retract the term" (2.24.219).[70] Sidney certainly specifies that the tumults he endorses are intended to protect the people against wrongdoers. General upheaval in a state should be accepted when it is a by-product of the protection of the people's interests.

[69] Scott, *Restoration Crisis*, 262.
[70] Wood draws his parallel between Machiavelli and Sidney on the basis of their mutual endorsement of civil conflict ("Value of Asocial Sociability," 292, 296–8).

He continues with a degree of Machiavellian vengeance: "If injustice there-fore be evil, and injuries forbidden, they are also to be punished; and the law instituted for their prevention, must necessarily intend the avenging of such as cannot be prevented." Sidney, in fact, admires those who will "con-tend" for their interests by punishing whoever will threaten them; therefore he embraces the passions that motivate the application of vengeance against wrongdoers and even accepts as inevitable those passions that motivate the wrongdoers in the first instance (219).

This issue of civil discord shows how far Sidney's thought is from Harrington's. The distinction proclaims itself when Sidney denies the very end that Harrington seeks: "'Tis in vain to seek a government in all points free from a possibility of civil wars, tumults, and seditions: that is a blessing denied to this life, and reserved to compleat the felicity of the next" (24.217). Thus, the tranquillity of a state that Harrington believes he has discovered, Sidney rejects as unattainable.[71]

The difference between Sidney and Harrington on this issue, however, ul-timately rests on their respective stances toward the passions. Sidney expects that not only a king but also the leading men in a commonwealth will use their positions to grasp at more power than the people have granted them, as well as to attempt to use their positions to accumulate ill-gotten prop-erty. He hopes and encourages the people to watch, to assess, and to punish when necessary. Such a vigilant people, as we have seen, must possess the spirit necessary "to contend" to satisfy their desires; such an active people is reminiscent of Machiavelli's depiction of the Roman plebeians who agitated for the agrarian law, for instance, against the wishes of the patricians. Their spiritedness derived from their passions – most often the passion for property and sometimes for glory. For Sidney, what belongs to the people is their lives, liberties, and properties. This is, of course, a Lockean and liberal formula-tion, but what stands behind it is the passions – preeminently, the desire for security. Thus, Sidney differs from Harrington ultimately in using the pas-sions to counteract the passions, in a way prefigured by Machiavelli. Sidney differs from Harrington in being a more authentic – although certainly a more reticent – Machiavellian. As a result, Sidney should be understood to be one of the English Machiavellians who brings back the Machiavellian appreciation for the passions that Harrington attempts to expel from the political realm.

Sidney, like Harrington, embraces the Machiavellian activity of aggressive war. This aspect of Sidney's Machiavellianism leads him, in a very important respect, away from the liberalism that Locke would outline. Willing to enable the people to satisfy their desires, Locke is unwilling to pursue the same avenues to that satisfaction. Whereas Sidney encourages aggressive wars,

---

[71] Houston, *Algernon Sidney*, 120; Wood, "Value of Asocial Sociability," 293 and 297; Worden, "Republicanism and Restoration," 170–1.

Locke does not. Unlike Locke, Sidney is scornful of republics based on trade, as his criticism of Venice has already indicated. And he praises Plato, for example, for not teaching "us how to erect manufactures, and to increase trade or riches; but how magistrates may be helpful to nations" (2.1.83). He prefers, of course, those republics outfitted for acquisitive war. Sidney, however, fails to consider how a state that pursues aggressive forays against other states can also furnish for its citizens safety and security.

Conversely, Locke shuns war. In fact, he outlines in the *Second Treatise* an understanding of the just rewards of conquest, which, if put into practice, would result in a significant reduction in plunder and, thus, discourage the ravages of war that remove farmers from the plow and merchants from the scale. First, Locke announces that an aggressor nation that conquers its quarry cannot have a right to the spoils.[72] This position is, of course, far removed from the view that Machiavelli and Sidney articulate, which proclaims that expansion not only is necessary but is a legitimate way for a nation to benefit its citizens. Moreover, Locke denies that those who are victorious in resisting the incursion of an unjust foe have a right to the spoils. Of course, they have a right to reparations, but even their seemingly just demand to have the cost of their defense repaid must be limited, because the wives and children of those who fought on the side of the unjust vanquished do not deserve to lose their estates as a result of an action in which they had no part. Nevertheless, Locke would agree with Sidney's declaration that

as the wisdom of a father is seen, not only in providing bread for his family, or increasing his patrimonial estate, but in making all possible provision for the security of it; so that government is evidently the best, which, not relying upon what it does at first enjoy, seeks to increase the number, strength, and riches of the people; and by the best discipline to bring the power so improved into such order as may be of most use to the publick. (2.23.209)

Thus, whereas Sidney asserts the legitimacy of pursuit of such increase through violence, Locke does not. Nevertheless, both seek the same end for politics – the attempt to satisfy human desire. That end entails the unleashing of the passions, a means to which Machiavelli too nods his assent. Therefore, all three embrace the notion that Machiavelli articulates in *The Prince*: it is a natural and ordinary thing to desire to acquire. What remains in dispute is precisely how one should pursue that acquisition – through conquest or through commerce.

---

[72] Locke, *Second Treatise*, para. 176. Of course, Hobbes, too, disapproves of such depredations as his condemnation of the Roman Republic's method of acquisition shows. See particularly, Hobbes, *Citizen*, 3 and 150, and my discussion in Chapter 2.

7

Cato's Thought as the Reconciliation of Machiavellian Republicanism and Lockean Liberalism

As influential as Sidney's thought was in America before and immediately after the Revolution, that of John Trenchard and Thomas Gordon, the authors of *Cato's Letters*, was even more so.[1] "Cato" also surpasses Sidney in his public adoration of Machiavelli. Whereas Sidney is calculatedly circumspect in referring to Machiavelli, Cato exhibits no compunctions about associating himself with the Florentine; he has frequent recourse to the Florentine's thought, frequently names his source, and even refers to him as a "great authority" (16.121).[2] Because Cato's influence was so wide and because he so overtly appeals to the thought of Machiavelli, it is necessary to ask what principles Cato derives and propounds from the Italian. Do his frequent appeals to the writings of this Renaissance thinker underscore his dedication to civic humanism and classical republicanism, or do they reveal, instead, his attempt to participate in a new and modern understanding of government and of the individual's place within it?

Given the immediate circumstances of the publication of *Cato's Letters*, it is all too easy to accept the notion that they are expressions of the former – of a nostalgic longing for a lost world of virtuous dedication to the homeland. The letters, which took the form of a series of articles that appeared in the *London Journal* and the *British Journal* from 1720 to 1723, originate as a response to the crisis of the South Sea Company.[3] In 1719 the company had been

---

[1] Karsten, *Patriot-Heroes*, 34. According to Bailyn, their influence in America "ranked with the treatises of Locke as the most authoritative statement of the nature of political liberty and above Locke as an exposition of the social sources of the threats it faced" (*Ideological Origins*, 36).

[2] *Cato's Letters: or, Essays on Liberty, Civil and Religious, and Other Important Subjects*, ed. Ronald Hamowy (Indianapolis: Liberty Classics, 1995). References to this work appear in the text in this chapter. The number of the letter appears first, followed by the page number.

[3] Trenchard and Gordon were members of what scholars term the "Real," "Old," "Opposition," or "Country" Whig tradition. See, e.g., Robbins, *Eighteenth-Century Commonwealthman*, 6; Pocock, *Machiavellian Moment*, 426–7; Bailyn, *Ideological Origins*, 35–6. For an

granted a monopoly of trade with the South Seas and South America when it assumed the national debt. Prominent individuals, including members of the court, invested in the company, and its managers manipulated the price of the stock to unsustainable levels. Eventually the bubble burst, with the result that investors in the stock lost their fortunes; corrupt public officials and disingenuous financiers were responsible. The initial letters in the series denounce the scandal and demand the harshest punishment possible for those implicated in it. Given this evidence, scholars often view *Cato's Letters* both as railings against the corruptions, deceits, and miasmas of the new world of finance and as emotional lamentations for the lost world composed of those engaged in simple and honest husbandry and virtuous civic action.[4] Other scholars, however, have disputed this claim, discerning in Cato's vehemence against the perpetrators of the scandal not a rejection of the new world of trade as such but rather the manner in which that world can be corrupted by governmental intrusion.[5]

Because *Cato's Letters* goes on to discourse not merely on the scandal but on a myriad of social, political, and religious topics, it is not necessary to look only to Cato's view of commerce and the South Sea bubble to gauge his position with respect to the old and new worlds. After a careful consideration of the political thought expressed in *Cato's Letters*, it becomes clear that Cato embraces the new. Not only do his reflections serve to belie any lingering allegiance to civic humanism deriving from the Aristotelian tradition of political thought often imputed to him, but they reveal him to be attached to the thought of such moderns as Hobbes and Locke; Cato's view of human nature derives largely from Hobbes, and his political principles derive largely from Locke.

In addition, however, as we have already noted, he voices his indebtedness to Machiavelli. As a result of this fundamental reliance on the thought of Machiavelli, as well on that of Hobbes and Locke, Cato's thought represents the final synthesis of Machiavellian republicanism with Lockean liberalism.[6]

---

examination of the various divisions and alliances among Whig and Tory, Court and Country, over the political issues of the day, see Dickinson, *Liberty and Property*, 121–92.

[4] This is the view of Pocock. See particularly, "*Machiavellian Moment* Revisited," 65.

[5] Hamowy maintains that Cato's ire is directed not against trade itself but instead "government intrusion into the world of trade." "Political corruption is not the result of a failure to constrain our private passions. Rather, it arises when our rights are either ignored or unprotected by law, conditions which occur as consequences of the dishonesty or lack of diligence of our magistrates" ("*Cato's Letters*, Locke, and Republican Paradigm," 281). Goodale ("Pocock's Neo-Harringtonians," 250–1); Pangle (*Spirit of Modern Republicanism*, 32–3); and Shelley Burtt (*Virtue Transformed: Political Argument in England, 1688–1740* [Cambridge: Cambridge University Press, 1992], 36, 69, and 82) make similar points with regard to Cato's denunciation of the scandal.

[6] Zuckert emphasizes the Lockean elements of *Cato's Letters*, and further claims, as do I, that the work represents a synthesis of Lockean political philosophy with another alternative. Whereas I claim that other element is Machiavelli's republicanism, Zuckert identifies it as

That synthesis begins to reveal itself in Cato's embrace of the human passions. Like Hobbes, he understands human beings as creatures of their passions, and to buttress this view, he has frequent recourse to distinctive elements of Hobbes's thought that proclaim the dominance of the passions in human psychology. Unlike Hobbes, however, but reflecting his dedication to elements of Machiavelli's thought, he does not flinch from ambition that manifests itself in the desire for glory. Cato embraces, in particular, Machiavelli's depiction of the human passions – particularly the passions of the ambitious few – and of their necessity to a vigorous state. Because he knows that men who seek preeminence can do good for the state as they seek to promote themselves, Cato, precisely like Machiavelli, is ambitious for ambition in his state. Therefore, whereas Hobbes shuns such ambition, Cato embraces it. Again like Machiavelli, he realizes that such ambition can be as dangerous as it is useful, and he proposes – still following Machiavelli – that ambition when it becomes threatening to the free life of a state be punished publicly and severely. Therefore, again in a most Machiavellian fashion, he refuses to recoil from the upheaval such ambition can cause to a state. Ultimately, when it comes to the means by which glory is to be gained, however, Cato distances himself from Machiavelli and reveals himself to be a true liberal. He renounces the battlefield as the venue where glory is to be won in order to embrace trade as the vehicle by which England can compete and best other nations. By renouncing acquisition through war in this manner, Cato retains Machiavelli's injunction to acquire but tames its spirit by making it commensurable with the liberal injunction to acquire for the sake of commodious living.

Cato's synthesis of Machiavellian republicanism and liberalism also features an aspect related not to the ambitious great, but to the many. Like Machiavelli, he seeks to include them in the life of a state. Cato intends their participation in politics not as a fulfillment of human beings' political nature; political participation is a means, not an end in itself. The means to which Cato puts their participation is the protection of their own interests, which necessitates their vigilance toward their rulers. Unlike Machiavelli, however, and reminiscent of Nedham's early anticipation of this synthesis, Cato has

---

"earlier Whig political science" (*Natural Rights and the New Republicanism*, 299, 314). This particular synthesis, according to Zuckert, produces a Lockean Cato, who shares such concerns of the earlier Whigs as "the mixed and balanced constitution, the balance of property, the various threats to the constitution deriving from standing armies and parliamentary corruption, and, finally, the preference for republicanism itself" (307). Although Zuckert does not study in detail the Machiavellian elements of Cato's thought, he recognizes the Florentine's influence on Cato (e.g., 309–10) and states that Cato's political science has much to do with that of "Machiavelli and Harrington, who must be freed from the Pocockian civic humanist interpretation if their relation to Cato is to be clear" (313). Pangle views Cato as combining a "ruthlessly Machiavellian psychology [with] repeated invocations of Hobbesian and Lockean political principles" (*Spirit of Modern Republicanism*, 32).

the people act on their liberties, and refrains from any notion that the people must be duped by their betters in order to produce favorable political outcomes. This difference between Cato and Machiavelli can be ascribed to the fact that, in contrast to Machiavelli, politics for Cato no longer requires the limitation of the people's desire to protect their lives and goods from the ravages of war; because war is no longer the necessary focus of a state, Cato can wholeheartedly embrace the people's desire for security and the accumulation of property in a way impossible for the militaristic Machiavelli. Although Nedham may be said to have anticipated to some degree this synthesis that Cato offers, the people's liberties in Cato's thought are much more fully articulated as rights, thanks to the obvious and direct influence of Locke's thought on Cato. In this way, Cato displays how a Machiavellian spirit can be harnessed to serve liberal ends.

Cato as Civic Humanist

Whereas Harrington, according to Pocock's account, is the prominent link in the civic humanist chain that brought Machiavellian civic humanism with its Aristotelian assumptions to England from Renaissance Italy, Cato is the critical link that facilitated the transfer of that form of thought from Europe to America.[7] The Cato who is to be found in the thousand or so pages of *Cato's Letters*, however, does not readily submit to that particular characterization of him. The depiction of him as a civic humanist is, at best, a one-sided interpretation that overlooks the depth and significance of his embrace of a Hobbesian psychology;[8] his denial that human beings can do otherwise than to act on their self-interest; and his statements that warn of demagogic appeals to virtue. Ultimately, Cato is very far from the civic humanist portrayal of him that attempts to align him with the ancients; as this and the next section show, Cato is a thoroughly modern thinker who works from premises largely drawn not from Aristotle but rather from Hobbes and Locke.

On Pocock's interpretation, however, Cato must be understood as succeeding to the civic humanist line of thought, and thus as "develop[ing] an unmistakably Machiavellian and neo-Harringtonian critique of corruption and of the republic which is its opposite."[9] In other words, a republic demands, on the part of its citizens, a dedication to the whole that will defy the corruption that occurs when individuals put their own interests above those of the whole.

---

[7] Pocock, "English Political Ideologies," 134–5, and *Machiavellian Moment*, 467–8. I offer a criticism of this particular interpretation of Cato in Sullivan, "Civic Humanist Portrait," 87–96.

[8] On Cato's indebtedness to Hobbes, see Dworetz, *Unvarnished Doctrine*, 104–5, 107.

[9] Pocock, *Machiavellian Moment*, 468.

This characterization of Cato's thought is entirely misleading; because he understands human beings as being thoroughly controlled by their passions, Cato will not accept exhortations to virtue as the solution to the promotion of good behavior in politics. Indeed, his understanding of the passions owes much to Hobbes, as he embraces the notions that human reason is instrumental to the passions and, thus, that the passions cloud the reason of individuals. It is not "to be expected," declares Cato, "that men disagreeing in interest, will ever agree in judgement. Wrong, with advantages attending it, will be turned into right, falsehood into truth; and, as often as reason is against a man, a man will be against reason: And both truth and right, when they thwart the interests and passions of men, will be used like enemies, and called names" (47.317). Here Cato reveals his allegiance to Hobbes's understanding of human nature by quoting, without attribution, Hobbes's statement in the epistle dedicatory to *The Elements of Law* ("as oft as reason is against a man, so oft will a man be against reason").[10] Harrington too embraces this sentiment, and his own quotation of this passage in *Oceana* similarly helps to reveal his own reliance on Hobbesian psychology.[11]

In addition, Cato accepts Hobbes's characterization of the passions as thoroughly roiling the human psyche. Cato declares both that "[t]he mind of man is restless, and cannot stand still, nor set bounds to its pursuits" (11.90) and that "men are never satisfied with their present condition, which is never perfectly happy; and perfect happiness being their chief aim, and always out of their reach, they are restlesly grasping at what they never can attain" (40.278). In further musing on this passionate character of human beings, Cato clearly echoes Hobbes's understanding that the passions so agitate human beings that there can be no rest from such agitation until death stills the passions.[12]

When we say, that if such a thing happened, we would be easy; we can only mean, or ought to mean, that we would be more easy than we are: And in that too we are often mistaken; for new acquisitions bring new wants; and imaginary wants are as pungent as real ones. So that there is the same end of wishing as of living, and death only can still the appetites. (40.278)

Elsewhere, he echoes Hobbes's assertion that "Felicity of this life, consisteth not in the repose of a mind satisfied" because "there is no such *Finis ultimus,* (utmost ayme,) nor *Summum Bonum,* (greatest Good,) as is spoken of in the Books of the old Morall Philosophers,"[13] when he recounts: "I laugh at the foolish philosophy of some sects in old Greece, who placed the *summum*

[10] Hobbes, *Elements of Law*, 19.

[11] See Chapter 4, note 75.

[12] See, for example, Hobbes's declaration that he places "for a generall inclination of all mankind, a perpetual and restlesse desire of Power after power, that ceaseth onely in Death" (Hobbes, *Leviathan*, 70).

[13] Ibid.

bonum, or chief happiness, in the absence of all passions or desires; which can be only a state of death, or perfect stupidity, whilst we are alive" (117.816).

Pocock himself notes a Hobbesian element in Cato's understanding of human nature when referring to the preceding passage from letter 40, but, nevertheless, he assures his readers that, despite this cynical aspect of Cato's thought, "the ideal of civic virtue is not abandoned."[14] In support of his interpretation, Pocock cites both Cato's praise for the selfless dedication to the common good that moved some political men in the past and his hope to find just such dedication in the men of the present:

I know that it is exceeding hard and rare, for any man to separate his passions from his own person and interest; but it is certain that there have been such men. Brutus, Cato, Regulus, Timoleon, Dion, and Epaminondas, were such, as were many more ancient Greeks and Romans; and, I hope, England has still some such. And though, in pursuing publick views, men regard themselves and their own advantages; yet if they regard the publick more, or their own in subserviency to the publick, they may justly be esteemed virtuous and good. (39.276–7)[15]

Pocock concludes from this statement that Cato is now safely ensconced in the now familiar civic humanist tradition that emphasizes the fundamentally political nature of human beings, which in turn demands that individuals sacrifice their private interests to the pursuit of the public good:

The passions now appear as the pursuits of private and particular goods, familiar to us from the whole tradition of Aristotelian politics and ethics; virtue is the passion for pursuing the public good, with which the lesser passions may compete, but into which they may equally be transformed. And corruption is the failure, or the consequences of the failure, to effect this transformation.[16]

Contrary to the impression that Pocock's exposition leaves, however, Cato is very far from embracing what Pocock depicts as "the whole tradition of Aristotelian politics and ethics" as the method by which free government is to be fostered and maintained. Indeed, Pocock neglects to report that Cato in this very same letter issues a dire warning regarding exhortations to virtue – precisely the type of exhortations Pocock's civic humanists constantly utter. Discerning a threat to liberty, Cato warns: "We have, all of us, heard much of the duty of subduing our appetites, and extinguishing our passions, from men, who by these phrases shewed at once their ignorance of human nature, and yet that they aimed at an absolute dominion over it" (39.273). Cato further declares here that "And though the mortifying of the appetites be a very plausible phrase, and, in a restrained sense, a laudable thing; yet he who recommends it to you does often mean nothing but this, *Make your*

[14] Pocock, *Machiavellian Moment*, 471.
[15] Pocock cites this passage at *Machiavellian Moment*, 471–2.
[16] Ibid., 472. Pocock also claims here that Cato's virtue "is a Machiavellian *virtù* in the sense that civic does not always accord with personal morality."

Passions tame, that I may ride them" (39.276; emphasis in original). He further confirms the necessity of such skepticism toward those who habitually make demands for self-abnegating virtue when he declares that "[g]enerosity, self-denial, and private and personal virtues, are in politicks but mere names, or rather cant-words, that go for nothing with wise men, though they may cheat the vulgar" (11.92). Such admonishments are attempts to tyrannize over those foolish enough to act on them.[17]

As his statement regarding the great men of Greek and Roman antiquity shows, Cato does admit that there are some outstanding political men who appear to put the public before their private interest. Appearance, though, is the key, because these men, as Cato insists is the case with all human beings, are, in fact, acting on their need to satisfy their passions. Cato explains more fully in the next letter that these men have not, in fact, subordinated their private passions to the public, but are rather acting on those private passions, because they wish to satisfy their desire for glory by heroically serving their country.

I own, that many have seemed to despise riches and power, and really declined the means of acquiring them: But they deceived themselves, if they thought this conduct of theirs was owing to a real contempt for the things themselves; when in truth it was only a dislike of the terms upon which they were to be had. Disinterestedness is often created by laziness, pride, or fear; and then it is no virtue.... Every passion, every view that men have, is selfish in some degree; but when it does good to the publick in its operation and consequence, it may be justly called disinterested in the usual meaning of that word. So that when we call any man disinterested, we should intend no more by it, than that the turn of his mind is towards the publick, and that he has placed his own personal glory and pleasure in serving it. (40.279)

Some leaders, then, are themselves ruled by more benign passions that can produce desirable outcomes for the whole, while at the same time they actually seek to benefit themselves.[18] As Cato affirms elsewhere: "I think it impossible for any man to act upon any other motive than his own interest: For every pursuit that we make must have for its end the gratification of some appetite, or the avoiding of some evil which we fear" (117.815).

Because human beings are so much the creatures of their passions, Cato will rely neither on admonitions to virtue nor on political leaders being consistently governed by those more benign passions that propel them to further the public good. He puts his faith instead in his knowledge that they will act on their passions and in the likelihood that those passions will be nefarious ones at that.[19] This knowledge must, in his view, be propounded to all. He

---

[17] Sullivan, "Civic Humanist Portrait," 89–90.
[18] Pangle, *Spirit of Modern Republicanism*, 31–2; Rahe, *Republics Ancient and Modern*, 433–4.
[19] Burtt offers a portrait of a Cato whose conception of "civic virtue is privatized, its roots given a self-interested, personally focused foundation; but it is not dispensed with altogether" (Burtt, *Virtue Transformed*, 76).

explains that his exposition of "[a]ll these discoveries and complaints of the crookedness and corruption of human nature are made with no malignant intention to break the bonds of society; but they are made to shew, that as selfishness is the strongest bias of men, every man ought to be upon his guard against another, that he become not the prey of another" (40.280). In other words, every man must watch the other; the governed must watch their governors, and governors must watch other governors.

In support of this proposition that the people must guard against the evil designs of their leaders, he asserts that "every private subject has a right to watch the steps of those who would betray their country; nor is he to take their word about the motives of their designs, but to judge of their designs by the event" (13.103). In support of his view of the need for rulers to guard other rulers, he refers to what he understands as the method of circumscribing the power of magistrates in free countries: it was "so qualified, and so divided into different channels, and committed to the direction of so many different men, with different interests and views, that the majority of them could seldom or never find their account in betraying their trust in fundamental instances. Their emulation, envy, fear, or interest, always made them spies and checks upon one another" (60.417). Good government results when an active citizenry is alive with vigilance and a body of ruling men discerns and acts on any undue accumulation of power by another. Neither of these parties need be motivated by anything other than its own selfish interests. Thus, for Cato renunciations of the selfish passions are far from necessary to produce good government in the manner that Pocock's civic humanists maintain. Self-interest when properly activated and channeled is all that is necessary to produce positive political outcomes:

[W]hilst men are men, ambition, avarice, and vanity, and other passions, will govern their actions; in spite of all equity and reason, they will be ever usurping, or attempting to usurp, upon the liberty and fortunes of one another, and all men will be striving to enlarge their own. Dominion will always desire increase, and property always to preserve itself; and these opposite views and interests will be causing a perpetual struggle: But by this struggle liberty is preserved, as water is kept sweet by motion. (70.504)[20]

Cato's Lockean Political Principles

Because Cato had access to the thought of Locke as contained in *The Second Treatise*, he need not derive these principles from the thought of Hobbes and

---

[20] Goodale challenges Pocock's interpretation of Cato's thought by arguing that it expresses the view that "it was the structure of the government and not the character of the people in power that ensured liberty" ("Pocock's Neo-Harringtonians," 248). It is just such an attempt at such structuring to which Cato is here alluding. In this, Cato can be said to be following Harrington's republicanism. See also Rahe, *Republicanism Ancient and Modern*, 431–2.

then transform them in order for them to support a government that was anything less than authoritarian, as did other English republican thinkers. Cato makes good use of his access to Lockean political principles: he argues repeatedly and consistently that the original condition of human beings is one of equality in the state of nature, that governments are created with the consent of human beings to alleviate the ills of that original condition, that governments must be judged by the conditions of that original contract, and that people may resist their government when it derogates from those conditions. Cato's political understanding is thoroughly Lockean. This fact must challenge, as scholars Ronald Hamowy and Michael Zuckert argue, Pocock's understanding of Cato as a civic humanist who resists the encroachment of such modern concepts against the ancient alternative, which claims that because human beings are by nature political animals, the polity must have a much wider province over the lives of the individuals who constitute it than the Lockean alternative would permit.[21] Contrary to this ancient understanding, Cato argues for a limited government whose purpose is to attempt to fulfill the needs and desires and to protect the rights of those individuals who have constituted it.

We have already seen Sidney approximate Locke's definition of equality that holds that nature decrees not that any particular individual is suited to rule while another is suited to be ruled, but rather that "all...should...be equal one amongst another without Subordination or Subjection."[22] Cato embraces this Lockean notion in a formulation strikingly similar to that of Sidney: "Men are naturally equal, and none ever rose above the rest but by force or consent" (45.306).[23] Thus, Cato endorses the understanding of Sidney and Locke that no one is born to rule others.

Cato, however, goes further in asserting the fundamental equality among human beings than does either Sidney or Locke. For Cato, equality rests not merely on the lack of a divinely or naturally designated ruler and ruled but also on the real similarities in faculties among human beings. He asserts, for example, that "Nature...constitutes no particular favourites with endowments and privileges above the rest" (45.306) and "[t]hat nature has made

---

[21] Hamowy, "Cato's Letters, Locke, and Republican Paradigm," 273–83, and Zuckert, Natural Rights and the New Republicanism, 300–19. In contrast to my analysis and that of Zuckert, Hamowy disputes in particular Pocock's characterization of Cato's view of economic activity. Although not making as sustained a case as Hamowy and Zuckert, Pangle too discerns Lockean elements in Cato (Spirit of Modern Republicanism, 32), and Rahe comments that "Cato's Letters owed far more to Locke than to any other figure" (Republics Ancient and Modern, 532). Cf. Dworetz, who maintains that although there are clearly Lockean elements in Cato's thought, "Cato's political liberalism seems ad hoc – not an integral part of his doctrine, as it is for Locke's" (Unvarnished Doctrine, 109).

[22] Locke, Second Treatise, para 4.

[23] It will be recalled that Sidney says that equality of right demands that one cannot be put under the domination of any other except "by his own consent, or by force" (Discourses Concerning Government 3.31.304).

men equal, we know and feel" (307).[24] In asserting that the equality of human beings rests also on the basis of nature's endowments, he draws close to Hobbes. Indeed, when Cato announces that "Nature has made [men] all equal, and most men seem well content with the lot of parts which nature has given them" (42.294), he replicates Hobbes's sentiment that the fact that people generally believe themselves wiser than the multitude "proveth...that men are in that point equall, than unequall. For there is not ordinarily a greater signe of the equall distribution of any thing, than that every man is contented with his share."[25] Therefore, Cato accepts the Lockean notion of equality that rests on the notion that no one is born to rule another, but then proceeds to add to it the Hobbesian assertion of equality of innate faculties.

Although inclining toward Hobbes on this aspect of equality, Cato far surpasses Sidney in earning his Lockean stripes when he treats the state of nature, the law that governs it, and the manner by which it furnishes a standard by which to judge political regimes. It will be recalled that Sidney does not use the term state of nature in his *Discourses*, although he certainly draws his political principles from a prepolitical condition. Cato, by contrast, uses the term frequently. He also maintains in a distinctively Lockean tone that the "first law of nature" is that of "self-preservation" (12.93; 33.239). Further, in a more detailed discussion of this law of preservation, and in a clear echo of Locke's description of the law of nature that enjoins each to preserve his life as well as those of his fellows,[26] Cato announces: "Nor has any man in the state of nature power over his own life, or to take away the life of another, unless to defend his own, or what is as much his own, namely, his property" (60.414). Moreover, he extends to those who inhabit the state of nature, in a line of thought distinctively Lockean, the power to execute that law against those who would violate it by threatening the security of others: "Every man in the state of nature had a right to repel injuries, and to revenge them; that is, he had a right to punish the authors of those injuries" (11.87).[27] The fact that Locke himself concedes that his assertion of the right to execute the law of nature against its violators "will seem a very strange Doctrine to some Men" attests to the distinctiveness of the doctrine that Cato seeks to borrow from Locke.[28]

Moreover, Cato uses the notion of consent as a basis for the formation of political society. He also indicates elsewhere that consent is not merely one basis of government but is, in fact, the only legitimate basis of it: "Government therefore can have no power, but such as men can give, and such as they

---

[24] On the issue of equality in Cato's thought, see also Robbins, *Eighteenth-Century Commonwealthman*, 122.

[25] Hobbes, *Leviathan*, 87.

[26] Locke, *Second Treatise*, para. 6.

[27] For Locke's treatment of the execution of the law of nature in the state of nature, see ibid., para. 7–9.

[28] Ibid., para. 9.

actually did give, or permit for their own sakes: Nor can any government be in fact framed but by consent, if not of every subject, yet of as many as can compel the rest" (60.413–14).

According to Cato's understanding, however, the people have the right to withdraw their consent from a government that does not fulfill the purposes for which it was formed. In this, as we will see, Cato follows Locke's doctrine of resistance. Cato builds his case for this doctrine by arguing that although the state of nature is superseded by the formation of societies, it still furnishes a standard that allows citizens to judge whether their government is fulfilling the purposes for which it was intended: "The entering into political society, is so far from a departure from his natural right, that to preserve it was the sole reason why men did so; and mutual protection and assistance is the only reasonable purpose of all reasonable societies" (62.427; see also 11.87, 62.427).

Cato emphasizes liberty, in particular, as a natural right that was insecure in the state of nature. Political society's guarantee of liberty is particularly important given that the promise of its protection was a primary inducement for entering into the state of political society. Moreover, Cato depicts liberty both as central to human happiness and as being bound up with the ability to hold and increase property. Of course, Cato's understanding of the right to liberty in all of these aspects is deeply indebted to Locke. Cato explains that he defines liberty as "the power which every man has over his own actions, and his right to enjoy the fruit of his labour, art, and industry, as far as by it he hurts not the society, or any members of it. . . . The fruits of a man's honest industry are the just rewards of it, ascertained to him by natural and eternal equity" (62.427). Magistrates cannot violate the law of nature by infringing the liberty of citizens: "[T]he nature of government does not alter the natural right of men to liberty" (60.416). Liberty benefits society as a whole by encouraging industry in the individuals who possess it, and benefits individuals by fostering their own happiness: "[L]iberty is the divine source of all human happiness. To possess, in security, the effects of our industry, is the most powerful and reasonable incitement to be industrious. . . . But where property is precarious, labour will languish" (432). "To live securely, happily, and independently," Cato declares, "is the end and effect of liberty; and it is the ambition of all men to live agreeably to their own humours and discretion" (68.483).

In this manner, Cato explains the purpose of politics by recourse to the reasons why naturally disassociated individuals would agree to enter into society. He states this more pointedly elsewhere: "So that to know the jurisdiction of governors, and its limits, we must have recourse to the institution of government, and ascertain those limits by the measure of power, when men in the state of nature have over themselves and one another: And no man can take from many, who are stronger than him, what they have no mind to give him" (60.414). In order to fulfill the purpose for which political society was intended, "the magistrate is entrusted with conducting and applying the united force of the community; and with exacting such a share of every man's property, as is necessary to preserve the whole, and to defend every man and his property from foreign and domestick injuries. These are the boundaries of the power of the magistrate, who deserts his function whenever he breaks them" (62.427). Thus, the state of nature establishes strict parameters around the authority of magistrates.

Magistrates, however, do not always observe those parameters: "[M]en quitted part of their natural liberty to acquire civil security. But frequently the remedy proved worse than the disease; and human society had often no enemies so great as their own magistrates; who, whereever they were trusted with too much power, always abused it, and grew mischievous to those who made them what they were" (33.236). When rulers so violate their trust, it must be considered that political society is "dissolved," because, as Cato explains: "It is a most wicked and absurd position, to say, that a whole people can ever be in such a situation, as not to have a right to defend and preserve themselves, when there is no other power in being to protect and defend them; and much more, that they must not oppose a tyrant, a traitor, an universal robber, who, by violence, treachery, rapine, infinite murders and devastations, has deprived them of their legal protection" (55.370). In explaining the right to defend and preserve themselves in such a dire situation, he has recourse to a doctrine of resistance very similar to Locke's, which Cato defends against its critics with the statement: "It is said, that the doctrine of resistance would destroy the peace of the world: But it may be more truly said, that the contrary doctrine would destroy the world itself." He continues that "[t]he law of nature does not only allow us, but oblige us, to defend ourselves" (42.292).

The doctrine of resistance, though, contains the problem of who is to judge when the rulers have exceeded their grant of authority so that they derogate from the purposes for which society is established. Cato attempts to resolve this problem with the solution that "[w]here no judge is nor can be appointed, every man must be his own; that is, when there is no stated judge upon earth, we must have recourse to heaven, and obey the will of heaven, by declaring ourselves on that which we think the juster side" (59.407–8). In settling this question, Cato clearly follows Locke's own answer to this problem: "[T]his Question, (*Who shall be Judge?*) cannot mean, that there is no Judge at all. For where there is no Judicature on Earth, to decide Controversies amongst Men, *God* in Heaven is *Judge*: He alone, 'tis true, is Judge of the Right. But *every Man* is *Judge* for himself, as in all other Cases, so in this."[29] Thus, Cato follows Locke in asserting that in such situations

[29] Ibid., para. 241. Zuckert (*Natural Rights and the New Republicanism*, 304) and Rahe (*Republics Ancient and Modern*, 532) also point to the similarity between this discussion of Cato and that of Locke and use it as evidence of Cato's genuine link to Locke.

individuals themselves are to decide by consulting their own consciences – a consultation that both thinkers refer to as an appeal to heaven.

Thus, Cato operates from a distinctively Lockean understanding of the purposes and limits of political society. Like Locke, Cato asserts that people leave the state of nature in order to preserve their natural rights. When those rights are threatened by the very officials who are elevated to protect them, the people have a right to resist and ultimately to form a new government. All of Cato's extensive borrowing from Locke serves to show further that Cato is not operating from a civic humanist understanding of government. For Cato, individuals pursue fulfillment – what he calls their happiness – in the liberty political society affords them to pursue their own interests and enterprises rather than in the civic humanist characterization of virtuous participation in the polity. Not the collective, but the individual – his rights, his desires, and his happiness – is the standard by which government is to be judged.

The Question of Cato's Republican Sympathies

Neither Locke nor Hobbes, of course, is noted for his republican sympathies, and Cato himself refuses to announce in favor of a republic in England. Nevertheless, he praises and endorses the thought of the noted republican Algernon Sidney,[30] a move, having once made, he later finds himself having to defend against accusations that such praise belies his own republican sympathies. He also adapts elements of Harrington's republic into his own understanding of government when he accepts Harrington's famous claim that property determines what political possibilities are attainable for a state. Harrington's own analysis of the distribution of property in England – which proves to Harrington the inevitability of a republican England – indicates instead to Cato its impossibility. Of course, the English political scene had changed drastically since Harrington, and even Sidney, wrote. The Bill of Rights and the Act of Settlement had defined and limited the powers of the monarchy, and thereby stabilized its rule. As a result, the possibility of a republic in England had been utterly eclipsed. Cato seems to resign himself to this fact, but his acceptance does not prevent him from admiring republics and those who endorse them.[31] Ultimately, however, mixed with his admiration for republics and republicans is not merely a realistic assessment of the possibility of a republican future in England but also a principled objection to what he sees as the constraints of republican life.

---

[30] Worden, *Roundhead Reputations*, 151.

[31] Worden regards *Cato's Letters* as one of "the principal despotistor[ies] of republican ideas in the earlier eighteenth century" ("Republicanism and the Restoration," 177), but describes that republicanism as "resigned to defeat, its aspirations being purely hypothetical" (*Roundhead Reputations*, 152).

His admiration for previous republicans, for instance, is particularly evident when he fills letter 26 with an extended passage from Sidney's *Discourses*. In introducing the passage, he offers an encomium to Sidney, "who has written better upon government than any Englishman, and as well as any foreigner." He praises Sidney as "a martyr for . . . liberty," who, having "asserted the rights of mankind, and shewed the odiousness of tyranny," fell victim to the "vile and corrupt court of our pious Charles II" (26.188). He then proceeds to quote from a passage of Sidney's *Discourses* that describes how liberty is threatened by evil monarchs who undertake to corrupt their people with blandishments and that lauds, in the process of this description, virtue and denounces corruption.[32]

At the beginning of the second letter devoted to the transmission of another passage from Sidney's *Discourses*, Cato finds it necessary to defend himself against those who, on the basis of his admiration of Sidney's heroism and political views as expressed in letter 26, accuse him of republicanism. Cato responds that the imputation is "dishonestly suggested"; the passages he transmits of Sidney "are not republican passages, unless virtue and truth be republicans." He then seems to belie his republican predilections by announcing his allegiance to the English monarchy on a republican basis: "Mr. Sidney's book, for the main of it, is eternally true, and agreeable to our own constitution, which is the best republick in the world, with a prince at the head of it." He appears, then, to be devoted to England because it is a type of republic. On this point, however, he equivocates in the continuation: "That our government is a thousand degrees nearer akin to a commonwealth (any sort of commonwealth now subsisting, or that ever did subsist in the world) than it is to absolute monarchy." The fact that England's government is closer to a republic than it is to an absolute monarchy hardly bolsters his earlier claim that England is a republic per se. A monarchy, of course, can be far from absolutism without being a republic. Nevertheless, he here concludes his comments on his own views of England's government with the declaration: "I hope in God never to see any other form of government in England than that which is now in England; and that if this be the style and spirit of a republican, I glory in it" (37.262). His statements here regarding his view of the republican qualities of the English constitution are not unambiguous; that very equivocation gives pause to those who might be inclined to view Cato as a republican.[33]

---

[32] See also Hamowy's discussion of Cato's use of Sidney, "*Cato's Letters*, Locke, and Republican Paradigm," 287–9.

[33] Dworetz fails to note any such equivocation on Cato's part, declaring that Cato was simply and clearly opposed to republicanism. He uses this position to embarrass the current "republican" interpretation of Cato's thought: "Nowadays, it's Cato's friends who wish to make him into something he was not. His declared antipathy for republican ideals has [not] deterred them from extolling his political thought as the principal source of American republicanism" (*Unvarnished Doctrine*, 106–7). In contrast to Dworetz, Zuckert rightly notes

He also transmits elements of a thinker even more overtly republican than Sidney: Harrington. Cato finds Harrington's principle of rotation critical to maintaining liberty in a monarchy. "I can see no means in human policy," declares Cato, "to preserve the publick liberty and a monarchical form of government together, but by the frequent fresh elections of the people's deputies." Without mentioning Harrington's name, he apparently nods to Harrington in particular when he continues, "This is what the writers in politicks call rotation of magistracy" (61.422). Without rotation, elected officials will forget the interests of those who remain in the station from which they have been elevated and will thus "by too sudden degrees become insolent, rapacious and tyrannical" (61.423).

Cato embraces another distinctive feature of Harrington's republic – that of its method of balancing interests. Harrington's use of dividing and choosing provides a particularly salient example of this method; the many and the few act on their self-interest, but find that they are forced to do so in a manner that responds to the interests of the opposing group. Thus, he promotes institutional arrangements not to do away with self-interest but rather to channel it. In this way, Harrington helps to develop the modern political principle of securing good government by having interests check other interests and passions other passions. Cato too evinces evidence of the same tendency. Although he has a much higher level of tolerance for tumults caused by the play of passions than does Harrington, he shows that he grasps the principle of balancing and channeling interests when, as we have seen, he declares "opposite views and interests will be causing a perpetual struggle: But by this struggle liberty is preserved" (70.504).[34]

Moreover, Trenchard reveals himself to be a particular acolyte of this strategy, when, in an earlier publication, he states that:

A Government is a mere piece of Clockwork, and having such Springs and Wheels, must act after such a manner: and therefore the Art is to constitute it so, that it must move to the public Advantage. It is certain that every Man will act for his own Interest; and all wise Governments are founded upon that Principle: So that this whole Mystery is only to make the Interest of the Governors and Governed the same.[35]

Cato's telling equivocations on the issue of republicanism, and, in challenging Dworetz's characterization, argues that, given his historical circumstances, any declaration in favor of a republic on Cato's part would be "impolitic in the extreme." Moreover, Zuckert, as do I, points to conditions in England unfavorable to such an establishment (*Natural Rights and the New Republicanism*, 313–14 and 374, n. 68). I differ from Zuckert, however, in pointing to what appears to be a principled objection in a divided mind regarding the constraints necessary for a true republic – particularly one of a Harringtonian character.

34 See the earlier section, "Cato as Civic Humanist," as well as my comments in note 20.
35 John Trenchard, *A Short History of Standing Armies in England*, 3d ed. (London: Printed for A. Baldwin, 1698), iii. Both Goodale ("Pocock's Neo-Harringtonians," 248) and Rahe (*Republics Ancient and Modern*, 432) refer to this earlier writing of Trenchard when making

Trenchard has either copied or intuited Harrington's own conclusion that declares that the secret of good government is to be found in its mechanistic perfection. This is particularly evident in Harrington's political application of the lesson he derives from the spectacle of cats trapped in a mechanism that forced each to do its part in a kitchen that worked very much like clockwork: "If the frame of your commonwealth be not such as causeth everyone to perform his certain function as necessarily as this did the cat to make green sauce, it is not right," Harrington intones.[36] Cato and Harrington are alike in refusing to lodge their hopes in government inducing individuals to renounce their private interests but, instead, in placing their hopes in the control and management of those interests so that they not only do not harm but, in fact, benefit the state.

Presumably, this prominent aspect of Harrington's republican theory can be put to use, as the principle of rotation illustrates, in monarchical England, which at times Cato claims is nearly a republic. Despite the consoling thought of England's nearness to republican government, Cato still admires republics. When faced with the need to declare where his sympathies lie, he declares in favor of England's form of monarchy, but not without a modicum of regret. Writing of the deceased Trenchard in the preface to the collected Cato's Letters, Gordon maintains that "As passionate as he was for liberty, he was not for a Commonwealth in England. He neither believed it possible, nor wished for it. He thought that we were better as we were, than any practicable change could make us." Gordon accepts but explicitly expresses regret for this situation when he comments, "I wish that he may have been mistaken; but the grounds of his opinion were too plausible" (pr. 31–2). Of course, the expression of such regret raises the possibility that if a republic were attainable in England, they would be its enthusiastic supporters.

Cato finally unveils the nature of those insurmountable obstacles to England's republican future in letter 85, which begins with the reflection that England is able to bear neither "full liberty, nor perfect slavery," "if ... liberty be understood" as "a republican form of government." This particular definition of liberty, which equates it exclusively with republican government, is certainly different from his other definitions of liberty, which reserve for it the ability to enjoy without interference the products of one's labor and to live securely and independently. Certainly, the type of liberty that the latter definition describes could be found in monarchical governments, whereas the former, of course, could not. That divergence between definitions is underscored in the continuation when he proceeds to associate liberty with monarchical government: "I conceive that liberty may be better preserved

the point of the extent to which Cato relies on the structure of government to produce favorable political outcomes. Rahe makes the further point of relating Cato's thought on this basis to the "political architecture" prominent in Harrington's (433).

[36] Harrington, Discourse upon this Saying, 744. See also Chapter 4, note 41.

by a well poised monarchy, than by any popular government that I know now in the world, whatever forms may exist in imagination." An element of doubt enters his analysis at this point: "[W]hether this be true or not, it is certainly true that no man in his wits will lose the benefits of a very good present establishment, and run infinite hazards, to try to get one a little better, if he could have any prospect of attaining it." He then proceeds to delineate the difficulties inherent in establishing a republic, including among his remarks the "present distribution" of property. According to his analysis, the distribution of property in England does not produce the type of equality necessary for a republic: "An equality of estate will give an equality of power; and an equality of power is a commonwealth, or democracy: An agrarian law, or something equivalent to it, must make or find a suitable disposition of property; and when that comes to be the case, there is no hindering a popular form of government" (85.613–14). In this manner, he adds his voice to Harrington's rather idiosyncratic support for the necessity of agrarian laws to sustain republican government.

He confirms elsewhere this analysis regarding the necessity of imposing and stringently maintaining equality of property as the basis for liberty. "As liberty can never subsist without equality, nor equality be long preserved without an agrarian law, or something like it," he explains, "so when men's riches are become immeasurably or surprizingly great, a people, who regard their own security, ought to ... oblige them to take down their own size, for fear of ... mastering [their community]." He corroborates this analysis, in Harringtonian fashion, by pointing to the decline of Rome: "If the Romans had well observed the agrarian law ... one man would never have ... established, as Caesar did at last, a tyranny in that great and glorious state" (35.253). In regard to the case of England, then, he concludes: "We have an excellent constitution at present; and if not the best which can be formed in an utopian commonwealth, yet I doubt the best that we are capable of receiving. The present distribution of property renders us incapable of changing it for the better; and probably any attempt to change it for the better, would conclude in an absolute monarchy" (80.584).

Thus, Cato clearly accepts Harrington's conclusions that the distribution of property determines the type of government a state can maintain and that a republic requires an agrarian law, but differs with him on whether England's distribution of property is fit for a commonwealth. According to Cato's assessment of the political landscape, the nobility and gentry of England simply hold too much property and possess too great privileges to permit a republican form of government. Moreover, the imposition of an agrarian law in England is unthinkable. He hopes that "no one amongst us has a head so wrong turned, as to imagine that any man, or number of men, in the present situation of affairs, can ever get power enough to turn all the possessions of England topsy-turvy, and throw them into average ... and without all this it is impossible to settle a commonwealth here." He adds as another undesirable feature of the imposition of an agrarian law in England the fact that its only advocates are those who have "no estates of their own, or means and merit to acquire them," and "would be glad to share in those of other people" (85.614). Thus, given all these considerations, he can decide in favor of the continued rule of England's monarchy at this point without "entering into the question, which is the best government in theory, a limited monarchy, or a democratical form of government" (85.616).

His borrowings from and discussions of his English republican predecessors express a real ambivalence on Cato's part: he appears to mix a realistic assessment of the impossibility of an English republic with a wistful regard for republican politics. His additional reflections suggest, however, that he has a principled objection to republican austerity as Harrington, for example, envisioned it.

One definition of liberty Cato provides in letter 85 links it inextricably with "a republican from of government" (613), but, as we have seen, he also frequently discusses a type of liberty that simply cannot exist in a republic of Cato's description and seems much more compatible with contemporary England. He declares elsewhere, for instance, "The privileges of thinking, saying, and doing what we please, and of growing as rich as we can, without any other restriction, than that by all this we hurt not the publick, nor one another, are the glorious privileges of liberty" (62.432). Obviously, this definition of liberty is simply incompatible with republican liberty as he presents it in letters 85 and 35; a citizen of a republic with an agrarian law as its basis simply cannot find his liberty in an ability to grow as rich as he can. A subject in Cato's England, though, certainly can. Perhaps for this reason, Cato expresses, even in the chapter where he associates liberty with republican government, regard for the manner in which a well-constructed monarchy can foster liberty ("But I conceive that liberty may be better preserved by a well poised monarchy, than by any popular government that I know now in the world, whatever forms may exist in imagination"), before he goes on to wonder whether this understanding of England is true (85.613). Despite Cato's equivocations that suggest a republican sentiment, his depiction of England's current form of liberty is certainly much more compatible with his treatments both of human nature and of the purpose of government as the promotion of individual desires. He too shuns elements of Harrington's domestic politics in the name of the satisfaction of the desires to acquire.

Cato's Machiavellian Teaching Regarding Vengeance and Return to First Principles

Whether England is a commonwealth with a king at its helm or whether it is the best monarchy in the world, Cato is quite willing to recur to the thought of another republican – Machiavelli – and to import elements of his depiction of the Roman Republic specifically and of republics generally into the operation of England. Indeed, perhaps Cato's adaptation of Machiavelli's republican-ism for England best expresses the quality of his republicanism. In embrac-ing Machiavellian republicanism, however, Cato does not leave Hobbes and Locke – who are not known themselves as partisans of republics – behind. Indeed, in some respects, elements of the thought of Hobbes and Locke can be said to encourage Cato's embrace of the Florentine. In particu-lar, as this and the next section illustrate, by accepting the Hobbesian notion of the manner in which human beings are driven by their passions, and by simultaneously refusing to renounce the passion for preeminence (as does Hobbes), Cato finds himself in need of Machiavelli's teaching regarding a republic's need for vengeance, punishment, and ingratitude. These qualities are needed as weapons against those rulers who attempt to step beyond the bounds and thereby infringe on the rights of the people. In Cato's view, then, the protection of liberal rights deriving from the thought of Locke requires Machiavellian vigilance and vengeance.[37]

The subject of how to deal with the managers of the South Sea Company moves Cato to a tirade of Machiavellian vengeance.[38] To allow such crimes to go unpunished would be to risk, in Cato's mind, the continued health of the commonwealth. In discussing the appropriate penalty for those who betray their homeland, Cato refers explicitly to Machiavelli's harsh teach-ing, reminding his readers that "Machiavel" insists that "a free government is not to be preserved but by destroying Brutus's sons" (16.121). Cato, like Nedham, displays a high regard for the extreme penalty Brutus demanded his own sons pay when they acted on their resentment of the new repub-lic by conspiring to reestablish the Tarquins as rulers in Rome; Brutus not only presided at his sons' trial but was also present at their execution.[39] As we know, Machiavelli transforms this particular case into a general rule regarding the necessity for republics to take extreme measures for the sake of the preservation of their freedom: "[T]here is no remedy more powerful, nor more valid, more secure, and more necessary, than to kill the sons of Brutus."[40] As we see, Cato eagerly applies this harsh maxim with which Machiavelli furnishes him. In a later letter, he attests to the potency of this remedy in the Roman case and hence suggests its desirability in modern times when he provokingly notes that "[a]fter the death of the sons of Brutus, . . . we hear no more of any conspirators in Rome to restore the Tarquins" (20.142).

---

[37] Rahe attributes these elements of Cato's thought solely to Locke's influence on him (*Republics Ancient and Modern*, 532).

[38] Pocock also links Cato's spirit of vengeance against the perpetrators of the South Sea debacle to Machiavelli's thought (*Machiavellian Moment*, 468).

[39] Livy, *Ab urbe condita* 2.3–5.

[40] Machiavelli, *Discourses* 1.16.4. Machiavelli tells the story of the execution of the sons of Brutus in *Discourses* 3.3 entitled "That It Is Necessary to Kill the Sons of Brutus If One Wishes to Maintain a Newly Acquired Freedom."

The implication is, of course, that a similarly harsh penalty against the guilty would have a similarly beneficial effect in England.

As even further inducement to take the harshest method possible, Cato draws from Machiavelli's teaching regarding the necessity for a state to have recourse to first principles. "Machiavel tells us," Cato reports, "that no government can long subsist, but by recurring often to its first principles." In this way, Cato displays a partiality for Machiavelli's teaching that counsels that complacency in a state can be overcome through public executions – including the execution of Brutus's sons – that remind all of their vulnerability. Displaying an acute awareness of the dangers of the complacency of which Machiavelli warns, Cato comments that a recurrence to the first principles

can never be done while men live at ease and in luxury; for then they cannot be persuaded to see distant dangers, of which they feel no part. The conjunctures proper for such reformations, are when men are awakened by misfortunes, and frighted with the approach and near view of present evils; then they will wish for remedies, and their minds are prepared to receive them, to hear reasons, and to fall into measures proposed by wise men for their security. (16.121)

The punishment of the malefactors responsible for the South Sea crisis, thus, will demonstrate to all citizens their vulnerability and the need for vigilance. During a time of crisis the people will be more likely to listen to wise men, such as Cato. At other times when danger does not appear to impinge on them, they will take their own security and wise counsel for granted. It is precisely at such a time that their governors are likely to take advantage of them.

The prescription Cato follows regarding the need for a return to first principles derives from *Discourses* 3.1, where Machiavelli is concerned with setting a frightening example for other likely malefactors. In fact, in this chapter he comments suggestively with regard to the decline of Rome that "as the memory of that beating is eliminated, men began to dare to try new things and to say evil."[41] Cato demonstrates that he has taken Machiavelli's lesson to heart and would not let such a memory fade when he declares that he himself would welcome a spectacle so frightening that its memory would furnish a restraint to other possible transgressors long into the future:

[Y]ou may, at present, load every gallows in England with directors and stock-jobbers.... A thousand stock-jobbers, well trussed up, besides the diverting sight, would be a cheap sacrifice to the Manes of trade; it would be one certain expedient to soften the rage of the people; and to convince them that the future direction of their wealth and estates shall be put into the hands of those, who will as effectually study to promote the general benefit and publick good, as others have, lately, most infamously sacrificed both to their private advantage. (2.42)

---

[41] Ibid., 3.1.3.

In this manner, such severe punishment would assure both that the spirits of the people are offered a catharsis and that men who hold such positions in the future will endeavor to act more responsibly. Given that such favorable results will flow from stern measures, Cato is emboldened to intone in his most authoritative Machiavellian accent that the opposite tack may occasion harm: "[M]ercy may be cruelty" (2.41).[42]

Cato's Machiavellian Teaching on Ingratitude

Although Cato's immediate historical circumstances demand such severity, he also offers general reflections on how a free state can avoid the danger that ambitious leaders pose at all times. Two letters of Cato in particular, 118 and 119, devoted to the subject of ingratitude, deal with this subject. He draws heavily on Machiavelli's own section on ingratitude in the *Discourses*, chapters 28–32 of the first book. The ostensible purpose of each treatment is to examine the phenomenon of gratitude in a republic: Machiavelli purports to examine why Rome was less ungrateful than Athens, whereas Cato undertakes to defend free states from the charge that they are more ungrateful to the men who perform great services for them than are arbitrary states. Because each discussion defends a type of state that the author deems grateful, each appears at times to presume gratitude to be a virtue for a state – something to be pursued rather than avoided. Nevertheless, a strong current in each discussion suggests that an excess of gratitude extended to powerful and talented men can be quite dangerous and that stern punishment is a potent antidote for their nefarious ambition.

Cato begins by treating a phenomenon that all states encounter: those who perform great services for them rarely regard the rewards they receive as adequate recompense. As a result, such men "being neither pleased with the measure nor duration of their power, where it is not boundless and perpetual, are apt to be struggling to make it so, though to the ruin of those who gave it for their own preservation, and to the overthrowing of every purpose for which it was given" (118.821). When a free people takes measures to protect liberty from the machinations of the ambitious, the people are thus termed ungrateful: "The dearest and most valuable things are most apt to create jealousies and fears about them: and the dearest of all being liberty, as that which produces and secures all the rest, the people's zeal to preserve it has been ever called ingratitude by such as had designs against it" (118.824).

Machiavelli too emphasizes the difficulty that states face in rewarding their leading men. In a chapter preceding his section on ingratitude, he provides the following encapsulation of that difficulty: "[A] free way of life proffers honors and rewards through certain honest and determinate causes, and outside these it neither rewards nor honors anyone; and when one has

---

[42] See particularly chapter 17 of *The Prince*. Sullivan, "Civic Humanist Portrait," 95–6.

those honors and those useful things that it appears to him he merits, he does not confess that he has an obligation to those who reward him." As a result of this difficulty, a free state has "partisan enemies and not partisan friends." Quite in keeping with the aspect of his thought that Cato finds so appealing, Machiavelli recommends the expedient of "kill[ing] the sons of Brutus."[43]

Thus, both Machiavelli and Cato begin their discussions of ingratitude by asserting that free states find themselves in a precarious position with respect to their great men. The abilities of talented men are needed to maintain the liberty of their state, but at the same time their ambitions are dangerous; too great rewards will make them insolent, too small will make them resentful. As a result, Machiavelli and Cato concur that a state can never be too suspicious. Cato expresses this sentiment as follows: "Considering what sort of a creature man is, it is scarce possible to put him under too many restraints, when he is possessed of great power" (33.234).

Cato's strict reliance on Machiavelli's treatment of ingratitude is evident from the fact that, in accord with Machiavelli's own strategy, he examines in detail, for the purpose of exonerating Rome, the cases of Coriolanus, Camillus, and Scipio. Machiavelli attempts to counter the charge of ingratitude that might be lodged against Rome in the cases of Coriolanus and Camillus by noting in *Discourses* 1.29 that they "were made exiles for the injuries that both had done to the plebs," thereby suggesting that their deserts were just.[44] Livy reports that Coriolanus injured the plebs when he argued that it should be denied corn during a dearth in the hope that its desperation would induce it to agree to the annulment of the law that established the office of the tribunes, the representatives of the people.[45] Camillus denied the plebs a full share of the plunder when he ordered that a tithe of the spoils from the capture of the town of Veii be used to fulfill a vow to Apollo.[46] As a result of these actions, both Romans were exiled from their city. Cato follows Machiavelli's lead when he finds that these extraordinary citizens were "guilty of ... partiality ... towards the nobles" (118.825).

Further, Machiavelli and Cato both agree that another conclusion is required in the case of Rome's treatment of Scipio. Machiavelli goes so far in distinguishing this case that he states that "there was no example [of ingratitude] other than that of Scipio." Nevertheless, Machiavelli excuses Rome even in this case by raising concerns regarding the prominence that the hero had attained: Rome was justified in taking the action against Scipio because "a city could not call itself free where there was a citizen who was

[43] Machiavelli, *Discourses* 1.16.3–4.

[44] Ibid., 1.29.3.

[45] Livy, *Ab urbe condita* 2.33–5.

[46] Ibid., 5.23 and 32. See *Discourses* 3.23, "For What Cause Camillus Was Expelled from Rome," for Machiavelli's exposition of Camillus's mistake.

feared by the magistrates."[47] Similarly, the English Cato, while acknowledging the man's accomplishments, states that the regard the people had for him set a dangerous precedent. Indeed, it "shook the foundations of Rome, and made way for the violent proceedings and usurpations of Marius, and afterwards of Caesar" (118.826). Cato, then, just like Sidney before him, sides with Machiavelli in condoning Rome's prosecution of Scipio. Therefore, even in the cases of these three prominent soldiers, whose victories proved so beneficial to Rome, Machiavelli and Cato either refuse to admit to instances of ingratitude or offer palliation for such instances.

Cato reveals another aspect of his Machiavellian sensibility in another passage of the same letter. He declares, for instance, that the dictator provided a great service to his city when he sentenced Spurius Melius [sic] to death for having endeavored to raise his stature in the state by distributing free grain to the Roman plebeians. Similarly, he commends Rome for throwing Manlius Capitolinus from the Capitol – the very Capitol he had once saved – for having become ill-contented with the honors his city had bestowed on him for his valor (118.822). Both of these punishments are cited by Machiavelli in *Discourses* 3.1 as examples of executions that brought Rome "back toward its beginning,"[48] and thus further highlight Cato's embrace of this Machiavellian teaching.

Cato's high regard for *Discourses* 3.1 surfaces yet again in this set of chapters when he finds irresistible the urge to apply these general reflections to recent events: "Even in England, the hanging of two or three great men among the many guilty, once in a reign or two, would have prevented much evil, and many dangers and oppressions, and saved this nation many millions" (119.828). He thus exhorts England to use the remedy that would have prevented, according to Machiavelli's assessment, the collapse of Rome: if stern punishments had "continued at least every ten years in that city, it follows of necessity that it would never have been corrupt."[49]

According to Cato, then, a state's expression of gratitude is less a virtue than a vice. He goes so far as to assert that "there is generally more crime and insecurity in not punishing well, than in not paying well; a fault too frequent in free states" (118.823–4). He is thus in firm agreement with Machiavelli that "men are kept better and less ambitious longer through fear of punishment."[50]

Having so emphasized the notion that gratitude is a dangerous luxury for a free state, Cato appears to have made more difficult the task of arguing his ostensible point that free states are less ungrateful than arbitrary princes. He calls on Machiavelli's help to extricate himself from this difficulty, explicitly

---

[47] Machiavelli, *Discourses* 1.29.3.
[48] Ibid., 3.1.3.
[49] Ibid.
[50] Ibid., 1.29.3.

deferring to the authority of Machiavelli's discussion of ingratitude in the *Discourses* for the only time in these two thoroughly Machiavellian letters: "Machiavel...says, that a great and successful general, under an arbitrary prince, has but two ways to escape the certain ruin which his glory, services, and renown, will else bring upon him: He must either quit the army, and, retiring from all power, live like a private man; or depose his master, and set up himself: Which last is generally the safer course" (120.830).[51] Cato's point is that whereas the free state waits for a false step or even the slightest sign of insolence from a glorious victor, an arbitrary prince will not; success itself is enough to trigger such a prince's wrath. One wonders, however, how Cato can maintain this distinction when he notes elsewhere that the democratic Athenians punished great men "though they could prove no other crime against them but that of being great men" (11.92).[52] Cato's deep concern for constraining the celebrated great seems to originate in his acceptance of a Machiavellian maxim: "Machiavel tells us, that it is rare to find out a man perfectly good or perfectly bad: Men generally swim between the two extremes" (80.583).[53] As we have seen, for safety's sake, Cato emphasizes the half of the formulation that asserts that no one is perfectly good. In the name of such safety, Cato is willing to take the "best defence which we can have against [men] being knaves," which "is to make it terrible to them to be knaves" (33.240).

Notions of Greatness and War in Their Machiavellian and Liberal Aspects

Unlike Harrington and Hobbes, who are particularly wary of the political upheaval that ambition and emulation can create, and thus who attempt to quash those passions completely, Cato, precisely like Machiavelli, understands the potential dangers but accepts and indeed fosters those passions nevertheless, given the tremendous benefits to the state of men who long for greatness. As we have seen, Cato follows Machiavelli in arguing that a state must be prepared to punish such men and to accept the unseemly upheaval such punishment entails. Both thinkers, as we have seen, also emphasize the benefit that such a shocking spectacle can have on the state. Therefore, Cato, like Machiavelli, honors greatness; in fact, they both appeal to the ambition for greatness for positive political results.

Although much less interested than Cato in admiring and recommending ambition in a state's leading men, Sidney shares with Cato the acceptance of the passions and the recognition of the resultant need to exercise vigilance and to inflict vengeance – in a most Machiavellian fashion – when the passions impel rulers beyond the bounds. In this regard, Cato and Sidney can

---

[51] Cato is referring to *Discourses* 1.30.
[52] Pangle, *Spirit of Modern Republicanism*, 31.
[53] Machiavelli makes this statement in 1.27 of the *Discourses*.

be said to join forces against Harrington's Hobbesian effort to expel from politics such passions and the upheaval they create. Politics for both of these English Machiavellians necessitates tumults; but, in their view, such tumult is all to the good.

Beyond this point, however, Cato diverges from Machiavelli and Sidney through his pursuit of peace rather than war. Cato seeks greatness in domestic politics and in the dangerous and valorous pursuit of foreign trade; he shuns the Machiavellian battlefield as a realm in which men should seek to glorify themselves and their homeland. In eschewing war and promoting the peaceful activity of trade – but in retaining the Machiavellian notion of the benefit of competition and greatness – Cato forges the final reconciliation between liberalism and Machiavellian republicanism.

In treating the characteristics of men who aspire to and achieve supreme greatness, Machiavelli emphasizes that they regard difficult circumstances – indeed, circumstances that would defeat others – merely as auspicious opportunities to display their prowess. Machiavelli's four great founders of *The Prince*, for instance, were all born into less than promising circumstances. These men, Moses, Cyrus, Romulus, and Theseus, were able to parlay their misfortunes into great fame, fame far surpassing what they would have garnered had they not – paradoxically – been so fortunate in encountering misfortune. If one studies their lives, Machiavelli concludes, "one does not see that they had anything else from fortune than the opportunity [*occasione*]."[54] Machiavelli teaches, then, that misfortune is merely opportunity to be seized by the ambitious.

Cato displays the same attitude toward misfortune and, in fact, uses the same words to describe it. In treating the current misfortunes of England, he enjoins his readers: "Let us make earning of our misfortunes, and accept our calamities as an opportunity thrown into our laps by indulgent providence, to save ourselves" (16.121). Just like Machiavelli, Cato regards misfortune as opportunity. One needs ability and ambition to transform such dire circumstances to the benefit of oneself and others.

In his *Discourses*, Machiavelli teaches the same lesson he teaches in *The Prince*, although in a slightly different way. Cato, in turn, faithfully transmits the same lesson in all its nuances. Machiavelli declares in the *Discourses* that a great man is fortunate in being confronted by a thoroughly corrupt city, because it affords him the possibility of great fame. He states, "if a prince seeks the glory of the world he ought to desire to possess a corrupt city – not to spoil it entirely ... but to reorder it. ... And truly the heavens cannot give to men a greater opportunity for glory, nor can men desire any greater."[55] Cato follows Machiavelli's lead in a letter addressed to the members of the House

---

[54] Machiavelli, *Prince* 6.23; *Opere*, 264.
[55] Machiavelli, *Discourses* 1.10.6.

of Commons by insisting that the current condition of England affords them the possibility of great fame:

Here is a scene of glory, an opportunity put by gracious heaven into your hands, to exercise your virtues, and to obtain a reputation far above the tinsel triumphs of fabulous and imaginary heroes. Virtuous men could not ask more of providence; nor could providence bestow more upon mortal men, than to set them at the head of a corrupted and almost undone people, and to give them the honour of restoring their power, and reforming their manners. (98.701)

Again, Cato understands misfortune as opportunity, and in order to motivate others to seize the opportunity, he holds out the lure of glory and reputation. Therefore, Cato will not renounce the pursuit of glory because, just as Machiavelli teaches, an individual's pursuit of this reward can benefit the state by giving rise to great accomplishments: "No man can be too ambitious of the glory and security of his country, nor too angry at its misfortunes and ill usage; nor too revengeful against those that abuse and betray it; nor too avaricious to enrich it, provided that in doing it he violates not the rights of others" (39.277). As he expresses suspicion for those who advocate the suppression of the passions, he regrets the loss that such suppression may engender: men "become cowards, by stifling the love of glory" (39.275). A state should encourage rather than quash such manifestations of the highest ambition.

Cato expresses this same sentiment elsewhere when he declares that "Emulation therefore, or the passion of one man to equal or excel another, ought to be encouraged." Quite in keeping with the strict watch he believes needs to be kept on such men, he offers two restrictions on how such emulation is to be encouraged: "First, that no man, let his merit be what it will, should take his own reward; secondly, that he should have no more than comes to his share" (43.296–7). Like Machiavelli, then, Cato recognizes the need both to foster ambition and to maintain a vigilant eye against its growth beyond safe levels.

Given Cato's extreme indebtedness to Machiavelli on the issue of the desirability of ambition in the men who populate a state, Cato shows remarkable independence in diverging from Machiavelli's insistence both that war is the foremost venue for ambition's exercise and that a state must seek increase through war. He accepts the necessity of increase, but a state is to garner that increase through trade rather than war. Thus, Cato seeks an entirely new outlet for the ambition he fosters and differs not only from Machiavelli but also from Machiavelli's most martial disciples, Harrington and Sidney.

In accordance with the Machiavellian view of the necessity to seek increase, Cato declares that "it is certainly the interest and duty of states, by all prudent and just methods to increase their wealth and power, and in consequence their security and protection" (87.626). Moreover, like Machiavelli,

Cato is quite forthright in his readiness to support one nation's attempt to augment its wealth and power at the expense of others. Nevertheless, he differs substantially with Machiavelli on the means by which such aggrandizement is to be achieved. Admitting that augmentation is to be had "either by arms or trade," he shuns war and seeks the refuge of trade. "War," he says, "is comprehensive of most, if not all the mischiefs which do or ever can afflict men: It depopulates nations, lays waste the finest countries, destroys arts, sciences, and learning." He readily admits, however, that war is an attempt "to gain the possessions of others," but he insists there is a better method by which to reap "the produce of their country, and the acquisitions of their labour and industry":

This is certainly more easily and effectually done by a well regulated commerce, than by arms. The balance of trade will return more clear money from neighbouring countries, than can be forced from them by fleets or armies, and more advantageously than under the odious name of tribute. It enervates rival states by their own consent, and obligates them, whilst it impoverishes and ruins them: It keeps our own people at home employed in arts, manufactures, and husbandry, instead of murdering them in wild, expensive, and hazardous expeditions, to the weakening their own country, and the pillaging and destroying their neighbours, and only for the fruitless and imaginary glory of conquest. (87.628–9)

In this remarkable passage, Cato has managed to combine the Machiavellian passion for the fray – the fray that will eventuate in the exaltation of the winner and the subjugation of the vanquished – with the Lockean sensibility that promotes comfort and peace, justice and humanity, through the industry of individuals.

It is the Lockean, however, who gains the upper hand in this particular contest for Cato's ultimate allegiance. For example, at other points, Cato allows the competitive edge to his praise of trade to fall away. In these places he offers his praise of peace in terms of public benefits rather than in those of the belligerent glorification of England (e.g., 89.639 and 86.619). Elsewhere, his Lockean allegiance is particularly evident when he mimics Locke's assertion regarding the productivity of cultivated land – land that is more likely to be worked when a nation is at peace than when at war: "One acre of ground well manured, cultivated, and sowed with corn, will produce ten times as much for the sustenance of man, as ten acres not cultivated, or ill cultivated" (87.631).[56] Cato goes further than does Locke, asserting in the sequel that a good artisan is ten times more productive than a cultivator.

Laying aside the benefits of peaceful employment, Cato also produces a more principled rejection of war. He declares, for example, that "[c]onquest,

---

[56] See Locke, *Second Treatise*, para. 37. Cato reduces Locke's example by a factor of ten; Locke's discussion uses ten cultivated acres and one hundred uncultivated ones. Zuckert too notes Cato's use of Locke's example (*Natural Rights and the New Republicanism*, 307).

or fighting for territory, is, for the most part, the most shameless thing in the world" (74.549). Moreover, war should not be the method by which the person of the ruler is decided: "[I]n all contests among conquerors about territory, if natural justice and common sense were to decide it, that prince ought to carry it, who can satisfy the people that he will use them best" (74.549). Interestingly, here Cato appears to apply more consistently Sidney's own principle. Although it was Sidney's claim that a people has the right to choose its governors, he was forced to lapse in the application of his own principle when he so pugnaciously favored an aggressive state. Of course, even when the conqueror is a republic, the vanquished have no voice in the choice of their rulers, and, thus, whereas consent may be the basis of rule in the conquering country, it certainly is not in the conquered country. In this manner, Sidney allowed his cherished principle of consent to be trampled by the intoxicating spirit of war.[57] Therefore, it can be said that the Lockean manner in which Cato rejects armed aggression allows for a more universal application of Sidney's own principles.

Liberalism with a Machiavellian Spirit

Cato's Machiavellianism distinguishes his brand of liberalism from liberalism as it is conventionally understood. Liberalism, in its concentration on the rights and liberties of individuals, is supposed to eschew the public realm. The individual finds his or her satisfaction in the cocoon of the private realm, but the Machiavellian in Cato will not stand for such isolation. In the spirit of Machiavelli he urges the people to take their place in politics by watching and challenging their leading men when they exceed the bounds. Just as in Machiavelli's depiction of republican Rome, the people of England engage in politics to fight for their interests. Thus, although political participation is quite salient in Cato's thought, it neither serves the satisfaction of human nature nor promises the attainment of happiness; instead, such participation is in the service of the rights of the people. Because Cato's politics are built on this liberal foundation, the individual is primary and furnishes Cato with his standard. The people can act on those rights, in Cato's view, by withdrawing their consent and resisting their government.

By contrast, in Machiavelli's depiction of the Roman Republic, the plebeians who entered the public realm to struggle with the patricians did not possess such claims against the patricians, who often manipulated the plebeians to their own ends – namely, the end of war, in which the most ambitious among them could strive to satisfy their desire for glory. Nevertheless, although the liberal notion of rights is completely foreign to Machiavelli's

---

[57] Sidney does, however, offer the conquered the consolation that they have a right to rebel. See, e.g., *Discourses* 3.36.

thought, Cato appeals to the Florentine's spirit to allow the people a prominent role in governance.[58]

Again, in sharp contrast to Harrington, Cato is not in the least chary of the Florentine's depiction of the chaotic Roman Republic. Indeed, he describes how liberty results when the various constituents of society contend for their interests. In fact, we have already considered a passage particularly illustrative of this point when treating the beneficial character of self-interest, but now we are ready to discern also its Machiavellian aspects. The particular passage runs: "Dominion will always desire increase, and property always to preserve itself; and these opposite views and interests will be causing a perpetual struggle: But by this struggle liberty is preserved, as water is kept sweet by motion" (70.504). Cato's point is a clear echo of 1.4 of the Discourses, where Machiavelli asserts that those who criticize Rome's tumultuousness do not recognize "those things that were the first cause of keeping Rome free." Such critics of Rome "do not consider that in every republic are two diverse humors, that of the people and that of the great, and that all the laws that are made in favor of freedom arise from their disunion."[59] In addition to embracing Machiavellian tumults that arise from the clash of two different parties in a state, Cato also borrows the Florentine's distinction between the few who covet dominion and the many who desire property. Despite his obvious reliance on Machiavelli, the passage also contains Cato's own contribution – that of the metaphor of the flowing water. The prospect of such contention in a state, which so attracts Cato, had so repelled Harrington that he designed his Oceana with the specific intent of preventing such "jostling."[60]

According to Cato, the people play that prominent and salutary role, as we have seen, by acting precisely on their self-interest. This demand on Cato's part that the people act on their interests is not as straightforward as it may first appear. The complication arises when the people must discern where their true interests lay and understand how to attain them. Cato explains that "[n]othing is so much the interest of private men, as to see the publick flourish" because "every man's private advantage is so much wrapt up in the publick felicity, that by every step which he takes to depreciate his country's happiness, he undermines and destroys his own: when the publick is secure, and trade and commerce flourish, every man who has property, or the means of acquiring property, will find and feel the blessed effects of such a circumstance of affairs" (89.638–9). Although this is the case, often people miss

---

[58] Dworetz emphasizes that Cato's use of fear derives from Hobbes. By not considering how much of Cato's concern with the positive effects of fear derives from Machiavelli's Discourses, Dworetz misses how Cato encourages civic participation on the part of the people by encouraging them to vigilance and vengeance. See particularly, Dworetz, Unvarnished Doctrine, 104–5.

[59] Machiavelli, Discourses 1.4.1.

[60] Sullivan, "Civic Humanist Portrait," 91–2.

this greater benefit for a smaller, more immediate one, because a "very small part of mankind have capacities large enough to judge the whole of things; but catch at every appearance which promises present benefit, without considering how it will affect their general interest; and so bring misfortunes and lasting misery upon themselves to gratify a present appetite, passion, or desire." Still, Cato does not ask for the renunciation of such appetites, but rather a better consideration of them:

How many are there, who do not prefer a servile office or pension before the general interest of their country, in which their own is involved; and so sacrifice their liberty and the protection which they receive from equal laws, for momentary and precarious advantages; and by such means lose or hazard a large inheritance, or make it much less valuable, for trifling benefits, which will not pay half the difference? (89.638)

In this manner, Cato advocates a greater, well-considered gain for the individual rather than a smaller, ill-considered one. To this end, he redefines the meaning of self-interest: "*[S]elf-interest*, in the ill sense of the word, ought to be new-defined, and made applicable only to those who prefer a small interest to a great one, or to such who take a wrong way to attain that great one" (117.816).[61] Therefore, if citizens can be made to understand that their own good results when the whole thrives, then Cato will praise the pursuit of one's self-interest. In order to undertake the task, the people's understanding must be enlarged and educated. The more that they observe and participate in public matters, the more they will understand where their true interests lie.

First, Cato demands that the people assume their proper place as sentinels for the protection of their interests. The South Sea crisis signals a lack of the proper watchfulness, but as he frequently notes, such a lapse must be turned to the good: "Our present misfortunes will rouse up our spirits, and, as it were, awaken us out of a deep lethargy" (18.131). Second, he demands that the people assume this position in the public realm with the proper attitude: "Political jealousy...in the people, is a necessary and laudable passion" (33.238). They must assume the worst of their leaders and be ready to act against those who undertake to cheat or otherwise harm them: "[E]very private subject has a right to watch the steps of those who would betray their country; nor is he to take their word about the motives of their designs, but to judge of their designs by the event" (99.103).

Clearly, the spirit of liberty that Cato demands from the people is one that is imbued with a Machiavellian spirit of vengeance. In writing of the South Sea crisis, he points out that the Roman commonwealth "was formerly...beholden" to a "spirit of jealousy and revenge...for the long preservation of its liberty." He draws from this the lesson that "liberty will never subsist long where this spirit is not" (2.41). Elsewhere he also calls on

---

[61] Emphasis in original.

that spirit and its power: "[A]s Machiavel well observes, When the people are dissatisfied, and have taken a prejudice against their governors, there is no thing nor person that they ought not to fear" (24.176).[62] For Cato, liberty – a liberty that is largely Lockean – must be sustained with a Machiavellian spirit.

[62] Pocock cites this passage and claims that this "thought is authentically Machiavellian, though it is not quite clear to what text this passage alludes" (*Machiavellian Moment*, 472, n. 31). Cato appears to paraphrase Machiavelli's statement in chapter 19 of *The Prince*: " . . . if [the people] are hostile and bear hatred for him, he should fear everything and everyone."

Conclusion

Hobbes and Machiavelli laid the foundations for this reconciliation of liberalism and republicanism. One sought peace above all, the other war. For the sake of peace, one favored the people; for the sake of war, the other promoted the interests both of the nobles and of the people to the extent compatible with that end. That end of Machiavelli, though, dictates that the love of glory and the desires for preeminence and domination flourish among the few – precisely those passions that produce those political occurrences, war and internal oppression, from which the many flee.

Because Cato's thought represents the final synthesis, one can use it to assess the degree to which these two thinkers achieved their ends. Cato shows us that Hobbes's purpose ultimately won out, although his means did not. Nevertheless, this is a significant win for Hobbes's ambitions. Moreover, perhaps because of the addition of Machiavellian ferocity in service of the people's interest in peace and commodious living – interests repulsive to Machiavelli – modernity's purposes have all the more potency. Rather than arming an all-powerful sovereign, the people are to protect themselves with a Machiavellian ferocity; the people's purposes are given a more vigorous protection because they guard their interests for themselves with an intense vehemence born of an acute fear – an understanding that derives from the analyses of both Machiavelli and Hobbes – of violent death in war and of tyrannical oppression at the hands of the few.

Hobbes's – and also Cato's – pursuit of peace can be linked with a central focus of modern thought, which sought to promulgate a new understanding of the place of human beings in the whole and a new conception of the good life. That conception encouraged people to discover the mysteries of the natural world and harness them for their prosperity and pleasure. This scientific and philosophic project was fundamentally linked to an understanding of the need for a reinterpretation of Christianity. It was not lost on the philosophers of early modernity that religious fanaticism can foster the most bitter wars. Human beings are often willing to wager their mortal

existence when their souls' immortal existence hangs in the balance, and
the European religious wars of the sixteenth and seventeenth centuries provide ample evidence of this phenomenon. Of course, such religious wars
fostered conditions ill-suited to the pursuit of science; its pursuit requires
leisure, and leisure, peace. Moreover, early modern philosophers saw that a
reinterpretation of Christianity could not only help to overcome this imped-
iment but could actually aid in the pursuit of peace and earthly prosperity.
That reinterpretation, though, makes the temporal and earthly – rather than
the spiritual – primary, and arises from the view of these thinkers that people must be turned from a concern with their heavenly existence to their
earthly one.

No philosopher is as widely credited with the formation of the modern
philosophic project as René Descartes, and Descartes and Hobbes share some
fundamental insights regarding peace, Christianity, and how earthly prosperity is to be secured. Early in the next century, Cato sees fit to transmit
some of their lessons. Cato, as we know, offers a message of peace. At times,
Cato also offers that message in terms remarkably similar to those of modern
philosophy's progenitors. Cato presents himself as one of their messengers
of peace.

Descartes and Hobbes on Peace, Prosperity, and Religion

Descartes explains, for example, that he formulated the very principles of
his modern philosophic and scientific project when he took a break from his
soldierly duties during the Thirty Years' War, a period in which Europe was
in a general conflagration between the armed forces of Catholicism and those
of Protestantism.[1] He speaks to the benefits of peace when he describes how
he himself sought haven in a commercial country to pursue the philosophic
and scientific inquiry that he had defined on that break from the war. He
relates that he takes Holland as his haven because "the long-continued war
has caused such order to be established that the armies which are maintained
seem only to be of use in allowing the inhabitants to enjoy the fruits of peace
with so much the more security." He continues that that country is also a
particularly hospitable venue for his work because "in the crowded throng of
a great and very active nation, which is more concerned with its own affairs
than curious about those of others," he lives "as solitary and retired as in
deserts the most remote."[2] Peace, commerce, and scientific inquiry prosper
together, he suggests. For Descartes, the scientists' purposes and those of the

---

[1] René Descartes, *Discourse on the Method of Rightly Conducting the Reason and Seeking for
Truth in the Sciences*, in *The Philosophical Works of Descartes*, trans. Elizabeth S. Haldane and
G. R. T. Ross (Cambridge: Cambridge University Press, 1973), 1:87.
[2] Ibid., 1:100.

people could be allied because they both embrace peace in service to their ends.[3]

Moreover, Descartes proclaims that the practical results of such inquiry could make human life more secure and enticing. Obviously, many of his fellow Europeans were not so intensely interested in earthly prosperity, as they used their mortal existence to win for themselves eternal life, which, in turn, fostered the wars in Europe. Thus, despite this mutual embrace of peace that flourished in parts of Europe, Descartes knew that in order for it to be truly effective, it had to be much more widely dispersed.

For Descartes, then, the people could only benefit from his scientific project if they concentrated less on the next life and more on this one. Confident that the scientists themselves could give the people inducements to turn their gaze from the transcendent to the earthly realm, Descartes makes just such an offer. In a decidedly Baconian voice, he proposes that we "render ourselves the masters and possessors of nature." The scientific conquest of nature, he foresees, will be a most charitable endeavor, bringing untold benefits to humanity. The benefits he foresees in the area of medicine are particularly striking, for example. In this field, "all that men know is almost nothing in comparison with what remains to be known; and that we could be free of an infinitude of maladies both of body and mind, and even also possibly of the infirmities of age, if we had sufficient knowledge of their causes, and of all the remedies with which nature has provided us."[4] Just like Christianity, then, Descartes dispenses charity and promises eternal life. His promised eternal life, though, will not come after death on earth but will rather forestall that very death. His charity promises an eternal earthly existence. Peace promotes science, which then weakens the hold of the teachings of the various Christian sects that promote war, which, in turn, will further enforce the peace.[5]

Hobbes too recognizes and attempts to deploy the same alliance as does Descartes. The pursuit of peace will conduce to the people's desires: "[I]t can never be that Warre shall preserve life, and Peace destroy it."[6] Hobbes here does not consider the possibility that some wars might preserve an eternal life. He too understands that in order to pursue peace, though, the people must be focused on temporal attractions: "The Passions that encline men to Peace, are...Desire of such things as are necessary to commodious living."[7] Those whose passions lead them to pursue science also embrace the

---

[3] I owe this formulation to my colleague Robert Devigne.

[4] Descartes, *Discourse on Method*, 1:119–20.

[5] For an interpretation of Descartes's philosophy that emphasizes how Descartes uses some aspects of Christian thought to overturn Christianity, see Laurence Lampert, *Nietzsche and Modern Times: A Study of Bacon, Descartes, and Nietzsche* (New Haven: Yale University Press, 1993), 145–271, particularly 146–7, 229–30, and 234.

[6] Hobbes, *Leviathan*, 110.

[7] Ibid., 90.

prospect of peace, because it is peace, after all, that allows them to pursue their passion: "*Leasure* is the mother of *Philosophy*; and *Common-wealth*, the mother of *Peace*, and *Leasure*."[8] Thus, Hobbes believes that the seekers after knowledge will be particularly attracted to his political proposals: "Desire of Knowledge, and Arts of Peace, enclineth men to obey a common Power: For such Desire, containeth a desire of leisure."[9] Of course, Hobbes intends to foster peace and leisure not for the old type of scholars of scholasticism, who, to Hobbes's mind, cavil about useless distinctions, but rather for a new type of inquirer: "The Light of humane minds is Perspicuous Words, but by exact definitions first snuffed, and purged from ambiguity; *Reason* is the *pace*; Encrease of *Science*, the *way*; and the Benefit of man-kind, the *end*."[10] Hobbes, like Descartes, intends for a new science that will benefit humankind.

The benefit, as Hobbes specifies, requires that perspicuous words replace the combination of Aristotelian metaphysics and Christian doctrine, which comprises the vocabulary of scholasticism. The combination, to his mind, not only produces ridiculous philosophic formulations but also undermines the cause of peace. The "doctrine of *Separated Essences*, built on the Vain Philosophy of Aristotle" induces Christians of his day to believe "that when a Man is dead and buried, they say his Soule (that is his Life) can walk separated from his Body, and is seen by night among the graves." Hobbes explains that "subtilty" in the pursuit of true causes is necessary because such superstition discourages citizens from peaceful obedience to law: "Or who will not obey a Priest" "rather than his Sovereign" when that priest can transform bread and wine to "make God"? "Or who, that is in fear of Ghosts, will not bear great respect to those that can make the Holy Water, that drives them from him? And this shall suffice for an example of the Errors, which are brought into the Church, from the *Entities*, and *Essences* of Aristotle."[11] If citizens do not obey their sovereign, they cannot have peace; the current interpretation of Christianity must be changed so that it fosters peace.

Hobbes's teaching itself could be said to be just such a transformation of the Christian understanding – an understanding that will foster peace and useful inquiry. Although the high-stakes battle for the souls of believers and nonbelievers alike induced Christians of many varieties to shed their own blood and that of their opponents on fields and streets near and far, Christianity itself proclaimed the importance of peace. It proclaims, after all, the birth of the Prince of Peace, as well as the centrality of love. As much as Hobbes's name was associated with atheism, as much as he denies the

[8] Ibid., 459.
[9] Ibid., 71.
[10] Ibid., 36.
[11] Ibid., 465.

existence of spirit,[12] and as much as he himself notes that "not to believe there were at all any spirits" "is very neere to direct Atheisme,"[13] he attempts to advance a central teaching of Christianity. Hobbes preaches peace and concord. He draws attention to their shared purposes, for example, when he cites several "places of Scripture" to support his claim "that the law divine, for so much as is moral, are those precepts that tend to peace."[14]

Machiavelli and His Bellicose English Protégés on War and Religion

As we have seen, Harrington and Sidney did not embrace this facet of modernity, as they had no intention of inducing human beings to become less warlike. Although they lived after the time of the European religious wars and of the Thirty Years' War, and they themselves had experienced civil war in their own country, these particular thinkers did not derive the same lessons on the essential nature of peace as did their countryman, Hobbes. Instead, they were in Machiavelli's camp arrayed against any alliance that the people could make that would forestall the pursuit of war. Not afraid to jettison critical aspects of Machiavelli's thought when they oppose his preferences, Harrington's dedication to the Florentine's thought on the issue of war appears to derive from Harrington's own predilections for a republic that conquers. Sidney, however, so fully accepts Machiavelli's logic that he appears to defer to Machiavelli as his philosophical authority on the issue. Thus, whereas the former seems to use Machiavelli as a convenient authority for a predetermined end, the latter seems to be a convert to this conclusion, moved by the power of Machiavelli's argument.

As Neville well recognized, however, Machiavelli also intends to dampen the hold of religious powers over the minds of human beings. Thus, Machiavelli is, in fact, aligned with Descartes and Hobbes in the endeavor to transform Christianity to permit it to serve as a resource for his political purposes. Nevertheless, in stark contrast to his modern successors, Machiavelli sought to transform the religion in order to bring about the precisely opposite result: the Italian uses such a transformation to spur his fellows to war.

In Machiavelli's view, the Christian religion, far from piquing human beings' bellicosity, robbed them of it. Machiavelli, in fact, laments that "[o]ur religion has glorified humble and contemplative more than active men" and "placed the highest good in humility, abjectness, and contempt of things

---

[12] Ibid., 463: "The World, (I mean not the Earth onely,... but the *Universe*, that is, the whole masse of all things that are) is Corporeall, that is to say, Body; and hath the dimensions of Magnitude, namely, Length, Bredth, and Depth: also every part of Body, is likewise Body, and hath the like dimensions; and consequently every part of the Universe, is Body."

[13] Ibid., 58.

[14] Hobbes, *Elements*, 100.

human." He continues sorrowfully that "men, so as to go to paradise, think more of enduring their beatings than of avenging them."[15] Therefore, Machiavelli sees the same phenomenon that Hobbes and Descartes do: Christians live their lives on earth in such a way as to gain entry into a spiritual paradise. Machiavelli, however, did not live through the long years of wars that followed the advent of Protestantism, when Christian soldiers were not fighting for their earthly homelands, but rather for their heavenly ones. It is easy to imagine following Neville's example and attempting to construct Machiavelli's reaction to events that occurred after his death.

In order to counter what he saw as the deleterious consequences of religion during his own time, Machiavelli also makes promises to the people in the spirit of a transformed Christianity that weakens the spiritual interpretation of the religion. He claims, after all, that an alternative interpretation of "our religion" could induce us "to love and honor [the fatherland] and to prepare ourselves to be such that we can defend it."[16] To this end, Machiavelli wishes to vitiate the deep appeal of Christianity's promise of an eternal spiritual paradise. In his view, the people should fight not for their spiritual homelands but rather for their earthly ones. Machiavelli, in fact, may be said to have set an instructive precedent for Descartes and Hobbes by extending promises similar to those of Christianity with the intent of vitiating the allure of some of its teachings. For example, as we have seen, Machiavelli himself makes incredible promises of eternity. Unlike Descartes, though, he proffers the prospect not of the eternal life of an individual but rather that of a republic. Whereas the Cartesian form of this promise requires peace, Machiavelli's form requires war. The Italian intends for individuals to offer to sacrifice their individual lives for the eternal life of their republic.[17] Indeed, Sidney appears to respond to Machiavelli's appeal for a religion that makes human beings active rather than passive when he declares that "God helps those who help themselves."[18]

Cato's Message of Peace and His Relation to Modernity's Progenitors

Cato rejects Machiavelli's form of a Christianity reinterpreted and embraces that of Hobbes, emulating the latter's ambivalence toward Christianity in a remarkable series of three successive letters, 77–79, that addresses the absurdity of religious superstition. The first, entitled "Of Superstitious Fears, and their Causes Natural and Accidental," takes up one of Hobbes's crusades: the alleviation of beliefs in spirits that deceitful individuals use to manipulate

---

[15] Machiavelli, *Discourses* 2.2.2.
[16] Ibid.
[17] For a discussion of Machiavelli's reinterpretation of Christianity for temporal ends, see Sullivan, *Machiavelli's Three Romes*, 147–71.
[18] Sidney, *Discourses* 2.23.210.

the credulous in order to further their own designs. Cato declares there that "we are not obliged, by any precept, moral or divine, to believe every thing which weak, crazed, or designing men tell us in his name; and the disbelieving their foolish and fantastical stories, is not questioning the power of God, but the veracity or judgment of the persons who tell them."[19]

Cato prefaces this declaration with a seemingly pious acknowledgment of the vastness of God's awe-inspiring creation: "The Earth itself is but as a mustard-seed to the visible world; and doubtless that is infinitely less in comparison of the invisible one. It is very likely, that its many fellow-planets, which move about the sun, as we do, are filled with inhabitants, and some of them probably with more valuable ones than ourselves."[20] This reflection pays homage to the universe's creator, and it does so with the biblical image of the mustard seed that appears in the Gospels of Matthew, Mark, and Luke.

There is a significant difference, however, between the use these Gospels, on the one hand, and Cato, on the other, make of the image. The New Testament announces: "The kingdom of heaven is like a grain of mustard seed...; it is the smallest of all seeds, but when it has grown it is the greatest of shrubs and becomes a tree, so that the birds of the air come and make nests in its branches."[21] In Cato's use of the metaphor, the mustard seed is the earth, only a small part of the material world. As a result, the earth's seeming vastness is eclipsed by that of the whole. By contrast, in the biblical use, the mustard seed is the kingdom of heaven that will itself grow to large proportions. Although Cato's image pays homage to the "Author of all nature," it certainly does not do so to the extent of the biblical.[22] Cato's interest is temporal, not spiritual; he speaks not of the kingdom of heaven but only of the material world. Of course, according to modern scientists and philosophers, human beings can and should subdue material nature – no matter how vast its expanse – for the benefit of the race.

Moreover, Cato's elaboration of the metaphor calls attention to the religious controversies of the previous century that arose from scientific investigation, because he actually conveys the picture of the universe that

---

[19] *Cato's Letters* 77.566. Hobbes declares: "[W]hen wee Believe that the Scriptures are the word of God, having no immediate revelation from God himselfe, our Beleefe, Faith, and Trust is in the church...; And they that believe that which a Prophet relates unto them in the name of God, take the word of the Prophet" (*Leviathan*, 49) and "for Fayries, and walking Ghosts, the opinion of them has I think been on purpose, either taught, or not confuted, to keep in credit the use of Exorcisme, of Crosses, of holy Water, and other such inventions of Ghostly men.... But evill men under pretext that God can do anything, are so bold as to say any thing when it serves their turn, though they think it untrue; It is the part of a wise man, to believe them no further, than right reason makes that which they say, appear credible" (*Leviathan*, 18–19).

[20] *Cato's Letters* 77.564.

[21] Matthew 13.31–2; see also Mark 4.30–2; Luke 13.18–19.

[22] *Cato's Letters*, 77.564.

that science produced. Galileo was condemned by the Inquisition and sentenced to life imprisonment for endorsing the Copernican theory of the solar system to which Cato refers: the Earth and other planets revolve around the Sun; the Earth is not the center of the universe. It was Galileo's prosecution for the crime of promulgating this view that, Descartes explains, caused him to wonder whether he should publish his own scientific discoveries during his lifetime.[23] Although Cato finds himself in a time and place in which he can state the discoveries of scientific investigation in such a matter-of-fact manner, he still finds it necessary to continue to attempt to curb religious enthusiasm. By conveying their teachings, Cato makes himself the messenger of his modern philosophic predecessors.

To this end of curbing religious enthusiasm, Cato repeats, in the second letter of this series, "The Common Notion of Spirits, their Powers and Feats, Exposed," Hobbes's mantra in terms strikingly similar: "I cannot conceive why the dreams of the old heathen philosophers should be adopted into the Christian system: or from what principles of reason or religion we should be told that the soul is *totum in toto*, and *totum in qualibet parte*; that is, that all of it is diffused through the whole body, and yet all of it is in every part of the body."[24] In addition, in the last letter of this series entitled "A Further Detection of the Vulgar Absurdities about Ghosts and Witches," he reveals a particularly ridiculous but nevertheless serious cruelty committed in the name of religion. In decrying the once-common practice in England of persecuting old women as witches, he observes that the practice is not so far distant. He notes that although during King Charles I's reign the number of such occurrences declined, the number increased at the time of the Civil Wars when the "new set of saints got into the saddle."[25] He emphasizes again later that not only Catholic countries but also Protestant ones are subject to such religious cruelty.[26] Cato's interest in the preservation of life and in peace require the curbing of superstitious fears and religious enthusiasm. In this respect, Cato shows himself to be very much the heir of Hobbes, and also of Descartes.

Unlike Machiavelli's challenge to Christianity, then, Cato's is meant to foster peace. Indeed, he sees it as necessary for religious superstition to be mitigated in order for his own political project to come to fruition; Cato needs to weaken the hopes and the fears for the next life, in order to induce

---

[23] Descartes, *Discourse on Method*, 1:118.

[24] *Cato's Letters* 78.570; cf. Hobbes, *Leviathan*, 466: "And in particular, of the Essence of a Man, which (they say) is his Soule, they affirm it, to be All of it in his little Finger, and All of it in every other Part (how small soever) of his Body; and yet no more Soule in the Whole Body, than in any one of those Parts. Can any man think that God is served with such absurdities?" For Hobbes's use of the term "Heathen Philosophers," see, e.g., *Leviathan*, 469 and 472.

[25] *Cato's Letters* 79.580.

[26] Ibid., 79.582.

the people to take their earthly lives seriously. This sounds Hobbesian, and to a very large extent it is.

Cato's Machiavellian Means to Modernity's Ends

Cato's project is not entirely Hobbesian, though, because he finds that Hobbes's means cannot bring about his end: Hobbes's all-powerful Leviathan threatens the civil peace it is meant to guarantee. In response to this problem, Cato formulates a political project that is a combination of Lockean and Machiavellian elements. Thus, although with Cato the influence of Machiavelli's romance with military adventure has dissipated, he remains very much the Florentine's intellectual heir. Like Machiavelli, for example, Cato embraces – in contrast to Hobbes – politics and the human passions that make politics possible. He praises the pursuit of individual and collective glory and denounces cowardice. He agrees with Machiavelli both that the greatest bravery is displayed when individuals reform states such that they benefit the people and, hence, that the greatest glory is to be achieved from such an enterprise.[27] Further, like Machiavelli, he understands that the same passions that produce such magnificent deeds can also give rise to nefarious ones, such as an attempt at tyranny. Thus, Cato, like Machiavelli, understands that the most ambitious are the authors not only of the greatest political outcomes but also of the greatest political crimes.

Although Cato has imbibed these Machiavellian lessons concerning the glory of benefiting the people and the double-sided character of the men who manifest the greatest political passions, he applies these lessons in ways very different from those of their source. Because Cato is a liberal thinker, he has an alternative understanding both of how politics is to benefit the people and of the meaning of tyranny. Cato understands political benefit as the protection of the liberal rights to life, liberty, and property and defines tyranny as their deprivation. Thus, liberal rights are there to greet Cato's extension of the parameters of the domestic political realm from those very restricted ones outlined by Harrington. Harrington's Hobbesian pursuit of domestic quiet permits domestic politics only to the extent necessary to sustain an army for acquisition.

Although rights protect the individual, maintain the individual's privacy, and separate the individual from the government, Cato emphasizes that such rights also require constant vigilance and collective action for their protection. To this liberal end, he uses decidedly Machiavellian means. He follows Machiavelli's injunction to bring the people into the political realm. Not only great men on rare occasions but also the people themselves on a regular basis are to be the guardians of their rights. To this purpose, as the intellectual heir of the Italian, Cato values the spirited self-assertion that such vigilant

[27] Machiavelli, *Discourses* 1.9, 10.

protection of rights demands, but he chains that spiritedness to the pursuit of safety. Behind this attempt to control the political manifestation of spirited self-assertion lies the assumption that the love of glory simply will not be extinguished from the human character and from politics. By contrast, Hobbes seems to assume that such passions, so threatening to internal and external peace, will be eradicated or at least channeled into other avenues so as to be rendered innocuous – perhaps even beneficial – but certainly irrelevant in the political realm. Cato refuses to believe that such passions will become politically irrelevant. He insists, instead, that the fulfillment of the desires of the people are at any time vulnerable precisely because the love of domination remains in the character of some. Cato, though, will have the same passions for distinction serve to protect the rights of the people: Cato will have individuals pursue peace, act on their rights, and recognize those of others, but he decidedly rejects Hobbesian quiescence. Although Hobbes's means cannot bring about the end of peace and security, some important aspects of Machiavelli's means can, in Cato's view.

Works Cited

Anthony, H. Sylvia. "*Mercurius Politicus* under Milton." *Journal of the History of Ideas* 27 (1966): 593–609.

Appleby, Joyce. *Liberalism and Republicanism in the Historical Imagination.* Cambridge: Harvard University Press, 1992.

Aristotle. *Nicomachean Ethics.* Loeb Classical Library. 1934.

  The Politics. Translated by Carnes Lord. Chicago: University of Chicago Press, 1984.

Ascham, Anthony. *Of the Confusions and Revolutions of Governments (1649).* Edited by G. W. S. V. Rumble. Delmar, N.Y.: Scholars' Facsimiles & Reprints, 1975.

Aubrey, John. *"Brief Lives," Chiefly of Contemporaries, Set down by John Aubrey, between the Years 1669 and 1696.* Edited by Andrew Clark. 2 vols. Oxford: Clarendon Press, 1898.

Bailyn, Bernard. *The Ideological Origins of the American Revolution.* 1967. Reprint and enlarged, Cambridge, Mass.: Belknap Press, 1992.

Baumgold, Deborah. "Hobbes's Political Sensibility: The Menace of Political Ambition." In *Thomas Hobbes and Political Theory,* edited by Mary G. Dietz, 74–90. Lawrence: University of Kansas Press, 1990.

Beard, Charles. *An Economic Interpretation of the Constitution.* 1913. Reprint, with a new introduction, New York: Macmillan, 1935.

Beller, Elmer A. "Milton and *Mercurius Politicus.*" *Huntington Library Quarterly* 5 (1941–2): 479–87.

Berkowitz, Peter. *Virtue and the Making of Modern Liberalism.* Princeton: Princeton University Press, 1999.

Bobbio, Norberto. *Thomas Hobbes and the Natural Law Tradition.* Translated by Daniela Gobetti. Chicago: University of Chicago Press, 1993.

Burtt, Shelley. *Virtue Transformed: Political Argument in England, 1688–1740.* Cambridge: Cambridge University Press, 1992.

Cicero. *De Officiis.* Loeb Classical Library. 1947.

Coby, J. Patrick. *Machiavelli's Romans: Liberty and Greatness in the "Discourses on Livy."* Lanham, Md.: Lexington Books, 1999.

Colbourn, H. Trevor. *The Lamp of Experience: Whig History and the Intellectual Origins of the American Revolution.* Chapel Hill: University of North Carolina Press, 1965.

Colish, Marcia L. "The Idea of Liberty in Machiavelli." *Journal of the History of Ideas* 32 (1971): 323–50.

Conniff, James. "Reason and History in Early Whig Thought: The Case of Algernon Sidney." *Journal of the History of Ideas* 43 (1982): 397–416.

Cotton, James. "James Harrington and Thomas Hobbes." *Journal of the History of Ideas* 42 (1981): 407–21.

———. "James Harrington as Aristotelian." *Political Theory* 7 (1979): 371–89.

Dagger, Richard. *Civic Virtues: Rights, Citizenship, and Republican Liberalism.* Oxford: Oxford University Press, 1997.

Davis, J. C. "Equality in an Unequal Commonwealth: James Harrington's Republicanism and the Meaning of Equality." In *Soldiers, Writers and Statesmen of the English Revolution*, edited by Ian Gentles, John Morrill, and Blair Worden, 229–42. Cambridge: Cambridge University Press, 1998.

———. "Pocock's Harrington: Grace, Nature and Art in the Classical Republicanism of James Harrington." *Historical Journal* 24 (1981): 683–97.

Descartes, René. *Discourse on the Method of Rightly Conducting the Reason and Seeking for Truth in the Sciences.* In *The Philosophical Works of Descartes*, translated by Elizabeth S. Haldane and G. R. T. Ross, 1:79–130. Cambridge: Cambridge University Press, 1973.

Dickinson, H. T. *Liberty and Property: Political Ideology in Eighteenth-Century Britain.* New York: Holmes & Meier, 1977.

Dworetz, Steven M. *The Unvarnished Doctrine: Locke, Liberalism, and the American Revolution.* Durham: Duke University Press, 1990.

Filmer, Robert. *Patriarcha and Other Writings.* Edited by Johann P. Sommerville. Cambridge: Cambridge University Press, 1991.

Fink, Z. S. *The Classical Republicans: An Essay in the Recovery of a Pattern of Thought in Seventeenth-Century England.* 2d ed. Evanston, Ill.: Northwestern University Press, 1962.

Fischer, Markus. *Well-Ordered License: On the Unity of Machiavelli's Thought.* Lanham, Md.: Lexington Books, 2000.

Fortier, John C. "Hobbes and 'A Discourse of Laws': The Perils of Wordprint Analysis." *Review of Politics* 59 (1997): 861–87.

———. "Last Word." *Review of Politics* 59 (1997): 905–14.

Frank, Joseph. *Cromwell's Press Agent: A Critical Biography of Marchamont Nedham, 1620–1678.* Lanham, Md.: University Press of America, 1980.

French, J. Milton. "Milton, Needham, and *Mercurius Politicus*." *Studies in Philology* 33 (1933): 236–52.

Fukuda, Arihiro. *Sovereignty and the Sword: Harrington, Hobbes, and Mixed Government in the English Civil Wars.* Oxford: Clarendon Press, 1997.

Goddard, Thomas. *Plato's Demon: Or, the State-Physician Unmaskt; Being a Discourse in Answer to a Book call'd Plato Redivivus.* London: H. Hills Jun. for Walter Keeilby, 1684.

Goldie, Mark. "The Civil Religion of James Harrington." In *Languages of Political Theory in Early-Modern Europe*, edited by Anthony Pagden, 197–222. Cambridge: Cambridge University Press, 1987.

Goodale, Jesse R. "J. G. A. Pocock's Neo-Harringtonians: A Reconsideration." *History of Political Thought* 1 (1980): 237–59.

Gunn, J. W. A. *Politics and the Public Interest in the Seventeenth Century*. London: Routledge & Kegan Paul; Toronto: University of Toronto Press, 1969.

Hamilton, James Jay. "Hobbes's Study and the Hardwick Library." *Journal of the History of Philosophy* 16 (1978): 445–53.

Hamowy, Ronald. "*Cato's Letters*, John Locke, and the Republican Paradigm." *History of Political Thought* 11 (1990): 273–94.

Hankins, James. Introduction to *Renaissance Civic Humanism*. Cambridge: Cambridge University Press, 2000.

Harrington, James. *The Art of Lawgiving*. In *The Political Works of James Harrington*, edited by J. G. A. Pocock, 599–704. Cambridge: Cambridge University Press, 1977.

The Commonwealth of Oceana and A System of Politics. Edited by J. G. A. Pocock. Cambridge: Cambridge University Press, 1992.

A Discourse upon this Saying... In *The Political Works of James Harrington*, edited by J. G. A. Pocock, 735–45. Cambridge: Cambridge University Press, 1977.

The Examination of James Harrington. In *The Political Works of James Harrington*, edited by J. G. A. Pocock, 855–9. Cambridge: Cambridge University Press, 1977.

A Note upon the Foregoing Eclogues. In *The Political Works of James Harrington*, edited by J. G. A. Pocock, 579–81. Cambridge: Cambridge University Press, 1977.

The Prerogative of Popular Government. In *The Political Works of James Harrington*, edited by J. G. A. Pocock, 389–566. Cambridge: Cambridge University Press, 1977.

The Rota. In *The Political Works of James Harrington*, edited by J. G. A. Pocock, 807–21. Cambridge: Cambridge University Press, 1977.

A System of Politics. In *The Political Works of James Harrington*, edited by J. G. A. Pocock, 833–54. Cambridge: Cambridge University Press, 1977.

Hartz, Louis. *The Liberal Tradition in America: An Interpretation of American Political Thought since the Revolution*. New York: Harcourt, Brace, 1955.

Herzog, Don. "Some Questions for Republicans." *Political Theory* 14 (1986): 473–93.

Hill, Christopher. "James Harrington and the People." In *Puritanism and Revolution: Studies in Interpretation of the English Revolution of the Seventeenth Century*, 299–313. London: Mercury Books, 1962.

Hilton, John L., Noel B. Reynolds, and Arlene W. Saxonhouse. "Hobbes and 'A Discourse of Laws': Response to Fortier." *Review of Politics* 59 (1997): 889–903.

Hirschman, Albert O. *The Passions and the Interests: Political Arguments for Capitalism before Its Triumph*. Princeton: Princeton University Press, 1977.

Hobbes, Thomas. *The Elements of Law Natural and Politic: Human Nature and De Corpore Politico*. Edited by J. C. A. Gaskin. Oxford: Oxford University Press, 1994.

Leviathan. Edited by Richard Tuck. Cambridge: Cambridge University Press, 1991.

On the Citizen [*De Cive*]. Edited and translated by Richard Tuck and Michael Silverthorne. Cambridge: Cambridge University Press, 1998.

Three Discourses: A Critical Modern Edition of Newly Identified Work of the Young Hobbes. Edited by Noel B. Reynolds and Arlene W. Saxonhouse. Chicago: University of Chicago Press, 1995.

Höpfl, Harro, and Martyn P. Thompson. "The History of Contract as a Motif in Political Thought." *American Historical Review* 84 (1979): 919–44.

Holmes, Stephen. *Passions and Constraints: On the Theory of Liberal Democracy.* Chicago: University of Chicago Press, 1995.

Houston, Alan Craig. *Algernon Sidney and the Republican Heritage in England and America.* Princeton: Princeton University Press, 1991.

Hulliung, Mark. *Citizen Machiavelli.* Princeton: Princeton University Press, 1983.

Isaac, Jeffrey C. "Republicanism vs. Liberalism? A Reconsideration." *History of Political Thought* 9 (1988): 349–77.

Jefferson, Thomas. *Writings.* New York: Library of America, 1984.

Kahn, Victoria. *Machiavellian Rhetoric: From the Counter-Reformation to Milton.* Princeton: Princeton University Press, 1994.

Karsten, Peter. *Patriot-Heroes in England and America: Political Symbolism and Changing Values over Three Centuries.* Madison: University of Wisconsin Press, 1978.

Knachel, Philip A. Introduction to *The Case of the Commonwealth of England, Stated,* by Marchamont Nedham. Charlottesville: University Press of Virginia published for the Folger Shakespeare Library, 1969.

Lampert, Laurence. *Nietzsche and Modern Times: A Study of Bacon, Descartes, and Nietzsche.* New Haven: Yale University Press, 1993.

Laslett, Peter. Introduction to *The Two Treatises of Government,* by John Locke. Cambridge: Cambridge University Press, 1988.

Livy. *Ab urbe condita.* Loeb Classical Library. 1967–84.

Locke, John. *The Second Treatise of Government* in *Two Treatises of Government.* Edited by Peter Laslett. Cambridge: Cambridge University Press, 1988.

Machiavelli, Niccolò. *Discourses on Livy.* Translated by Harvey C. Mansfield and Nathan Tarcov. Chicago: University of Chicago Press, 1996.

——— . *Florentine Histories.* Translated by Laura F. Banfield and Harvey C. Mansfield. Princeton: Princeton University Press, 1988.

——— . *The Prince.* Translated by Harvey C. Mansfield. 2d ed. Chicago: University of Chicago Press, 1985.

——— . *Tutte le opere.* Edited by Mario Martelli. Florence: Sansoni, 1971.

Macpherson, C. B. *The Political Theory of Possessive Individualism: Hobbes to Locke.* Oxford: Oxford University Press, 1962.

Manent, Pierre. *An Intellectual History of Liberalism.* Translated by Rebecca Balinski. Princeton: Princeton University Press, 1995.

Mansfield, Harvey C. *Machiavelli's New Modes and Orders: A Study of the "Discourses on Livy."* Ithaca: Cornell University Press, 1979. Reprint, Chicago: University of Chicago Press, 2001.

——— . *Machiavelli's Virtue.* Chicago: University of Chicago Press, 1996.

——— . *Taming the Prince: The Ambivalence of Modern Executive Power.* New York: Free Press, 1989.

Mansfield, Harvey C., and Nathan Tarcov. Introduction to *Discourses on Livy,* by Niccolò Machiavelli. Chicago: University of Chicago Press, 1996.

McCormick, John P. "Machiavellian Democracy: Controlling Elites with Ferocious Populism." *American Political Science Review* 95 (2001): 297–313.

Montesquieu, Charles de Secondat, baron de. *The Spirit of the Laws.* Translated and edited by Anne M. Cohler, Basia Carolyn Miller, and Harold Samuel Stone. Cambridge: Cambridge University Press, 1989.

Moyle, Walter. *An Essay upon the Constitution of the Roman Government*. In *Two English Republican Tracts*, edited by Caroline Robbins, 201–59. Cambridge: Cambridge University Press, 1969.

Myers, Peter C. *Our Only Star and Compass: Locke and the Struggle for Political Rationality*. Lanham, Md.: Rowman & Littlefield, 1998.

Nadon, Christopher. "Aristotle and the Republican Paradigm: A Reconsideration of Pocock's *Machiavellian Moment*." *Review of Politics* 58 (1996): 677–98.

Nedham, Marchamont. *The Case of the Commonwealth*. Edited by Philip A. Knachel. Charlottesville: University Press of Virginia published for the Folger Shakespeare Library, 1969.

The Case of the Commonwealth. London: E. Blackmore and R. Lowndes, 1650.

The Case of the Kingdom Stated. 2d ed. London, 1647.

The Excellencie of a Free State. London, 1767.

[*Mercurius Politicus*.] *Annales Reipublicæn Anglicanæ, or A Relation of the Affairs and Designs by the Common-wealth of England, Scotland, and Ireland. With Intelligence from Forraigne Parts* by Mercurius Politicus. London: Thomas Newcomb, 1650–60.

A True State of the Case of the Commonwealth. Exeter: The Rota, 1978.

Neville, Henry. *The Isle of Pines*. London, 1668.

A Parliament of Ladies with Their Lawes Newly Enacted. London: 1647.

Plato Redivivus: or, A Dialogue Concerning Government. In *Two English Republican Tracts*, edited by Caroline Robbins, 61–200. Cambridge: Cambridge University Press, 1969.

A True Copy of a Letter Written by N. Machiavill, in Defence of Himself, and his Religion. London, 1691.

The Works of the Famous Nicholas Machiavel, Citizen and Secretary of Florence. London, 1680.

Oakeshott, Michael. "Introduction to *Leviathan*." In *Rationalism and Politics and Other Essays*, 221–94. New York: Basic Books, 1962. Reprint, with a foreword by Timothy Fuller, Indianapolis: Liberty Press, 1991.

"The Moral Life in the Writings of Thomas Hobbes." In *Rationalism in Politics and Other Essays*, 295–350. New York: Basic Books, 1962. Reprint, with a foreword by Timothy Fuller, Indianapolis: Liberty Press, 1991.

Pangle, Thomas L. *The Spirit of Modern Republicanism: The Moral Vision of the American Founders and the Philosophy of Locke*. Chicago: University of Chicago Press, 1988.

Pettit, Philip. *Republicanism: A Theory of Freedom and Government*. Oxford: Oxford University Press, 1997.

Pincus, Steven C. A. "Neither Machiavellian Moment nor Possessive Individualism: Commercial Society and the Defenders of the English Commonwealth." *American Historical Review* 103 (1998): 705–36.

Plato. *The Republic of Plato*. Translated by Allan Bloom. New York: Basic Books, 1968.

Pocock, J. G. A. *The Ancient Constitution and the Feudal Law: A Study of English Historical Thought in the Seventeenth Century: A Reissue with a Retrospect*. Cambridge: Cambridge University Press, 1987.

"Authority and Property: The Question of Liberal Origins." In *Virtue, Commerce, and History: Essays on Political Thought and History, Chiefly in the Eighteenth Century,* 51–71. Cambridge: Cambridge University Press, 1985.

"A Discourse of Sovereignty: Observations on the Works in Progress." In *Political Discourse in Early Modern Britain,* edited by Nicholas Phillipson and Quentin Skinner, 377–428. Cambridge: Cambridge University Press, 1993.

"The Historical Introduction" to *The Political Works of James Harrington,* 1–152. Cambridge: Cambridge University Press, 1977.

"Machiavelli, Harrington and English Political Ideologies in the Eighteenth Century." In *Politics, Language, and Time: Essays on Political Thought and History,* 104–47. New York: Atheneum, 1971. First published in *William and Mary Quarterly,* 3d. ser., 22 (1965): 549–83.

The Machiavellian Moment: Florentine Political Thought and the Atlantic Republican Tradition. Princeton: Princeton University Press, 1975.

"*The Machiavellian Moment* Revisited: A Study in History and Ideology." *Journal of Modern History* 53 (1981): 49–72.

"Virtue and Commerce in the Eighteenth Century." *Journal of Interdisciplinary History* 3 (1972): 119–34.

Raab, Felix. *The English Face of Machiavelli: A Changing Interpretation, 1500–1700.* London: Routledge & Kegan Paul, 1964.

Rahe, Paul A. "Antiquity Surpassed: The Repudiation of Classical Republicanism." In *Republicanism, Liberty, and Commercial Society, 1649–1776,* edited by David Wootton, 233–69. Stanford: Stanford University Press, 1994.

"An Inky Wretch: The Outrageous Genius of Marchamont Nedham." *National Interest* 70 (2002–3): 55–64.

"Quentin Skinner's 'Third Way.'" *Review of Politics* 62 (2000): 395–8.

Republics Ancient and Modern: Classical Republicanism and the American Revolution. Chapel Hill: University of North Carolina Press, 1992.

Raymond, Joad. "The Cracking of the Republican Spokes." *Prose Studies* 19 (1996): 255–74.

"'A Mercury with a Winged Conscience': Marchamont Nedham, Monopoly and Censorship." *Media History* 4 (1998): 7–18.

Remer, Gary. "James Harrington's New Deliberative Rhetoric: Reflection of an Anticlassical Republican." *History of Political Thought* 16 (1995): 532–57.

Robbins, Caroline. "Algernon Sidney's *Discourses concerning Government*: Textbook of Revolution." *William and Mary Quarterly,* 3d ser., 4 (1947): 267–96.

The Eighteenth-Century Commonwealthman: Studies in the Transmission, Development and Circumstance of English Liberal Thought from the Restoration of Charles II until the War with the Thirteen Colonies. Cambridge: Harvard University Press, 1959.

ed. Introduction to *Two English Republican Tracts.* Cambridge: Cambridge University Press, 1969.

Rodgers, Daniel T. "Republicanism: The Career of a Concept." *Journal of American History* 79 (1992): 11–38.

Ryan, Alan. "Hobbes and Individualism." In *Perspectives on Thomas Hobbes,* edited by G. A. J. Rogers and Alan Ryan, 81–105. Oxford: Oxford University Press, 1988.

"Hobbes's Political Philosophy." In *The Cambridge Companion to Hobbes,* edited by Tom Sorell, 208–45. Cambridge: Cambridge University Press, 1996.

Sandel, Michael. *Democracy's Discontent: America in Search of a Public Philosophy.* Cambridge, Mass.: Belknap Press, 1996.

Saxonhouse, Arlene W. "Hobbes and the Beginnings of Modern Political Thought." In *Three Discourses: A Critical Modern Edition of Newly Identified Work of the Young Hobbes,* by Thomas Hobbes, 123–54. Chicago: University of Chicago Press, 1995.

Schochet, Gordon J. "Intending (Political) Obligation: Hobbes and the Voluntary Basis of Society." In *Thomas Hobbes and Political Theory,* edited by Mary G. Dietz, 55–73. Lawrence: University of Kansas Press, 1990.

Patriarchalism in Political Thought: The Authoritarian Family and Political Speculation and Attitudes Especially in Seventeenth-Century England. New York: Basic Books, 1975.

Schwoerer, Lois G. "The Literature of the Standing Army Controversy, 1697–1699." *Huntington Library Quarterly* 28 (1965): 187–212.

Scott, Jonathan. *Algernon Sidney and the English Republic, 1623–1677.* Cambridge: Cambridge University Press, 1988.

Algernon Sidney and the Restoration Crisis, 1677–1683. Cambridge: Cambridge University Press, 1991.

"The Rapture of Motion: James Harrington's Republicanism." In *Political Discourse in Early Modern Britain,* edited by Nicholas Phillipson and Quentin Skinner, 139–63. Cambridge: Cambridge University Press, 1993.

Shklar, Judith N. "Liberalism of Fear." In *Liberalism and the Moral Life,* edited by Nancy L. Rosenblum, 21–53. Cambridge: Harvard University Press, 1989.

Sidney, Algernon. *Court Maxims.* Edited by Hans W. Blom, Eco Haitsma Mulier, and Ronald Janse. Cambridge: Cambridge University Press, 1996.

Discourses Concerning Government. Edited by Thomas G. West. Indianapolis: Liberty Classics, 1990.

Skinner, Quentin. "Conquest and Consent: Thomas Hobbes and the Engagement Controversy." In *The Interregnum: The Quest for Settlement, 1646–1660,* edited by G. E. Aylmer, 79–98. Hamden, Conn.: Archon Books, 1972.

"The Idea of Negative Liberty: Machiavellian and Modern Perspectives." In *Renaissance Virtues,* vol. 2 of *Visions of Politics,* 186–212. Cambridge: Cambridge University Press, 2002. First published as "The Idea of Negative Liberty: Philosophical and Historical Perspectives." In *Philosophy in History: Essays on the Historiography of Philosophy,* ed. Richard Rorty, J. B. Schneewind, and Quentin Skinner, 193–221. Cambridge: Cambridge University Press, 1984.

"The Ideological Context of Hobbes's Political Thought." *Historical Journal* 9 (1966): 286–317.

Liberty before Liberalism. Cambridge: Cambridge University Press, 1998.

Machiavelli. New York: Hill and Wang, 1981. Reprint, *Machiavelli: A Very Short Introduction.* Oxford: Oxford University Press, 2000.

"Machiavelli on *Virtù* and the Maintenance of Liberty." In *Renaissance Virtues,* vol. 2 of *Visions of Politics,* 160–85. Cambridge: Cambridge University Press, 2002. First published as "Machiavelli on the Maintenance of Liberty." *Politics* 18 (1983): 3–15.

"Machiavelli's *Discorsi* and the Pre-humanist Origins of Republican Ideas." In *Machiavelli and Republicanism,* edited by Gisela Bock, Quentin Skinner, and Maurizio Viroli, 121–41. Cambridge: Cambridge University Press, 1990.

"The Paradoxes of Political Liberty." In *The Tanner Lectures on Human Values* 7, edited by Sterling M. McMurrin, 227–50. Salt Lake City: University of Utah Press.

Reason and Rhetoric in the Philosophy of Hobbes. Cambridge: Cambridge University Press, 1996.

"The Republican Ideal of Political Liberty." In *Machiavelli and Republicanism*, edited by Gisela Bock, Quentin Skinner, and Maurizio Viroli, 293–309. Cambridge: Cambridge University Press, 1990.

The Renaissance. Vol. 1 of *The Foundations of Modern Political Thought*. Cambridge: Cambridge University Press, 1978.

Slomp, Gabriella. *Thomas Hobbes and the Political Philosophy of Glory*. New York: St. Martin's Press, 2000.

Smith, Steven B. *Spinoza, Liberalism, and the Question of Jewish Identity*. New Haven: Yale University Press, 1997.

Sommerville, Johann P. *Politics and Ideology in England, 1603–1640*. London: Longman, 1986.

Thomas Hobbes: Political Ideas in Historical Context. New York: St. Martin's Press, 1992.

Spinoza, Baruch. *Political Treatise*. In *The Chief Works of Benedict de Spinoza*, 1:279–387. Translated by R. H. M. Elwes. 2 vols. London: George Bell and Sons, 1891.

Strauss, Leo. *The Political Philosophy of Hobbes: Its Basis and Its Genesis*. Translated by Elsa M. Sinclair. Chicago: University of Chicago Press, 1952.

Thoughts on Machiavelli. Chicago: University of Chicago Press, 1958.

Sullivan, Vickie B. "The Civic Humanist Portrait of Machiavelli's English Successors." *History of Political Thought* 15 (1994): 73–96.

"Machiavelli's Momentary 'Machiavellian Moment': A Reconsideration of Pocock's Treatment of the *Discourses*." *Political Theory* 20 (1992): 309–18.

Machiavelli's Three Romes: Religion, Human Liberty, and Politics Reformed. DeKalb: Northern Illinois University Press, 1996.

"Symposium: The Republican Civic Tradition." *Yale Law Journal* 97 (1988): 1493–1723.

Tarcov, Nathan. *Locke's Education for Liberty*. Chicago: University of Chicago Press, 1984.

Tawney, R. H. "Harrington's Interpretation of His Age." *Proceedings of the British Academy* 27 (1941): 199–223.

Thomas, Keith. "The Social Origins of Hobbes's Political Thought." In *Hobbes Studies*, edited by K. C. Brown, 185–236. Cambridge: Harvard University Press, 1965.

Toland, John. *Tetradymus*. London, 1720.

Toth, Kathleen. "Interpretation in Political Theory: The Case of Harrington." *Review of Politics* 37 (1975): 317–39.

Trenchard, John. *A Short History of Standing Armies in England*. 3d ed. London: Printed for A. Baldwin, 1698.

Trenchard, John, and Thomas Gordon. *Cato's Letters: or, Essays on Liberty, Civil and Religious, and Other Important Subjects*. Edited by Ronald Hamowy. 2 vols. Indianapolis: Liberty Classics, 1995.

Trenchard, John, and Walter Moyle. *An Argument, Shewing that a Standing Army is Inconsistent with a Free Government, and Absolutely Destructive to the Constitution of the English Monarchy*. London, 1697.

Trevor-Roper, Hugh. "The Gentry, 1540–1640." *Economic History Review Supplement*, no. 1 (1953): 1–55.

Tuck, Richard. *Hobbes*. Oxford: Oxford University Press, 1989.

"Hobbes and Locke on Toleration." In *Thomas Hobbes and Political Theory*, edited by Mary G. Dietz, 153–71. Lawrence: University of Kansas Press, 1990.

Natural Rights Theories: Their Origin and Development. Cambridge: Cambridge University Press, 1979.

Philosophy and Government: 1572–1651. Cambridge: Cambridge University Press, 1993.

Viroli, Maurizio. *From Politics to Reason of State: The Acquisition and Transformation of the Language of Politics, 1250–1600*. Cambridge: Cambridge University Press, 1992.

Machiavelli. Oxford: Oxford University Press, 1998.

von Maltzahn, Nicholas. "Henry Neville and the Art of the Possible: A Republican Letter Sent to General Monk (1660)." *Seventeenth Century* 7 (1992): 41–52.

Ward, Lee. "Rhetoric and Natural Rights in Algernon Sidney's *Discourses Concerning Government*." *Interpretation* 28 (Winter 2000–1): 119–45.

West, Thomas G. Foreword to *Discourses Concerning Government* by Algernon Sidney. Indianapolis: Liberty Classics, 1990.

Wettergreen, John A. "James Harrington's Liberal Republicanism." *Polity* 20 (1988): 665–87.

"Note on the Intention of James Harrington's Political Art." *Interpretation* 2 (1971): 64–78.

Wood, Anthony à. *Athenae Oxonienses, An Exact History of all the Writers and Bishops who Have Had Their Education in the University of Oxford*. 3d ed. 4 vols. London, 1820.

Wood, Gordon. *The Creation of the American Republic, 1776–1787*. Chapel Hill: University of North Carolina Press, 1969. Reprint, New York: W. W. Norton, 1972.

Wood, Neal. "Hobbes and the Crisis of the English Aristocracy." *History of Political Thought* 1 (1980): 437–52.

"The Value of Asocial Sociability: Contributions of Machiavelli, Sidney and Montesquieu." In *Machiavelli and the Nature of Political Thought*, edited by Martin Fleisher, 282–307. New York: Atheneum, 1972.

Wootton, David. Introduction to *Political Writings of John Locke*. New York: Mentor, 1993.

"The Republican Tradition: From Commonwealth to Common Sense." Introduction to *Republicanism, Liberty, and Commercial Society, 1649–1776*, edited by David Wootton, 1–41. Stanford: Stanford University Press, 1994.

Worden, Blair. "Classical Republicanism and the Puritan Revolution." In *History and Imagination: Essays in Honor of H. R. Trevor-Roper*, edited by Hugh Lloyd-Jones, Valerie Pearl, and Blair Worden, 182–200. New York: Holmes & Meier, 1981.

"The Commonwealth Kidney of Algernon Sidney." *Journal of British Studies* 24 (1985): 1–40.

"English Republicanism." In *The Cambridge History of Political Thought, 1450–1700*, edited by J. H. Burns with the assistance of Mark Goldie, 443–75. Cambridge: Cambridge University Press, 1991.

"Factory of the Revolution." *London Review of Books* 20 (5 February 1998): 13–15.

"Harrington's *Oceana*: Origins and Aftermath, 1651–1660." In *Republicanism, Liberty, and Commercial Society, 1649–1776*, edited by David Wootton, 111–38. Stanford: Stanford University Press, 1994.

"James Harrington and *The Commonwealth of Oceana*." In *Republicanism, Liberty, and Commercial Society, 1649–1776*, edited by David Wootton, 82–110. Stanford: Stanford University Press, 1994.

"Marchamont Nedham and the Beginnings of English Republicanism, 1649–1656." In *Republicanism, Liberty, and Commercial Society, 1649–1776*, edited by David Wootton, 45–81. Stanford: Stanford University Press, 1994.

"Milton and Marchamont Nedham." In *Milton and Republicanism*, edited by David Armitage, Armand Himy, and Quentin Skinner, 156–80. Cambridge: Cambridge University Press, 1995.

"Milton's Republicanism and the Tyranny of Heaven." In *Machiavelli and Republicanism*, edited by Gisela Bock, Quentin Skinner, and Maurizio Viroli, 225–45. Cambridge: Cambridge University Press, 1990.

"Republicanism and the Restoration, 1660–83." In *Republicanism, Liberty, and Commercial Society, 1649–1776*, edited by David Wootton, 139–93. Stanford: Stanford University Press, 1994.

Roundhead Reputations: The English Civil Wars and the Passions of Posterity. London: Penguin Press, 2001.

The Rump Parliament, 1648–1653. Cambridge: Cambridge University Press, 1974.

"'Wit in a Roundhead': The Dilemma of Marchamont Nedham." In *Political Culture and Cultural Politics in Early Modern England: Essays Presented to David Underdown*, edited by Susan D. Amussen and Mark A. Kishlansky, 301–37. Manchester: Manchester University Press, 1995.

Wren, Matthew. *Consideration on Mr. Harrington's Common-wealth of Oceana: Restrained to the First Part of the Preliminaries*. London: Printed for Samuel Gellibrand, 1657.

Zagorin, Perez. *A History of Political Thought in the English Revolution*. London: Routledge & Kegan Paul, 1954. Reprint, New York: Humanities Press, 1966.

Zuckert, Michael P. *Launching Liberalism: On Lockean Political Philosophy*. Lawrence: University Press of Kansas, 2002.

Natural Rights and the New Republicanism. Princeton: Princeton University Press, 1994.

Index

Printed in the United States
81570LV00003B/31-63